Asynchronous On-Chip Networks and Fault-Tolerant Techniques

Asynchronous On-Chip Networks and Fault-Tolerant Techniques

Wei Song and Guangda Zhang

CRC Press
Taylor & Francis Group
Boca Raton London New York

CRC Press is an imprint of the
Taylor & Francis Group, an **informa** business

First edition published 2022
by CRC Press
6000 Broken Sound Parkway NW, Suite 300, Boca Raton, FL 33487-2742

and by CRC Press
4 Park Square, Milton Park, Abingdon, Oxon, OX14 4RN

CRC Press is an imprint of Taylor & Francis Group, LLC

© 2022 Wei Song and Guangda Zhang

ISBN: 978-1-032-25575-0 (hbk)
ISBN: 978-1-032-25741-9 (pbk)
ISBN: 978-1-003-28478-9 (ebk)

DOI: 10.1201/9781003284789

Typeset in Latin Modern
by KnowledgeWorks Global Ltd.

To Chunzhen and Chao for their patience and love.
To Mingyi and Jersey for bringing joy into our life.

Contents

Preface

We have entered an era of multicore processors as the single-core performance has reached its ceiling along with the slowing down of the Moore's Law. Current mainstream commercial processors, such as Intel Core and Xeon, and AMD Ryzen and Epyc, are all multicore processors which contain up to 64 processing cores. In the foreseeable future, the number of cores in a processor will continue to increase.

When the number of cores reaches tens to hundreds, a significant portion of the total design effort would be dedicated to making the core-to-core communication speed and energy efficient. Although currently almost all processors use synchronous on-chip networks built by synchronous circuits, asynchronous on-chip networks may become useful or even necessary in the near future. In synchronous on-chip networks, the global clock needs to be distributed over long distances with little clock skew, which becomes a challenge as the network scales. It is estimated that the clock tree could consume 20% to 50% of the total power in synchronous circuits while the synchronous on-chip network could consume 33% to 36% of total power. To reduce the total power consumption, it is common to let individual processing cores implemented in their own clock and power domains, and run at their own clock frequencies dynamically tuned according to real-time work load. In this scenario, an asynchronous on-chip network might be a better candidate than a synchronous one.

This is a book about how to design a high throughput and fault-tolerant asynchronous on-chip network for multicore and many-core processors. The state-of-the-art way of designing and optimizing asynchronous on-chip networks is to mimic the structure of synchronous on-chip networks. However, the timing division multiplexing (TDM) techniques extensively utilized in synchronous networks introduce extra synchronization and largely increase the speed penalty in asynchronous on-chip networks. Instead of TDM, we would like to introduce spatial parallelism into asynchronous networks to improve their throughput performance without incurring the synchronization penalties.

There is one annoying problem with the asynchronous on-chip networks built by quasi-delay-insensitive (QDI) circuits: They are sensitive to faults. A fault does not only corrupt a data packet, it also obstructs the handshake protocol essentially needed for correct data transmission, disrupts the normal data flow and may finally produce a deadlock paralyzing the whole network. The second half of this book is dedicated to this issue. A fault-tolerant coding method is proposed to tolerate transient faults. When a deadlock is caused by a fault, the location of the fault is first accurately pinpointed using a fault detection circuit and the network is then functionally resumed by isolating the faulty components.

This book is intended for researchers, engineers and students who research QDI and speed-independent (SI) circuits, asynchronous on-chip networks and switching networks built on QDI and SI circuits, fault-tolerant QDI circuits and finally the fault-tolerant asynchronous on-chip networks.

The organization of the book follows a self-contained manner. Chapters are carefully ordered in a way that necessary background knowledge and related topics are introduced and discussed before an advanced technique is described. Readers can read through the book without resorting to related research papers and books, but they are provided in the bibliography for further references.

Introduction provides a context for the topics described in this book, including our motivation in doing these researches, their applications in current and future computer systems and the state of the art in related areas.

Asynchronous Circuits introduces the concept of asynchronous circuits, the timing assumptions used in different types of asynchronous circuits and the implementation of asynchronous circuits.

Asynchronous Networks-on-Chip describes all the general concepts of on-chip interconnects necessary for understanding this book. This chapter also introduces asynchronous on-chip networks.

Optimizing Asynchronous On-Chip Networks improves the throughput performance of asynchronous on-chip networks by introducing spatial parallelism into the router design.

Fault-Tolerant Asynchronous Circuits begins to analyze the effect of faults on asynchronous circuits, and presents the state-of-art fault-tolerant techniques for asynchronous circuits. It shows that faults not only corrupt data but can also bring down the whole asynchronous network.

Fault-Tolerant Coding introduces the fault-tolerant encoding for asynchronous circuits and proposes a fault-tolerance delay-insensitive redundant check code for QDI interconnections that can tolerate transient faults.

Deadlock Detection describes how to detect a deadlock caused by a fault on asynchronous on-chip networks and how to locate the faulty link. This is the prerequisite for a network to recover from a fault-caused deadlock.

Deadlock Recovery presents deadlock recovery techniques, including an asynchronous router design and on-chip network design that can recover from a deadlock caused by faults.

Summary concludes the book and introduces the future work.

This book is based on our Ph.D. research work done in the Advanced Processor Technologies (APT) group in the School of Computer Science at the University of Manchester. We are greatly indebted to our supervisors, Dr. Doug Edwards and Dr. Jim Garside. They brought us into the world of asynchronous circuit designs, carefully guided us with their wide knowledge and insight and constantly encouraged us using their deep passion in research. We would like to express our gratitude also to the colleagues in the APT group for their direct and indirect help to this research.

Wei Song and Guangda Zhang
October 2021

CHAPTER 1

Introduction

The advancing semiconductor technology makes it possible to integrate more and more processing cores on a single chip to achieve continuously increasing chip performance, posing a growing demand for scalable and efficient interconnection. On-chip networks (OCNs) or Networks-on-Chip (NoCs) have emerged as a promising candidate to support large-scale on-chip communication. Most existing NoCs are built synchronously, which could be restricted by issues induced by the growing clock distribution as the network scales. As an alternative, event-driven asynchronous circuits which are controlled by handshake protocols rather than global clocks, can be employed to implement NoCs. Removing the clock, asynchronous NoCs have many attractive advantages over synchronous ones.

In the deep sub-micron era, reliability has become a challenge faced by the scaling electronics. Accompanied with the shrinking device dimensions, factors like the lowering voltage supply, the increasing clock frequency and the growing density of chips, have a negative impact on the chip reliability. Electronic systems are more susceptible to *faults*. *Fault tolerance* has become an essential objective for critical digital systems.

Fault tolerance has been systematically studied in traditional synchronous NoCs, but rarely in asynchronous ones. Using one timing-robust class of asynchronous circuits — the quasi-delay-insensitive (QDI) circuits — to implement the NoC, QDI NoCs can naturally tolerate delay variation, which is attractive for large-scale

DOI: 10.1201/9781003284789-1

NoCs. Faults have more complicated and devastated impact on QDI NoCs compared with synchronous NoCs, which is a challenging issue needed to be resolved. This book talks about the fault-tolerant on-chip networks implemented by asynchronous circuits, and targets providing holistic, efficient, resilient and cost-effective fault-tolerant solutions to asynchronous NoCs.

1.1 ASYNCHRONOUS CIRCUITS

Asynchronous circuits work in a clockless and self-timed manner. They are designed under certain timing assumptions, which describe their tolerance to the delay variance of gates and wires. This book concentrates on one specific timing-robust type of asynchronous circuits, the quasi-delay-insensitive (QDI) circuit, which tolerates arbitrary positive delay on all gates and wires except for some forks that are assumed isochronic (wires that have equal latency to all its fanouts). Since its strong tolerance to delay variation, QDI circuit remains functioning under extreme working conditions, such as sub-threshold supply voltage and ultra low/high temperature, naturally tolerates process variation which becomes increasingly troublesome for synchronous circuits, and requires less static timing analysis than all other types of asynchronous circuits, not to mention the synchronous ones. In addition, QDI circuit is presumably low power because it wastes no power on the clock tree and consumes nearly zero power when it is not actively in use.

Although asynchronous circuits have a long history of over 50 years [163], most very large-scale integration (VLSI) circuits are synchronous due to the mature electronic design automation (EDA) support. Since registers and latches in synchronous circuits are synchronized by the global clock, they are the natural timing boundaries by which a circuit can be divided into paths. All these paths are driven by the same clock and operate concurrently and independently. EDA tools, especially synthesis tools, are therefore able to improve speed by optimizing these paths individually. On the other hand, the latches in asynchronous circuits are driven by handshake protocols (circuits). The operation of one latch is normally triggered by events generated from other latches. It is difficult to optimize the speed of asynchronous circuits due to the lack of clear timing boundaries to break large circuits into small analyzable pieces as in synchronous circuits. Some asynchronous synthesis tools have been proposed recently, such as Petrify [57] and Balsa [73], to translate behavioral hardware descriptions into low level netlists. However, high-speed asynchronous circuits are almost always manually designed [182, 212, 219].

Shrinking transistor geometry brings opportunities for asynchronous circuits. As the number of transistors in a single die increases corresponding to the prediction of Moore's Law, the area and power overhead of synchronizing the whole chip with one global clock is unacceptable and beyond the control of current EDA tools. Future multicore processors should be globally asynchronous and locally synchronous (GALS) designs where synchronous intellectual property (IP) blocks talk with each other using an asynchronous communication infrastructure. 49% of the global signals will be driven by asynchronous circuits by the year 2024 [104]. Variation is another problem. The decreasing transistor size increases power density which leads to temperature and power variations [98]. Process variation worsens the situation with non-deterministic cell latency. The worst case timing analysis in synchronous circuits generates over-pessimistic speed estimation [31]. Asynchronous circuits are tolerant to variations and provide average speed performance.

Designing asynchronous circuits is not an easy task compared with their synchronous counterparts. Without the mature support of commercial EDA tools, asynchronous circuits are usually fully or partially manually crafted. For this reason, this book demonstrates how to design QDI circuits from scratch by describing all implementations in gate-level Verilog HDL using normal gates available in any standard cell libraries.

1.2 ASYNCHRONOUS ON-CHIP NETWORKS

Current multicore processors use on-chip networks as their communication fabric. Most networks-on-chip (NoCs) are synchronous networks where network components are driven by the same or several global clocks. Thanks to the timing assumptions allowed by the global clock and mature EDA tools, these synchronous NoCs are fast and area efficient. However, there are several design challenges in synchronous NoCs that are difficult to resolve:

- *Support for heterogeneous networks*: Unlike chip multi-processor (CMP) systems where every network node is a homogeneous processor element, a multiprocessor system-on-a-chip (MPSoC) is a heterogeneous system where network nodes are IP blocks with different functions and hardware structures. These IP blocks are provided and tested with different clock frequencies, area sizes and even working voltages. These differences complicate the network topology, compromise the latency performance of synchronous networks and make chip timing closure difficult to reach.

- *Low power consumption*: It is crucial to reduce the power consumption of an SoC as it determines the maximum standby time of a device. The clock tree of synchronous on-chip networks consumes a significant amount of energy [153], and it is getting worse along with the shrinking transistor geometry.

- *Tolerance to variation*: Process, temperature and voltage variations affect future sub-micron VLSI designs significantly [133, 138]. According to the international technology roadmap for semiconductors, the delay uncertainty caused by variations in the sign-off timing closure will reach 32% in 2024 [104]. Traditional static timing analysis is going to be replaced with statistical timing analysis methods [31] to cope with the dropping yield rate and the over-conservative timing estimation. Synchronous on-chip networks alleviate this effect by considering variations in their task mapping procedure [138]. However, this works only in homogeneous networks and the routers are still working at the worst estimated speed.

Instead of using synchronous on-chip networks, asynchronous on-chip networks are a promising solution to the above challenges. The communication components in an asynchronous on-chip network are built with clockless asynchronous circuits. Data are transmitted according to certain handshake protocols largely insensitive to delay variations [231]. Because of this delay insensitivity, the interface between all IP blocks to the global asynchronous on-chip network is unified by the same synchronous to/from asynchronous interface. The fact that all synchronous blocks are isolated by the asynchronous network simplifies chip-level timing closure. Also, thanks to the delay insensitivity, an asynchronous on-chip network is naturally tolerant to all variations as the delay uncertainty caused by these variations cannot affect the function of those handshake protocols. Finally, since no clock is needed in asynchronous circuits, an asynchronous on-chip network consumes zero dynamic power when no data is in transmission.

However, asynchronous networks [11, 22, 28, 67, 75] are often slower than the synchronous on-chip networks with similar structures and resources [153]. Although the global clock in synchronous circuits is power consuming, it is a speed- and area-efficient approach to synchronize combinational operations. Asynchronous circuits rely on handshake protocols to control data transmission. Combinational operations are explicitly detected and guarded to ensure the insensitivity to delay. The circuits used in detecting combinational operations introduce area and speed overhead. Delay insensitive asynchronous circuits are intrinsically slow.

Another issue is that the state-of-the-art way of designing asynchronous on-chip networks is to asynchronously reproduce the structures of synchronous on-chip networks. As synchronous on-chip networks synchronize data with no speed penalty, timing division multiplexing (TDM) techniques [58] are extensively utilized. Simply reproducing such TDM structures in asynchronous on-chip networks introduces extra completion detection circuits and causes speed penalties.

Although the speed penalty of completion detection is unavoidable, as the promising advantages of asynchronous circuits are derived from those delay insensitive handshake protocols, the scale of the synchronization in asynchronous circuits can be limited to small transmission units, such as a single pipeline. The speed penalty is therefore alleviated. The following question is how to build asynchronous networks with such limited synchronization.

This book introduces techniques to improve network throughput by employing spatial parallelism in asynchronous on-chip networks at different levels. Channel slicing is a new pipeline structure that alleviates the speed penalty of synchronization by removing it in bit-level data pipelines. It is also possible to further improve speed using the lookahead pipeline style if the QDI timing assumption is slightly relaxed. Spatial division multiplexing (SDM) is a flow control method that improves network throughput by removing the synchronization between flits of different packets, which is required by TDM methods on the contrary. The main cost of using SDM is a significantly increased crossbar inside each router. To reduce this area overhead, the crossbar can be replaced with novel switch structures, such as a novel 2-stage Clos switch dynamically reconfigured by an asynchronous dispatching algorithm.

1.3 FAULT-TOLERANT ASYNCHRONOUS ON-CHIP NETWORKS

On one hand, the advancing semiconductor technology boosts the chip performance and permits more processing cores to be integrated. On the other hand, accompanied with the shrinking device dimensions, all of the factors like the lowering power voltage, the increasing clock frequency and the growing density of chip impose a negative impact on the chip reliability [37].

In the deep sub-micron era, variations in manufacturing and operating conditions have a proportionately greater effect than before. Shrinking transistor dimensions means that variations in the actual manufacturing, such as dopant levels and crystal boundaries, influence transistor and wire properties with time [37]. Growing chip density results in a high heat flux across the die, creates hot spots with a high temperature, which affects the circuit performance and accelerates the device aging process. Reducing supplying voltage gives greater susceptibility to various noise sources [37, 56]. Increasing clock frequency raises the probability that noise creates faults on circuits. As a result, the sensitivity of electronic devices to environmental variations is significantly increased and the device aging process is accelerated.

It has been reported that the mean values of soft error rate (SER) of three circuits under a 40 nm process are 2.2E-4 FIT, 4.7E-4 FIT and 1.2E-4 FIT, respectively (1 FIT = 1 fail per 1 billion hours) [257]. The 24 *MByte* of Level 3 Cache in an Intel Processor encountered 0.2~2 errors per year under the SER of 0.0001~0.001 FIT/bit [221]. An SER in the order of 0.001 FIT/bit has also been observed on the Altitude SEE test European platform [10]. It was predicted that the SER per logic state bit could increase 8% in each technology generation [95]. The SER in static random-access memory would increase 6~7× from 130 *nm* to 22 *nm* process [102]. In 65 *nm* technology, the radiation can cause a 6.45× increase in SER when the supply voltage decreases from 1.0 *V* to 0.33 *V* [187]. It is believed that both the SER and the aging speed would increase as the technology continues scaling [37, 56, 84, 173]. Although researchers disagree on the absolute number of faults in particular circuits on particular processes, they all agree that the trend is for faults to increase as processes shrink. Electronic systems are more susceptible to *faults* [18], including *transient, intermittent* and *permanent* faults depending period of lasting [162]. The 2015 ITRS takes *reliability* as one main challenge faced by the next generation electronics and stresses the importance of a runtime protection [39]. Consequently, *fault tolerance* has become an essential design objective for critical digital systems, especially in highly specialized fields such as aerospace, military and medical equipment.

The fault tolerance of synchronous NoCs has been extensively studied. Faults typically cause data errors (or packet loss). These errors can normally be detected and corrected within several clock cycles. A clock signal provides a timing reference for error detection and correction. Detecting the error or packet loss, a retransmission can be requested to obtain the right packet [229]. However, there is no such timing reference in an asynchronous NoC. The QDI implementations are robust to timing variations but not to faults. A fault may pollute a transmitting packet, corrupt the handshake protocol and disrupt the normal data flow, which is a new challenge faced by asynchronous circuit designers. A single fault could even break the handshake protocol and results in a *fault-caused physical-layer deadlock*. This deadlock is different from the well-known network layer one induced by the cyclic dependence of multiple competing packets [61, 63]. Most conventional fault tolerant or deadlock management techniques for synchronous NoCs cannot work in a *deadlocked* state. The fault tolerance of asynchronous NoCs has not been thoroughly studied. Various styles of asynchronous NoCs have been proposed but rarely do they have fault-tolerance capabilities [11, 30, 67, 75, 200, 212].

Faults can be classified into *transient, intermittent* and *permanent* faults depending on their duration [56]. Transient faults usually last for a short time and behave as positive or negative glitches (0→1→0 or 1→0→1) [18, 111]. Permanent faults will influence the victim gates or wires forever. Most permanent faults can be modeled as "stuck-at" faults [5, 137], where the logic level of a net is always 0 or 1. Intermittent faults usually happen as an early manifestation of permanent ones with the aging process [56]. They can appear as either transient or permanent during error detection or correction.

In the presence of faults, QDI NoCs behave differently from synchronous ones. A fundamental difference between synchronous and QDI circuits is the timing reference used in the transmission of data symbols.

- In synchronous circuits, a data symbol typically has a constant time per bit which can be agreed — and maintained for a known time — between the transmitter and the receiver. Corruption of the transmission will therefore affect a known number of bits. Thus faults on a synchronous NoC may corrupt packets being transmitted, lead packets to wrong destinations, result in packet loss or cause data errors. Nevertheless, the erroneous data symbol or faulty behavior can be easily detected and further corrected or recovered.

- There is no such timing reference in QDI circuits. Faults can insert or possibly delete symbols besides corrupting them. Managing these faulty cases represents a new challenge faced by QDI NoCs. Meanwhile, it is obvious that a permanent fault will stall the handshake and cause a physical-layer deadlock. Its detection and recovery has not been thoroughly studied in a NoC environment. More seriously, a transient fault cannot only cause data errors but also deadlock a QDI NoC, which has been neglected by the asynchronous community. These all increase the challenge of fault detection and recovery in QDI NoCs.

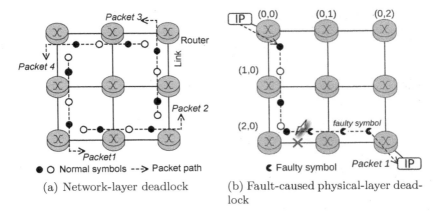

(a) Network-layer deadlock

(b) Fault-caused physical-layer dead-lock

Figure 1.1   Network-layer and physical-layer deadlocks in a QDI NoC.

Deadlock is fatal to a NoC without any management mechanisms [61]. It can reduce the network performance, paralyze its function and eventually cause the chip to be discarded. The well-known *network-layer* deadlock due to the cyclic dependence of packets or restricted routings [63] can happen in all NoCs. Figure 1.1a shows an example where four packets hold and request network resources in a cyclic fashion, which is a network-layer deadlock. It can be resolved by using specific turn models or providing extra escape channels [63]. This network-layer deadlock is common in all NoCs and not the target of this book. In QDI NoCs, a fault may break the handshake protocol, resulting in a physical-layer deadlock, which is particular to QDI NoCs. Taking a simple (*req, ack*) handshake process for example, if the sender sends out a request to the receiver but without getting acknowledged, the sender does not know whether this is caused by a fault or delay because QDI circuit is insensitive to delay variations. It would keep waiting for the lost *ack*, resulting a physical-layer deadlock. Figure 1.1b illustrates a faulty case that a fault on a transmitting packet deadlocks the reserved data path in the network. Note that it is the adaptability of a QDI circuit to timing variations that makes it more vulnerable to this kind of deadlock-type faults. This physical-layer deadlock cannot be easily resolved by higher-layer techniques for network-layer ones.

This book studies the impact of different faults on QDI NoCs, including transient and permanent ones, and proposes thorough and systematic fault-tolerant solutions to protect QDI NoCs. The achieved fault-tolerance capability and the incurred performance and hardware overhead are two main factors considered in the evaluation.

1.3.1   Protection for QDI Links

A large-scale NoC may contain a large number of long link wires, which are common in large-scale Systems-on-Chip (SoCs). Exposed to the external environment, they can be easily affected by various noise or fault sources and become the victim of timing variations or transient faults [14]. These chip-level long interconnects can be implemented as QDI pipelines to achieve high bandwidth and timing-robustness. However, a transient fault can be accepted as a valid signal in a QDI system, leading to the insertion, deletion or corruption of a data symbol. Fault-tolerant codes have been widely used to protect on-chip communication [229]. Codes also perform an important role in QDI circuits where delay-insensitive (DI) codes are used to build data symbols to encode the timing information. Most existing state-of-the-art fault-tolerant codes proposed for asynchronous circuits either compromise the timing-robustness of QDI circuits or incur large area and speed overhead. This book presents a novel delay-insensitive redundant coding (DIRC) scheme to protect QDI communication from transient faults, which can be easily adopted by existing DI or QDI interconnects without destroying their intrinsic timing-robustness. The protected QDI links can be constructed flexibly to satisfy various fault-tolerance requirement, with a moderate and reasonable hardware overhead.

1.3.2   Deadlock Detection

Both permanent and transient faults could break the handshake process in QDI NoCs and generate a physical-layer deadlock, which has more serious consequences to the system than pure data errors. The management of this fault-caused physical-layer deadlock is significantly important to the chip life-span but it has barely been studied. To resume from a physical-layer deadlock, the network must go through two phases: deadlock *detection* and *recovery*. *Detection* of a fault-caused physical-layer deadlock is difficult in a QDI NoC. In a deadlocked state, error syndromes for fault analysis cannot be easily collected. Locating a specific defective wire or gate is difficult. The ideal situation is that the faulty component can be precisely located so that a recovery method can be further applied to bypass or replace the faulty component, which consequently resumes the network functionality. Therefore, an efficient and flexible detection method is necessary. It should be able to not only precisely locate the fault in the QDI NoC, but also differentiate the fault-caused physical-layer deadlock from other similar network scenarios, including the upper network-layer deadlock and the network congestion. When both transient and permanent faults are considered, an accurate model is needed to differentiate deadlocks caused by different faults, so as to enable the *fault diagnosis*. The proposed techniques should be able to detect, diagnose and locate the fault as long as the fault deadlocks the network.

1.3.3 Network Recovery

As the fault position has been located, the next step is to recover the network function according to the deadlocked state of the handshake protocol and the network protocol. Figure 1.1b shows one possible deadlock case where a fault deadlocks a reserved long packet path composed of the faulty link and other healthy network sources. A direct system reboot can temporarily remove this deadlock, but it is expensive and cannot deal with the deadlock caused by permanent faults. Therefore, a fine-grained recovery strategy is necessary to remove the deadlock and isolate the faulty component. The recovery contains two main processes: (1) deadlock removal, which recovers the stalled packet flow in the deadlocked packet path, releasing blocked healthy network resources and eliminating the deadlock and (2) faulty link isolation: instead of using upper network-layer methods such as fault-tolerant routings to detour the faulty link, this book proposes a fine-grained recovery technique at the lower physical layer to isolate the faulty component and restore the network function. Upper layer recovery techniques can further be used to improve the network performance after the loss of the faulty component. When transient and intermittent faults deadlock the network, the isolated link should be resumed when the fault fades.

CHAPTER 2

Asynchronous Circuits

Both synchronous and asynchronous circuits are *sequential circuits* which have internal states stored in latches (registers) or memories. The key difference between these two is the way how storage elements are triggered. The storage elements in asynchronous circuits are driven by handshakes rather than global clocks. According to the delay assumptions and the protocols utilized to implement the handshakes, asynchronous circuits present different levels of tolerance to delay variation. This chapter introduces the classification and the implementation of some asynchronous circuits necessary for the understanding of the rest of this book.

2.1 CIRCUIT CLASSIFICATION

It is well understood that all storage elements in a synchronous circuit are synchronously driven by a small number of global clocks. Consequently, any circuits whose storage elements are triggered by other means, such as by local signals, should be considered as asynchronous. Instead of denoting a single type, the term *asynchronous circuit* represents actually a large number of circuit styles. It would be extremely difficult, if ever possible, to explore and classify all types of asynchronous circuits. This book therefore focuses on the commonly utilized types of asynchronous circuits whose storage elements are triggered by local events communicated according to certain *handshake protocols*. Sometimes, these types of asynchronous circuits are also called *event-driven* circuits while synchronous circuits are *clock-driven*.

DOI: 10.1201/9781003284789-2

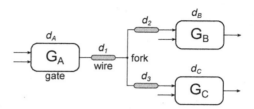

Figure 2.1   A circuit model with gate and wire forks [231].

Some types of asynchronous circuits offer strong tolerance to delay variation, which is one of the major benefits provided by asynchronous circuits. This tolerance derives from the rather strong assumption that gates and wires may incur positive but unbounded delay, which is unsupportable in synchronous circuits. To create functional logic while still allowing unbounded delay on gates and wires, some extra assumptions are usually used to selectively relax the original strong delay assumption and this relaxation decides the level of delay tolerance offered by the implemented circuit. As a result, asynchronous circuits are usually classified by the delay relaxation applied on them [231].

2.1.1   Delay-Insensitive

Delay-insensitive (DI) circuits are designed without introducing any relaxation on the original strong assumption. As an example, all the gate delay (d_A, d_B and d_C) and wire delay (d_1, d_2 and d_3) in Figure 2.1 are positive and unbounded. Consequently, the logic function of the circuit is independent of delay. This makes DI circuits invulnerable to any forms of delay variation. However, the delay assumption is so strong that it constricts the possible formations of circuits. Only C-elements and inverters can be used in DI circuits [140] while nearly all basic gates used in synchronous circuits, such as AND, OR, XOR, etc., are not DI. This has severely limited the use of DI circuits in practice.

2.1.2   Quasi-Delay-Insensitive

Quasi-delay-insensitive (QDI) circuits relax the original delay assumption by allowing *isochronic forks* [231]. A wire is an isochronic fork when the delays from the common driver to all sinks are equal. In the example shown in Figure 2.1, the fork is isochronic if $d_2 = d_3$. Strictly speaking, isochronic fork is a conceptual idea as no fork is rigidly isochronic. However, we consider a wire as an practical isochronic fork when the skew (delay variation between sinks) is small enough. Note that an isochronic fork may still incur an unbounded delay but it allows a signal to be simultaneously transmitted to multiple sub-circuits, which is a fundamental requirement for designing communication channels for data. QDI circuits are the most delay insensitive asynchronous circuit style that can be used to design complicated logic functions in practice.

Among all the types of asynchronous circuits, QDI circuits are the most attractive type, since it can implement complicated logic functions and provide strong tolerance to delay variations, where the latter becomes a serious issue with the shrinking transistor geometry. QDI circuits have been used to construct many point-to-point on-chip interconnects [11, 12, 224] and networks [53, 77, 227], and are the preferred type for asynchronous circuits in this book.

2.1.3   Speed-Independent

Speed-independent (SI) circuits assume all wires incur zero delay ($d_1 = d_2 = d_3 = 0$ in Figure 2.1) while the delays of gates are still positive and unbounded. This timing assumption might look unrealistic as wires do have positive delays. In deep sub-micron process, wire delay may be even longer than gate delay. The underlying idea is to assume all forks are isochronic and have the wire delay lumped into the delay of the gate driving it. If the lumped delay of gate G_A in Figure 2.1 is denoted as d'_A, SI assumes $d_2 = d_3$ and $d'_A = d_A + d_1 + d_2$. Since QDI assumes some, but not all, forks are isochronic, SI is a further relaxed delay assumption and SI circuits are less tolerant to delay variation compared with QDI circuits.

One advantage of adopting SI circuits is that they can be synthesized from behavioral circuit models described in signal transition graphs (STGs) [52, 57]. This allows complicated controllers to be designed with the help of circuit synthesis software. In certain scenarios, designers might choose to deliberately weaken the difference between QDI and SI circuits by considering all wires as isochronic forks, especially for the asynchronous controllers automatically synthesized by software. In this sense, SI circuits are also QDI.

2.1.4 Relaxed QDI

Since DI, QDI and SI circuits assume gate delays are unbounded, the completion of the operation on a sub-circuit must be explicitly monitored by an extra circuit, namely a completion detection circuit. These completion detection circuits incur speed and area overhead which can be substantial especially when a significant number of operations are to be synchronized. To reduce this overhead, designers might exploit the delay relations between operations that are synchronized [219, 220, 237, 262] and to simplify the completion detection circuit. Circuits designed in this manner are usually called relaxed QDI circuits. For an example, if two operations A and B are required to be synchronized and it is known that operation A always completes before B, then the completion detection circuit can be reduced to checking the completion of B only, leaving the completion of A undetected. As long as the assumptions on delay relations are not violated, relaxed QDI circuits are still tolerant to delay variations just like DI, QDI and SI circuits.

2.1.5 Self-Timed

In a sense, all asynchronous circuits are self-timed as they do not rely on the global clocks but we normally use the term to refer the asynchronous circuits that assume gates and wires have bounded delays. Since the delay is bounded, completion detection circuits can be replaced by matched delay lines by worst-case delay analysis. The resulting circuits are normally more area, speed and even power efficient than their QDI equivalent. However, the bounded delay assumption compromises their tolerance to delay variations. Moreover, self-timed circuits may require special (manual) treatment in the layout process to ensure that the estimated bounded delay assumption is not violated.

2.2   HANDSHAKE PROTOCOLS

In asynchronous circuits, data are transmitted on data channels according to certain types of handshake protocols, which control when a data is put on a channel by a sender and when the data is considered captured by a receiver. A transfer of data starts with an *initiator* asserting a request (*req*) on the channel. On the other end of this channel, the *target* responds the request with an acknowledgment (*ack*). Depending on the direction where data flow, a channel is either a *push* channel where data flow with the request as shown in Figure 2.2a, or a *pull* channel where data go along with the acknowledgment as shown in Figure 2.2b [13].

2.2.1   Return-to-Zero

Let us consider a push channel. To start a data transfer, the initiator can assert a positive voltage on *req* (*req*+) along with data and wait for a positive *ack* (*ack*+) as the confirmation of receiving the data. Data are required to remain valid and stable during this period. In this scenario, both *req* and *ack* must be withdrawn to zero to start the next transfer. As a result, the whole data transfer cycle needs four phases as shown in Figure 2.3: $req+ \rightarrow ack+ \rightarrow req- \rightarrow ack-$. We normally describe this type of

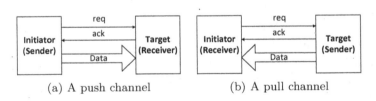

(a) A push channel   (b) A pull channel

Figure 2.2   Channel models of asynchronous circuits.

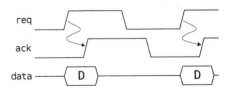

Figure 2.3   4-Phase handshake protocol.

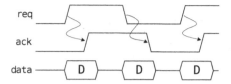

Figure 2.4   2-phase handshake protocol.

channels complying with the *4-phase* handshake protocol, or utilizing the return-to-zero (RTZ) signaling or level signaling.

2.2.2   Non-Return-to-Zero

Requiring the withdrawal of *req* and *ack* before the start of the next data transfer can be a waste of bandwidth as no data is transferred during these two phases. Therefore, some channels adopt a *2-phase* protocol, which is also called non-return-to-zero (NRZ) signaling or transition signaling. As described by the name, a data transfer cycle needs only two phases: a transition on *req* and a transition on *ack*, as shown in Figure 2.4. Whenever there is a transition on *req*, no matter positive or negative, data are put on the channel and stay stable until they are captured, indicated by a transition on *ack*.

In theory, 2-phase is better than 4-phase because data are delivered in two phases instead of four phases, which means a 2-phase channel might be faster and more energy efficient than a 4-phase channel. However, it has some implementation problems: Implementing a 4-phase channel requires only level triggered circuits, which can be constructed using gates from standard cell libraries. On the contrary, implementing a 2-phase channel requires gates triggered by both positive and negative edges, which must be customarily designed at transistor level [236]. In other words, it can be complicated and difficult to implement 2-phase channels. Fault tolerance is another problem. In 4-phase channels, storage components are active and vulnerable to transient faults 50% of time in the worst case but it is 100% of time for 2-phase channels as the storage components are always ready for new data. 4-phase protocol is less vulnerable to transient faults than 2-phase protocol [209].

Consequently, 4-phase protocol is the most utilized handshake protocol in asynchronous circuits [2, 11, 28, 67, 75, 196, 200, 212, 223, 244] and is the preferred handshake protocol in this book.

2.3 DATA ENCODING

Like handshake protocols, data encoding is an important concept in asynchronous designs. Figure 2.5 illustrates a general asynchronous pipeline, which comprises a *control* path and a *data* path. The control path contains the latch control circuit which triggers the latching operations on the data path, which processes the actual data. The term *data encoding* refers to how information is represented on the *data* path. It is closely relevant to delay models (DI, QDI, SI or self-timed) and has a significant impact on the circuit area, speed and energy efficiency. Besides, codes play an important role in fault-tolerance field [229]. According to the timing assumptions of asynchronous circuits, data encodings can be classified into DI [251] and non-DI ones.

2.3.1 Non-Delay-Insensitive Codes

As the simplest non-DI codes, *bundled-data* codes [13], also known as single-rail codes, encode information in the usual binary format: one wire per each bit of information. They are also commonly utilized in traditional synchronous circuits.

Bundled-data encoding has high coding efficiency compared with the others as all codes are valid codes. Arguably, this is also a drawback because bundled-data codes cannot differentiate stable

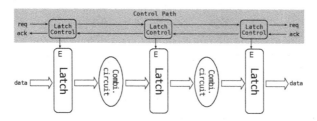

Figure 2.5   Control and data paths of an asynchronous pipline.

data from changing data. They normally need a separate control signal to identify the availability of data but the latency of this control signal is unrelated to the data path, which leads to reduced timing robustness. To make the control signal correlated to the data being processed on the data path, delay gates are normally added on the control path to ensure that the control signal is always later than data. This leads to several issues: The assumption that control signal is always slower than data actually breaks the assumption of unbounded delay normally adopted by asynchronous circuits. Delay gates cannot be automatically and efficiently added by current EDA tools, which increases the burden of circuit designers. Traditional timing analysis tools cannot correctly analyze such delay gates and enforce the timing relation by default. Manual timing analysis and verification is normally required after layout. Although some techniques have been proposed to make the control delays vary according to the data being processed, such as speculation completion [174] or delay selection [231], they unavoidably further complicate the timing model.

2.3.2 Delay-Insensitive Codes

In DI, QDI and relaxed QDI circuits, data bits from a sender may arrive at the receiver at any time and in any order, and the receiver knows when all bits are arrived and ready for latching. This reflects the timing-robustness of these circuits. One of the crucial issues for this communication is to detect when a full data code has arrived [48]. To achieve this target, delay-insensitive codes expand their encoding spaces; therefore, only a portion of the code are valid. The circuit implementation should also guarantee that the transition between two valid codes always follows a path containing only invalid codes. As a result, whenever a different valid code is detected on the data path, the latch knows that a new data arrives.

2.3.2.1 *1-of-n Encoding*

Different from the binary representation of data, 1-of-n encoding occupies n wires ($n \geq 2$) and have only n valid codes all in the one-hot format and a *spacer* (or *NULL*) where all wires are zero.

Table 2.1   1-of-4 code.

	Binary	1-of-4
0	00	0001
1	01	0010
2	10	0100
3	11	1000

Spacers do not represent any data information. They are used to separate two adjacent data symbols if 4-phase handshake protocol is employed. Therefore, 1-of-n encoding delivers $\log_2 n$ bits of information in each valid code.

As an example, Table 2.1 shows the encoding space of the 1-of-4 codes. Every valid code is composed of four data bits but only one of them is one. So each code contains two bits of information. In some literature, 1-of-2 encoding is also called dual-rail codes as the number of wires is two.

For 1-of-n codes, choosing a larger n increases the amount of information encoded in each code. Since the data are one-hot coded, only one data wire transits during one data transfer and the power consumption is nearly the same for different selections of n. Increasing the number of data wires in a 1-of-n pipeline improves energy efficiency. However, using a extremely large n is bad for area efficiency due to the logarithmic relation between n and the information bits. In practical asynchronous on-chip networks, n is usually fewer than five [11, 197].

2.3.2.2   m-of-n Encoding

The m-of-n codes are a superset of 1-of-n codes but usually refer to cases of $2 \leq m < n$. A valid m-of-n code contains m ones on a total of n data wires. The total number of valid codes is therefore $\binom{n}{m}$. Since $\binom{n}{m}$ is larger than $\binom{n}{1}$ when $n \geq 4$ and $n - 1 > m > 1$, m-of-n encoding can deliver more information than 1-of-n encoding with the same wire count, which might lead to lower area overhead.

Table 2.2   2-of-7 code.

	Binary	2-of-7
0	0000	000-0101
1	0001	000-0110
2	0010	000-1001
3	0011	000-1010
4	0100	001-0001
5	0101	001-0010
6	0110	001-0100
7	0111	001-1000
8	1000	010-0001
9	1001	010-0010
10	1010	010-0100
11	1011	010-1000
12	1100	100-0001
13	1101	100-0010
14	1110	100-0100
15	1111	100-1000

Table 2.2 shows an example of a 2-of-7 code [12]. An asynchronous pipeline using this 2-of-7 code delivers four bits of information per transaction, which is equivalent to a wide pipeline built from two 1-of-4 pipelines but with one less data wire. When utilized for delivering data between circuits, m-of-n codes can incur less area overhead while retaining the energy efficiency.

However, m-of-n codes might not be the good candidates for implementation combinational operations [217]. Conventional combinational circuits, especially those synchronous ones, use binary code, which can be directly transformed into 1-of-2 or 1-of-4 codes. However, it is difficult to do calculation in 2-of-7 or general m-of-n codes. Translating m-of-n to dual-rail leads to extra encoding and decoding circuits. Since the area reduction of using m-of-n codes in complex combinational circuits is normally smaller than the area overhead introduced by code translation, m-of-n pipelines are normally only used in long distance communications.

Table 2.3   LEDR code.

	Phase	Wires
0	odd	01
1	odd	10
0	even	00
1	even	11

2.3.2.3   Other DI Encoding

Both 1-of-n and m-of-n codes can be used to implement 2-phase and 4-phase asynchronous circuits but they are not the only encoding available. Some encoding schemes are especially invented for 2-phase circuits. Level-encoded dual-rail (LEDR) signaling [65] is one of the popular 2-phase DI codes which require no return-to-zero phase. As shown in Table 2.3, it encodes two data wires: *data* and *parity*. The *data* holds the real bit value while *parity* indicates the phase. The encoding alternates between two phases: *even* and *odd*. For example, the encoding of bit 1 is 10 in odd phase and 11 in even phase. The introduction of phase provides a necessary distance between adjacent codes and such distance is carefully designed to be one. An improved version is proposed in [149], which is left for interested readers.

2.3.3   Code Evaluation

Here we try to conduct a theoretical comparison of different encoding schemes using two metrics: *code rate* and *toggle rate*.

The code rate (R) is used to measure the coding efficiency [251]: The number of information bits delivered by each data wire. It is calculated using Equation 2.1, where n is the number of wires and M is the number of valid codes.

$$R = \frac{\log_2 M}{n} \tag{2.1}$$

The toggle rate (T) is another metric usually used to evaluate the dynamic energy cost of the encoding. It is normally calculated as the average number of bit transitions needed to deliver one bit of

Table 2.4   Comparison of data encodings under 4-phase protocols.

Encoding	Delay-insensitive	M	R	T
Bundled-data	No	2	1	0.5
Dual-rail: 1-of-2	Yes	2	0.5	2
1-of-4	Yes	4	1	1
2-of-4	Yes	6	0.65	1.5
3-of-6	Yes	20	0.72	1.4
Incomplete 3-of-6	Yes	16	0.67	1.5
2-of-7	Yes	21	0.63	0.9
Incomplete 2-of-7	Yes	16	0.57	1

information. Toggle rate is closely related to the number of phases. Utilizing the 4-phase protocol normally doubles the toggle rate than the 2-phase protocol version of the same encoding. Assuming the 4-phase protocol is used, the toggle rate for m-of-n codes is presented in Equation 2.2

$$T = \frac{2m}{\log_2 M} \qquad (2.2)$$

Table 2.4 presents an estimation of the code rates and the toggle rates of common used code encoding schemes using 4-phase protocols. Bundled data provide the highest code rate and the lowest toggle rate; however, it is not delay insensitive. For the delay insensitive 1-of-n and m-of-n encoding, 1-of-4 provides the best code rate and toggle rate combination although 2-of-7 may further reduce the toggle rate. General speaking, 1-of-n codes can be efficiently utilized in combination operations while m-of-n codes is more suitable for the pure data communication between circuits thanks to its potentially low toggle rate.

2.4   ASYNCHRONOUS PIPELINES

The general structure of asynchronous pipelines has already been depicted in Figure 2.5. Depending on the implementation of the latches and the correlation between the data path and the control path, we build different styles of asynchronous pipelines. In fact, since the number of these different styles of pipelines is too large

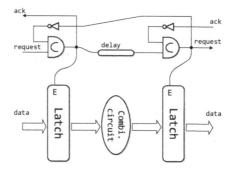

Figure 2.6   A 4-phase bundled-data pipline.

Figure 2.7   2-input C-element.

and we just cannot cover them all in this book, we concentrate on describing the bundled-data pipeline and the multi-rail pipelines as they are more utilized than others.

2.4.1   Bundled-Data Pipeline

Bundled-data pipelines encode data in the binary format as described in Section 2.3.1. A simple bundled-data pipeline is presented in Figure 2.6. For an N-bit bundled-data pipeline, the wire count of data is N. The number of available symbols is 2^N and every symbol is valid. Since the data path cannot differentiate stable data from changing data, the triggering of the latches relies solely on the control logic on the control path.

The simplest latch triggering circuit is to use Muller C-elements as Figure 2.7 shows. Such a pipeline is also called a Muller pipeline or a single-rail pipeline. The Muller C-element is one of the most utilized primitives in asynchronous circuits. Described by the transition table (Table 2.5), a C-element behaves like a combined logical AND and latch. The next state of output q^* updates when both

Table 2.5   Transition table of a 2-input C-element.

a_0	a_1	q^*
0	0	0
1	1	1
0	1	q
1	0	q

input pins have the same value, otherwise the output value retains its previous value q.

The waveform of this bundled-data pipeline is depicted in Figure 2.3. The C-elements in the control pipeline trigger data latches only when the data from the previous pipeline stage is valid (*request+*) and the next pipeline stage is ready for new data (*ack−*). Since the control path has no way to actually detect the data arrival events, some delay gates are added on *request* path to ensure that latches are triggered after data are arrived and stable. As mentioned in Section 2.3.1, the use of delay gates is one of the major problems of implementing a bundled-data pipeline and it makes the pipeline delay sensitive. The latches on the data path are level triggered latches complying with the 4-phase handshake protocol.

It is possible to implement 2-phase bundled-data pipelines, such as the micropipeline first invented by Ivan Sutherland [236]. A micropipeline can utilize the Muller pipeline as the trigger control logic but the data latches are double-edge triggered. These double-edge triggered latches are usually transistor level designs which are unavailable in pure standard cell design flows.

2.4.2   Multi-Rail Pipeline

Multi-rail pipelines represent a family of pipeline styles utilizing the 1-of-n and m-of-n encoding schemes. Circuit implemented using multi-rail pipelines are often QDI (or relaxed-QDI) as they resolve two of the major reasons why bundled-data pipelines are not QDI: the binary encoding cannot indicate the arrival of data and the control path triggers latches without detecting the data arrivals. As described in Section 2.3.2, delay-insensitive codes, such

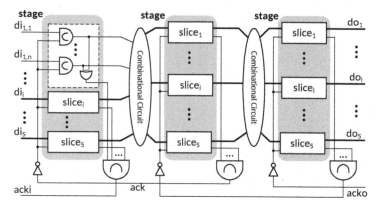

Figure 2.8   A 4-phase 1-of-n multi-rail pipeline.

as m-of-n encoding, expand their encoding space to differentiate valid codes from invalid ones. As long as the transition between any two valid symbols is connected by invalid symbols, data can indicate its availability. This is then used by the control path to trigger latches properly after the arrivals of new data symbols.

Figure 2.8 demonstrates the general structure of a 4-phase 1-of-n multi-rail pipeline. Each pipeline stage is composed of S latch slices, each of which is an asynchronous latch (or half buffer latch) built from n C-elements that can store one 1-of-n symbol [231]. The total data width of the pipeline is therefore $S \cdot \log_2 n$.

When using the 4-phase protocol, a pipeline stage stays in the following three states:

- **spacer**: all S codes are spacers (all 0s);

- **incomplete data**: this is an intermediate state between a spacer and a complete data where some of the S codes are valid while others are spacers;

- **complete data**: all S codes are valid.

As shown in Figure 2.9, the data transition on a pipeline stage always follows the sequence of "*spacer → incomplete data → complete data → incomplete data → spacer*".

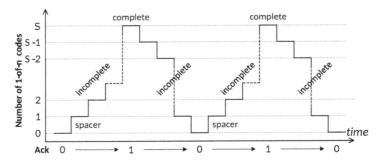

Figure 2.9   State transitions of a 4-phase multi-rail pipeline stage.

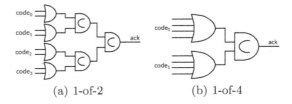

(a) 1-of-2   (b) 1-of-4

Figure 2.10   Completion detectors for 1-of-n codes.

The half buffers are triggered by the acknowledge signal (ack) driven by the next pipeline stage. When the data latched on the current stage is safely captured by the next stage ($ack+$), it can be released. Vice versa, a new data can be latched when the data on the next stage is released ($ack-$). Consequently, the control path of a multi-rail pipeline does not require a *req* signal as the bundled-data pipeline does. The latches in one pipeline stage is triggered and synchronized by the ack signal, which should indicate the arrival of a complete data or a spacer.

Such indication is generated by a completion detector (CD). Figure 2.10 illustrates the implementation of the CDs for 4-bit wide 1-of-2 and 1-of-4 pipeline stages. Each of the first level of OR gates detects the validness of a single 1-of-n code. When all 1-of-n codes are valid, the output of C-element tree becomes high. It returns low when all slices capture spacers. Compared with Figure 2.8, the tree of 2-input C-elements is an equivalent implementation of the multi-input C-element. The CD of 1-of-2 pipelines is one level deeper than CD of 1-of-4 pipelines.

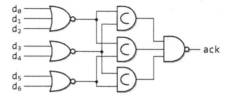

Figure 2.11 Completion detection circuit of a 2-of-7 pipeline latch slice.

Similar to 1-of-n codes, m-of-n codes can be used to implement the data paths for multi-rail pipelines. When m-of-n codes are used, the internal structure of a latch slice is similar to those shown in Figure 2.8. The CDs are more complicated thanks to their complex encoding. Instead of using a single n-input OR gate as in a 1-of-n latch slice, Figure 2.11 depicts one possible implementation of the CD in a 2-of-7 latch slice [12] according to the encoding detailed in Table 2.2.-

2.4.3 Performance Comparison

2.4.3.1 Pipeline Delay

Pipeline delay is the forward latency of delivering a valid data from one end of an empty pipeline to the other end. It represents the delay performance of the pipelines stages. Empty multi-rail pipeline stages capture data whenever they are ready. Bundled-data pipelines insert delay gates on the control path to ensure that latch triggers are slower than data. As a result, bundled-data pipelines normally demonstrate longer pipeline delay than multi-rail pipelines. However, it is not true when complicated combinational circuits are implemented. The using of multi-rail pipelines, especially the m-of-n pipelines, leads to slow combinational circuits. When the extra delay caused by these slow combinational circuits is longer than the added delay on the bundled-data control path, bundled-data pipelines show better speed performance.

2.4.3.2 Pipeline Throughput

Just like any pipelines, when the speed of data production overruns the speed of consumption, the pipeline will gradually be overfed. As a result, incoming data cannot be latched immediately as pipeline stages are busy processing the previous data. In this scenario, the speed performance of a pipeline is determined by the speed of handshake (the loop path delay of adjacent pipeline stages) instead of the pipeline delay. The reverse of the period is the maximum throughput. It is obvious that pipeline stages may have different periods. The stage with the maximum period determines the maximum throughput because other pipeline stages are always waiting for the slowest one when the pipeline is heavily loaded. The slowest loop path is the *critical cycle* of the pipeline.

For long distance serial pipelines, 2-phase pipelines are normally faster (in terms of throughput) than 4-phase pipelines because no reset on request lines is needed. Bundled-data pipelines may suffer from the large data skew in long distance transmission.

For wide pipelines without complicated combinational circuits, bundled-data pipelines outperform QDI multi-rail pipelines. Although the added delay gates introduce extra latency, this overhead can be reduced if the extra delay is accurately matched with the actual delay of the data path and the data path itself is carefully routed to minimize the wire skew. On the other hand, the completion detection circuits needed to synchronize the latch slices lead to significant delay.

If complicated combinational circuits are implemented between pipeline stages, the delay overhead of using a multi-rail pipeline can be large. Similar to pipeline delay, bundled-data pipelines normally achieve better throughput thanks to their fast combinational circuits.

2.4.3.3 Area and Power Consumption

Bundled-data pipelines utilize binary coding and the combinational circuits are the same as those in synchronous circuits. Multi-rail pipelines, on the other hand, need extra data latches in pipeline stages due to the expanded symbol space, require encoders and decoders when m-of-n codes are used, and lead to large combinational circuits. In other words, multi-rail pipelines introduce significant area overhead due to their inefficient data encoding. The benefit of using multi-rail pipelines is their compliance with the

QDI delay assumption while all bundled-data implemented circuits are self-timed.

For long distance serial pipelines, m-of-n pipelines consume less area than dual-rail or 1-of-n pipelines. To achieve a reasonable latency, buffers and inverters are inserted on the long wires to increase driving strength and reduce transition time. These buffers are the major area overhead. The m-of-n codes reduce the wire count as well as the area. However, when complex functions are needed, the use of m-of-n codes should be generally avoided because of their unaffordable area overhead in combinational circuits.

No clock is needed in asynchronous circuit styles therefore no dynamic power is consumed when the circuit is idle. The leakage power is proportional to the area. The key issue is the dynamic power consumed in active circuits, which is related to the toggle rate. Bundled-data pipelines represent data in binary code. On average 50% of data wires flip very cycle. Multi-rail pipelines represent data in 1-of-n or m-of-n codes. In each 4-phase multi-rail pipeline, one wire (dual-rail or 1-of-n) or m wires (m-of-n) must toggle twice every cycle. All pipelines have some extra toggles introduced by the *ack* line and the *request* line (only in bundled-data pipelines).

Based on the toggle rates in Table 2.4, bundled-data pipelines consume less power than multi-rail ones. Normally, 2-phase pipelines consume less dynamic power than 4-phase ones as the toggle rate is halved. The power consumption comparison between m-of-n and 1-of-n pipelines is hard to evaluate. In theory, the toggle rate of m-of-n codes can be smaller than 1-of-n codes. On the other hand, m-of-n pipelines require complicated completion detection circuits which causes extra power consumption.

2.5 IMPLEMENTATION OF ASYNCHRONOUS CIRCUITS

2.5.1 Functional Analysis

Petri nets [167, 192] are the most utilized mathematical tools to describe and analyze the behavior of an asynchronous circuit. In a broader scope of computer science, Petri nets are proposed to analyze the operation of all concurrent systems. Without the intrinsic synchronization of clock, the behavior of an asynchronous circuit is exactly a concurrent system.

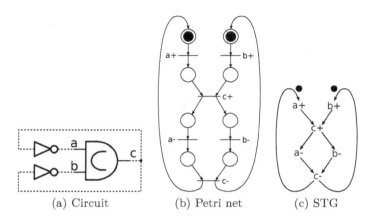

(a) Circuit   (b) Petri net   (c) STG

Figure 2.12   Functional analysis of a simple 2-input C-element.

Briefly speaking, a Petri net is a graph composed of two types of nodes, transitions and places, and directed arcs connecting them. Figure 2.12b depicts the Petri net describing a simple asynchronous circuit containing only one C-element and two inverters (Figure 2.12a). With sufficient number of initial tokens, a Petri net can be executed equivalently to the operation of the corresponding circuit. In the execution, a transition fires (executes) when each of its input places hold at least one token. The execution of this transition consumes one token from each of its input places and generates one token for each of its output places. The labels besides the transitions denote the corresponding events occurring on the circuit when transitions fire.

When the number of tokens that can be held by one place is limited to one, namely 1-bounded, a simple Petri as shown in Figure 2.12b net can be simplified into a signal transition graph (STG) as depicted in Figure 2.12c. A desirable benefit of using a STG is the possibility to synthesize a speed-independent circuit from it. Petrify [57] is one of the most utilized tools capable of doing so. Several controller circuits designed in this book are synthesized from STGs using Petrify.

Petri net can be used to describe the abstract model of certain class of asynchronous circuit. For example, Figure 2.13 describes the behavior of a generic allocator which accepts four incoming

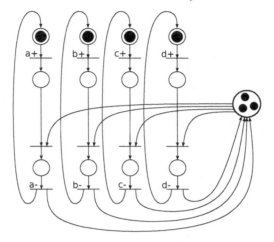

Figure 2.13   Petri net of an abstract allocator/arbiter.

requests from a, b, c and d. Since there is a maximum of three tokens held by the allocator, only three of the four requestors can be granted concurrently. If the number of tokens is reduced to one, the same Petri net then describes an arbiter.

It is important to note that there are many variants of Petri nets which can be used to describe asynchronous circuit, but only a small portion of them can be used to generate speed-independent circuit using Petrify [57]. Figure 2.13 is an example of such Petri nets that cannot be directly used for circuit synthesis. STGs, as the synthesizable variant of Petri nets, normally hold the following properties [231]:

- **Input free choice**: The selection among alternatives must be controlled by mutually exclusive inputs.

- **1-Bounded**: A place will never hold more than one token.

- **Liveness**: There are always executable transitions.

- **Consistent state assignment**: A signal always transits between + and − following any executable path.

- **Persistency**: A transition is always executed when it is able to fire.

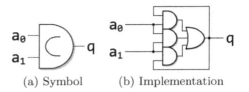

| (a) Symbol | (b) Implementation |

Figure 2.14 Symmetric 2-input C-element (C2).

Table 2.6 Transition table of a symmetric 2-input C-element.

a_0	a_1	q^*
0	0	0
1	1	1
0	1	q
1	0	q

For more details related to STG and the circuit synthesis procedure, please refer to Section 6.2 of [231].

2.5.2 Common Circuit Components

2.5.2.1 Basic Components

In addition to basic logic gates like AND, OR, NOT, etc. and latches, asynchronous circuits commonly use some extra basic elements. The most common one is the Muller C-element [163, 231], also known as a C-element or C-gate. It is a fundamental control and state-holding element that has been extensively used.

The most common form of C-elements is a symmetric 2-input C-element (C2). Figure 2.14a depicts its symbol, Figure 2.14b presents on possible implementation of it using standard cells, Table 2.6 reveals the transition table and Listing 2.1 shows how we can actually implement it in Verilog HDL.

In relaxed-QDI circuits, some symmetric C-elements can be optimized into asymmetric C-elements for improved speed performance and area consumption. Depending on the extra delay assumption, a symmetric 2-input C-element can be optimized into

```
module c2 (a0, a1, q);
    input a0, a1;          // two inputs
    output q;              // output
    wire [2:0] m;          // internal wires

    nand U1 (m[0], a0, a1);
    nand U2 (m[1], a0, q);
    nand U3 (m[2], a1, q);
    assign q = ~&m;
endmodule
```

Listing 2.1   A symmetric 2-input C-element

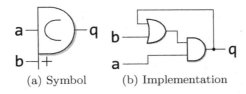

(a) Symbol   (b) Implementation

Figure 2.15   2-input C-element with a plus input (C2p).

either a 2-input C-element with a plus input (C2p) or a 2-input C-element with a minus input (C2n).

A 2-input C-element with a plus input (C2p) can be used instead of a normal symmetric C-element when one of its inputs affects only the positive transition of the output. Figure 2.15a depicts a 2-input C-element with a plus input, Figure 2.15b presents on possible implementation of it using standard cells, Table 2.7 reveals the transition table and Listing 2.2 shows how we can actually implement it in Verilog HDL. According to the transition table, the positive transition on the output $q+$ requires both inputs to be high but the negative transition $q-$ happens whenever a becomes low disregarding the value of b. According to the implementation shown in Figure 2.15b, The level of gates on the input a is reduced to one as the value of input b is not checked during the $q-$ transition. This reduces the area and improves the timing on a.

Similarly, a 2-input C-element with a minus input (C2n) can be used instead of a normal symmetric C-element when one of its inputs affects only the negative transition of the output. Figure 2.16a depicts a 2-input C-element with a plus input, Figure 2.16b presents

Table 2.7   Transition table of a 2-input C-element with a plus input (C2p).

a	b	q^*
0	0	0
1	1	1
0	1	0
1	0	q

```
module c2p (a, b, q);
input a;        // the normal input
input b;        // the plus input
output q;       // output
wire m;         // internal wire

or  U1 (m, b, q);
and U2 (q, m, a);
endmodule
```

Listing 2.2   2-input C-element with a plus input (C2p)

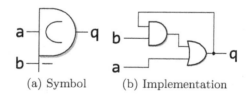

(a) Symbol   (b) Implementation

Figure 2.16   2-input C-element with a minus input (C2n).

on possible implementation of it using standard cells, Table 2.8 reveals the transition table and Listing 2.3 shows how we can actually implement it in Verilog HDL. The negative transition on the output $q-$ requires both inputs to be low but the positive transition $q+$ happens whenever a becomes high disregarding the value of b. The level of gates on the input a is reduced to one as the value of input b is not checked during the $q+$ transition, which reduces the area and improves the timing on a.

Table 2.8 Transition table of a 2-input C-element with a minus input (C2n).

a	b	q^*
0	0	0
1	1	1
0	1	q
1	0	1

```
module c2p (a, b, q);
    input a;        // the normal input
    input b;        // the minus input
    output q;       // output
    wire m;         // internal wire

    and U1 (m, b, q);
    or  U2 (q, m, a);
endmodule
```

Listing 2.3   2-input C-element with a minus input (C2n)

Note that the number of inputs for a C-element is not limited to two. For a multiple input symmetric C-element, we normally implement it using a tree of 2-input C-element. One such example of implementing a 4-input C-element is depicted in Figure 2.10a. The input combinations of asymmetric C-element are not limited as well. For example, Figure 2.17 shows the symbol and implementation of a 3-input C-element with a plus input (C3p), Figure 2.18 shows the symbol and implementation of a 3-input C-element with two plus inputs (C3p2), and Figure 2.19 shows the symbol and implementation of a 3-input C-element with one plus and one minus inputs (C3p1n1).

The Mutex Exclusion (ME) element [231] is another important asynchronous cell. It has been widely used in the arbitration circuit of existing asynchronous designs [11, 43, 88, 115, 223]. Figure 2.20 presents its symbol and one possible implementation [231]. It reads two requests and grants the one arriving first. If they arrive at the same time, the ME may enter a metastable state before

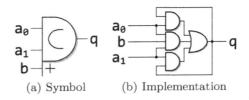

(a) Symbol   (b) Implementation

Figure 2.17   3-input C-element with a plus input (C3p).

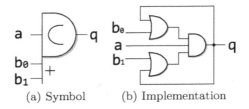

(a) Symbol   (b) Implementation

Figure 2.18   3-input C-element with two plus inputs (C3p2).

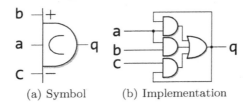

(a) Symbol   (b) Implementation

Figure 2.19   3-input C-element with one plus and one minus inputs (C3p1n1).

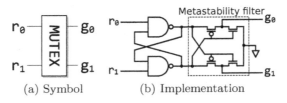

(a) Symbol   (b) Implementation

Figure 2.20   Mutex Exclusion (ME) element [231].

making an arbitrating decision. As the timing is flexible, a metastability filter (Figure 2.20b) is added to detect metastability and delay any decision until it has resolved. However, this metastability filter is a dedicated transistor level design that does not have an

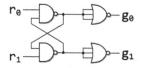

Figure 2.21   A standard cell implementation of a ME element.

```
module mutex (r0 , r1 , g0 , g1);
   input r0, r1;
   output g0, g1;
   wire g0n, g1n;

   nand U1 (g0n, r0, g1n);
   nand U2 (g1n, r1, g0n);
   nor   F1 (g0, g0n, g0n, g0n);   // dont touch!
   nor   F2 (g1, g1n, g1n ,g1n);   // dont touch!
endmodule;
```

Listing 2.4   Standard cell implementation of a ME element

equivalent standard cell implementation. To produce a similar filter effect, Figure 2.21 demonstrates another implementation that can be implemented using standard cells only. The multiple input NOR gate effectively lowers the threshold of an equivalent inverter [115]; therefore, a grant is produced only when the input of the NOR gate becomes a relatively strong 0.

The Verilog HDL implementation is revealed in Listing 2.4. Note that the NOR gates for the metastability filter should be replaced with the name of the actual NOR gates in the target cell library and these two gates should be labeled *dont touch* to avoid being optimized into simple inverters.

2.5.2.2   Arbiters

Arbiters are an important class of combinational components in asynchronous on-chip networks where arbitration occurs frequently.

The multi-way ME arbiter is fast and area efficient with a small number of requests. It is utilized extensively in asynchronous on-chip networks [67, 225]. A single ME element is a 2-way ME arbiter.

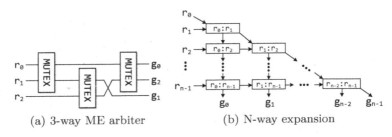

(a) 3-way ME arbiter   (b) N-way expansion

Figure 2.22   Multi-way ME arbiter.

Multiple ME elements are used when extra requests are arbitrated. Figure 2.22a depicts a 3-way ME arbiter which grants one resource to one of the three requests. Since every pair of requests is checked by a ME element, the arbiter ensures that when one request is granted, all other requests are blocked. The 3-way ME arbiter can be expanded into an arbitrary N-way ME arbiter shown in Figure 2.22b [115]. The total number of ME elements in an N-way ME arbiter is $\binom{N}{2}$ where N is the number of requests.

Multi-way ME arbiters have several advantages over other arbiter structures. Since the number of MEs on every request is equal, requests have the same minimum arbitration delay. Multi-way ME arbiters are strictly fair. They are fast and area efficient when the number of requests is small. However, multi-way ME arbiters are no longer area efficient when the number of requests increases to a certain amount, and other arbitration structures should be selected.

The tree arbiter is also an expandable arbiter structure. It is area efficient and able to handle a large number of requests. Figure 2.23a shows the diagram of a tree arbiter with six requests. It is expanded from the basic ME element. The six requests are first divided into two groups and their combined requests are guarded by the ME. Then the tree arbiter grows into a binary tree. Each arbiter block, as shown in Figure 2.23b [109], divides its requests into two sub-groups until there is only one request in each sub-group.

In Figure 2.23b, the negative grant signals $\bar{g}_0$ and $\bar{g}_1$ are driven by two C2n elements. They guarantee that the output grant signal $\bar{g}_0$ or $\bar{g}_1$ is low (active) only when this arbiter block is granted (low on $\bar{g}$) and the internal ME has chosen the corresponding request through signals ng_0 or ng_1. When the granted request is released,

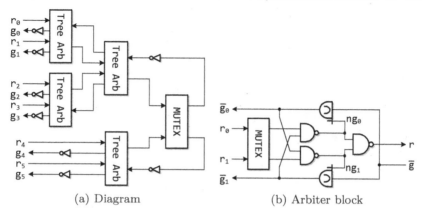

(a) Diagram

(b) Arbiter block

Figure 2.23   Tree arbiter.

the combined request r drops and later the positive voltage on $\bar{g}$ (inactive) drives both $\bar{g}_0$ and $\bar{g}_0$ to high.[1]

Tree arbiters are strictly fair arbiters when the binary tree is balanced; otherwise, the leaf requests near to the root ME element are more likely to be granted than others. The area of a tree arbiter is linear with the number of requests as every new request leads to a new arbiter block. A request is granted when all the arbiter blocks on its route to the root ME element select it. Thus the minimum arbitration delay is proportional to the depth of each request. If the tree arbiter is balanced, the depth of the tree is $\lceil \log_2 N \rceil$ where N is the number of requests. Therefore, the delay of tree arbiters increases logarithmically.

As first introduced in [139], the ring arbiter is an asynchronous "round-robin" arbiter. Figure 2.24 [212] shows an implementation of a ring arbiter developed by Martin [139]. In this ring arbiter, each request from a user is connected to an individual arbiter block as shown in Figure 2.24b. The ring has one and only one token. A request must secure the token in order to be granted. If a request arrives at an arbiter block without a token, the block forwards this

---

[1]In the original design [109], symmetric C-elements are used instead of asynchronous C-elements. Because ng_0 and ng_1 rise long before $\bar{g}$ returns to high, it is not necessary to check the values on ng_0 and ng_1 in practical circuits. Using asymmetric C-elements reduces delay and area.

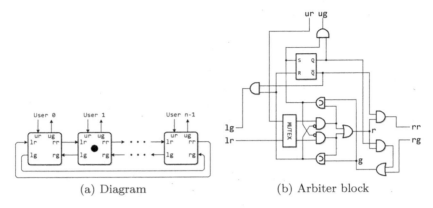

(a) Diagram   (b) Arbiter block

Figure 2.24   Ring arbiter.

request to its neighbor in order to hold a token. In this implementation, the forward process goes clockwise.

The arbiter block has a similar internal structure to the tree arbiter block. Both of them have two request inputs and one combined request output, which is the forward request to its neighbor in a ring arbiter. These two input requests, one from the local user and the other one from its anti-clockwise neighbor, are selected by a ME element. The winner first checks the local token storage, which is the set-reset (RS) latch in Figure 2.24b. A grant is immediately returned if there is a token stored locally, otherwise the combined request is forwarded to the neighbor.

Ring arbiters have a special advantage over other asynchronous arbiters: it remembers the last granted request and selects users in a round-robin fashion. The minimum arbitration delay for a request depends on the location of the token. On average, the distance between the active request and the token is $N/2$ where N is the number of requests. Thus delay is proportional to the number of requests in total. Obviously, the area of a ring arbiter is also proportional to the number of requests in total.

Another way to build a ring arbiter is to let the token circle the ring. A request is granted when the token arrives at its arbiter block [136]. It is shown that using the circling token scheme reduces

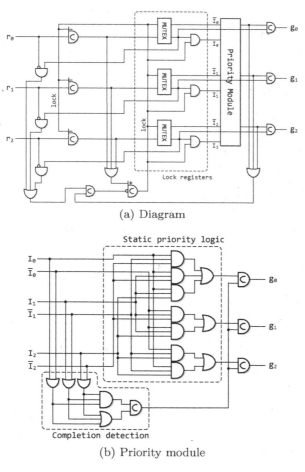

(a) Diagram

(b) Priority module

Figure 2.25 Static priority arbiter.

arbitration latency by half but increases the power consumption significantly when requests are infrequent.

When different priority levels are assigned to requests, a priority arbiter is required. Figure 2.25 shows a 3-way static priority arbiter (SPA) [43]. It has two parts: request capture logic and a priority module. The capture of requests is controlled by *lock* which is generated by the asymmetric C-element at the bottom. Initially *lock* is low and the column of asymmetric C-elements output is low. Incoming requests go through the column of C-elements and MEs.

At the same time, *lock* is driven high, blocking other MEs without an incoming request. Since multiple requests can arrive simultaneously and be captured by multiple MEs, the priority module grants the request with the highest priority. After the request is served, the withdrawal of the corresponding r triggers the release of *lock*, which consequently resets the corresponding asymmetric C-elements in the left column. Later the corresponding g is released. If new requests have been locked by those MEs, *lock* returns to high immediately.

The priority module shown in Figure 2.25b is configured to grant all requests with approximately the same probability. Other priority configurations can be easily achieved by modifying the AND and OR matrix. It is also possible to reconfigure the priority dynamically [43].

Static priority arbiters are fast and area efficient. The arbitration delay depends on the request capture delay and the delay of the priority module. As the positive transition on lock and the locking requests in MEs occur concurrently, the request capture time is short and independent on the number of requests. The delay of the priority module can be long if the number of requests is large.

2.5.2.3 Allocators

Although arbiters are capable of allocating one resource to multiple requests, they cannot allocate multiple resources concurrently, which is a common requirement for implementing asynchronous on-chip networks. In these scenarios, asynchronous allocators are utilized instead of arbiters. Several state-of-the-art asynchronous allocators are introduced. In the description, the resource is named a "client" to avoid the same initial letter with requests.

The virtual channel admission control (VCAC) module used in the QNoC project [67] allocates multiple virtual channels (clients) to several requests; it is an allocator design. Figure 2.26 shows the schematic of a VCAC allocator that can match m clients to n concurrent requests in a sequential way. It contains an n-way ME arbiter and an m-way SPA configured with linear priority.

The allocation runs in three steps: Firstly, one incoming request is selected by the n-way ME arbiter. Secondly, if there are available

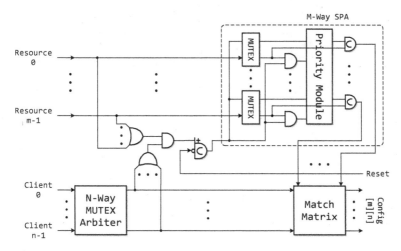

Figure 2.26   Virtual channel admission control.

clients, the m-way SPA is enabled and an available client is chosen for the selected request. Finally, the request and the client are matched inside the match matrix which then generates a configuration (or grant).

Because the VCAC allocator is capable of matching only one pair of request and client at one time, the generated configuration must be latched outside the allocator. The corresponding request and client inputs are also withdrawn once the configuration is captured. A pulse on reset is also generated to allow the SPA to choose another client.

The VCAC allocator is area efficient and fast but has some timing issues. The release of requests and clients is not guarded; therefore, VCAC is not strictly QDI. Only one pair of request and client can be matched at one time, which can be a bottleneck in a busy system. The VCAC allocator is not prioritized. It is believed that SPA is used in VCAC due to its reset capability which makes its peripheral circuit easy to design. However, the area overhead of a SPA is larger than a fair (non-prioritized) arbiter such as a multi-way ME arbiter or a tree arbiter.

A multi-resource arbiter is QDI [88, 89, 211]. As shown in Figure 2.27, multi-resource arbiters and VCAC have similar structures.

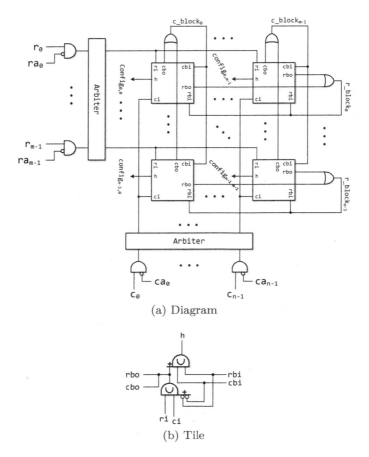

(a) Diagram

(b) Tile

Figure 2.27   Multi-resource arbiter.

Both have two arbiters and a match matrix, but the match matrix of a multi-resource arbiter is more complicated than that of VCAC. Every tile in the match matrix of a multi-resource arbiter is a speed-independent circuit which ensures the corresponding request and client can rise and drop independently.

Like VCAC, a multi-resource arbiter matches clients to requests in a sequential way. At first, the arbiters on requests and clients select a winner pair of request (ri) and client (ci) independently. Then the asymmetric C-element in the corresponding tile (Figure 2.27b) drives rbo and cbo to high. These two signals trigger the corresponding blockage signals r block and c block in Figure 2.27a, which block all the tiles in the same row and column of the chosen request and client. Once the tile receives the blockage signals meaning that other tiles are safely blocked, the configuration h is generated.

The allocated pair of request and client must be withdrawn as soon as possible to allow other requests to be served. The configuration is stored outside the multi-resource arbiter. The peripheral circuit has to raise the corresponding acknowledge signals ra and ca to withdraw the allocated request and client. In the match matrix, the blockage signals rbi and cbi guarantees that the lower asymmetric C-element in Figure 2.27b is disabled until the previous allocation is safely withdrawn.

The major advantage of the multi-resource arbiter over VCAC is its robustness. Multi-resource arbiters are QDI and the timing relation between requests and clients are fully decoupled. As a result, the arbiters on requests and clients run independently. However, the tile based match matrix is area consuming. When the number of requests or clients is large, the blockage signals in the match matrix may fail to release all tiles soon enough when false configurations are produced. The reason is related to the QDI delay assumption. The blockage signals r_block and c_block no longer fit the isochronic fork assumption in a large design. A blockage ring can resolve this problem but it introduces extra area overhead [211].

2.5.3 Metastability and Synchronization

Although nearly all digital circuits can be designed and implemented using pure asynchronous circuits, most designs are implemented using synchronous circuits, while asynchronous circuits must work along with its synchronous counterparts. A common issue that needs to be carefully resolved is the *metastability* issue.

When data are delivered across the asynchronous/synchronous boundary or even between two synchronous modules driven by independent clocks, the storage unit (register or latch) on the receiver side might capture a wrong value if the transitions on the data wires occur inside a small vicinity of the trigger event for the storage unit (such as the positive clock edge for a normal D-type flip-flop). In

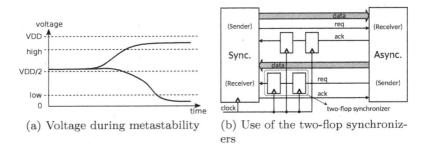

(a) Voltage during metastability

(b) Use of the two-flop synchronizers

Figure 2.28 Metastability and synchronization.

this scenario, the voltage of a data wire at the trigger time might sit just in between the high and low voltage threshold, which is neither 1 nor 0. A storage unit is an inverter loop that boosts the polarity of the input voltage using positive feedback. As shown in Figure 2.28a, the output of this inverter loop will converge to a certain but unknown value [115]. If the final converged value does not match with the input data, an error bit is produced due to metastability. In addition, if the output of this storage unit is used by following circuits before the output converges, this metastability problem may propagate to the downstream storage unit, leading to extra errors. Compared with a bit error, the propagation of metastability is more problematic as the former can be rectified by resampling the input data while the outcome of the latter is hardly controllable.

To stop the propagation of metastability, the most utilized and probably the most reliable solution is to add a two-flip-flop synchronizer [85] on the control signal as depicted in Figure 2.28b. Note that synchronizers are not added on the control signals toward the asynchronous side because asynchronous circuit can avoid metastability by using the incoming control signals to trigger the latch operation.

The use of synchronizers does not eliminate the bit errors produced by metastability but significantly reduces its probability of occurrence. The mean time between failures (MTBF) of using the two-flip-flop synchronizer can be estimated as [66, 85]:

$$MTBF = \frac{T e^{T/\tau}}{T_W f_D} \tag{2.3}$$

where T is the clock period, τ is the settling (setup/hold) time of the flip-flop, T_W is a factor related to the time window of susceptibility and f_D is the transition rate of the incoming data wire. The estimated MTBF of the two-flip-flop synchronizer is around 10^{204} years [85] when used with the 0.18 μm technology. For technologies using smaller geometries, an extra stage of flip-flop might be needed for high-reliable applications.

2.5.4 Optimization with Traditional EDA Tools

In most scenarios, the QDI implementation of an asynchronous design should work without any forms of timing optimization or analysis. Some researchers might even believe the use of traditional synchronous EDA tools for asynchronous designs should be deliberately avoided. In our opinions, traditional synchronous EDA tools, especially the synthesis tools, can be used to improve the speed performance of the produced asynchronous circuit but a carefully designed set of constraints should be provided to guide the synthesis tools.

Before diving into the details, we need to understand how the traditional synthesis tools work. In synchronous designs, the circuit is divided into timing paths using the clock signal. Each path starts from either the output pin of a flip-flop (latch) or an input port and ends at either the data input pin of a flip-flop (latch) or an output port.[2] After being provided with a target clock frequency, the synthesis tool calculates the latency of all timing paths and endeavors to reduce the paths longer than the clock period. For this mechanism to work, no feedback wire is allowed on any of the timing paths. All loops of combinational circuits must be broken by at least one flip-flop or declared false path[3] otherwise.

---

[2]Let us overlook the clock path here for simplicity. They are considered ideal during synthesis any way.

[3]When a timing path is declared false, the synthesis tool will not calculate its delay. Only area and power optimization is applied the path.

Unlike synchronous circuits, combinational loops are everywhere in asynchronous circuits. If we naively feed the design to a synthesis tool without telling it how to break the loops, the tool would report all loops found in the design and break these loops in a rather random and uncontrolled manner. Speed optimization based on the timing calculation using arbitrarily broken loops is obviously unacceptable. Instead, designers must choose proper locations to break individual loops and convey this information to the tool by constraints.

2.5.4.1 Loop Elimination

There are two levels of loops that need to be eliminated: the loops inside basic components and the loops in designs in general. Since basic components, such as C-elements and ME elements, are used all over the design, the loops inside them should be handled inside the components, while other loops depend on the function of individual designs and should be handled case by case.

Let us take the symmetric 2-input C-element (Figure 2.14 and Listing 2.1) as an example. According to the naming pattern used by the Synopsys Design Compiler:

$$\textbf{type} \; name(Z, A, B, C, D, ...) \tag{2.4}$$

There are two internal feedback loops: (1) $q \to \text{U2.B} \to \text{U2.Z} \to q$ and (2) $q \to \text{U3.B} \to \text{U3.Z} \to q$.

Assuming the speed of C-element should be optimized to speed up the path from inputs (a_0 and a_1) to output (q), the internal loops should be broken without affecting the external timing calculation. Therefore, the following constraint can be used to break the internal loops at U2.B and U3.B in all symmetric 2-input C-elements:

```
foreach_in_collection celln \
  [get_references -hierarchical c2_*] {
  set_disable_timing [get_object_name $celln]/U2 \
    -from B -to Z
  set_disable_timing [get_object_name $celln]/U3 \
    -from B -to Z
}
```

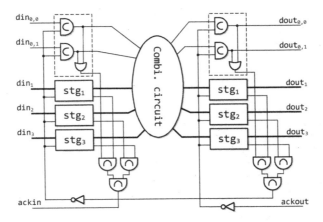

Figure 2.29   A simple dual-rail pipeline.

The get_references command collects all symmetric 2-input C-elements,[4] and the two set_disable_timing commands tell the synthesis tool to avoid estimating the delay of any paths through U2.B → U2.Z and U3.B → U3.Z, which effectively break the internal loops. Note that breaking these internal loops does not lead to overly long delay on these two loops. Normally, there are global constraints on the total power, the total area and the maximal capacity and transition time on each wire. These constraints would prohibit the synthesis tool to deliberately prolong the delay of a circuit. Considering the simple structure of the C-element, there is no need to add special constraint to regulate the delay of the internal loops. In fact, doing so may significantly prolong the overall running time for synthesis with no observable timing improvement.

We use a general dual-rail pipeline as an example to explain how to break loops outside the basic elements. The circuit structure is depicted in Figure 2.29 with the detailed implementation of one pipeline stage revealed in Listing 2.5. The data latch used in the pipeline stage is implemented in symmetric C-elements but the module name is changed from c2 to dc2 to indicate its use as data

---

[4]Timing constraints are applied after the whole design is uniquified. As a result, a numeric suffix is automatically appended to all c2 modules.

```
module ctree (co, ci); // a C-tree
   parameter DW = 2;
   input [DW-1:0] ci;
   output         co;
   wire [2*DW-2:0] dat;
   genvar i;
   assign dat[DW-1:0] = ci;
   generate for (i=0; i<DW-1; i=i+1) begin:AT
   c2 CT(.a0(dat[i*2]), .a1(dat[i*2+1]),
         .q(dat[i+DW]));
   end endgenerate
   assign co = dat[2*DW-2];
endmodule

module dc2 (d, a, q); // data latch
   input   d, a;
   output  q;
   wire [2:0] m;
   nand U1(m[0], a, d);
   nand U2(m[1], d, q);
   nand U3(m[2], a, q);
   assign q = ~&m;
endmodule

module pipe( din, ackin, dout, ackout);
   parameter DW = 32;
   input   [DW-1:0][1:0]  din;
   output  [DW-1:0][1:0]  dout;
   input   ackout;
   output  ackin;
   wire [DW-1:0] tack;
   genvar        i;
   generate for (i=0; i<SCN; i++) begin:DD
     dc2 DC0(din[i][0], ackout, dout[i][0]);
     dc2 DC1(din[i][0], ackout, dout[i][0]);
     assign tack[i] = |dout[i];
   end endgenerate
   ctree #(.DW(DW)) ACKT(.ci(tack), .co(ackin));
endmodule
```

Listing 2.5   Implementation of a dual-rail pipeline stage

latches. The tree of C-elements needed for generating the ackin
signal use the normal c2 modules.

One combinational loop exists for each pipeline stage: dout →
ackin → previous stage → din → dout. It is easy to make an
analogy between synchronous and asynchronous circuits here. The
ackout is used as the trigger for the data latch, which behaves
exactly like a clock signal to synchronous data latch. Consequently,
it is natural to understand that we need to break the timing at
din → dout. Considering that we need to break the internal loops
inside each dc2 cells, the combined constraints can be described as:

```
foreach_in_collection celln \
  [get_references -hierarchical dc2_*] {
    set_disable_timing [get_object_name $celln]/U1 \
      -from B -to Z
    set_disable_timing [get_object_name $celln]/U2 \
      -from A -to, Z
    set_disable_timing [get_object_name $celln]/U2 \
      -from B -to Z
    set_disable_timing [get_object_name $celln]/U3 \
      -from B -to Z
}
```

In summary, for loops in the designs, we should utilize special
names to easy the search for the specific location where timing
paths should be broken. When such renaming is not possible for
not enough, synthesizers also allow specifying cells using the hierarchical names.

2.5.4.2 Speed Optimization

Assuming all combinational loops are broken at proper locations by
constraining the synthesizer, we now discuss how we can improve
the speed performance using the synthesizer as well. The key is to
define individual timing path groups by specifically specifying the
starting and ending points.

Let us use the dual-rail pipeline example again. First of all, we
can ask the synthesizer to put the starting and ending points of
timing groups into different collections:

```
set DPD []
set DPA []
foreach_in_collection celln \
  [get_references -hierarchical dc2_*] {
    append_to_collection DPD \
      [ get_pins [get_object_name $celln]/U1/B]
```

```
append_to_collection DPD \
  [ get_pins [get_object_name $celln]/U2/A]
append_to_collection DPA \
  [ get_pins [get_object_name $celln]/U1/A]
append_to_collection DPA \
  [ get_pins [get_object_name $celln]/U3/A]
}

set IODI [filter [get_ports *i*] "@port_direction == in
  "]
set IODO [filter [get_ports *o*] "@port_direction ==
  out"]
set IOAI [filter [get_ports *i*] "@port_direction ==
  out"]
set IOAO [filter [get_ports *o*] "@port_direction == in
  "]
```

With these constraints, we have 6 collections of points: data input pins for pipeline stages (DPD), ack input pins for pipeline stages (DPA), data ports on the input side (IODI), data ports on the output side (IODO), ack ports on the input side (IOAI), and ack ports on the output side (IOAO).

With the help of them, we can then define timing constraints for different timing groups:

```
set DATA_dly 1.0
set ACK_dly 1.6

set_max_delay [expr ${DATA_dly} * 1.00] \
  -from ${DPA}   -to ${DPD}   -group G_DATA
set_max_delay [expr ${ACK_dly} * 1.00]  \
  -from ${DPA}   -to ${DPA}   -group G_ACK
set_max_delay [expr ${DATA_dly} * 0.30] \
  -from ${IODI}   -to ${DPD}   -group G_DATA
set_max_delay [expr ${ACK_dly} * 0.75]  \
  -from ${DPA}   -to ${IOAI}   -group G_ACK
set_max_delay [expr ${DATA_dly} * 0.70] \
  -from ${DPA}   -to ${IODO}   -group G_DATA
set_max_delay [expr ${ACK_dly} * 0.25]  \
  -from ${IOAO}   -to ${DPA}   -group G_ACK
```

DATA_dly and ACK_dly define two expected latency values for the forward data path and backward acknowledge path on each pipeline segment. The latency for the acknowledge paths is set longer than it for data paths because the asynchronous circuits of NoC components are data transmitting circuits light in calculation. The trees of C-elements on the acknowledge paths are actually the most time consuming circuit on most pipeline stages. The following `set_max_delay` instructions constrain the individual latency for different path groups. The general data paths DPA → DPD and acknowledge paths DPD → DPA belong to the data path group G_DATA and acknowledge path group G_ACK respectively and are constrained with the default latency. Input data paths IODI → DPD and output data paths DPD → IODO belong to G_DATA as well and are constrained with 30% and 70% of the default data path latency respectively. Similarly, input acknowledge paths DPA → IOAI and output acknowledge paths IOAO → DPA belong to G_ACK and are regulated at 75% and 25% of the default acknowledge path latency respectively. This set of constrains ensure that all paths in the synchronous circuits have a default timing requirement just like setting the clock period in the synthesis for synchronous circuit.

Sometime, we would need to regulate special path groups with extra constrains. This could be done by moving the related paths to separate path groups and applying different latency values. It is also helpful to prioritize the synthesis engine to optimize the knowing critical path before other paths. This could be done by increasing the default weight for the group of critical paths. Assuming the data path group G_DATA is the critical path group, we can use:

```
group_path -weight 1.5 -critical_range 40 -name G_DATA
```

to increase the weight to 1.5 and force the synthesizer to simultaneously consider 40 paths in this group if the timing is not satisfied.

CHAPTER 3

Asynchronous Networks-on-Chip

The number of transistors on a single die has doubled periodically for several decades as predicted by Moore's law but the design complexity is becoming unmanageable. Traditional SoC systems were hierarchically built from processors, functional units, intellectual property (IP) blocks and bus-based communication infrastructures. When tens to hundreds of these hardware components are packed into one system, a hierarchical bus is not scalable enough to support the huge amount of communication and becomes the major throughput bottleneck. To overcome this problem, researchers have proposed the idea of on-chip network or network-on-a-chip (NoC) from the 1990s [24, 62, 96, 177]. In such a NoC system, SoC subsystems use buses as their local communication method but the data traveling across the boundary of a sub-system are encapsulated into packets and delivered to the target sub-system by a scalable network-based communication infrastructure [62]. As a scalable and efficient on-chip interconnection fabric to support the communication of large-scale multi-core systems [62, 107, 152], NoCs have been widely used in both chip multi-processors (CMP) and multi-processor system-on-chip (MPSoC) [32, 253]. In this chapter, the background of NoCs and the recent developments of asynchronous on-chip networks are introduced.

3.1 CONCEPTS OF NETWORKS-ON-CHIP

A NoC or on-chip network is the chip level communication infrastructure that connects tens to hundreds of sub-systems. As shown in Figure 3.1, a sub-system has its own bus, processor, memory/cache or other function blocks. Such a sub-system, namely a processing element (PE), communicates with other PEs through the on-chip network consisting of routers and links. The network interface in each PE, acting as a bridge, converts and delivers data between the on-chip network and the local sub-system.

Depending on the structure of PEs, a NoC can be classified into two categories: homogeneous NoCs and heterogeneous NoCs. All PEs in a homogeneous NoC use the same internal structure; therefore, they have the same size and the chip is symmetric, whereas the PEs in a heterogeneous NoC may use different structures. The size of a PE is therefore variable and the chip floorplan is hardly symmetric. Chip multi-processors are normally homogeneous NoCs as every PE is a processor [249]. On the other hand, MPSoCs are generally heterogeneous NoCs because PEs have different functions [53].

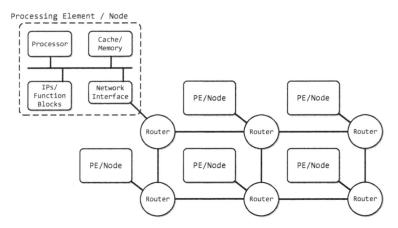

Figure 3.1   Architecture of a NoC.

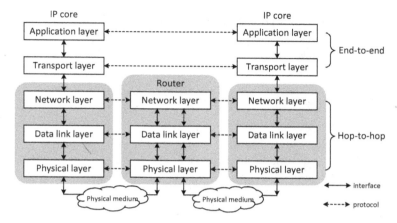

Figure 3.2 A modified OSI reference model [241].

3.1.1 Network Layer Model

As shown in Figure 3.2, it is possible to describe a NoC using a modified open systems interconnection (OSI) model as normally adopted in traditional macro networks [241]:

- *Physical layer* is the layer above the physical medium, which transmits raw bit streams and specifies the electrical/physical properties of the connection.

- *Data link layer* groups bit streams into small blocks to provide reliable hop-to-hop transmission over the physical medium. Flow control methods, which decide the allocation of network resources [63], are defined in this layer.

- *Network layer* decides the path by which a packet reaches its destination, where the routing lies.

- *Transport layer* deals with the packet loss or packet reordering to ensure reliable end-to-end communication.

- *Application layer* defines how application programs use the network.

However, there is currently no consensus on the division of layers in NoCs. According to another well-accepted layer division [71], the lower network structure can be divided as *physical layer, switching layer* and *routing layer*, which are equivalent to the lower three layers defined by the OSI model. This book concentrates on the design and implementation of the lower three layers, including the physical layer, the data link layer and the network layer, while the other two upper layers are out of the scope.

In terms of fault-tolerance, a fault occurring on the physical medium may first manifest on the bottom physical layer. Without proper fault-tolerant techniques, the resulting error may later show up on upper layers. Adding fault-tolerance capability on different layers to stop faults infiltrating upper layers is necessary to reduce the impact on the whole network. In the literature, it is common to co-manage multiple layers to provide systematic protection, so as to increase the reliability of the network [260, 261]. When the interconnect is implemented using asynchronous circuits, a fault on the physical layer can corrupt the basic handshake protocol and lead to an insolvable system failure, in which case the protection from high layers (including the network layer and upper layers) cannot work effectively. Providing fault-tolerance from the bottom up is necessary to keep an asynchronous NoC working in a faulty environment, which is the ultimate objective of this book.

3.1.2 Network Topology

"Network topology refers to the static arrangement of channels and nodes in an interconnection network — the roads over which packets travel." [63] The topology of a NoC determines the global layout and fundamentally affects the strategies and performance of higher layers. Selecting a topology is the first step of building a NoC.

A node in a NoC is either a switch node which is basically a router delivering packets from input ports to output ports, or a terminal node which contains a PE generating and receiving packets. A network is a direct network when every router is connected to one or more PEs, otherwise, it is an indirect network where some routers are connected only with other routers.

The ring network shown in Figure 3.3a is a direct network. PEs in this network can be addressed by a vector. Routing algorithms are simple as every pair of PEs has only two possible paths:

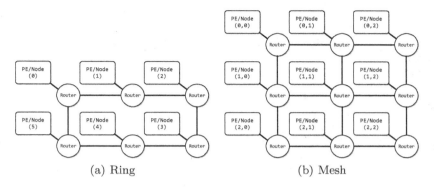

Figure 3.3   Examples of direct networks.

clockwise and anti-clockwise. The maximum distance between two PEs is $\lfloor N/2 \rfloor$ where N is the number of PEs. It is beneficial to use the ring topology with a small N thanks to its simple structure and low hardware overhead but the distance between two PEs can be intolerably long when N is large.

Mesh is one of the most utilized topologies in direct on-chip networks. Figure 3.3b shows a 3×3 mesh network where every PE is addressed by a two-dimension index (x, y). Compared with ring networks, mesh networks have two major advantages: one is the reduced communication distance. For two PEs located at (x_1, y_1) and (x_2, y_2), the minimal distance is the taxicab distance $(|x_1 - x_2| + |y_1 - y_2|)$. Thus the maximum distance is $2(\sqrt{N} - 1)$ where N is the number of PEs. When N is larger than 12 (a 4×3 mesh), mesh networks have shorter distances than ring networks. The other is the scalable throughput performance. The paths between a pair of PEs are not deterministic in mesh networks. The number of channels per PE in a mesh network is $\lim\limits_{N \to +\infty} \frac{2\sqrt{N}(\sqrt{N}-1)}{N} = 2$ while it is only one in a ring network. Mesh networks doubles the amount of communication resource. The network throughput should increase consequently if data packets are directed to all channels in a balanced way.

Most MPSoC designs use direct networks [53]. The design of a direct network is modularized. Every router is connected to a PE. As long as the interface between PEs and routers is unified, all routers are functionally equivalent and PEs can be designed

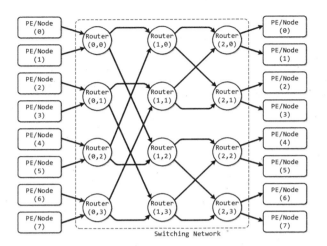

Figure 3.4   A butterfly network.

independently. This is essential to meet the short time-to-market requirement for current MPSoC designs.

Unlike MPSoC systems, many CMP systems prefer indirect networks. Figure 3.4 depicts a butterfly network [63]. In the figure, the PEs in the left column are in fact the same PEs in the right column. Duplicating them in the figure is a simplified way of showing the butterfly network between PEs. In a practical implementation, the butterfly network is folded [208].

Butterfly networks are one class of indirect networks. All pairs of PEs are connected by deterministic paths with equal communication delays. The butterfly network between PEs can be replaced with other switching networks, such as crossbars [185], Clos networks [208], Beneš networks, etc. All of these switching networks provide fixed communication delay between all pairs of PEs. In some switching networks, such as the butterfly networks and crossbars, only one path exists between any pair of PEs. In other switching networks, such as Clos networks and Beneš networks, multiple paths are available. Compared with direct networks, these indirect networks provide equal minimal communication delay between all PEs but the network implementation is not modularized. The

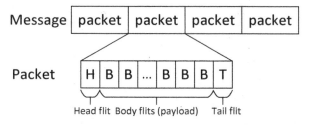

Figure 3.5   Message, packet and flit in NoCs.

routers and channels in an indirect network must be carefully calibrated to provide equal delays and fair resource allocation.

3.1.3 Switching Techniques

Network topology provides communications with different paths. Communications are launched concurrently and paths are selected individually. Contention occurs when more than one communication chooses the same resource at the same time. If we consider a communication is composed of a series of messages, switching techniques decide how network resources, including the channel bandwidth and input/output buffers in a router, are allocated to messages and how messages traverse the network.

For a NoC, before a *message* is injected to the network, it is usually first disassembled into *packets*, which can be further divided into multiple, fixed-length *flits*,[1] including a *head* flit containing the destination address information, *body* flits containing the data information (or payload) and a *tail* flit indicating the end of a packet, as illustrated in Figure 3.5. Correspondingly, network resources can be organized in different sizes. There are two classes of switching techniques: *circuit switching* and *packet switching* [63, 152]. In some literature, the algorithms utilized in the dynamic allocation of network resource are called flow control methods. The choice of switching and control flow extensively influence the router structure.

---

[1] As a subdivision of a packet, a flit is the basic unit of bandwidth and storage allocation used by most flow control methods [63].

3.1.3.1 Circuit Switching and Packet Switching

The major difference between circuit switching and packet switching is whether a path is allocated beforehand. In a circuit switching network, a path between the transmitting PE and the receiving PE, namely a *virtual circuit* [152], is allocated before transmitting the payload of a packet. On the contrary, a packet switched network sends out a packet immediately after it is produced while the path for this packet is dynamically allocated on the fly. The flow control methods in packet switched networks do not guarantee that enough resources are available before delivering payload.

The path allocation in a circuit switched network can be static: the path configuration is prefabricated or statically configured during the setup stage [132, 234, 254]. It is also possible to allocate path dynamically. One way is using handshake protocols [28, 175, 252]. The initiating PE sends a request to the target PE. This request packet reserves the network resources on the path which it has traversed. When it reaches the target PE, an acknowledge returns through the same path denoting that a path is reserved. The other way is by reconfiguring the switches by instructions from the connected PEs [246].

Circuit switched networks are area and energy efficient compared with packet switched networks. Paths are statically configured for a long time or even the whole life time. As a result, routers do not analyze data most of the time and switch configuration is simple. Little or no energy is consumed by reconfiguring switches. No buffer is needed because two communications cannot share any resource at the same time. The transmission delay and throughput is generally predictable, which is essential for providing guaranteed services (GS) [63]. However, a significant portion of the available throughput is wasted when a communication pauses temporarily or some resources are reserved by an ongoing path request. When the network is heavily loaded, circuit switched networks suffer from long communication latency and significant power overhead in the path reservation process [252].

By contrast, *packet switching* does not reserve a physical path before the message transmission. Packets can be transmitted to the destination through different routes, improving the link utilization compared to the circuit switching. Without the set-up phase, multiple packets may try to use a link at the same time, leading to *contention* that only one packet can be served at one time while the others have to wait the link to be released. This may result in variable packet transmission delays, making it difficult to guarantee the quality-of-service (QoS) [152].

Rather than allocating a path before transmitting the payload of a packet, packet switching dynamically allocates resources to the packets. Therefore, multiple packets belonging to the same message might be transmitted to the destination through different routes, improving the link utilization compared to the circuit switching. Since resources are not pre-allocated, it is unavoidable that multiple packets may compete for the same resource and leads to a contention, particularly when a network is heavily loaded. This results in variable packet transmission delays, making it difficult to guarantee the QoS [152].

The flow control method used in packet switching resolve contention by temporarily allocating the resources to one packet and reserves some buffers for the blocked one. Depending on the buffer space reserved in each allocation procedure, a packet switched network can be classified into three types: a store-and-forward network where buffers are reserved in units of packets, a wormhole network where buffers are reserved in units of flits and a virtual cut-through [113] network where buffers are reserved in units of flits but enough buffer space is ensured to store a whole packet.

Figure 3.6 illustrates an example of different packet switched networks. The router in Figure 3.6a has only three ports: A, B and C. Input ports and output ports are dynamically connected through the crossbar, which is reconfigured by the switch allocator. A buffer is inserted between each input port and the crossbar. If the router is used in store-and-forward or virtual cut-through networks, the buffer is enough for a whole packet, otherwise it is only able to store one flit (in wormhole networks). The packets in this example have a fixed length of four flits: one header flit denoting the target PE, two data flits carrying the data payload and a tail flit indicating the end of the packet. Assuming that networks are implemented in synchronous circuits, each port can transmit only one flit in every cycle. Two packets A and B arrive at the router from input ports

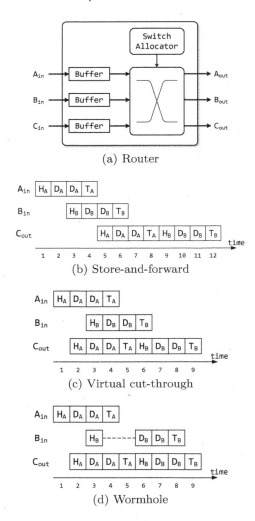

(a) Router

(b) Store-and-forward

(c) Virtual cut-through

(d) Wormhole

Figure 3.6   Packet switched flow control.

A_{in} and B_{in} at the first and the third clock cycle respectively. Both of them ask for the output port C_{out}. Contention is thus generated.

As shown in Figure 3.6b, the router in a store-and-forward network starts to transmit a packet only when all its flits are received. Since packet A arrives before packet B, the output port C_{out} is first allocated to A but it is only utilized at the fifth clock cycle when all parts of packet A are received. Consequently, packet B is temporarily stored in buffers and is transmitted when packet A is transmitted. The idea of store-and-forward is straightforward but it leads to long packet transmission latency and waste of resources. In this example, the output port C_{out} is allocated but not utilized for three clock cycles.

Virtual cut-through reduces the long latency by allowing routers to transmit a packet whenever a flit is received. As shown in Figure 3.6c, the output port C_{out} starts to transmit packet A immediately after the header flit is received. Although virtual cut-through reduces packet transmission delay, the buffer size is not reduced. Virtual cut-through requires enough buffer space for every packet. Thus a packet is stored in only one router when it is blocked. In some networks, a packet can be extremely long and the area overhead of this requirement is then intolerable.

The wormhole flow control method relaxes the size requirement to one flit in the minimal case. Figure 3.6d demonstrates the outcome of limiting the size of buffers to one flit. Packet A is transmitted before packet B but now only the header flit of packet B is stored in the router. Other flits of packet B are blocked and temporarily buffered in preceding routers. In this example, both virtual cut-through and wormhole can deliver two packets in nine clock cycles.

3.1.3.2 Virtual Channel

The wormhole flow control flow control method reduces buffers significantly. However, it has head-of-line (HOL) issues introducing long packet transmission delay when networks are heavily loaded.

Figure 3.7a shows an example of how HOL prolongs the packet transmission latency. Three communications (A, B and C) are initiated concurrently. Packets A and B compete for the east output port of router R_2. The other packet, packet C, has contention with packet B and will be transmitted through the west input port of router R_1 immediately after packet B. All packets have the same length of four flits. Initially both packets A and B arrive at ports $R_2.N$ and $R_1.W$ respectively at the first clock cycle.

The result data flow is depicted in Figure 3.7b. In router R_2, packet A is one clock cycle earlier than packet B and is thus served

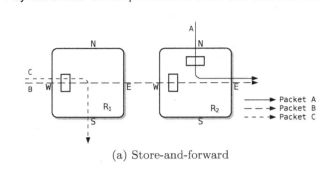

(a) Store-and-forward

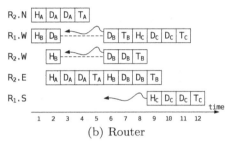

(b) Router

Figure 3.7   Head-of-line problem.

first. As a result, packet B is blocked waiting for the output port $R_2.E$ to be available again. In the meanwhile, the first two flits of packet B, H_B and D_B , are stored in the buffers connected to ports $R_2.W$ and $R_1.W$ respectively. As described, packet C is waiting for packet B. As packet B is blocked, packet C is also blocked by the contention in router R_2, although packet C does not go through R_2 at all. This is the HOL problem introduced by the wormhole flow control method.

If the buffer space is large enough for a whole packet, the virtual cut-through flow control method can be used and packet C would be delivered three clock cycles ahead (indicated by the arrows in Figure 3.7b). In this case, the whole packet B is temporarily stored in the buffers in router R_2 while packet C is in transmission.

The nature of HOL is: when a packet is blocked in one router and the router does not have enough buffer space to store the blocked packet, parts of the blocked packet are stored in other routers and corresponding switches and channels are occupied.

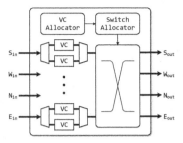

Figure 3.8   VC router.

These occupied resources then block other packets who are active and asking for these resources at the same time.

Virtual channel (VC) is an extensively utilized flow control method which significantly alleviates the HOL problem [58]. The basic idea of VC is to share channels among multiple packets. When one packet is blocked, the packet must not occupy the channels which are otherwise reserved in wormhole networks; therefore, other packets can utilize these channels at the same time. However, the flits belonging to the blocked packet cannot be thrown away. Extra buffers are inserted and the buffers connecting to each input port are divided into groups, each of which is called a virtual channel and stores flits of an individual packet.

A VC router is shown in Figure 3.8. It has four bidirectional ports: south, west, north and east. Two VCs are inserted between each input port and the crossbar. Channels and the crossbar is shared by both VCs. The allocation of VCs is controlled by a VC allocator.

When two packets compete for the same channel, they are allocated different VCs. Both packets are transmitted through the same channel using different VCs. Obviously only one flit is delivered in every cycle. Thus the shared channel is occupied by both VCs in a time divided manner. When one packet is blocked wherever in the network, the other packet can fully utilize the channel.

To further illustrate the impact of VCs, the same example in Figure 3.7 is implemented again using VC routers as demonstrated in Figure 3.9. All VCs and crossbars are allocated by fair

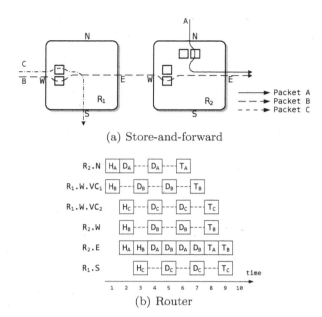

(a) Store-and-forward

(b) Router

Figure 3.9   Resolving head-of-line with VCs.

round-robin arbiters. Packets A and B share the channel connected to the east output port of router R_2, which is therefore alternately used by both packets. The same sharing procedure occurs on the channel connected to $R_1.W$. Packets B and C occupy different VCs and are delivered alternately. Finally, all packets are transmitted in nine cycles, which is three cycles shorter than using wormhole routers.

3.1.3.3   Other Flow Control Methods

VC is a popular flow control method in NoCs [28, 53, 67, 75, 122, 166] but it is not the only flow control method.

Time division multiplexing (TDM) is another extensively utilized flow control method [92].[2] It divides time into time slots and

---

[2]Strictly speaking, VC is also a TDM method because channels are shared by multiple VCs in a time divided manner. In the literature, TDM usually refers to its narrow meaning of sharing channels according to explicitly defined time slots.

multiple packets share the same channel by occupying some slots. The number of slots allocated to a packet defines the maximum throughput available to the packet. The transmission delay of every packet is predictable. However, the network throughput may be wasted when some slots are not allocated or the allocated slots are not used.

Rather than sharing a channel among multiple packets in a time divided manner, spatial division multiplexing (SDM) divides every link into several sub-links and allocates sub-links to packets [90, 132]. In this way, multiple packets traverse the same link concurrently using different sub-links. However, packets are effectively serialized as every sub-link provides only a portion of the total bandwidth. Although using SDM prolongs the transmission delay of a single packet, the overall throughput increases because no contention occurs until all sub-links of a link are allocated.

This book proposes the use of wormhole switching with SDM to design fault-tolerant QDI NoCs. As an advantage of using SDM, a permanent fault pollutes only one sub-link while the other sub-links of the same link are healthy. By isolating the defective sub-link, the other fault-free ones can still be used to transfer packets, showing a promising fault-tolerance nature. In a QDI NoC, if a fault destroys the handshake process and creates a faulty acknowledge informing the pre-fault router of unavailable buffers, the remaining flits in the packet path upstream of the fault cannot progress, leading to a *physical-layer* deadlock different from the network-layer one caused by cyclic dependence of packet transmission (Section 3.1.4.2). As a result, all remaining flits of the packet upstream of the fault are fault-free but cannot progress, while the fault may transmit to the destination along the built path and the downstream path will not be released without receiving a tail flit (blocked before the fault). Detection of this fault-caused physical-layer deadlock and recovery of the network from broken handshakes is an unexplored challenge faced by QDI NoCs. These will be described with details in Chapters 7 and 8.

3.1.3.4 *Quality of Service*

Quality of service (QoS) is an important concept in NoCs. The communications in a network have different requirements, such as delay or throughput. For the whole system to work properly, a network needs to provide certain guaranteed services (GS) to meet the requirements of these communications.

Some communications require reaching their targets before certain deadlines, such as an interrupt signal that must arrive at its destination before a certain latency deadline. The networks supporting this service are called delay-guaranteed networks. Circuit switched or TDM networks are good candidates for this requirement because the maximum latency for delivering a packet can be accurately estimated. Packet switched networks using other flow control methods, such as VC and SDM, provide only soft delay-guaranteed services where the probability that a packet reaches its destination before a deadline can be statistically analyzed but not guaranteed.

Some forms of communication, such as multimedia data streams, can tolerate some delay variance but are sensitive to throughput. The networks that satisfy this requirement are called throughput-guaranteed networks. Nearly all flow control methods can provide some level of through-guaranteed services by assigning high priorities to the data with the throughput requirement over others.

When there is no specific communication requirement, it is beneficial to deliver all packets as soon as possible. These types of communication are called best-effort (BE) traffic. Wormhole, VC and SDM flow control methods are good at providing such services.

3.1.4 Routing Algorithms

A routing algorithm determines the path via which a packet traverses a network of certain topology [62, 107, 152]. It is an important research topic in NoCs as a poor routing algorithm is more likely to congest the network by overloading some communication resources while leaving others unused. However, the problem is so complicated that no routing algorithm can perfectly balance all communications in all circumstances. A routing algorithm that fits one traffic pattern may congest the same network if the pattern changes. Unfortunately, the traffic pattern is not always pre-known at design time and can vary dramatically at run-time.

Furthermore, when considering the potential occurrence of faults, the network topology might be temporarily or permanently altered when a fault occurs. This change can further convert a deadlock-free routing algorithm into a deadlocking one [59]. Obviously, the network throughput would be significantly affected in this situation.

3.1.4.1 Deterministic and Non-Deterministic

Routing algorithms can be classified into two categories: deterministic routing algorithms and non-deterministic routing algorithms. The packets of any pair of PEs in a network always go through the same path when using a deterministic routing algorithm while they may go through different paths if a non-deterministic routing algorithm is used. The advantage of deterministic routing algorithms is their simplicity. They do not require complicated routing calculation circuits in routers. They are also capable of routing communications in non-regular networks where some non-deterministic routing algorithms may not work. However, they lack flexibility in their paths. A network can easily be congested when multiple communications simultaneously request the same resource. They may generate deadlock as well when the network topology is altered by faults [59]. In these situations, using non-deterministic routing algorithm is a better choice.

Most deterministic routing algorithms use source routing. The packet sender knows where the target is and specifies a route there. The usual way to implement source routing is to record the chosen path in the header flit. Every router on the path analyzes the header flit, finds out the recorded output port, removes the turn in the record, and forwards the modified header flit to the next router. Source routing has been utilized in many NoC designs [22, 25, 28, 249] because it can be used in all topology and introduces extremely low hardware overhead. However, the path recorded in the header flit may increase the packet size. If the path is extremely long, multiple header flits are needed to record the path, which incurs extra delay and energy.

There is a solution to avoid this issue if the topology is regular (ring, mesh or torus [60]). A class of source routing algorithms, namely dimension-ordered routing (DOR) [61], can be used without recording the whole path within the header flit but just the address of the target. Packets are delivered to targets through the edge of the minimal line (ring) or rectangle (mesh or torus) that can be drawn between the source and the target. To obtain the correct output port, routers simply compare the target address in the header flit with their own addresses. As an example, if a packet is sent from (x_1, y_1) to (x_2, y_2) in a 2D-mesh, the selected path will be either $(x_1, y_1) \rightarrow (x_2, y_1) \rightarrow (x_2, y_2)$ (XY-DOR) or $(x_1, y_1) \rightarrow (x_1, y_2) \rightarrow (x_2, y_2)$ (YX-DOR) depending on which dimension is traveled first.

DOR algorithms have many advantages over other routing algorithms: Since DOR algorithms are source routing algorithms, they introduce extremely low area overhead. Meanwhile, DOR algorithms are also distributed routing algorithms as the routing decisions are made by routers. It is not necessary to pre-define the whole path and store it within the header flit as other source routing algorithms. The selected paths by DOR algorithms are minimal paths leading to the shortest packet delay when networks are not busy. Due to these advantages, DOR algorithms have been extensively utilized in many NoC designs [67, 75, 153, 160, 165, 212, 223].

A major problem of deterministic routing algorithms is their lack of path flexibility, which leads to congestion and prolonged packet delay when network traffic is not uniform. Non-deterministic routing algorithms, on the other hand, can divert packets away from their original paths and thus distribute traffic to all resources. Depending on how path diversion is introduced, non-deterministic routing algorithms can be classified into two categories: oblivious routing algorithms and adaptive routing algorithms.

Oblivious routing algorithms route packets without regarding the states of the network [62].[3] Valiant's randomized routing algorithm [248] can balance the load of any traffic pattern in nearly all topologies. For each packet, an intermediate node is randomly selected, and the packet is first delivered to the intermediate node

---

[3]Some literature believes deterministic routing algorithms are also oblivious routing algorithms. Literally it is right but in this book oblivious routing algorithms refer to the non-deterministic and non-adaptive routing algorithms only.

and then to the target node. As the randomly selected node can be anywhere inside the network, the diversion is hardly a minimal path. The minimal oblivious routing randomly (ROMM) algorithm [170] restricts the intermediate node to be one inside the minimal rectangle between the sender and the receiver, thus the diversion is also minimal. ROMM can outperform DOR algorithms in some unbalanced traffic patterns [218].

The stochastic routing algorithm is another well-known oblivious routing algorithm [34, 72]. A packet is duplicated and forwarded to multiple output ports in every router at which it has arrived. The result is that the packet is flooded from the sender to the whole network. This algorithm has strong tolerance to on-chip faults and it guarantees that a packet is delivered to the target as long as the target is still reachable. However, the flood wastes resources and throughput is extremely low. It is possible to constrain the flood to improve throughput while reserving the tolerance to faults [175, 194, 228].

Adaptive routing algorithms route packets according to the states of the network. According to whether there are any routing restrictions, adaptive routings can be further classified into *fully* and *partially* ones. Different algorithms divert packets for different reasons. Some algorithms try to balance the load and improve throughput [50, 97] while others provide tolerance to on-chip faults by diverting or retransmitting packets when a channel or a router is broken [91, 204, 267]. Since fault-tolerant adaptive routing [103] detours packets only when faulty component is detected and located, they normally provide a better fault-tolerance capability than oblivious routing algorithms. After all, the price of using adaptive routing algorithms can be expensive. The states of the network, such as congested buffers and channels, or broken channels and switches, need to be collected before they can be used to generate diversions. Extra area, energy and delay overhead is introduced consequently.

3.1.4.2 Deadlock and Livelock

Deadlock and livelock are harmful by-products potentially caused by some routing algorithms or faults. Their occurrences paralyze

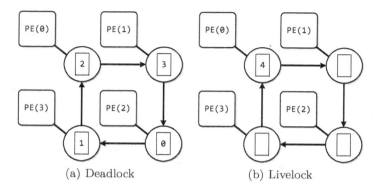

(a) Deadlock   (b) Livelock

Figure 3.10   Deadlock and livelock.

a part or even the whole network. To some extent, a practical NoC design must either prove that its routing algorithm is safe from deadlock or livelock, or demonstrate that it can recover when deadlock or livelock occurs. When analyzing the deadlock possibility of a routing algorithm, the traffic pattern itself is assumed to be free of message-dependent deadlock [16, 55] and the network is assumed fault-free. Due to the limited buffer size in practical network interfaces, a deadlock occurs when a network interface fails to receive enough data in order to produce a response. This deadlock is introduced by the dependence between packets, which cannot be eliminated by deadlock-free routing algorithms alone. If some faults occurs on the network and it becomes permanently damaged, the topology of the network might be changed. It would be difficult to analyze the possible deadlock in this situation as the fault can occur on any network components. However, some routing algorithms might be able to adapt to the altered topology especially when the possibility of faults has already been considered at the design stage of the network.

An example of deadlock and livelock is shown in Figure 3.10, which is a simple unidirectional ring network containing four PEs. Deadlock occurs when the channel dependency graph of a network is cyclic [61] — a group of concurrent packets are individually holding some resources which are mutually waited for by others in the same group. Since no packet releases its resources before obtaining

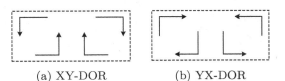

(a) XY-DOR   (b) YX-DOR

Figure 3.11   Turn models of DOR algorithms.

the necessary resources occupied by others, all packets in the group stop. In Figure 3.10a, four packets targeting different PEs have consumed all buffers in all routers. Since every packet is waiting for the buffer in its clockwise neighbor to become free, no packet can be transmitted.

In a fault-free environment, guaranteeing deadlock freedom of the NoC is an essential topic in the network layer. Two strategies have been proposed to deal with the deadlock: deadlock avoidance and deadlock recovery [6, 129, 144]. Deadlock avoidance has been extensively used in NoC designs where packet routing or flow control methods are restricted in a way that cyclic dependence is prevented [50, 87, 97], so that the whole network is deadlock-free. DOR algorithms are the most utilized deadlock-free routing algorithms as there is no cyclic dependence in their turn model (Figure 3.11). If the routing algorithm itself cannot eliminate the cyclic dependence, virtual channels can be used to avoid the deadlock by specifying an escape channel for each port [61].

Instead of deadlock-avoidance, a network may choose to allow deadlock to happen but recover from it afterward. Differentiating the real deadlock from congestion at runtime is the main challenge. The cost of recovering from a deadlock can be huge as it normally requires dropping multiple packets to release the network resources causing the deadlock. If the location of a deadlock cannot be accurately specified (which is usually a hard task), extra packets are unnecessarily dropped and later re-transmitted, leading to waste of network throughput. Considering the fact that deadlock rarely happens if the network traffic is restricted well below its saturation point, deadlock recovery can be more attractive than deadlock avoidance due to its lower cost in hardware implementation [6].

However, a deadlock-free network may still face deadlocks when permanent faults occur and alter the network topology. Adaptive routing algorithms can cope with faults by changing their routing strategies [36, 91, 267] but expensive fault detection circuits are required. Oblivious routing algorithms are naturally tolerant to faults but they also need complicated strategies to avoid deadlocks [72, 175, 194, 228]. This book is then dedicated to resolve this problem for asynchronous on-chip networks.

Besides deadlock, livelock happens one or more packets are continuously traversing the network without reaching its or their target(s). Figure 3.10b demonstrates an example of how livelock can occur in a ring network. A packet continuously circles the ring clockwise targeting a nonexistent PE(4). This may look ridiculous but it is possible when a transient fault attacks the header flit or a permanent fault disconnects PE(4) from the ring network.

3.2 ASYNCHRONOUS NETWORKS-ON-CHIP

Several asynchronous on-chip networks have been proposed and implemented in recent years. After introducing some basic concepts special to asynchronous on-chip networks, this section will review some of these existing network designs.

3.2.1 Taxonomy of Asynchronous On-Chip Networks

According to the implementation of network components, asynchronous NoCs can be generally classified into globally asynchronous and locally synchronous (GALS) NoCs and fully-asynchronous NoCs [119, 168, 198, 230]. Note that both the SoCs using GALS NoCs and the SoCs using fully-asynchronous NoCs are GALS systems because the global on-chip network behaves in an asynchronous manner.

Figure 3.12a illustrates an exemplary GALS NoC [119] where routers are implemented by synchronous circuit and the whole network is divided into multiple synchronous domains possibly driven by different clock signals. As the communication fabric between domains, the inter-router links are implemented asynchronously using handshake protocols. Depending on the practical design

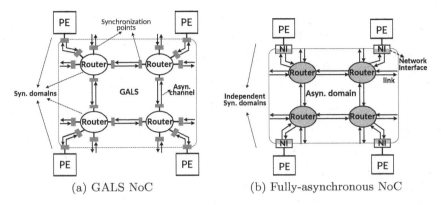

(a) GALS NoC   (b) Fully-asynchronous NoC

Figure 3.12   Asynchronous NoCs.

requirement, the router and its attached PEs may or may not use the same local clock.

A NoC is fully-asynchronous when both routers and links are asynchronous circuits controlled by handshake protocols. Figure 3.12b depicts such a SoC using a fully-asynchronous NoC. PEs, which usually contain multiple synchronous IP cores and are implemented by synchronous circuit, are connected to the asynchronous network through network interfaces (NIs) acting as the bridge between the synchronous and asynchronous worlds. Since PEs are implemented in their individual clock domains isolated by the asynchronous network while the internal communication of the network does not require synchronization, the use of a fully-asynchronous NoC simplifies the chip-level timing closure. However, implementing and verifying complicated network protocols on a fully-asynchronous NoC is more difficult than that on a synchronous or GALS NoC due to the lack of clock, and the resulting area can be large [67, 230]. The fault-tolerance capability of fully-asynchronous NoCs is another challenge which has not been thoroughly studied, which is the objective of this book.

Considering the design of NIs for fully-asynchronous NoCs, there are three different ways to implement an interface between synchronous and asynchronous circuits: pausible clocks, synchronizers and asynchronous first-in-first-out (FIFO) buffers [119].

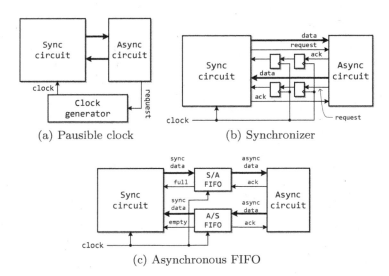

(a) Pausible clock   (b) Synchronizer

(c) Asynchronous FIFO

Figure 3.13   Synchronous and asynchronous interface.

The pausible clock scheme is simple to understand. The major issue of data transmission between synchronous and asynchronous circuits is the metastability problem [44]. Let us consider a group of synchronous flip-flops (FFs) that capture data from asynchronous circuits. The data may arrive at any time as asynchronous circuits are not synchronized. If the data arrive exactly at the positive transition of the global clock, FFs may go into metastability state during which the output values are not stable and wrong data may be generated. The pausible clock scheme resolves this problem by deferring the clock when metastability may occur. As shown in Figure 3.13a, the synchronous circuit is driven by a local clock generator. When asynchronous data are ready, they make a request to the local clock generator. If the data are going to clash with the clock, the clock will be postponed until the asynchronous data can be safely captured. Hence the metastability problem is avoided [164, 243].

The pausible clock scheme has some advantages over other interfacing methods. It is the only scheme that can fully eliminate metastability. The data latency between asynchronous and synchronous circuits is extremely small as asynchronous data are usually captured in the same cycle. The local clock generator also provides the possibility to implement dynamic voltage and frequency scaling (DVFS) [21], which can significantly reduce the power consumption of the synchronous sub-system. However, the pausible clock scheme restricts the highest clock frequency because the clock period is required to be longer than the clock tree delay [68]. It is also not practically viable for fabless designers due to the requirement for the careful calibration of the local clock generator [119].

Synchronizers are extensively utilized in synchronous circuits [85]. The basic two-flip-flop synchronizers shown in Figure 3.13b are usually inserted on the control signals crossing clock boundaries to increase the mean time between failures (MTBF), although they cannot eliminate the metastability problem. The same method can be used on the asynchronous signals heading to synchronous circuits. For signals from synchronous circuits to asynchronous circuits, no synchronizers are needed as asynchronous circuits are event-triggered.

The sync/async interface built from synchronizers introduces the minimum area overhead of all interface schemes but the throughput is the lowest. Using the two-flip-flop synchronizer shown in Figure 3.13b, the sync/async interface introduces two extra clock cycles in every data transmission. Several attempts have been made to reduce the synchronization delay by new synchronizer structures [67, 68] or by duplicating the interface to compensate the throughput loss [195]. Some asynchronous on-chip networks use synchronizer based interfaces [27, 195].

If long latency can be tolerated and high throughput is the major design concern, the sync/async FIFO scheme is the best choice. As shown in Figure 3.13c, a synchronous to asynchronous FIFO (S/A FIFO) and an asynchronous to synchronous FIFO (A/S FIFO) are inserted on forward and backward paths respectively. Unlike synchronizers, sync/async FIFOs have no throughput degradation, and the buffers inside the FIFOs balance the speed difference between synchronous and asynchronous sides. However, FIFOs introduce area overhead and prolong the synchronization latency. This scheme has been utilized in several asynchronous on-chip networks [213, 243].

No matter which interface scheme is selected, the channels between routers and network interfaces are pure asynchronous circuits. As a result, the routers in a mesh network are modular designs independent from their local PEs. This book concentrates on the asynchronous architecture and the enhancement of fault-tolerance for these asynchronous routers.

3.2.2 Previous Asynchronous NoCs

3.2.2.1 SpiNNaker

The SpiNNaker system is a universal spiking neural network architecture aiming to simulate the human brain activities in real time [169, 197, 242]. As shown in Figure 3.14a, ten to thousands of SpiNNaker chips interconnect with each other in a mesh network. Every SpiNNaker chip is linked with its south (S), southwest (SE), west (W), north (N), northeast (NE) and east (E) neighbors. The channels between chips are 2-phase asynchronous pipelines using the 2-of-7 data encoding method [217].

The internal structure of a SpiNNaker chip is demonstrated in Figure 3.14b. 18 Synchronous processors are connected by two on-chip networks: a communication NoC and a system NoC. As shown in the upper half of Figure 3.14b, the communication NoC is a

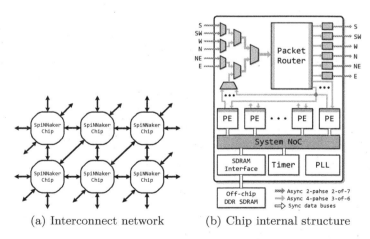

(a) Interconnect network   (b) Chip internal structure

Figure 3.14   SpiNNaker System.

part of the system-level interconnection network. The synchronous packet router in each chip receives spike signals from its six neighbors and the local 18 PEs [255]. These signals are delivered by 4-phase 3-of-6 pipelines and are merged by a tree of bandwidth aggregators [195]. Running at 200 MHz, the packet router is capable of processing all spike signals and forwarding them to their destinations. The system NoC is shared by the 18 local PEs inside a chip. Implemented using an asynchronous CHAIN network [11, 81], it allows PEs to access the off-chip memory concurrently.

The SpiNNaker system demonstrates an example of how asynchronous communication systems can be smoothly integrated with traditional synchronous bus systems. The inter-chip 2-phase 2-of-7 asynchronous channels reduce power consumption and communication delay between chips. On-chip communications are delivered by 4-phase 3-of-6 asynchronous channels leading to simple control circuits. Complicated computations are handled by synchronous circuits. Neurons and spike signals are simulated and generated by synchronous processors. The routing and broadcasting of spikes is calculated in the synchronous packet router.

However, in the aspect of networks, only the inter-chip interconnection network is fully scalable. Both on-chip networks use central communication structures whose throughput is limited by the central communication devices, such as the packet router in the communication NoC and the SDRAM interface in the system NoC. The on-chip networks would be saturated when the accumulative throughput requirement of all PEs exceeds the throughput capability of the central communication devices. Such central communication fabric is less scalable to support a large number of PEs than the on-chip networks using mesh topology.

3.2.2.2 ASPIN

The asynchronous scalable programmable interconnection network (ASPIN) is an asynchronous packet-switched on-chip network supporting clustered and shared memory MPSoCs [1, 214]. It is a direct mesh network. An ASPIN router is depicted in Figure 3.15 [212]. It uses the basic wormhole flow control method. Its switches have been simplified by removing disabled turns defined in the XY routing.

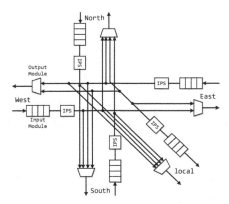

Figure 3.15   ASPIN router.

The router comprises ten hard macros: an input module and an output module in each direction. Data between hard macros are delivered by 4-phase dual-rail pipelines. An input module includes a FIFO and an intermediate pipeline stage (IPS). The FIFO contains several bundled-data pipeline stages controlled by the fully decoupled control circuit [82]. Extra dual-rail to bundled-data and bundled-data to dual-rail converters are added before and after the FIFO respectively. IPS is a simple dual-rail pipeline stage inserted to cope with the long wire delay between input and output modules. An output module is a multiplexer connecting input modules to the output port. The multiplexer is controlled by a ring arbiter [139].

ASPIN is a fast and area efficient NoC system. Long wire delays between input and output modules have been compensated by inserting intermediate pipeline stages. Area consuming buffers are replaced by area efficient bundled-data pipelines. The fully decoupled control circuit further doubles the storage efficiency. Complicated dual-rail control circuits have been manually designed in the fully customized hard macros. The ten macros can be carefully placed to balance long wires and improve throughput. The estimated period of such NoC using a 90 nm technology was reported 0.88 ns, which is equivalent to 1.131 GHz [212].

However, the fully customized hard macros and special designed asynchronous cells are not usually affordable in standard cell based design flows. Ten hard macros per router also implies a heavy burden in chip floorplanning. The reported 0.88 ns period is extracted from a claimed latency accurate simulation, which uses transport delay models where gate delays are scaled down to 90 nm and are fixed without considering the output load and input transition time of individual gates. The actual period could be much longer due to the scaling process and the inaccurate gate delay estimation.

3.2.2.3 QoS NoC

The QoS NoC [75, 77] is the only published asynchronous VC router that strictly follows the structure of synchronous VC routers shown in Figure 3.8. All data channels are QDI 4-phase 1-of-4 pipelines. Every input buffer has four VC buffers assigned with different priorities. The SPA arbiters inside output ports [76] always allocate the output port to the VC with the highest priority in all concurrent requests.

QoS NoC is an early effort to provide QoS in asynchronous on-chip networks. The full QDI implementation consumes low power and provides tolerance to variations. However, the period of a 8-bit QoS NoC router in 0.18 μm is around 4 ns [75], which is much slower than ASPIN. It will be shown in Chapter 4 that VC compromises throughput significantly.

3.2.2.4 ANOC

The asynchronous network-on-chip (ANOC) [22] is also a QDI VC router providing QoS support. The ANOC router shown in Figure 3.16 and the router in the QoS NoC have similar structures

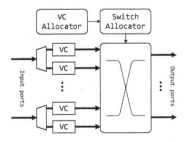

Figure 3.16   ANOC router.

except for the central switch. In the QoS NoC router, VCs in one input buffer are arbitrated and multiplexed; therefore, the central switch is a 5×5 crossbar. On the other hand, the ANOC router connects all VCs to the central switch. As every direction is equipped with two VCs, the central switch is a 10 × 5 crossbar. VCs in one direction are also assigned with different priorities and output ports arbitrate these VCs using static priorities, which is similar to the QoS NoC.

The extended switch in ANOC improves throughput. The ANOC router has been implemented using a 0.13 µ*m* standard cell library with an augmented asynchronous cell library [145]. The router has been packaged into a hard IP core and utilized in the MAGALI and the FAUST chips [53]. The period reported in [22] is around 4 ns.

It has the same throughput problem as the QoS NoC. The augmented asynchronous cell library is another design problem. Building asynchronous circuits using only synchronous standard cell libraries is more adaptable although using special asynchronous cells significantly improves power, area and speed [145].

3.2.2.5 MANGO

The message-passing asynchronous NoC providing guaranteed service through Open Core Protocol (OCP) interfaces (MANGO) [27–29] is the first asynchronous NoC providing circuit-switched guaranteed services while also supporting packet-switched best-effort traffic. The router structure is shown in Figure 3.17. Every router

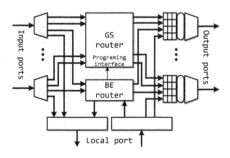

Figure 3.17   MANGO router.

has a local port and four other ports. The local port supports five services levels: four different GS service levels and one BE service. Other ports use VC buffers for different services and eight VCs are implemented (seven GS VCs and one BE VC). Unlike other input-buffered asynchronous routers, MANGO routers are output-buffered. VC buffers are thus implemented inside output ports. The central switch is expanded like the one in ANOC but is divided into two separated switches: a GS router for circuit-switched GS services and a BE router for packet-switched BE traffic. The GS router is dynamically configured by packets from the BE router. The eight VCs in each output ports are dynamically scheduled by an asynchronous latency guarantee algorithm, which provides latency and throughput guarantees for all GS VCs. All circuits use self-timed bundled-data protocols. Implemented using a 0.12 μm standard cell library, the MANGO router runs at equivalent 795 MHz (around 1.26 ns period).

Compared with other asynchronous NoCs that provide QoS using VCs, MANGO guarantees a maximum packet delay for each service level. The asynchronous latency guarantee algorithm running in each output port ensures that VCs with higher priorities cannot starve other VCs with lower priorities [29]. On the contrary, the static priority arbiters utilized in QoS NoC and ANOC allow the highest QoS level to occupy a shared channel as long as it is busy.

However, the output-buffered switch introduces significant area overhead and is the most area consuming part in the router. The self-timed bundled-data implementation is less tolerant to variations than QDI implementations.

3.2.2.6 QNoC

The QoS NoC (QNoC) [67] provides multiple VCs in each service level. The router structure is depicted in Figure 3.18. Its structure is similar to the ANOC router shown in Figure 3.16 but every service level (SL) has several equal-priority VCs. The central switch is expanded to allow the input VCs (VC-IP) in one service level to communicate directly with the output VCs (VC-OP) in the same service level. The VC arbiter (VCA in Figure 3.18) in each service

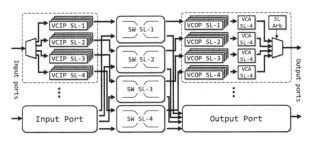

Figure 3.18   QNoC router.

level selects one VC-OP from all active VC-OPs every cycle. The SL arbiter in each output port selects one VC using a static priority arbiter. All buffers and channels use self-timed 4-phase bundled-data pipelines. The period of a QNoC router implemented using a 0.18 μm standard cell library is around 4.8 ns.

CHAPTER 4

Optimizing Asynchronous On-Chip Networks

Most of current asynchronous on-chip networks resemble the router structures and the flow control methods explored thoroughly in synchronous on-chip networks. Specifically speaking, low-level asynchronous pipelines are synchronized to implement wide pipelines and virtual channels using time division multiplexing are widely adopted. The synchronization introduced by these techniques significantly compromises the throughput of asynchronous on-chip networks. This chapter explores the possibilities of using spatial parallelism rather than timing division methods to improve throughput. The proposed techniques concentrate on the lower two network layers: the physical layer and the data link layer.

4.1   CHANNEL SLICING

Asynchronous channels and pipelines are the basic elements of asynchronous on-chip networks. The throughput of an asynchronous circuit is determined by the slowest pipeline stage. This section tries to introduce spatial and timing concurrency into the circuits of the physical layer. Two new techniques, channel slicing

DOI: 10.1201/9781003284789-4

and lookahead pipeline style, are proposed to reduce the period of basic asynchronous pipelines.

4.1.1 Synchronization Overhead

Many asynchronous pipeline styles have been utilized in asynchronous on-chip networks. Self-timed 4-phase bundled-data pipelines have been used in MANGO [30], ASPIN [212] and QNoC [67]. QDI 4-phase dual-rail pipelines have been used in AS-PIN. QDI 4-phase 1-of-4 pipelines have been used in ANOC [22] and QoS NoC [75]. QDI 4-phase and 2-phase m-of-n pipelines have been used in SpiNNaker [197]. As described in Section 2.4.1, bundled-data pipelines need detailed timing analysis and careful delay insertion. Compared with 4-phase pipelines, 2-phase pipelines reduce period but introduce complicated combinational circuits (see Section 2.2). QDI 4-phase pipelines are promising candidates for asynchronous on-chip network due to their moderate area overhead and tolerance to variations.

In all asynchronous routers using QDI 4-phase pipelines, wide pipelines are built by synchronizing multiple bit-level pipelines as the 4-bit dual-rail pipeline shown in Figure 4.1. The synchronized pipelines are easy to control because data on all bit-level pipelines (slices) are synchronized. However, the completion detection (CD) circuit, normally a C-element tree, introduces extra delay and prolongs the period.

Assuming rising time and falling time are equal, the period T of the 4-phase dual-rail pipeline, depicted in Figure 4.1, can be calculated as:

$$T = 4t_{\mathrm{buf}} + 2(t_{\mathrm{pcd}} + t_{\mathrm{syn}}) + 2t_{\mathrm{data}} + 2t_{\mathrm{ack}} \qquad (4.1)$$

In this equation, t_{buf}, t_{data} and t_{ack} are the delays of a buffer cell, the combinational circuit on data wires and the combinational circuit on ack wires, respectively. t_{pcd} and t_{syn} are the delays of the completion detection circuits inside one slice and among slices (the C-element tree). The buffer cells in multi-rail pipelines are normally 2-input C-elements. Thus, the buffer latency t_{buf} is equal with the latency of a 2-input C-element t_{C}. For a wide dual-rail pipeline of

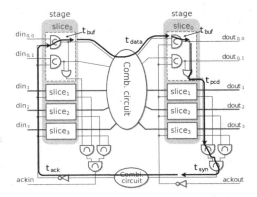

Figure 4.1 4-bit 4-phase dual-rail pipeline.

N bits, the latency of the C-element tree is:

$$t_{\text{syn}} = t_{\text{C}} \cdot log_2 \left\lceil \frac{N}{2} \right\rceil \tag{4.2}$$

4-phase pipelines use return-to-zero signaling. The period T includes a positive cycle for data transmission and a negative cycle for data withdrawal. Assuming gate rising time and falling time are equal, T is obtained by doubling the loop path latency.

To evaluate the delay overhead of synchronizing bit-level pipelines (or slices), the period is divided into two parts: the period of a single dual-rail pipeline ($T_{\text{dual-rail}}$), and the extra delay caused by the synchronization (Δ). In Figure 4.1, Δ is the extra delay caused by the C-element tree ($2t_{\text{syn}}$). In this way, synchronization overhead can be represented as:

$$\frac{\Delta}{T_{\text{dual-rail}}} = \frac{t_{\text{C}} \cdot \log_2 \left\lceil \frac{N}{2} \right\rceil}{2t_{\text{C}} + t_{\text{OR}} + t_{\text{data}} + t_{\text{ack}}} \tag{4.3}$$

where t_{OR} is the completion detection delay in a single dual-rail pipeline — the delay of a 2-input OR gate.

In Equation 4.3, the denominator $T_{\text{dual-rail}}$ is the minimum period without synchronization, which is independent of N. The numerator Δ is the synchronization overhead, which increases logarithmically with N. Increasing the data width of a wide pipeline leads to slow pipelines. From another aspect, routers are not computation heavy circuits. The combinational circuits between two pipeline stages are simple multiplexers and de-multiplexers. Their delays t_{data} and t_{ack} are small, as well as the minimum period $T_{\text{dual-rail}}$. Synchronization overhead is significant in simple circuits like asynchronous routers.

Increasing the wire count of a single 1-of-n or m-of-n pipeline seems to increase the total data width without introducing synchronization overhead. However, a 1-of-n pipeline using more than five data wires is not area efficient. The completion detection circuit of a single m-of-n pipeline introduces a similar delay overhead.

4.1.2 Channel Slicing

The pipelined completion process [143] is a QDI pipeline style which moves the completion detection circuit outside the loop path of pipeline stages. A simplified implementation of the pipelined completion process in a 2-bit dual-rail pipeline is presented in Figure 4.2. Compared with normal synchronized dual-rail pipelines, extra C-elements (colored in grey) are inserted between slices and the synchronization circuits. Each slice has its own *ack* line generated by these extra C-elements. Hence, individual slices generate acknowledge signals in parallel with pipeline synchronization. To ensure the data transmitted on all slices are still synchronized, the extra C-elements are guarded by the result of the synchronization

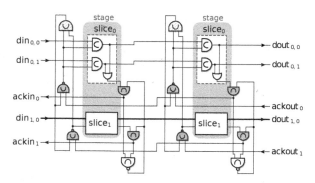

Figure 4.2   Pipelined completion process.

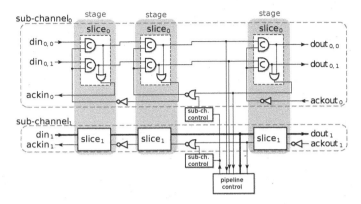

Figure 4.3   Channel slicing.

C-element tree. An extra synchronization C-element tree (shaded by slash lines) is also inserted in the sending pipeline stage to guarantee that data are not released before they are captured.

The pipelined completion process can be applied to all QDI pipelines even with complicated combinational circuits. Individual slices have their own *ack* lines and are semi-decoupled from each other. The data sent by different slices in the same stage are still synchronized. Extra C-elements and an extra C-element tree are used to guarantee synchronization while decoupling pipelines.

Similar to the pipelined completion process, channel slicing is an aggressive technique that fully decouples slices whenever possible. An abstract implementation of channel slicing is shown in Figure 4.3. The vertically divided pipelines where data can be delivered independently, namely sub-channels, are fully decoupled. Every sub-channel has its own *ack* line. The synchronization C-element tree is removed in all stages and no extra C-elements are inserted. For the pipeline stages where complicated combinational circuit is implemented or control is data dependent, extra sub-channel control circuits are added on each slice in this stage to temporarily stop individual sub-channels if synchronization is required on certain occasions. The pipeline control circuit receives the data from all sub-channels along with the *ack* lines. Synchronization can be regenerated when necessary.

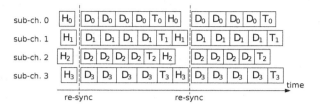

Figure 4.4   Data flow on a channel sliced pipeline.

Compared with the pipelined completion process, channel slicing is expected to introduce much lower area overhead. Extra control circuits and synchronization circuits are inserted only in the stages requiring synchronization. These circuits re-establish the synchronization only when it is necessary. Thus, the period of channel slicing is shorter than that of the pipelined completion process most of the time because the *ack* signals are directly generated by sub-channels. However, the circuit implementation of the pipeline control circuit tightly depends on the local logic function while the pipelined completion process generally fits all pipeline situations.

Channel slicing is suitable for asynchronous routers for two reasons: 1) Most pipeline stages in an asynchronous router are simple pipelines without complex combinational calculation or data related control logic. 2) For a packet, only the header flit and the tail flit need to be detected and analyzed; data flits, which are the main body of a packet, are normally delivered without being read.

The major design issue of using channel slicing in asynchronous routers is re-synchronization. Unlike the pipelined completion process, sub-channels in channel sliced pipelines are fully decoupled. Without re-synchronization, parts of a new flit can be transmitted by fast sub-channels while the old flit is under transmission by slow sub-channels as shown in Figure 4.4, where two packets are transmitted by a 4-bit channel sliced pipelines. Routers need to analyze the header flit for routing decisions. Thus, sub-channels should be re-synchronized when the header flit arrives. After a path is reserved in the central switch, sub-channels deliver data independently at their fastest speeds. The detailed implementation of channel slicing in a wormhole router will be revealed in Section 4.1.4.

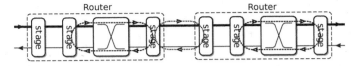

Figure 4.5　Critical cycles in asynchronous on-chip networks.

4.1.3　Lookahead Pipeline

The data paths of asynchronous on-chip networks can be simplified into pipeline stages and switches as shown in Figure 4.5. Several pipeline stages are placed in every input buffer and output buffer. Input and output buffers are connected by switches inside routers and long wires outside routers.

The throughput of synchronous circuits is determined by the slowest data path — the critical path. Likewise, the throughput of asynchronous circuits is determined by the slowest loop path between two adjacent pipeline stages — the critical cycle. Data paths of asynchronous on-chip networks normally have two types of critical cycles as shown in Figure 4.5: the loop path through the central switch inside a router (dash line) and the loop path between two adjacent routers (dotted line). The loop paths between routers are comparatively easy to handle if they are the throughput bottleneck. More pipeline stages can be inserted on long wires to reduce the period. It is also preferable to use other asynchronous pipeline styles if allowable, such as 2-phase pipelines [217], high-speed QDI pipelines [182] and wave-pipelined data links [69]. On the other hand, the loop path through the central switch is difficult to cope with. No intermediate pipeline stages can be inserted and using other pipeline styles complicates the switch control logic. This is the critical cycle that needs special treatment.

The lookahead pipeline [219] is a relaxed QDI pipeline style providing fast data rates by allowing the data wires and the *ack* line to be reset simultaneously. Since a router is normally shipped in the form of a hard IP core in large GALS projects, using relaxed QDI pipelines inside a router improves throughput without introducing any design overhead outside the router IP block.

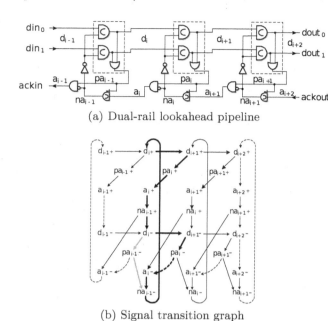

(a) Dual-rail lookahead pipeline

(b) Signal transition graph

Figure 4.6   Lookahead pipeline.

A dual-rail lookahead pipeline and its STG are shown in Figure 4.6. It has the basic structure of a QDI dual-rail pipeline but extra AND gates and C-elements are added on *ack* lines. The AND gate in pipeline stage i allows the *ack* signal a_i to be reset when pipeline stage $i + 2$ has safely captured the data transmitted in the current cycle; therefore, stage i can receive a new data while stage $i + 1$ is releasing its data buffers. The C-element ensures that the *ack* signal is not reset too fast, otherwise stage $i + 1$ fails to receive new data.

The critical cycle of this dual-rail lookahead pipeline is depicted in bold black lines in the STG (Figure 4.6b), while part of the original critical cycle of a QDI dual-rail pipeline is depicted in bold grey lines. Since the dependence between a_i- and pa_i- does not exist in lookahead pipelines, it is drawn as a dash line. In the original QDI pipelines, *ack* line a_i is reset after the release of data d_{i+1} indicated by pa_i-. The lookahead pipelines allow d_{i+1} to be withdrawn concurrently with a_i-, which reduces period by 25% in the best case.

However, this STG is not speed-independent. Transition a_i+ and transition a_i- are located in two parallel paths. The STG itself cannot ensure that a_i- occurs after a_i+. Two timing assumptions must be satisfied for the correct operation [220, 225].

Ack setup time: Expressed in Equation 4.4, the first timing assumption ensures that the positive pulse on a_i is long enough for the asymmetric C-element to capture it.

$$t_{d_{i+1}+\rightarrow a_i-} - t_{d_{i+1}+\rightarrow a_i+} > t_{\text{setup}} \tag{4.4}$$

where t_{setup} is the setup time for a C-element (an asymmetric C-element in this case). Assuming all C-elements incur the same cell delay, Equation 4.4 can be expressed in gate delays and simplified into:

$$2 \cdot t_{\text{C}} + t_{\text{AND}} > t_{\text{setup}} \tag{4.5}$$

where t_{C} and t_{AND} are the delays of a C-element (or an asymmetric C-element) and an AND gates, respectively. Obviously Equation 4.5 is easy to satisfy in gate-level implementations.

Data override: Since the reset of a_i occurs concurrently with the release of d_{i+1}, the new data on d_i must not arrive before the old data on d_{i+1} are released. Assuming $t_{d_i+\rightarrow d_{i+1}+}$ is equal with $t_{d_i-\rightarrow d_{i+1}-}$, this timing requirement can be expressed as:

$$t_{d_i-\rightarrow na_i-} + t_{na_i-\rightarrow d_i+} > t_{\text{setup}} \tag{4.6}$$

which can be further described in gate delays:

$$t_{\text{CD}} + 2 \cdot t_{\text{C}} + t_{\text{INV}} > t_{\text{setup}} \tag{4.7}$$

where t_{CD} is the delay of the completion detection circuit in each pipeline stage (an OR gate in dual-rail pipelines). Since the left side of Equation 4.7 is half the period of the fastest dual-rail pipeline, it is longer than the setup time of a C-element. The data override assumption is already met by hardware.

4.1.4 Channel Sliced Wormhole Router

In this section, a wormhole router using channel sliced pipelines and the lookahead pipeline style in its internal critical cycle is designed and implemented to demonstrate the throughput improvement along with design overhead [225].

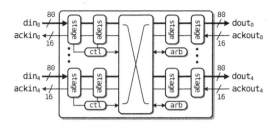

Figure 4.7 A channel sliced wormhole router.

4.1.4.1 Router Structure

The internal structure of a channel sliced wormhole router is shown in Figure 4.7. It has five bidirectional ports for four adjacent neighbors and the local processing element (PE). A 2-stage pipelined buffer is connected to each input and output port. Input buffers and output buffers are connected by a central switch controlled by the arbiters in the output ports. Besides buffers, every input port has a router analyzing the target address of incoming packets using the XY routing algorithm and a controller sending routing requests to the target output arbiters. In this implementation, each port delivers 32 bits per cycle using 16 4-phase 1-of-4 pipelines. 1-of-4 pipelines are preferred as they consume less energy than dual-rail pipelines and less area than m-of-n pipelines. Using the channel slicing technique, every 1-of-4 pipeline is a sub-channel with its own sub-channel controller.

According the wormhole flow control method, a packet is divided into flits. The flit format is explained in Table 4.1. The address of the target node is represented in eight binary digits which are enough to identify a 16×16 mesh network. The X and Y addresses are further translated into 1-of-4 codes and stored in the least significant bits of the header flit. The rest of the header flit is used for data. A variable number of data flits may follow the header. Following the data payload, the packet is ended by a tail flit indicating the end of a packet (EOP), in which the *eop* bit of every sub-channel is set high.

As described in Section 4.1.2, all pipeline stages are spatially divided into unsynchronized sub-channels. In the wormhole router

Table 4.1   Flit format.

			Sub-channels		
type	0	1	2	3	4 ~ 15
header	tar_X[1:0]	tar_X[3:2]	tar_Y[1:0]	tar_Y[3:2]	byte[2:0]
body			byte[4i + 7:4i + 3]		
tail	EOP	EOP	EOP	EOP	EOP

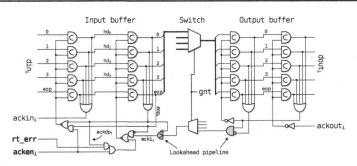

Figure 4.8   Data path of the ith sub-channel.

implementation, only the second pipeline stages of each input buffer are synchronized when the tail flit of the preceding packet is transmitted and the header flit of the new packet is going to be analyzed. A sub-channel controller is inserted in the second pipeline stage of each sub-channel and a router controller is inserted in each input buffer to control the XY router and establish synchronization.

The circuit structure of the ith single sub-channel in both input and output buffers is demonstrated in Figure 4.8. The second pipeline stage is controlled by two signals in the bottom left corner of Figure 4.8: $acken_i$ and rt_err. The active low signal $acken_i$ is driven by the sub-channel controller of each sub-channel. A negative $acken_i$ allows the second pipeline stage to capture new data. It is driven high to block the sub-channel when a header flit is expected or is being analyzed. If a decoded routing request is not valid due to wrong addresses or on-chip faults, rt_err is driven high denoting the packet should be dropped. In this case, $acken_i$ is still driven low to activate the sub-channel, but the ack line generated

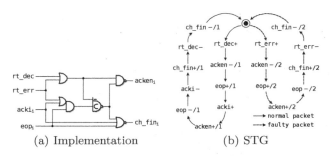

(a) Implementation   (b) STG

Figure 4.9   Sub-channel controller.

by the second pipeline stage ($ackdp_i$) is connected back to the second pipeline stage. The ack line from the output buffers ($acki_i$) is inactive during the process as no valid routing request is produced. The second pipeline stage is converted into a flit sink consuming all flits until the tail flit.

The tail flit of each packet is detected concurrently in all sub-channels, regardless of the validity of the routing request. Once a sub-channel has delivered its share of the tail flit, indicated by the eop_i bit, its $acken_i$ is driven high. Consequently, the next flit is captured and blocked in the first pipeline stage forcing re-synchronization.

The lookahead pipeline style is utilized in the pipeline stages connected to the central switch — the critical cycle (Figure 4.5). An AND gate is added in the first stage of the output buffer generating the early evaluated ack signal ($acki_i$). An asymmetric C-element is added on this ack line on the receiver side ensuring new data do not override the old data. This implementation exactly follows the dual-rail lookahead pipeline shown in Figure 4.6.

The $acken_i$ signal of an individual sub-channel is generated by the sub-channel controller shown in Figure 4.9. This control circuit reads four inputs: the correct routing decoding flag rt_dec and the faulty routing decoding flag rt_err from the XY router in each input port, the ack line $acki_i$ from the central switch, and the eop_i bit of the second pipeline stage. Two signals are generated: the active low ack enable signal $acken_i$ and the packet termination flag ch_fin_i which is high when the sub-channel has delivered its share of the

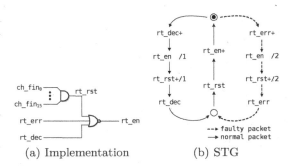

Figure 4.10   Router controller.

tail flit. The implementation depicted in Figure 4.9a is synthesized from the STG shown in Figure 4.9b using Petrify [57].

As shown in the STG, a sub-channel is enabled after a routing request is decoded, either right or wrong, and remains active until the tail flit is transmitted. The second pipeline stage releases the tail flit after it is blocked, making sure no further flits are transmitted. The packet termination flag ch_fin_i is set after the release of the tail flit and unset when the previous routing request is withdrawn.

Every input port has an XY router analyzing the header flit of incoming packets. It is controlled by the router controller demonstrated in Figure 4.10. It generates an active high router enable signal rt_en by reading the routing requests rt_dec and rt_err, and the packet termination flags ch_fin_i from all sub-channels. The circuit implementation is also synthesized from the STG illustrated in Figure 4.10b. The router is enabled when all sub-channels have delivered and released their shares of the tail flit, and is disabled once a routing request is decoded, either right or wrong. The decoded request is captured by some C-elements inside the router.

Figure 4.11 depicts the XY router in the south input port and its connection with the arbiter inside the east output port. The target addresses tar_X and tar_Y are read from $hd_0 \sim hd_3$ (Figure 4.8), which are the output of the first pipeline stage in the input buffer. Note that rt_en is only high when the second pipeline stage has released the tail flit and been disabled. Therefore, the data on $hd_0 \sim hd_3$ must be the header flit blocked in the first stage. The addresses

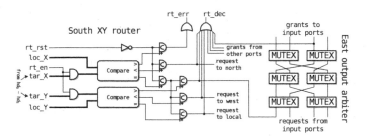

Figure 4.11   XY router and output arbiter.

are compared with the local addresses *loc_X* and *loc_Y* using two 1-of-4 comparators. They are implemented in one-hot circuits using a structure similar to the dual-rail comparators in ASPIN [212]. The comparison results are translated into routing requests and captured by the C-elements controlled by *rt_rst*, which resets the routing requests after releasing the tail flit. Valid routing requests are forwarded to corresponding arbiters in output ports while invalid requests trigger the *rt_err* signal and withdraw the packet. Signal *rt_dec* is set immediately after valid requests and remains high until corresponding arbiters in output ports are released.

4.1.4.2 *Performance Evaluation*

The channel sliced wormhole router has been implemented using a 0.13 μm standard cell library. All parts of the router are described in synthesizable Verilog HDL. The router controller and sub-channel controllers are synthesized from their STGs using Petrify [57], while other parts are manually written in gate-level netlists.

The area after synthesis is around 14.3k gates (0.057 mm^2). The period of data flits is 1.7 ns providing the maximum throughput of 18.8 Gbit/Port/s. The average latency for a data flit traversing the router is 1.7 ns. For the header flit, a minimum of 0.8 ns is required to analyze the target address and request to the arbiter in the corresponding output port.

Besides the channel sliced (ChSlice) wormhole router using lookahead (LH) pipelines, a traditional wormhole router using synchronized pipelines and a wormhole router using channel slicing

Table 4.2   Router area (in gates)..

	Input buffer	Output buffer	Switch	Overall
No ChSlice or LH	4.3k	4.4k	2.4k	11.3k
ChSlice only	5.8k	4.5k	3.2k	13.9k
ChSlice and LH	6.2k	4.5k	3.3k	14.5k

only have been implemented. The area of these routers is presented in Table 4.2.

Channel slicing introduces 23% area overhead compared with the traditional router using synchronized pipelines. The area of the central switch increases due to the enlarged wire count. The synchronized 1-of-4 pipeline needs 66 wires (64 data bits, one *eop* bit and one *ack* line). Channel slicing uses independent sub-channels with individual *eop* and ack lines. The total wire count is increased to 96 (64 data bits, 16 *eop* bits and 16 *ack* lines). Consequently, the switch is enlarged. The total number of C-elements in channel sliced pipelines and synchronized pipelines are equal. Although an extra C-element is added in each individual sub-channel for the *eop* bit, this area overhead is compensated by the removal of the synchronization circuit. The area of output buffers does not vary in all routers. The area overhead of input buffers is mainly due to the sub-channel controllers. Since sub-channel controllers are added only in the last pipeline stage in the input buffers, increasing the length of buffers introduces no further area overhead.

The lookahead pipeline style brings no significant area overhead. Only the area of input buffers is slightly increased. It is believed that the asymmetric C-element added on *acki* in Figure 4.8 is the major cause. This C-element is located on the critical cycle and its driving strength has been optimized for speed performance.

As shown in Table 4.3, channel slicing and lookahead pipelines improve throughput significantly. These speed results are produced by averaging the period and router delays of sending a packet from the south input to the east output, which has the worst router delay. Channel slicing and lookahead pipelines reduce the period by 24.1% and 17.2% respectively. The router using both channel slicing and lookahead pipelines delivers data flits at equivalent 588 MHz,

Table 4.3   Speed performance.

	Period	Frequency	Router latency	Routing
No ChSlice or LH	2.9 ns	345 MHz	2.8 ns	0.8 ns
ChSlice only	2.2 ns	455 MHz	2.1 ns	0.8 ns
ChSlice and LH	1.7 ns	588 MHz	1.7 ns	0.8 ns

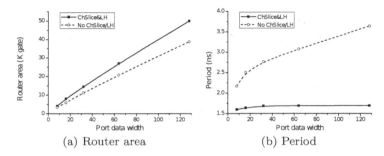

(a) Router area   (b) Period

Figure 4.12   Area and speed with various data widths.

which is 1.7 times of the equivalent frequency of the traditional router using synchronized pipelines.

A major disadvantage of using synchronized pipelines is the deteriorated throughput with increasing data width. The sub-channels in channel sliced pipelines are unsynchronized most of the time. Unlike synchronized pipelines, increasing data width leads to no significant throughput degradation. Figure 4.12 shows the router area and speed with various data widths. The router area is linear with data width as expected. The period of the channel sliced router remains around 1.7 ns, while it increases to more than 3.5 ns in the router using synchronized pipelines. Channel slicing is a desirable technique in wide QDI pipelines.

4.2   SPATIAL DIVISION MULTIPLEXING

The preceding section introduced two techniques which are ready for use in the physical layer to improve the throughput of asynchronous pipelines. This section proposes a new flow control method in the switching layer — spatial division multiplexing

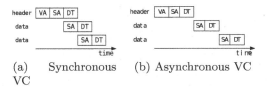

(a) Synchronous (b) Asynchronous VC
VC

Figure 4.13   Data flow of VC.

(SDM). The performance advantages and design overhead of SDM will be compared against the virtual channel (VC) flow control method, which is extensively adopted in most asynchronous on-chip networks.

4.2.1   Problems of the Virtual Channel Flow Control

Virtual channel (VC) is the most utilized flow control method in synchronous on-chip networks thanks to its capability of alleviating the head-of-line (HOL) problem. However, utilizing VC in asynchronous on-chip networks introduces significant design overhead and the throughput improvement is far from satisfactory. Although VC has already been employed in numerous asynchronous on-chip networks [22, 30, 67, 76], all of them use VCs to provide QoS support rather than improve throughput. VC is not a desirable method for high throughput asynchronous on-chip networks.

An asynchronous VC router suffers from three different disadvantages: slow switch allocation, large area overhead and long pipeline synchronization latency.

4.2.1.1   Slow Switch Allocation

The switch allocation in asynchronous VC routers significantly compromises throughput. As shown in Figure 4.13a, the transmission of a flit in synchronous VC routers proceeds in three steps: VC allocation (VA), switch allocation (SA) and data transmission (DT) [63]. Only header flits require the VC allocation step during which the VC allocator reserves a VC in the target output port. Since all VCs share the central switch in a time divided manner, all flits need to compete for a path in the switch before transmitting

Table 4.4   Buffer area.

	Latches	Latch type	Area
synchronous router	$D \cdot W$	flip-flop	$2820 \ \mu m^2$
asynchronous dual-rail	$4D \cdot W$	C-element	$10140 \ \mu m^2$
asynchronous 1-of-4	$4D \cdot W$	C-element	$8040 \ \mu m^2$
asynchronous 2-of-7	$2D \cdot W$	C-element	$9760 \ \mu m^2$

data. In a synchronous VC router, all VCs are synchronized by the global clock. VA, SA and DT are pipelined and accomplished in three clock cycles. As shown in Figure 4.13a, a flit can pre-order a path while another flit is under transmission.

An asynchronous VC router cannot pipeline the switch allocation with data transmission because a path cannot be pre-allocated to a VC before it is released. As a result, the absolute time consumed by each flit is the accumulated delay of SA and DT rather than a single clock cycle in synchronous VC router. Figure 4.13b depicts the asynchronous data flow. The latency of switch allocation has been directly added into the critical cycle. Network throughput is compromised significantly.

4.2.1.2 Large Area Overhead

It is well known that buffers are the major area overhead in synchronous VC routers [171]. Asynchronous buffers consume more area than their synchronous counterparts, leading to an even larger area overhead.

Table 4.4 illustrates the area overhead of synchronous and asynchronous buffers using different data encoding methods. The second and third columns reveal the type and number of latches needed for a buffer to store D data flits with data width of W bits. All asynchronous buffers are 4-phase QDI pipelines using C-elements as storage components. Wide pipelines are built by synchronizing multiple bit-level pipelines. A single asynchronous pipeline stage is a half buffer stage. Two asynchronous pipeline stages are equivalent to one synchronous pipeline stage using flip-flops. A minimum of $2D$ pipeline stages are required for D flits. The C-element tree in

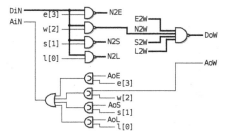

Figure 4.14　Crossbar in asynchronous VC routers.

the synchronization circuit introduces extra area overhead. The last column in Table 4.4 demonstrates the minimum area of implementing buffers for four 32-bit flits ($D = 4$, $W = 32$) using a 0.13 μm cell library. Obviously, asynchronous buffers are significantly larger than synchronous buffers.

4.2.1.3 Long Pipeline Synchronization Latency

As described in Section 4.1.1, synchronization overhead is the extra latency incurred by synchronizing multiple bit-level pipelines into a wide pipeline. In asynchronous VC routers, the central switch is re-allocated in every data cycle. Thus, pipeline stages must be synchronized in every data cycle and channel slicing cannot be used.

In addition to the synchronization overhead in pipelines, the frequent re-allocation of the central switch also introduces extra area and extra latency in the critical cycle. Figure 4.14 depicts the crossbar implementation in QoS NoC [75]. Since the crossbar configuration signals ($e[3]$, $w[2]$, $s[1]$ and $l[0]$) are withdrawn with data, extra C-elements must be inserted on the ack lines to ensure AiN drops after AoW (or other ack signals). If the path is allocated to a packet rather than a flit, such as the wormhole routers in Section 4.1.4, the configuration signals can be withdrawn after $AiN-$ and no extra C-element is needed.

4.2.2 Spatial Division Multiplexing

The latency overhead of VC routers is related to synchronization — the synchronization among bit-level pipelines, and the synchronization between switch allocation and data transmission. Instead

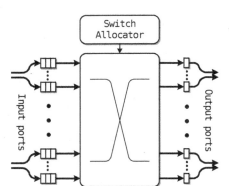

Figure 4.15   SDM router.

of introducing timing concurrency which leads to synchronization, the spatial division multiplexing (SDM) flow control method brings spatial parallelism which alleviates the HOL problem without introducing extra synchronization. It has been utilized in synchronous on-chip networks to improve throughput [90] or to provide QoS support [132]. It will be shown that using SDM in asynchronous on-chip networks provides better best-effort throughput than using VC.

The structure of an SDM router is shown in Figure 4.15. Every port or buffer is spatially divided into multiple virtual circuits [132].[1] Assuming the data width of each port is W bits and every port is divided into M virtual circuits, the data width of a single virtual circuit is W/M bits. Every virtual circuit delivers a packet independently in a serialized manner without sharing any resources with other virtual circuits. When one packet is blocked in one router, only the virtual circuit allocated to this packet is wasted. Other packets can go through the same port using other unblocked virtual circuits. Hence, the HOL problem is alleviated.

SDM routers introduce no synchronization overhead. Since virtual circuits are exclusively allocated to packets, no resource is shared. The path reserved in the central switch holds for the whole

---

[1]To avoid the ambiguity between virtual channel and virtual circuit, the abbreviation VC represents only virtual channel in this book.

transmission duration of a packet. Thus, switch allocation is made once per packet without introducing extra latency. Furthermore, the data width of each virtual circuit is a portion of the port data width. SDM, in fact, reduces the synchronization overhead among bit-level pipelines.

Long packet transmission latency and large switch area are the major design overhead of SDM routers. Since packets are serialized to fit the data width of a single virtual circuit, the packet transmission latency is prolonged. The packet transmission latency t_P can be expressed as:

$$t_P = t_R \cdot h + T \cdot l \cdot M + t_A \qquad (4.8)$$

where t_R is the router latency; h is the number of hops between packet sender and receiver; T is the period of data paths; l is the number of flits in a packet; M is the number of virtual circuits in one port; t_A is the extra latency introduced by HOL problems. When the number of virtual circuits in one port increases, packet latency rises with the increasing M. However, t_A, T and t_R are reduced as the HOL problem is alleviated and the synchronization overhead is decreased with small data width. The latency overhead is not significant when the network size is large (large h), packets are short (small l) or the network is heavily loaded (large t_A).

SDM routers use large central switches. In an SDM router with P ports, $M \times P$ input virtual circuits are connected to $M \times P$ output virtual circuits leading to a $MP \times MP$ crossbar. The area of a crossbar is proportional to the number of cross-points[2] inside it. Accordingly, the area of the crossbars inside wormhole routers and SDM routers can be calculated as:

$$A_{\text{wormhole}} = P^2 W \cdot A_{\text{CP}} \qquad (4.9)$$
$$A_{\text{SDM}} = M^2 P^2 W (W/M) \cdot A_{\text{CP}} = MP^2 W \cdot A_{\text{CP}} \qquad (4.10)$$

where A_{CP} is the equivalent area of a single cross-point. The area of the crossbar in an SDM router is proportional to the number of virtual circuits.

---

[2]A cross-point is a single switching element in an array of elements comprising the switch.

Although SDM introduces large switches, this area overhead is expected smaller than that of VC routers for three reasons:

- The size of the buffers in SDM routers is not increased; therefore, the large central switch is the major area overhead. As shown in the area breakdown of the wormhole router in Table 4.2, switches are smaller than buffers. Hence, increasing the size of switches leads to smaller routers than increasing the size of buffers, assuming the same number of VCs/virtual circuits are implemented.

- VC routers also increase the size of switches. If extended switches (Section 3.2.2.4) are used, such as ANOC [22], MANGO [28] and QNoC [67], the size of the switch is exactly the same as that of the SDM switch when the number of VCs is M. Even when the normal $P \times P$ switch is used as in the QoS NoC router [77], extra multiplexers are added on the outputs of input buffers leading to an area overhead of $MPW \cdot A_{\mathrm{CP}}$.

- As it will be presented in Section 4.3.4.1, utilizing a 2-stage Clos switch reduces the size of the switch to:

$$A_{\mathrm{SDM+Clos}} = (P^2 + MP)W \cdot A_{\mathrm{CP}} \qquad (4.11)$$

which introduces the same area overhead as the extra multiplexer in QoS NoC routers.

4.2.3 SDM Router

This section describes the hardware details of a relaxed-QDI SDM router. This router has been synthesized into gate-level netlists using a 0.13 μm cell library. The area and speed performance are revealed accordingly.

4.2.3.1 Router Structure

The overall structure of an SDM router has already been presented in Figure 4.15. The buffer in each input port is divided into M independent input buffers for individual virtual circuits, each of which is W/M bits wide. Every one of them has its own XY router and

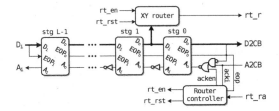

Figure 4.16   Input buffer for a virtual circuit.

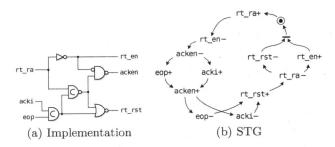

(a) Implementation   (b) STG

Figure 4.17   Router controller in an SDM router.

router controller. The structure of an input buffer for a virtual circuit is shown in Figure 4.16 [226]. It has L stages of buffers. The 0th pipeline stage is connected to the central switch and controlled by the local router controller. Incoming header flits are blocked in the 1st pipeline stage and analyzed by the local XY router, whose internal structure has been illustrated previously in Figure 4.11. The decoded route requests rt_r are sent to the switch allocator. A path inside the central switch is successfully reserved when a notification is received from rt_ra. The local router controller can temporarily pause the pipeline by setting the active low signal $acken$ to high when a new header flit is expected.

Figure 4.17 shows the router controller circuit synthesized from its STG using Petrify [57]. Initially, the buffer is blocked waiting for a new header flit. Once a path is reserved in the central switch, indicated by rt_ra+, the XY router is disabled (rt_en-) and the buffer is activated ($acken-$). After the packet is delivered, the tail flit drives both eop and $acki$ to high. Triggered by the tail flit, the router controller sequentially blocks the buffer and withdraws the tail flit ($acken+$), resets the decoded routing request (rt_rst+), and finally restarts the XY router (rt_en+) for the succeeding packet.

The output buffer of each virtual circuit contains only one pipeline stage, which decouples the critical cycle from the inter-router channels. The central switch is an $MP \times MP$ crossbar dynamically configured by P switch allocators, one for each output port. Since the router controllers in input buffers guarantee that the decoded routing requests remain stable until the whole packet is delivered, no extra C-element is needed in the crossbar.

The switch allocator is the most complicated component in an SDM router. Unlike a wormhole router where every output buffer heads to a different direction, an SDM router has up to M virtual circuits implemented in every output port heading to the same direction. The central switch allocator can be separated into P distributed allocators, but every distributed allocator is required to allocate M output virtual circuits to MP input virtual circuits, which cannot be done by asynchronous arbiters. Currently, the only QDI allocator capable of such allocation task is the multi-resource arbiter [88] previously mentioned in Section 2.5.2.3.

Figure 4.18 demonstrates a switch allocator for one output direction. It has two parts: a multi-resource arbiter in the lower layer (Figure 4.18a) and a configuration capture matrix in the upper layer (Figure 4.18b). The multi-resource arbiter reads requests from rt_r and matches them to available virtual circuits indicated by vc_rdy. As described in Section 2.5.2.3, the match process proceeds in a sequential way: only one pair of rt_r_i and vc_rdy_j is matched at one time. The match result is denoted by $h_{j,i}$. In order to match another pair, the corresponding rt_r_i and vc_rdy_j are withdrawn immediately after the result $h_{j,i}$ is captured in the configuration capture matrix.

The configuration capture matrix is depicted in Figure 4.18b. The switch configuration signals cfg are generated by the matrix of C-elements, which are triggered by h. When a configuration $cfg_{j,i}$ is produced, the corresponding virtual circuit ready flag vc_rdy_j is withdrawn and the acknowledgment to the input virtual circuit rt_ra_i is set. The acknowledgment is also connected to the multi-resource arbiter in order to release $h_{j,i}$.

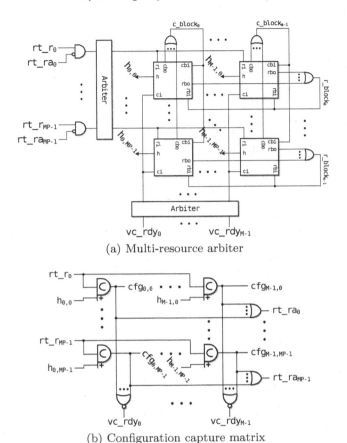

(a) Multi-resource arbiter

(b) Configuration capture matrix

Figure 4.18   Switch allocator in an SDM router.

4.2.3.2 Performance Evaluation

An QDI SDM router has been implemented using 0.13 μm cell library. The router has five bi-directional ports compatible with normal mesh topology. The data width of each port is set to 32 bits. Four virtual circuits are implemented in each port. Every input buffer has two pipeline stages.

In the flit definition for wormhole routers as described in Table 4.1, a header flit contains an 8-bit address field and three bytes of data. In the SDM router, every port and buffer are divided into four virtual circuits, each of which is eight bits wide. Thus, every original 32-bit flit in the network using wormhole routers are serialized into four 8-bit flits in the network using SDM routers. For the header flit, the first serialized flit contains the 8-bit address to avoid extra routing latency. The router can provide more than four virtual circuits although extra area and latency overhead is introduced. Assuming N bits are required to decode a route request, using a virtual circuit which is less than N bits wide divides the N bits into multiple flits. In this case, the XY router has to wait for multiple flits before producing a routing request, introducing an undesirable serialization latency.

The router area derived from the post-synthesis netlist is 71956 μm^2 (equivalent to 17.99k gates). Using the estimated gate delay from the synthesizer, the evaluated period of the SDM router is 4.1 ns. The router latency for data flits is 2.49 ns. The XY router and the switch allocator require 0.51 ns and 3.21 ns, respectively, to decode a route request and reserve a path.

4.2.4 Comparison between SDM and VC

This section provides behavioral level models for wormhole, SDM and VC routers; therefore, they can be simulated in large networks with various configurations. Area and latency estimation models are derived from different router architectures. The latency estimation is used in SystemC simulations for accurate throughput performance [226].

4.2.4.1 Area Model

The area of a router with P ports can be expressed as:

$$A = P \cdot (A_{\mathrm{IB}} + A_{\mathrm{OB}}) + A_{\mathrm{CB}} + A_{\mathrm{A}} \qquad (4.12)$$

where A_{IB}, A_{OB}, A_{CB} and A_{A} are the area of an input buffer, an output buffer, the crossbar and all allocators.

As shown in Figure 4.16, an input buffer contains L buffer stages, an XY router and a router controller. A buffer stage is built from multiple 4-phase 1-of-4 pipelines. Assuming the data width is W, every buffer stage needs $2W+1$ C-elements to store data and the *eop* bit. The completion detection circuit requires extra $0.5W - 1$

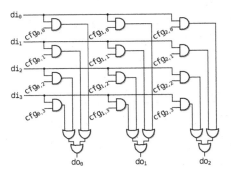

Figure 4.19   A 1-bit 4×3 crossbar.

C-elements to generate the common *ack* signal. Accordingly, the area of an input buffer in a wormhole router can be expressed as:

$$A_{\mathrm{IB,WH}} = L \cdot (2.5W A_{\mathrm{C}} + A_{\mathrm{EOP}}) + A_{\mathrm{R}} + A_{\mathrm{RC}} \qquad (4.13)$$

where A_{C}, A_{EOP}, A_{R} and A_{RC} represent the area of a 2-input C-element, the extra logic introduced by the *eop* bit, the XY router and the router controller, respectively.

An output buffer is a single buffer stage.

$$A_{\mathrm{OB,WH}} = 2.5W A_{\mathrm{C}} + A_{\mathrm{EOP}} \qquad (4.14)$$

M virtual circuits are implemented in an SDM router, each of which is W/M bits wide. As a virtual circuit delivers packets independently, it is a fully functional input buffer but with a narrow data width. The area of the input and output buffers of SDM routers can be calculated as follows:

$$A_{\mathrm{IB,SDM}} = M \cdot \left[L \cdot \left(\frac{2.5W}{M} \cdot A_{\mathrm{C}} + A_{\mathrm{EOP}} \right) + A_{\mathrm{R}} + A_{\mathrm{RC}} \right] \qquad (4.15)$$

$$A_{\mathrm{OB,SDM}} = 2.5W A_{\mathrm{C}} + M A_{\mathrm{EOP}} \qquad (4.16)$$

As shown in Figure 4.19, a crossbar consists of an AND gate matrix and several OR gate trees. The size of the AND gate matrix and the number of the OR gate trees are determined by the number of ports and the wire count of each port. The crossbar inside a wormhole router has P ports, while the one in an SDM router has

MP ports. Assuming all 2-input gates have the same area, the area of crossbars is as follows:

$$A_{\text{CB,WH}} = (2W + 2)(2P^2 - P)A_{\text{g}} \tag{4.17}$$

$$A_{\text{CB,SDM}} = \left(\frac{2W}{M} + 2\right)(2M^2P^2 - MP)A_{\text{g}} \tag{4.18}$$

where A_{g} is the equivalent area of a 2-input gate.

It is difficult to provide accurate area estimation for allocators. The area depends on the structure of the allocator and the number of clients/resources. Assuming all routers use the multi-resource arbiter, whose area is roughly proportional to the arbitration scheme, the area can be estimated as:

$$A_{\text{A,WH}} = P^2 A_{\text{arb}} \tag{4.19}$$

$$A_{\text{A,SDM}} = M^2 P^2 A_{\text{arb}} \tag{4.20}$$

where A_{arb} is the equivalent area overhead of a single arbitration point for one client and one resource.

Several wormhole and SDM routers have been implemented. Using the area reported from the post-synthesis netlists, the parameters in Equation 4.13 to 4.20 are extracted as follows (in unit of μm^2):

$$A_{\text{C}} = 14.7 \quad A_{\text{EOP}} = 11 \quad A_{\text{R}} = 440 \quad A_{\text{RC}} = 45 \quad A_{\text{g}} = 2.45$$
$$A_{\text{arb}} = 86$$

The detailed area and the estimation error of the area model are illustrated in Table 4.5. A wormhole router and an SDM router have been designed and synthesized. The crossbar and the switch allocator are simplified by removing unnecessary turn models in the XY routing algorithm. The actual area models have been adjusted accordingly. It is shown that the area models successfully estimate the area of all router components within a maximum error of 1.7% except for the switch allocator in the wormhole router. This significant error is due to the different allocator structure. The multi-way MUTEX arbiters used in wormhole routers consume much less area than multi-resource arbiters. Since allocators take only a small portion of the total area and the overall area of a router is more

Table 4.5 Area consumption.

	Wormhole			SDM		
	actual	model	error	actual	model	error
input buffer	14303	14295	0.0%	21995	21900	-0.4%
output buffer	5935	5935	0.0%	6000	6100	1.7%
crossbar	4356	4366	0.0%	21744	21697	-0.2%
switch allocator	772	1376	78.2%	22208	22016	-0.9%
total	25366	25927	2.4%	71956	71713	-0.3%

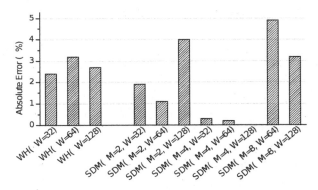

Figure 4.20   Area estimation error.

important than the area breakdown, this estimation error can be tolerated.

Figure 4.20 reveals the area estimation error of routers with various configurations. In all configurations, the estimation error is lower than 4.9% (SDM router $M = 4$ and $W = 64$). It is shown that the area models are adequate to estimate the area of routers in various configurations.

4.2.4.2 Latency Model

The throughput of an asynchronous pipeline is constrained by the period of its critical cycle. Hence, a latency model for the critical cycle is essential to achieve accurate throughput estimation. As described in Section 4.1.3, the critical cycle in asynchronous routers is the path around the pipeline stages connected to the central switch. Assuming rising time and falling time are the same in all gates, the latency T of the critical cycle can be expressed as:

$$T = 4t_C + 4t_{CB} + 2t_{CD} + 2t_{AD} + t_{CTL} \qquad (4.21)$$

where t_C is the propagation latency of a C-element used to store data, t_{CB} is the propagation latency of the crossbar, t_{CD} is the propagation latency of the completion detection circuit, t_{AD} is the latency of the isochronic fork on the receiver end of the *ack* line, namely the *ack* driver latency, and t_{CTL} is the extra latency caused by the router controller.

Linear delay models are used to approximate these latencies. The C-elements are connected to the crossbar. Thus, t_C is linear with the number of ports of the crossbar.

$$t_{C,WH} = l_C + k_C(P + 1) \qquad (4.22)$$
$$t_{C,SDM} = l_C + k_C(P + 1) \qquad (4.23)$$

where l_C is the latency of a C-element with zero load and k_C is the extra latency introduced by every extra fanout. Similarly, the *ack* driver latency t_{AD} is linear with the wire count of one buffer stage.

$$t_{AD,WH} = l_{AD} + k_{AD}(2W + 1) \qquad (4.24)$$
$$t_{AD,SDM} = l_{AD} + k_{AD}(2W/M + 1) \qquad (4.25)$$

where l_{AD} and k_{AD} are the latency of the *ack* driving gate and the extra fanouts.

The crossbar contains an AND gate matrix and several OR gate trees. The depth of the OR gate tree is determined by the number of input ports. Assuming all OR gates have the same propagation latency:

$$t_{CB,WH} = l_{CB} + k_{CB} \cdot log_2(P) \qquad (4.26)$$
$$t_{CB,SDM} = l_{CB} + k_{CB} \cdot log_2(MP) \qquad (4.27)$$

where l_{CB} and k_{CB} are the propagation latencies of an AND gate and an OR gate respectively.

The completion detection circuit contains a C-element tree. The latency of this tree is proportional to its depth. The final common *ack* signal drives the gates to all input ports; therefore, its fanout is proportional to the number of ports. The latency estimation must consider the impact by both effects.

$$t_{\text{CD,WH}} = l_{\text{CD}} + l_{\text{C}} \cdot log_2(W/2) + k_{\text{CD}} \cdot P \qquad (4.28)$$

$$t_{\text{CD,SDM}} = l_{\text{CD}} + l_{\text{C}} \cdot log_2\left(\frac{W}{2M}\right) + k_{\text{CD}} \cdot MP \qquad (4.29)$$

where l_{CD} and k_{CD} are the zero load latency of a completion detection circuit without any C-elements (the latency of two OR gates) and the extra fanout latency.

The router controller in wormhole or SDM routers halts the input buffer only once per packet to analyze incoming header flits. Once a path allocation is made for a packet, pipelines run at full speed and no extra control latency is introduced ($t_{\text{CTL}} = 0$). However, the controller in a VC router halts the data path in every cycle to reconfigure the crossbar, which leads to non-zero t_{CTL}.

All parameters are extracted from gate-level simulations back-annotated with latency provided by synthesis. The implemented routers have removed all unnecessary turns in the crossbar according to the XY routing algorithm. Wire latency is counted as part of gate latency. The extracted parameters are listed as follows (in unit of ns):

$$l_{\text{C}} = 0.15 \qquad k_{\text{C}} = 0.01 \qquad l_{\text{CB}} = 0.074 \qquad k_{\text{CB}} = 0.044$$
$$l_{\text{CD}} = 0.23 \qquad k_{\text{CD}} = 0.004 \qquad l_{\text{AD}} = 0.17 \qquad k_{\text{AD}} = 0.005$$

The practical speed performance and the estimation errors of the latency models are shown in Table 4.6. Compared with the errors of the area models, the latency estimation causes larger errors for several reasons: the practical latency of a gate is not linear; the load is not exactly proportional to fanout; the propagation time of a gate is related to the input transition time which is difficult to estimate statically.

Figure 4.21 shows the latency estimation errors of routers with various configurations. Most errors are smaller than 6.5%. The significant errors occur when large data width ($W/M > 32$) is used.

Table 4.6   Router latency (ns).

	Wormhole			SDM		
	actual	model	error	actual	model	error
cycle period	4.22	4.130	-2.1%	4.10	3.978	-3.0%
router latency	2.29			2.49		
route decoding	0.44			0.51		
switch allocation	0.78			3.21		
t_C	0.22	0.200	-9.1%	0.34	0.320	-5.9%
t_{CB}	0.16	0.162	1.3%	0.26	0.250	-3.8%
t_{CD}	0.79	0.846	7.6%	0.57	0.594	4.2%
t_{AD}	0.53	0.495	-6.6%	0.27	0.255	-5.5%
t_{CTL}	0.00			0.00		

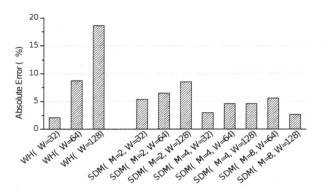

Figure 4.21   Latency estimation error.

These wide pipelines cause design rule violations (max capacitance and max transition time) on *ack* lines. Buffer trees are inserted to eliminate these violations in synthesis. Significant errors are introduced as these buffer trees do not fit in the linear latency model. To cope with this problem, all simulations using data width larger than 32 bits are carefully compensated.[3] It is important to notice

---

[3] When wide pipelines are used ($W/M > 32$), the compensated *ack* driver latency t'_{AD} is used in simulations. $t'_{AD} = t_{AD} + e_{AD}$, where e_{AD} is the correction factor of t_{AD}. Using the estimation errors in wormhole routers, e_{AD}

that technology and cell libraries have strong impact on latency. The parameters must be extracted again if a different cell library is used.

4.2.4.3 Model for VC Routers

Here, we produce a similar conceptual area and latency estimation model for VC routers. Assuming the asynchronous VC router uses the internal structure of an ANOC router [22] (Figure 3.16), it comprises P input buffers, an extended $MP \times P$ crossbar, P output buffers, a VC allocator and a switch allocator. It uses the input buffering scheme and each input buffer contains M VCs.

Using the same assumptions for wormhole and SDM routers, the area model of a VC router is expressed as follows:

$$A_{\mathrm{IB,VC}} = M \cdot A_{\mathrm{IB,WH}} \tag{4.30}$$

$$A_{\mathrm{OB,VC}} = A_{\mathrm{OB,WH}} \tag{4.31}$$

$$A_{\mathrm{CB,VC}} = (2MP^2 - P) \cdot (2W + 2) \cdot A_{\mathrm{g}} \tag{4.32}$$

$$A_{\mathrm{A,VC}} = (M^2 P^2 + MP) \cdot A_{\mathrm{arb}} \tag{4.33}$$

The area in Equation 4.33 includes two parts: the VC allocator and the switch allocator. As described in [188], the arbitration scheme of a fair VC allocator is $MP \times MP$ because MP output VCs are dynamically allocated to MP input VCs. The arbitration scheme of the switch allocator is $M \times P$ because an output port is requested by a maximum of M input VCs simultaneously.

A VC router using the input buffer scheme has the same critical cycle traversing the crossbar as wormhole and SDM routers. The latency of the critical cycle can be approximated as follows:

$$t_{\mathrm{C,VC}} = t_{\mathrm{C,WH}} \tag{4.34}$$

$$t_{\mathrm{CD,VC}} = l_{\mathrm{CD}} + l_{\mathrm{C}} \cdot log_2(W/2) + k_{\mathrm{CD}} \cdot MP \tag{4.35}$$

$$t_{\mathrm{AD,VC}} = t_{\mathrm{AD,WH}} \tag{4.36}$$

$$t_{\mathrm{CB,VC}} = t_{\mathrm{CB,WH}} \tag{4.37}$$

---

is extracted as -0.2 ns, -0.74 ns and -1.82 ns for the data widths of 64-bit, 128-bit and 256-bit respectively.

Similarly, we can estimate the delays for a 32-bit 5-port asynchronous VC router with four VCs are listed as follows (in unit of ns):

$$t_C = 0.20 \quad t_{CB} = 0.16 \quad t_{CD} = 0.89 \quad t_{AD} = 0.50 \quad t_{CTL} = 0.78$$
$$\text{cycle period} = 5.01 \qquad \text{route decoding} = 0.44$$
$$\text{VC allocation} = 3.21 \qquad \text{switch allocation} = 0.78$$

Asynchronous VC routers have the longest period in all router architectures. Both VC and wormhole router suffer from the longest *ack* driver latency and the deepest C-element tree in the completion detection circuit. The crossbar in a VC router introduces extra latency as an SDM router does. The fact that the crossbar is reconfigured in every cycle introduces extra control latency. The value of this extra control latency t_{CTL} comes from the switch allocation latency of the wormhole router assuming multi-way MUTEX arbiters are used in switch allocators. As a VC allocator has the same arbitration scheme as the switch allocator in an SDM router, their latencies are assumed the same.

4.2.4.4 Performance Analysis

An 8×8 mesh network has been built with latency accurate SystemC models. All simulations use the random uniform traffic pattern. Every network node sends packets uniformly to other nodes in a Poisson sequence.

Figure 4.22a shows the average packet transmission latency with various injection rates. All routers are equipped with two stages of input buffers except for the VC router which is also simulated with four stages. The payload size of a packet is set to 64 bytes. Four virtual circuits/VCs are implemented. It is shown that both VC and SDM improve throughput but SDM outperforms VC. The SDM router provides the best saturation throughput of 346 MByte/Node/s, which is around 1.7 times that of the wormhole router. However, the minimum packet transmission latency in an idle network is prolonged because the data width of a virtual circuit is only a portion of the total data width. Packets are delivered in a serialized way. The minimum packet latency of SDM

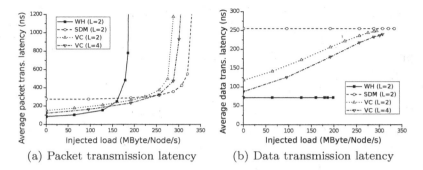

(a) Packet transmission latency   (b) Data transmission latency

Figure 4.22   Transmission latency with various network load ($P =$ 5, $W = 32$, $M = 4$).

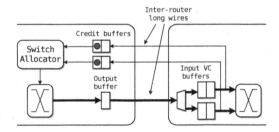

Figure 4.23   Credit based back-pressure method.

routers is 275 ns, which is 3.2 times that of using wormhole routers and 1.8 times that of using VC routers.

VC routers suffer from the credit loop latency when their input VC buffers are short. Every asynchronous buffer stage is a half buffer stage. Thus a full buffer stage needs two half buffer stages. Most VC routers use the credit based back-pressure method [22, 28, 67, 75] as shown in Figure 4.23. The switch allocator in one output port allocates the output buffer to input VCs only when the corresponding input VC buffer in the next router has available buffer space. The credit buffers in one output port record the available buffer space of all input VC buffers in the next router using tokens. A token is consumed when a flit is transmitted to the next router and a token is return when the input VC buffer in the next router transmits a flit. When input VC buffers are short, such as only one full buffer stage, the credit buffer of every VC has only one token.

Under low network load, it is likely that only one VC buffer in all VC buffers is utilized. In this case, a new flit has to wait until the token consumed by the previous flit is returned to the corresponding credit buffer. The latency of the loop path is called the credit loop latency. Inferred from the synchronous credit loop calculation (Equation 16.1 in [63]), the credit loop latency t_{crt} in an asynchronous VC router can be expressed as:[4]

$$t_{\text{crt}} = L \cdot t_{\text{C}} + 2t_{\text{w}} + t_{\text{CTL}} + T \qquad (4.38)$$

where t_{w} is the latency of the inter-router long wires. Adopting the long wire latency in ASPIN [212], the credit loop latency of the VC router is around 1.3 periods. As a result, at least two full buffer stages are required to avoid the credit stall under low network load. Figure 4.22a shows that adding two more half buffers (two stages of full buffers in total) reduces the packet transmission latency to 122 ns; however, it does not raise throughput significantly and introduces extra area overhead by doubling the buffer size. When the network is heavily loaded, multiple VCs are utilized simultaneously.

When a flit of one VC is waiting for a new token, the flits of other VCs can utilize the output buffer as long as they have tokens available in the credit buffers. Thus, the credit stall is unlikely to compromise the saturation throughput.

Packet transmission latency comprises two parts: the time consumed to reserve a path to the target PE and the time consumed to transmit data. Figure 4.22b shows the data transmission latency. In wormhole and SDM routers, links and buffers are exclusively allocated to packets. Resources are not shared during data transmission and the data transmission latency is not affected by network load. On the contrary, switches in VC routers are shared by all VCs in a time divided manner. The data transmission latency increases when the network is heavily loaded. This result reveals the potential of using SDM to reduce the latency jitters when hard latency guaranteed services are required.

---

[4]Equation 4.38 is provided as an explanation to the credit loop latency. It is not intended for accurate latency estimation because different switch allocator and input buffer implementations significantly affect the latency calculation.

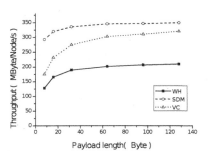

Figure 4.24 Throughput with various payload sizes ($P = 5$, $W = 32$, $L = 2$, $M = 4$).

Figure 4.24 demonstrates how the payload size affects the saturation throughput. Every packet has a fixed amount of control overhead, such as the target address in the header flit. Short packets are not efficient as the payload transmitted in each packet is small. The saturation throughput rises with payload length. This increase is not linear. The saturation throughput approaches its maximum when payload is larger than 64 bytes. Therefore, the payload size is fixed to 64 bytes in all following simulations. SDM outperforms VC and provides the highest throughput of 350 MByte/Node/s in the 128-byte case.

Both VC and SDM alleviate the head-of-line (HOL) problem. It is known that long distance communications are more vulnerable to contention than local communications. Figure 4.25 demonstrates

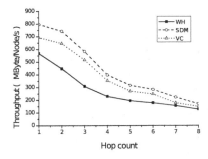

Figure 4.25 Throughput with various communication distances ($P = 5$, $W = 32$, $L = 2$, $M = 4$).

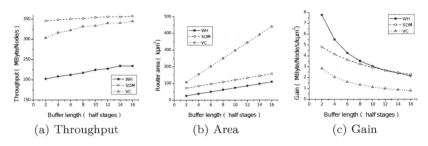

(a) Throughput   (b) Area   (c) Gain

Figure 4.26 Network performance with various buffer lengths ($P = 5$, $W = 32$, $M = 4$).

the throughput variation with different communication distances. In this simulation, network nodes send packets uniformly to all nodes certain hops away. The saturation throughput drops significantly with the increasing communication distance. Both VC and SDM achieve better performance improvement in local traffic patterns than in long distance communication patterns. When the communication distance is eight hops, using VC shows little throughput boost but SDM still raises the throughput by 33.9%.

Buffer size is an important design parameter. Increasing buffer length boosts throughput as more packets can be stored in the network when contention occurs. However, buffers consume significant area. Figure 4.26 reveals the throughput improvement by increasing the buffer length. Both the saturation throughput and the area overhead rise linearly. Figure 4.26c shows the gain of throughput per unit of area. Here the gain is defined as:

$$\text{Gain} = \frac{\text{throughput}}{\text{router area}} \tag{4.39}$$

Higher gain indicates better area-to-throughput efficiency. The gain of all router architectures drops along with buffer length. It is not efficient to improve throughput by adding buffers. The basic wormhole router shows the best area efficiency with short buffers. When long buffers are implemented ($L \geq 12$), SDM routers achieve the best area efficiency. In all cases, VC routers suffer from the worst area efficiency.

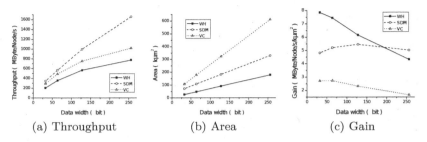

(a) Throughput (b) Area (c) Gain

Figure 4.27   Network performance with various port data widths
($P = 5$, $L = 2$, $M = 4$).

In addition to adding buffers, increasing data width also raises
throughput but the increase is not linear. Transmitting packets in
wide pipelines suffers from the increased control overhead because
the number of flits per packet is decreased. The delay incurred
by reconfiguring the central switch in a router is independent of
data width. In an overloaded network, decreasing the number of
flits per packet leads to frequent switch reconfiguration, which, in
turn, compromises throughput. Furthermore, wide pipelines introduce extra synchronization overhead. Figure 4.27 reveals the impact
of increasing data width. Router area increases linearly with data
width. Compared with wormhole and VC routers, SDM routers
show a steadier throughput increment because their C-element trees
in the completion detection circuits are shorter. Figure 4.27c shows
the gain of throughput per area unit. Although wormhole routers
still show the best gain with narrow pipelines, the gain of SDM
routers increases with data width until 128 bits. When the data
width is over 200 bits, SDM demonstrates the best area efficiency.

Since both VCs and virtual circuits use the wormhole flow control method, VC routers and SDM routers have similar scalability
to network size with wormhole routers. As provided in Section 3.3.1
in [63], Equation 4.40 gives the upper bound on throughput Θ in
random uniform traffic.

$$\Theta \leq \Theta_{\text{ideal}} \leq \frac{2W B_{\text{C}}}{T N^2} \qquad (4.40)$$

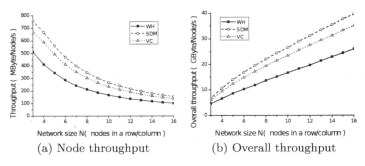

(a) Node throughput   (b) Overall throughput

Figure 4.28   Network scalability ($P = 5$, $W = 32$, $L = 2$, $M = 4$).

where B_C is the minimal channel count over all bisections of the network and N^2 is the total number of nodes in a mesh network. Since B_C is linear with N in a mesh network, the upper bound on throughput Θ and the overall throughput of all nodes in the network ΘN^2 can be simplified into:

$$\Theta \leq \frac{k}{TN} + C \tag{4.41}$$

$$\Theta N^2 \leq \frac{kN}{T} + C' \tag{4.42}$$

where k, C and C' are constants.

Figure 4.28 reveals the practical throughput and overall throughput of networks with different sizes. Figure 4.28a verifies the inverse relation between Θ and N, and the overall throughput in Figure 4.28b is approximately linear with N. Note that Equation 4.42 provides only the upper bound on overall throughput. Although VC routers have larger period than wormhole routers, they show better overall throughput thanks to their capability of resolving HOL problems. All flow control methods present similar scalability to network size.

Increasing the number of virtual circuits or VCs allows more packets to be delivered concurrently and raises throughput. Figure 4.29 demonstrates the packet transmission latency versus network load for SDM and VC routers with various numbers of virtual

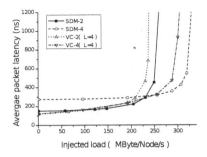

Figure 4.29 Throughput with various number of virtual circuits or VCs ($P = 5$, $W = 32$, $L = 2$).

circuits and VCs. The estimated router area is listed as follows (in unit of μm^2):

| SDM(M=2) | 38153 | SDM(M=4) | 71713 |
| VC(M=2) | 49896 | VC(M=4) | 103250 |

Both VC routers and SDM routers benefit significantly from the increased number of VCs/virtual circuits. Their throughput increase by 26.6% and 26.8%, respectively. It is also shown that the minimum packet transmission latency of SDM routers increases with the number of virtual circuits. Since the total data width of a port is fixed, increasing the number of virtual circuits reduces the data width of a single virtual circuit. Data are serialized to fit the small data width leading to increased overall transmission latency.

4.3   AREA REDUCTION USING CLOS NETWORKS

Section 4.2 proposes to use spatial division multiplexing (SDM) rather than virtual channel (VC) in asynchronous on-chip networks for high throughput. It is shown that SDM achieves better throughput and consumes less area than VC. The major area overhead of an SDM router is the central switch, the size of which is proportional to the number of virtual circuits. This section provides a solution capable of reducing this area overhead by using Clos switching networks instead of crossbars. A novel 2-stage Clos switch is proposed, which consumes the smallest area in almost all router configurations — a perfect switch structure for asynchronous SDM routers.

4.3.1 Clos Switching Networks

A switching network is a switch architecture which dynamically connects input ports to output ports. Clos networks are a class of multi-stage switching networks [54] providing the theoretically optimal solution for high-radix switches.

Clos networks were first used in telephone networks where high-radix switches were statically configured. The later asynchronous transfer mode (ATM) networks and internet protocol (IP) networks achieve high throughput using packet switching technologies [47]. A Clos network designed for current optical backbone networks has already reached peta-bit throughput [45].

Clos networks have already been utilized in intra- and inter-chip interconnection networks. Transistor scaling increases the available bandwidth on-chip. It is found that a router with many narrow ports is more efficient than a router with a few wide ports [91, 114]. A folded-Clos network is used in the Cray BlackWidow multiprocessor to support high bandwidth communications [208] and Beneš networks (multi-stage Clos networks) [23] are used in a synchronous SDM on-chip network to provide delay-guaranteed services [132].

This section tries to reduce the area overhead of the crossbar in an SDM router using Clos networks. Similar work has been done in [132] where a synchronous SDM router uses a Beneš network as the central switch. Although a significant area reduction is reported, the multi-stage Beneš network cannot be reconfigured at runtime. This section will demonstrate an asynchronous Clos scheduler which can dynamically reconfigure unbuffered 3-stage Clos networks.

Figure 4.30 illustrates the potential area reduction of using Clos networks. As the area of a switch is proportional to the number of cross-points inside the switch, the area overhead of using different switch structures in a 5-port 32-bit SDM router is evaluated in the number of cross-points. It is shown that the single stage crossbar structure is more area efficient than multi-stage switching networks when the switch radix is small. When more than three

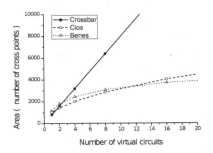

Figure 4.30   Area of different switches.

virtual circuits are implemented, the general 3-stage Clos networks and the multi-stage Beneš networks require smaller area than crossbars. In other words, crossbars are the optimal switch structure for wormhole and VC routers but not SDM routers due to the increasing switch radix. Multi-stage Clos networks have the potential for area reduction in SDM routers.

The internal structure of general 3-stage Clos networks is depicted in Figure 4.31. The terminologies describing the internal components of a Clos network are listed as follows:

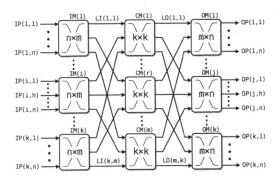

Figure 4.31   General 3-stage Clos network.

IM	Input module at the first stage.
CM	Central module at the second stage.
OM	Output module at the third stage.
n	Number of input ports (IPs)/OPs in each IM/OM.
k	Number of IMs/OMs.
m	Number of CMs.
i	Index of IMs ($0 < i \leq k$).
j	Index of OMs ($0 < j \leq k$).
r	Index of CMs ($0 < r \leq m$).
h	Index of IPs/OPs in an IM/OM ($0 < h \leq n$).
IM(i)	The (i)th IM.
OM(j)	The (j)th OM.
CM(r)	The (r)th CM.
IP(i, h)	The (h)th IP in IM(i).
OP(j, h)	The (h)th OP in OM(j).
LI(i, r)	The link from IM(i) to CM(r).
LO(r, j)	The link from CM(r) to OM(j).
C(n, k, m)	A Clos network has m CMs and k IMs/OMs with n IPs/OPs.
N	The total number of IPs/OPs ($N = nk$).

The first stage contains k IMs, each of which is an $n \times m$ crossbar. In the second stage, m CMs are statically connected to IMs and each CM is a $k \times k$ crossbar. The third stage contains k OMs, each of which is an $m \times n$ crossbar statically connected to CMs. When the size of a switching module is large, it can be replaced by an embedded Clos network and, therefore, the overall Clos network has more than three stages (a well-known class of such Clos networks are Beneš networks [23]).

According to the connection capability, switching networks can be classified into three categories [47]: *Blocking*, the switches have possible connection states such that an available I/O pair cannot be connected because of internal blocking; *strict non-blocking (SNB)*, the switches ensure the connection of any available I/O pairs without altering any established connections; *rearrangeable non-blocking (RNB)*, the switches ensure the connection of any available I/O pairs with possible modification of established connections. A three-stage Clos network with n CMs ($m = n$) is a RNB network, while it is an SNB network when the number of CMs is larger than $2n - 1$ [47].

Similar to crossbars, the area of a switching network is proportional to the number of cross-points. Both SNB and RNB Clos networks consume the minimum area when $k = \sqrt{2N}$:

$$A_{\text{Clos,SNB}} \geq \left[2(2N)^{1.5} - 4N\right] \cdot W \cdot A_{\text{CP}} \qquad (4.43)$$

$$A_{\text{Clos,RNB}} \geq (2N)^{1.5} \cdot W \cdot A_{\text{CP}} \qquad (4.44)$$

where W is the wire count of each port and A_{CP} is the equivalent area of a single cross-point. RNB Clos networks consume the minimum area overhead but introduce throughput degradation if established connections are not allowed to be reconfigured.

There are two classes of routing algorithms for Clos networks [46]; *optimal algorithms*, which provide guaranteed results for all matches but with a high complexity in time or implementation, and *heuristic algorithms*, which provide all or partial matches in low time complexity. Although optimal algorithms guarantee the connection of any I/O pairs, they require a global view of all modules and take a long time to reconfigure. They are normally used in statically configured Clos networks [132]. On the other hand, heuristic algorithms are fast and spatially distributed. Most dynamically reconfigurable Clos networks utilize heuristic algorithms [45, 46, 49, 51, 178, 179, 205].

Buffer insertion is a usual way of improving throughput in Clos networks. According to the stage where buffers are inserted, a Clos network can be a space-space-space network without buffers, a memory-space-memory network with buffer insertion in IMs and OMs, or a space-memory-space network with buffer insertion in CMs. Space-space-space networks introduce no buffer overhead but provide the worst throughput. Space-memory-space networks normally show better throughput than memory-space-memory networks because the buffers in CMs resolve the contention in CMs; however, this scheme requires a re-sequencing function in OMs because data issued to OMs are out-of-order. Memory-space-memory is the most utilized scheme in ATM networks. Buffers in IMs and OMs improve throughput without the out-of-order problem, but the OMs are required to speed-up m times to avoid throughput degradation (the detailed comparison of buffer insertion schemes and memory speed-up can be found in [47, 179]).

Only three-stage space-space-space Clos networks are researched in this section. The tight area budget of on-chip networks disallows any extra buffers except for the input/output buffers. Nevertheless, the routing algorithms for space-space-space Clos networks can be easily adopted in memory-space-memory or space-memory-space Clos networks.

4.3.2 Dispatching Algorithm

Every CM in a Clos network is shared by all I/O pairs, since every I/O pair has m possible path configurations and each of them goes through a different CM. In the worst case, all the nk IPs would try to utilize the same CM ignoring that one CM is capable of setting up only k paths. Hence an efficient routing algorithm must dispatch requests evenly to all CMs otherwise throughput is compromised. Heuristic algorithms process a request from $IP(i_1,h_1)$ to $OP(j_2,h_2)$ in two stages [205]: Module matching first reserves a path from $IP(i_1,h_1)$ to an $LO(r, j_2)$ which is connected to $OM(j_2)$. Then port matching connects $LO(r,j_2)$ and $OP(j_2,h_2)$ in $OM(j_2)$. Since it is the module matching stage that chooses the target CM, it determines the request distribution which directly affects throughput. The sub-algorithm used in module matching, namely the dispatching algorithm, is a key research issue.

4.3.2.1 Concurrent Round-Robin Dispatching

The data transmitted in the synchronous Clos networks used in ATM and IP networks are routed in units of a cell — a small and fixed sized fraction of a packet. Multiple cells are transmitted synchronously from IMs to OMs in one cell time. The reconfiguration of switches is scheduled concurrently with data transmission in a pipelined manner. The new configuration generated in the current cell time takes effect in the next cell time. The latency of generating a new configuration for the Clos network is therefore hidden. A cell time lasts one or multiple cycles depending on the complexity of the routing algorithm.

The concurrent round-robin dispatching (CRRD) algorithm [178] is one of the classic algorithms extensively utilized in synchronous Clos networks. As indicated by its name, the CRRD algorithm places independent round-robin arbiters on each LI (output link arbiter), IP (input port arbiter) and LO. A simplified description of CRRD is illustrated as follows [178]:

- Phase 1: Matching within IMs.

  - The 1st iteration:
    ① Non-idle IPs send requests to all output link arbiters.
    ② Each output link arbiter independently selects an IP.
    ③ Each non-idle IP accepts one LI from the received grants.
  - The (i)th iteration $(i > 1)$.
    ① Unmatched IPs send requests to all output link arbiters.
    ② and ③ are the same with the 1st iteration.

- Phase 2: Matching within CMs.

  - Matched LIs send requests to CMs. Each LO in CMs selects one request and returns a grant.
  - In the next cell time, the granted IPs send their cells and other IPs try again.

CRRD ensures that the requests in all IMs are dispatched to all CMs with the same probability using the parallel iterative matching (PIM) algorithm [9] in the matching within IMs.

Figure 4.32 demonstrates an example of the matching within an IM using CRRD. Initially all IPs receive new packets and all LIs are available. As shown in Figure 4.32a, IPs send requests to all available LIs. The output link arbiter in each LI grants one IP according to the received requests. Since these output link arbiters run independently, uneven request distribution where multiple LI arbiters select the same IP can be easily generated as depicted in Figure 4.32b. For those IPs receiving more than one grant, such as IP$(i, 1)$ in Figure 4.32c, their input port arbiters choose an LI and release others. In this way, the unmatched IPs are able to request again in the next iteration as shown in Figure 4.32d.

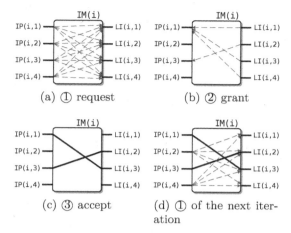

Figure 4.32   Matching within an IM.

The even distribution of CRRD relies on the number of iterations. In the worst scenario when only one match is made in each iteration, an IM needs n iterations to match all IPs. In practice, the number of iterations is also limited by the cell time. It is common that each iteration takes one clock cycle. A cell time must be longer than n cycles to guarantee the even distribution.

Although the requests from one IM are evenly distributed to all CMs, two requests from different IMs asking for the same OM can be distributed to the same CM competing for the same LO. CRRD produces even request distribution but this distribution is oblivious to the possible contention inside CMs.

4.3.2.2   Asynchronous Dispatching

Reconfiguring an asynchronous Clos network has some fundamental difficulties. The incoming packets arrive asynchronously and should be processed asynchronously. A path is allocated for a packet rather than a cell. Moreover, the scheduler must handle multiple packets concurrently and independently as packets can arrive at any time.

As a solution to these difficulties, a new asynchronous dispatching (AD) algorithm is proposed. In this algorithm, the matching within IMs and the matching within CMs are separated into two independent sub-algorithms running concurrently. All modules are event-driven. Independent arbiters are placed on each LI (output link arbiter), IP (input port arbiter) and LO as the CRRD algorithm does, but these arbiters are multi-way MUTEX arbiters and tree-arbiters.

In the CRRD algorithm, if a request fails to reserve a path due to the contention in CMs, it automatically tries again in the next cell time. However, an asynchronous request cannot withdraw itself until it is served. Directly adopting the CRRD algorithm in asynchronous Clos networks introduces severe arbitration latency because the contention in one CM causes at least one request to wait a whole packet transmission time rather than a cell time even when other CMs are available. To reduce such latency overhead, the AD algorithm introduces a state feedback scheme. Once an LO is occupied or released, the information is broadcast to all IMs. Since IMs are informed of the availabilities of LOs in all CMs, they dispatch requests only to the CMs currently with available LOs. The contention in CMs is accordingly avoided. A simplified description of the asynchronous dispatching algorithm is described as follows:

- Sub-algorithm 1: Matching within IMs.

  - A new packet arrives at IP(i, h).
  - IP(i, h) waits until at least one target LO is available.
  - IP(i, h) sends requests to all output link arbiters leading to the available LOs.
  - Output link arbiters return grants to IP(i, h).
  - IP(i, h) selects a path and withdraws requests to other output link arbiters.

- Sub-algorithm 2: Matching within CMs.

  - A request is forwarded from an IM.
  - The target LO returns a grant to the IM and reconfigures the CM once it is available.
  - The updated states are broadcast to all IMs.

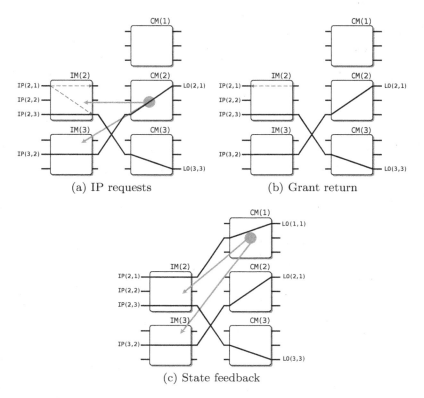

(a) IP requests

(b) Grant return

(c) State feedback

Figure 4.33   Asynchronous dispatching algorithm.

The sub-algorithm running in the IMs uses the same PIM algorithm in CRRD (an asynchronous and event-triggered version) to ensure that requests are evenly distributed to all CMs. The sub-algorithm running in the CMs is also an asynchronous version of the phase 2 in the CRRD algorithm but the state changes of CMs are broadcast to IMs.

An example of the state feedback scheme of the AD algorithm is presented in Figure 4.33. The Clos network in the example is a $C(3, 3, 3)$ network. Some links in this network have already been occupied, such as the links on the path from IP(2, 3) to LO(3, 3) and the path from IP(3, 2) to LO(2, 1). A new packet is received by IP(2, 1) in IM(2) requesting an OP in OM(1). By receiving the state feedback from all CMs, IM(2) knows that CM(2) is not available for the new packet because LO(2, 1) is occupied. Thus, the request from IP(2, 1) heading to OM(1) is not sent to LI(2, 2) (which is linked to CM(2)). This is the major difference between CRRD and AD. As other CMs are available, IP(2, 1) requests to LI(2, 1) and LI(2, 3) as illustrated in Figure 4.33a. Obviously, the arbiter on LI(2, 3) does not respond to this request as LI(2, 3) is occupied. As shown in Figure 4.33b, only the arbiter on LI(2, 1) returns a grant to IP(2, 1). Finally in Figure 4.33c, a request from IP(2, 1) is sent to CM(1) through LI(2, 1). The LO(1, 1) in CM(1) is correspondingly reserved. This new path reconfiguration is then broadcast to all IMs.

The state feedback scheme, which is the major difference between CRRD and AD, can improve throughput by avoiding the contention in CMs. However, it cannot resolve the contention among the requests processed simultaneously because they use the same state feedback. In other words, the state feedback avoids contention between established paths and future requests but cannot resolve the existing contention. If contention occurs, multiple requests from different IMs are sent to the same CM competing for the same LO. In this case, the arbiter on the LO grants only one request and forces others to wait until the granted request is withdrawn. The arbitration latency for the blocked requests is prolonged but they will be served eventually.

It should be noticed that the number of simultaneous requests in asynchronous Clos networks is significantly smaller than synchronous Clos networks due to their asynchronous nature. In synchronous Clos networks, all requests are synchronized; therefore, the number of simultaneous requests is the total number of active requests. Asynchronous Clos networks are not synchronized. When the network load is low, the time to establish a path is much shorter than the time to transmit a packet. The process of establishing a path can be recognized as an event. It is rare for two events to occur at exactly the same time. When the network is saturated, the number of simultaneous requests increases as many requests are blocked. Nevertheless, the number of simultaneous requests is still much smaller than the number in synchronous Clos networks as nearly half IPs are busy transmitting data (49% throughput in uniform traffic as will be shown in Figure 4.36). Using the placed and routed implementations of the synchronous and asynchronous Clos schedulers in Section 4.3.3.1, the CM contention rate (the ratio of the number of conflicted requests sent to CMs to the number of all CM requests) of the saturated Clos networks is extracted from post-layout simulations. The rates are 56.7% and 24.9% for the synchronous and asynchronous schedulers, respectively. It is shown that the state feedback scheme reduces the contention significantly.

4.3.2.3   Performance of CRRD and AD

Both AD and CRRD are implemented to reconfigure a C(4, 8, 4) space-space-space Clos network in behavioral level SystemC models. The Clos networks are injected with various traffic patterns. Some assumptions are employed to produce a fair comparison between synchronous and asynchronous Clos networks:

- *Pseudo-random arbiters are utilized in both models.*
  Synchronous and asynchronous circuits have fundamental differences. The implementation of synchronous dispatching algorithms uses round-robin arbiters while that of asynchronous algorithms uses multi-way MUTEX and tree arbiters. All these arbiters are hardware designs approximating random arbiters. Pseudo-random arbiters are directly utilized in SystemC models.

- *A request is withdrawn immediately after a path is allocated for it.*
  The data transmission in synchronous Clos networks and in asynchronous Clos networks has fundamental differences. In synchronous Clos networks, switch reconfiguration and data transmission are pipelined. Thus, network throughput is independent of path allocation latency as long as it is shorter than a cell time. On the contrary, switch reconfiguration and data transmission cannot be pipelined in asynchronous Clos networks because a path reservation cannot be arranged before the path is available. Long path allocation latency leads to low network throughput. As a result, even when the same routing algorithm is implemented in both synchronous and asynchronous Clos networks with the same path allocation

latency, asynchronous Clos networks show worse network throughput than synchronous Clos networks. Since routing algorithms (including dispatch algorithms) rather than the whole Clos network are the major research objective in this section, the throughput difference due to the pipelined switch allocation is eliminated by assuming no data is actually transmitted (a path is released immediately after allocation).

- *A packet comprises only one cell.*
  A path in a synchronous Clos network is allocated for transmitting a cell while it is allocated for a packet in an asynchronous Clos network. The packet size is set to one cell to eliminate this difference.

Non-blocking uniform traffic is a synthetic traffic pattern to reveal the sources of throughput loss in different dispatching algorithms. The traffic pattern ensures that no OP is concurrently requested by more than one IP; therefore, no contention is produced by the traffic pattern. The expected saturation throughput should be 100% (all packets injected are transmitted with the minimum delay) in a non-blocking Clos network controlled by an optimal algorithm. Any throughput loss observed in evaluation is caused by the imperfection of heuristic algorithms. The non-blocking uniform traffic can be described as:

$$E[\rho(t, s, d)] = \frac{E[\rho(t, s)]}{N} \qquad (4.45)$$

$$\sum_{s=1}^{N} \rho(t, s, d) \leq 1 \qquad (4.46)$$

where N is number of IPs/OPs, $\rho(t, s)$ is the normalized load injected in IP(s) at time t, and $\rho(s, d)$ is the normalized load from IP(s) to OP(d) at time t. All IPs are injected complying with a Poisson process with a fixed injection rate ρ:

$$\rho = \int_{t=0}^{\infty} \rho(t, s) dt = E[\rho(t, s)] = \rho(s) \qquad (4.47)$$

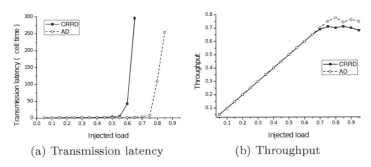

(a) Transmission latency   (b) Throughput

Figure 4.34   Performance under non-blocking uniform traffic.

ρ is the normalized injection rate of the Clos network value from 0 to 1. A packet is injected to an IP in every cell time[5] when $\rho = 1$ and no packet is injected when $\rho = 0$. As described by Equation 4.45, the load of an IP is uniformly distributed to all OPs. Equation 4.46 is a non-blocking constraint ensuring that no OP is overloaded at any time.

Figure 4.34 shows the packet transmission latency and through-put with non-blocking uniform traffic. The number of iterations in the CRRD dispatching algorithm is set to four to ensure the max-imum throughput [178]. The saturation throughput of CRRD and AD is 70% and 76% respectively. AD demonstrates better through-put than CRRD thanks to the state feedback scheme. Nevertheless, both algorithms show throughput loss even when the traffic is non-blocking. There are two reasons for this throughput loss: Firstly, established paths cannot be modified; therefore, the RNB C(4, 8, 4) network is blocking. Secondly, heuristic algorithms, such as the CRRD algorithm, produce contention.

Increasing the number of central modules converts a RNB net-work into an SNB one. Since no alterations to the established paths are needed to build a new path in an SNB network, the contention caused by dispatching algorithms is the only source of throughput loss. Figure 4.35 depicts the throughput increase gained by adding extra central modules. C(4, 8, $m \geq 7$) Clos networks are SNB. It

---

[5]Since a packet comprises one cell, a cell time is the minimum transmission latency of a packet. It is used as a virtual time unit in behavioral simulations.

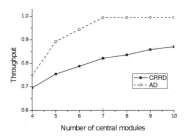

Figure 4.35   Throughput increases along with the number of CMs.

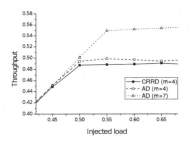

Figure 4.36   Throughput under uniform traffic.

is shown that the AD algorithm introduces no throughput loss in an SNB network, but the CRRD algorithm cannot provide 100% throughput even with ten central modules.

The traffic patterns in practical applications are blocking. Uniform traffic is one of the most analyzed patterns. It can be defined by Equation 4.45 and 4.47. All IPs are injected with a packet sequence complying with the same Poisson process as the nonblocking uniform traffic. The load on one IP is also uniformly distributed to all OPs, but OPs are not protected by the non-blocking constraint described in Equation 4.46. Consequently, OPs are overloaded occasionally.

Figure 4.36 reveals the throughput with uniform traffic. The saturation throughput of using CRRD and AD in a C(4, 8, 4) Clos network is 48.9% and 49.7%, respectively. AD shows 0.8% higher throughput than CRRD. It is known that the optimum

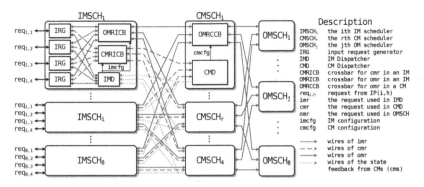

Figure 4.37   An asynchronous Clos scheduler for C(4,8,4).

saturation throughput of an input-queued switch[6] is 58.6% [112]. As shown in Figure 4.36, using AD in an SNB Clos network achieves 55.4% throughput, which is only 3.2% lower than the optimum throughput. Reducing the number of central modules introduces 5.7% throughput loss. In summary, the behavioral level simulations shows that the asynchronous dispatching algorithm demonstrates better throughput than the concurrent round-robin dispatching algorithm.

4.3.3   Asynchronous Clos Scheduler

In this section, we design an asynchronous scheduler capable of dynamically configuring a 32-port $C(4, 8, 4)$ space-space-space Clos network using the asynchronous dispatching algorithm.

4.3.3.1   Implementation

The overall structure of the Clos scheduler is shown in Figure 4.37. It adopts a distributed structure where every switch module has its own scheduler, such as the input module scheduler (IMSCH), the central module scheduler (CMSCH) and the output module scheduler (OMSCH).

---

[6]The original analysis was done on crossbars using input queues (FIFOs). A space-space-space Clos network is equivalent to an input queued crossbar.

An IMSCH comprises n input request generators (IRGs), an input module dispatcher (IMD) and two $n \times m$ bidirectional crossbars. An IRG converts the request from an IP (req) into three independent requests — IM request (imr), CM request (cmr) and OM request (omr) — for IMSCH, CMSCH and OMSCH, respectively. It also controls the timing of these requests in order to enforce safe reconfiguration operations. An IMD dynamically reconfigures an input module adhering to the asynchronous dispatching algorithm. It receives the imr signals generated by IRGs and produces the reconfiguration signal $imcfg$. Meanwhile, the cmr forwarding crossbar (CMRICB) and the omr forwarding crossbar (OMRICB) deliver cmr and omr to the second stage, the central modules, according to $imcfg$. Note that all request signals have their ack lines, namely ack for req, $imra$ for imr, $cmra$ for cmr and $omra$ for omr.

An CMSCH includes a central module dispatcher (CMD) and a $k \times k$ bidirectional crossbar — the omr forwarding crossbar in CM (OMRCCB). A CMD dynamically re-configures a central module and OMRCCB adhering to the asynchronous dispatching algorithm. It receives the cmr forwarded from IMs, generates the local CM reconfiguration $cmcfg$ and broadcasts its state back to IMs through the CM state feedback signal cms.

The structure of an OMSCH is similar to that of a CMD. It receives the omr forwarded from CMs and dynamically re-configures an output module.

Any IP in a Clos network can request any one of the nk OPs. As shown in the basic structure of a Clos network depicted in Figure 4.31, the nk OPs are grouped into k OMs. The asynchronous dispatching algorithm allocates a path from the requesting IP to the target OM. Then, the OMSCH allocates a path towards the target OP. Accordingly, the request from an IP should be converted into two requests: one for the dispatching algorithm to identify the OM and the other one for the OMSCH to identify the OP. This work is handled by the input request generator (IRG) connected to each IP.

The structure of an IRG is illustrated in Figure 4.38a. A one-hot encoder translates an incoming request into two requests encoded in one-hot: a 1-of-k request for imr and cmr and a 1-of-n request for omr. C-elements are added to request and ack lines to ensure

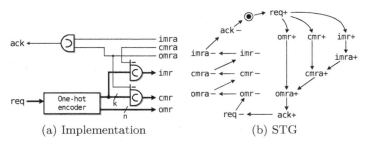

(a) Implementation   (b) STG

Figure 4.38   Input request generator.

the timing order as shown in Figure 4.38b. The requests to all switch modules are sent simultaneously but the order of releasing switch modules has to be guaranteed. Specifically, the OM must be released before the CM and the CM must be released before the IM. Otherwise, the next request can be mis-routed.

An input module dispatcher (IMD) dynamically reconfigures an IM using the asynchronous dispatching algorithm. It receives imr from IRGs, allocates LIs to IPs according to the state feedback cms from CMs, and generates the configuration $imcfg$ along with the ack line $imra$. As shown in Figure 4.39a, it consists of four components: a request-generate matrix, an M-N match allocator, a request enable tree and an ack generate tree. The request-generate matrix filters out the requests to unavailable CMs. The M-N match allocator randomly allocates LIs to incoming requests. Consequently the requests are acknowledged by the ack generate tree. The algorithm running in the M-N match allocator has a feedback loop inside which the feedback signal $ipren$ is generated by the request enable tree.

Figure 4.39b demonstrates the internal structure of the request-generate matrix. An incoming request from IP(h) is denoted by k bits, $\{imr_{h,k}, \cdots, imr_{h,1}\}$, each of which denotes a request to a target OM. The state feedback from CMs is identified by a $m \times k$ matrix cms where a positive $cms_{r,j}$ represents that the LO(r, j) in CM(r) is already occupied. Since any I/O pair has m different paths through the m CMs, every $imr_{h,j}$ is verified with m LOs denoted by $\{cms_{m,j}, \cdots, cms_{1,j}\}$ using the asymmetric C-elements. The output of the request-generate matrix is a matrix of request

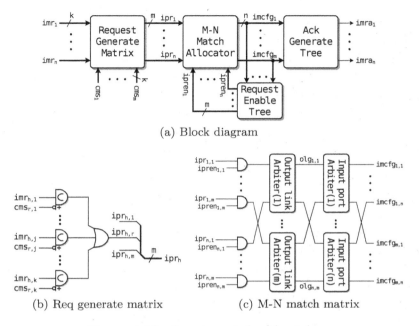

(a) Block diagram

(b) Req generate matrix (c) M-N match matrix

Figure 4.39   Input module dispatcher.

bits *ipr* where a positive $ipr_{h,r}$ denotes an active request from IP(h) to CM(r). Every $ipr_{h,r}$ is OR-reduced from the results of the C-elements. Since incoming requests are encoded one-hot, only one bit in the k bits imr_h can be high. The OR-reduced *ipr* is able to represent all active requests.

Figure 4.39c shows the M-N match allocator which is able to match m resources to n clients concurrently. It is an asynchronous implementation of the parallel iterative matching algorithm [9] using a structure similar to the speed-independent forward acting $n \times m$ arbiter [186]. It consists of two columns of multi-way MUTEX arbiters: one column of m output link arbiters and another column of n input port arbiters. Input requests *ipr* are shuffled and sent to output link arbiters. The output link arbiter of every LI chooses an IP independently. Since an IP can initiate multiple requests in the *ipr* matrix if multiple CMs are available, the arbitration results of the output link arbiters, represented by the *olg* in Figure 4.39c, have to be arbitrated again using the input arbiters in the second column. They ensure that one IP is matched with one and only one LI. In case when multiple output link arbiters choose the same IP, the configuration *imcfg* would withdraw the corresponding request enable signals *ipren*, which consequently withdraws the requests to the output link arbiters not selected by the input arbiter. These LIs can therefore be used by other IPs.

The generation of *ipren* from *imcfg* is processed in the request enable tree. An OR gate tree is built for each *ipren*:

$$ipren_{h,r} = \neg \left(\bigcup_{l=1,l\neq r}^{m} imcfg_{l,h} \right) \qquad (4.48)$$

Therefore, $ipren_{h,r}$ is immediately withdrawn when any LI but LI(r) is allocated to IP(h).

The *ack* line *imra* is also generated from *imcfg* in the *ack* generate tree. Similar to the request enable tree, an OR gate tree is built for each *imra*:

$$imra_h = \bigcup_{l=1}^{m} imcfg_{l,h} \qquad (4.49)$$

It should be pointed out that the M-N match allocator is relaxed-QDI rather than QDI. The multi-resource arbiter [88, 89, 211] (Section 2.5.2.3) is the only QDI allocator available so far that can allocate multiple resources to multiple clients. A modified version of the multi-resource arbiter was used in the previous Clos scheduler [224]. However, it has several design problems: The area of the multi-resource arbiter is so large that the area of IMDs consumes 67.2% of the total area of the Clos scheduler. The handshake protocol of the multi-resource arbiter is not fully satisfied in the Clos scheduler and the ring based multi-resource arbiter proposed in [211] generates livelock.[7] The allocation speed of a multi-resource arbiter is slow because only one IP is served at one time. Contrarily,

---

[7]If the multi-resource arbiter is utilized in IMD, the state feedback signals *cms* are used as client request signals. A client request cannot be released before receiving an *ack* generated from *imcfg*. Since the state of CMs can be altered because of other IMs, the non-withdrawal requirement is not satisfied. A false client request can occur and trigger livelock especially when the ring based multi-resource arbiter is used.

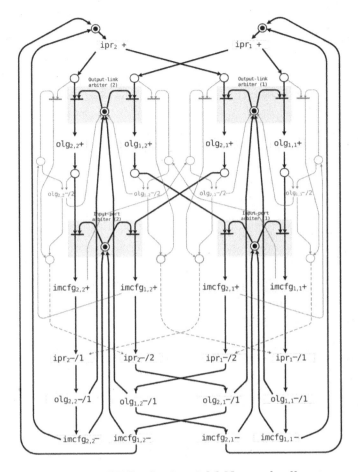

Figure 4.40   STG of a 2×2 M-N match allocator.

the M-N match allocator serves multiple IPs concurrently. It uses a similar structure as the forward acting $n \times m$ arbiter [186] but is simplified using timing assumptions.

The timing assumption required for the M-N match allocator is due to the unguarded withdrawal of requests and *olg*. Figure 4.40 shows the STG of a 2×2 M-N match allocator with two requests (ipr_1 and ipr_1) and two resources. The state feedback is not considered in this STG for simplicity reasons; therefore, a request is always forwarded to all output link arbiters. The withdrawal of requests and *olg* is shown in slim gray lines. When both output link arbiters have chosen the same request, the generated *imcfg* will release one of them. As an example, assuming both output link arbiters have chosen ipr_1, $olg_{1,1}$ and $olg_{1,2}$ are driven high. Only one of them can pass the input arbiter (1). Assuming the second resource is selected, $imcfg_{2,1}$ is set and a token is produced to release $olg_{1,1}$. In a more complicated situation, $olg_{1,1}$ may not be high as output link arbiter (1) is currently reserved by ipr_2. However, a token is still produced to withdraw the duplicated ipr_1 because ipr_2 can drop at any time and makes the output link arbiter (1) select ipr_1 .

To prohibit any false configuration from being produced, the withdrawal procedure must finish before $ipr-$, which is denoted in Figure 4.40 by dashed gray lines. However, implementing such completion detection leads to a significant number of C-elements and OR gates inserted into the allocator. Considering that the withdrawal procedure should be finished as soon as possible in order to allocate the resources to other requests, the latency of the withdrawal procedure is actually the equivalent cycle time of an iteration in the asynchronous PIM algorithm. This latency is far shorter than the serving time of a request. It is safe to let the withdrawal procedure be unguarded. The timing assumption of the safe but unguarded request withdrawal can be expressed as follow:

$$t_{(imcfg+ \ \to \ olg-)} < t_{(imcfg+ \ \to \ ipr-)} \qquad (4.50)$$

Considering the timing sequence shown in Figure 4.38b, the right side of Equation 4.50 is the accumulative latency of reserving the rest of a path in CMs and OMs, along with the whole data transmission. The left side of Equation 4.50 is merely the accumulative latency of the request enable tree and an output link arbiter. The speed evaluation in Section 4.3.3.2 will demonstrate that the latency of the right side is far longer than the left side even without data transmission. Enough timing margin has been provided by the design to ensure the timing assumption without inserting matched delay lines.

A central module dispatcher dynamically reconfigures a central module according to the *cmr* forwarded from input modules. It

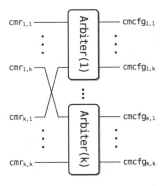

Figure 4.41   Central module dispatcher.

also broadcasts its state alteration to all input modules. The bidirectional crossbar OMRCCB in a central module scheduler (Figure 4.37) delivers *omr* to output modules. An output module scheduler dynamically reconfigures an output module corresponding to the forwarded *omr*.

A central module dispatcher and an output module scheduler have similar internal structures. They all contain a group of arbiters to generate the dynamic configuration and groups of OR gate trees. Figure 4.41 demonstrates the arbiters in a central module dispatcher. They receive *cmr* and produce *cmcfg*. In an output module scheduler, the same structure is used to produce *omcfg* according to *omr*.

A central module dispatcher also generates the *ack* lines *cmra* and the state feedback *cms*. Each bit of these signals is produced by an OR gate tree using the following equations:

$$cmra_i = \bigcup_{l=1}^{k} cmcfg_{l,i} \tag{4.51}$$

$$cms_j = \bigcup_{l=1}^{k} cmcfg_{j,l} \tag{4.52}$$

Similarly, the *ack* lines for *omr* are produced by OR gate trees in output module schedulers using the following equation:

$$omra_r = \bigcup_{l=1}^{n} omcfg_{l,r} \qquad (4.53)$$

4.3.3.2 Performance

The asynchronous Clos scheduler for a $C(4,\ 8,\ 4)$ space-space-space Clos network is implemented and compared against a reproduction of the synchronous Clos scheduler using the CRRD algorithm [178]. Both designs are written in Verilog HDL, synthesized, placed and routed using a 0.13 μm standard cell library. Accurate latency, throughput and power consumption are obtained from back-annotated post-layout simulations.

The synchronous Clos scheduler runs at a maximum of 300 MHz after optimization. The clock period in post-layout simulations is set to 3.5 ns (285 MHz) to leave a timing margin and avoid significant area overhead on optimizing critical paths. The number of iterations in the CRRD algorithm is dynamically re-configurable but fixed to four in simulations for the maximum throughput performance. The cell time in the synchronous Clos network is 17.5 ns according to the following equation:

$$t_{\text{cell}} = t_{\text{clock}} \cdot (I + 1) \qquad (4.54)$$

where I is the number of iterations.

The post-layout area of both Clos implementations is illustrated in Table 4.7. The area of the asynchronous Clos scheduler using the multi-resource arbiter is also listed in Table 4.7.

It is shown that the asynchronous Clos scheduler is smaller than its synchronous counterpart. This small area is caused by several reasons:

- The CRRD algorithm runs in multiple iterations. The intermediate states between iterations are stored in flip-flops.

- Since the path allocation and the data transmission are pipelined, the Clos configuration generated for the next cell time is stored in flip-flops.

Table 4.7   Area of a scheduler for a C(4, 8, 4) Clos network (μm^2).

	Async. (M-N match)	Async. (multi-resouce) [224]	Sync. [178]
single IMD	3862	21882	3186
single CMD	4879	8437	6498
single OMSCH	985	1258	1375
single IRG	160	196	N/A
Total	88057	260740	115262

- A clock tree is need to drive all flip-flops.

- The storage elements in asynchronous circuits are C-elements which are smaller than the flip-flops used in synchronous circuits.

Due to these reasons, all asynchronous scheduler components consume less area than synchronous ones, except for the input module dispatcher. The request-generate matrix in every IMD filters out the requests to unavailable LOs using the state feedback from CMs. Each request-generate matrix contains $n \times k \times m$ asymmetric C-elements, incurring extra area. It is also shown that the new asynchronous Clos scheduler using the M-N match allocator achieves a significant area reduction of 66% from the previous implementation which uses the multi-resource arbiter [224].

The detailed latency of allocating a path using the asynchronous Clos scheduler is labeled in the simplified STG shown in Figure 4.42. The transitions from $req+$ to $ack+$ denote that a path

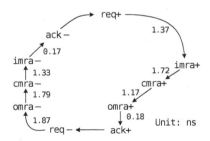

Figure 4.42   Detailed allocation latency.

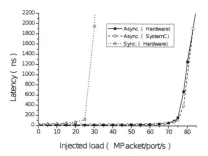

Figure 4.43   Latency of Clos schedulers.

is reconfigured for an incoming packet while the transitions from $req-$ to $ack-$ denote that the path is safely released. The delay of the data transmission of a packet, occurring between $req+$ and $req-$, is variable depending on the payload size of the packet. The delays labeled in the STG are averaged from allocating paths from different IPs to various OPs in an idle Clos network. Extra delays can be introduced when the Clos network is loaded with heavy traffic.

As shown in Figure 4.42, the asynchronous Clos scheduler can reserve a path in 4.44 ns and release it in 5.16 ns. The minimum allocation period is 9.6 ns, which is shorter than the 10.1 ns period of the previous design [224]. Apropos of the timing assumption of the safe but unguarded request withdrawal in the M-N match allocator, the latency $t_{(imcfg+ \rightarrow olg-)}$ in Equation 4.50 is around 0.69 ns, which is far shorter than the 6.73 ns latency of the right side without data transmission.

Assuming requests are withdrawn immediately after paths are reconfigured (the same assumption used in behavioral simulations), Figure 4.43 reveals the allocation latency with different injected loads. The detailed delays in Figure 4.42 are back-annotated into the behavioral level SystemC model. The latency of the back-annotated behavioral model is also shown in Figure 4.43. All schedulers are injected with uniform traffic pattern.

As shown in Figure 4.43, the back-annotated SystemC model of the asynchronous Clos network accurately matches the post-layout simulation. It is also shown that the asynchronous Clos scheduler

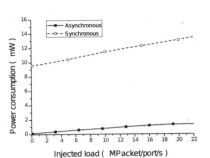

Figure 4.44   Power consumption of Clos schedulers.

provides larger saturation throughput with shorter allocation latency than the synchronous Clos scheduler. The asynchronous Clos scheduler can allocate a maximum of 77.3 MPacket/port/s while it is 27.3 MPacket/port/s for the synchronous Clos scheduler with four iterations.

Figure 4.44 reveals the power consumption of both schedulers with different injected load. The asynchronous Clos scheduler consumes significantly lower power than the synchronous Clos scheduler. The clock tree in the synchronous Clos scheduler consumes 8.34 mW, which is 63.6% of the total power consumption when the scheduler is injected with 20 MPacket/port/s load. In average, allocating 1 M packets in the asynchronous Clos scheduler consumes 64.4 μJ, which is 35.8% of the energy consumed by the synchronous Clos scheduler allocating the same number of packets. The average energy for 1 M packets in the synchronous Clos scheduler is 180 μJ.

4.3.4   SDM Router Using 2-Stage Clos Switch

4.3.4.1   Asynchronous 2-Stage Clos Switch

Using Clos networks reduces the area overhead of SDM routers. However, simply substituting the crossbar in an SDM router with a space-space-space Clos network is not the best solution. A 3-stage Clos network consumes the minimum area when $k = \sqrt{2N}$. The optimum k for a practical switch in an SDM router is usually not an integer, which leads to non-minimum Clos networks. On the other hand, the crossbar of a router using dimension-ordered

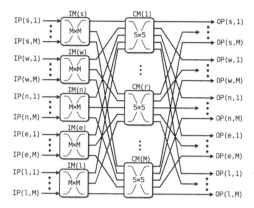

Figure 4.45   A 2-stage Clos switch.

routing (DOR) routing algorithms can be simplified by removing disabled turns. Such area reduction cannot be directly applied to a 3-stage Clos network.

A novel 2-stage Clos switch structure for a 5-port SDM router is depicted in Figure 4.45. Rather than building an optimum Clos network by setting the number of input modules to $\sqrt{2N}$, it is fixed to the number of directions. In a mesh network using 5-port routers, this number is fixed to five (south, west, north, east and local). Every direction has an input module sized $V \times V$, where V is the number of virtual circuits implemented in each direction. The central stage comprises V 5×5 central modules. An output module can be implemented for each direction. However, the virtual circuits in each output module are equivalent as they have the same output direction. LOs can be directly connected to OPs; therefore, output modules are not necessary and removed. The 2-stage Clos network is RNB because the number of central modules is equal to the number of virtual circuits in an input module. The area of a switch is proportional to the number of cross-points. The area of the 2-stages Clos switch is:

$$A_{\text{Clos,2-stg}} \leq (PV^2 + VP^2) \cdot (W/V) \cdot A_{\text{CP}} \qquad (4.55)$$

where P is the number of directions, W is the wire count of each virtual circuit, and A_{CP} is the equivalent area of a single cross-point.

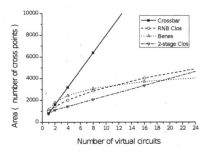

Figure 4.46   Area of different switches.

Compared with the space-space-space Clos network, the 2-stage Clos switch has several advantages:

- As shown in Figure 4.46, the 2-stage Clos switch consumes the smallest area in 5-port SDM routers as long as $V \leq 18$.

- The 2-stage structure simplifies the Clos scheduler and reduces the allocation latency.

- Every central module is equivalent to the crossbar in a wormhole router. The disabled turns can be removed in central modules for further area reduction.

- The latency of transmitting data through the switch is also reduced due to the removal of output modules.

4.3.4.2   Router Implementation

In this section, an asynchronous 5-port SDM router using the 2-stage Clos switch (SDM-Clos) is presented. As shown in Figure 4.47, the router has five bidirectional ports (directions): south, west, north, east and local. Every input port is connected to an input buffer and every output port is connected to an output buffer. The input buffer contains several pipeline stages to buffer incoming flits. A pipeline stage is implemented in each output buffer to decouple the timing between the internal switch and external links. Input and output buffers are spatially divided into V virtual circuits operating independently. The channel slicing technique has been

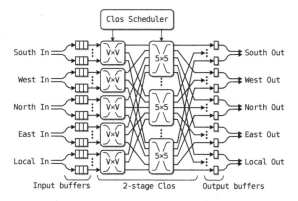

Figure 4.47 An SDM router using a 2-stage Clos switch.

utilized in each virtual circuit and the lookahead pipeline is used to implement the pipeline stages connected to the central switch in the same way as described in Section 4.1.3. Input and output buffers are dynamically connected through the 2-stage Clos switch, which is controlled by a Clos scheduler using the asynchronous dispatching algorithm.

The internal structure of the input buffer for a virtual circuit is illustrated in Figure 4.48. It is developed from the input buffer of an SDM router as shown in Figure 4.16. Every pipeline stage is spatially divided into C sub-channels. As described in Section 4.1.2 and 4.1.4, every sub-channel is a single multi-rail pipeline. In this implementation, it is a 4-phase 1-of-4 pipeline with its own *eop* bit and *ack* line. The data width of each sub-channel is two bits; therefore, the total data width of a virtual channel is $2C$.

Sub-channels run independently most of the time except for when a tail flit is detected and, therefore, a new header flit is going to be analyzed by the XY router (the same one used in Section 4.1.4 and Section 4.2.3). The control sequence has been depicted by the STG depicted in Figure 4.17b. Individual sub-channels have to detect the tail flit independently using their own *eop* bits and pause themselves afterwards. Corresponding control logic in the original router controller (Figure 4.17a) is duplicated and developed into sub-channel controllers located in sub-channels.

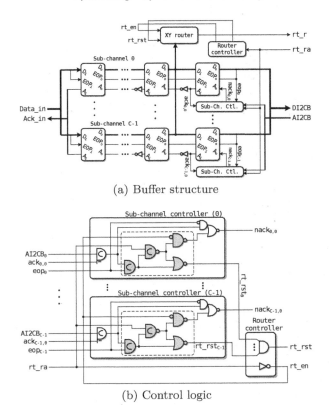

(a) Buffer structure

(b) Control logic

Figure 4.48 Input buffer for an virtual circuit.

The connection between sub-channel controllers and the router controller is shown in Figure 4.48b. The last pipeline stage of each sub-channel is controlled by a sub-channel controller. It reads the *ack* from the central switch (AI2CB), the *eop* output, the *ack* line driven by the last pipeline stage (ack_0) and the *ack* from the Clos scheduler (rt_ra). In response, it generates the *ack* line driving the last pipeline stage ($nack_0$) and its own router reset flag rt_rst. In the sub-channel controllers shown in Figure 4.48b, the gates colored in gray are duplicated from the original router controller in Figure 4.17a. They ensure that the operation of each sub-channel complies with the STG of the original router controller. The asymmetric C-elements on AI2CB and ack_0 wires are the asymmetric C-elements added in the lookahead pipeline as shown in Figure 4.6a.

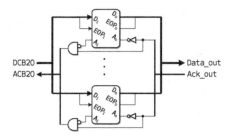

Figure 4.49   Output buffer for a virtual circuit.

It prohibits the pipeline stage from capturing new data before releasing the old one. The *ack* line driving the last pipeline stage, $nack_0$, is generated using the same logic as shown in Figure 4.48. It allows the sub-channel to run freely until a tail flit is detected.

All sub-channels are re-synchronized through the router controller, which is also shown in Figure 4.48b. Signal rt_rst_i turns high when sub-channel i has detected the tail flit. The AND gate in the router controller guarantees that the XY router is reset only when every sub-channel has received its share of the tail flit. This AND gate should be replaced with a C-element tree in a strictly QDI design. Considering the long latency of analyzing the header flit and reserving a path in the 2-stage Clos switch, it is safe to use the AND gate to reduce area and latency. The router controller generates the rt_en signal from rt_ra.

The structure of the output buffer of a virtual circuit is shown in Figure 4.49. It contains one pipeline stage which decouples the timing between the central switch and the long inter-router links. Like the input buffers, the buffer stage in output buffers is spatially divided into sub-channels. The AND gate in each sub-channel generates the early evaluated *ack* line required by the lookahead pipeline. The same circuit has been used in Figure 4.8.

The 2-stage Clos switch and its scheduler are optimized assuming the XY routing algorithm is used. Each central module in the 2-stage Clos switch is equivalent to a crossbar in a wormhole router. It can be optimized by removing the turns forbidden by the routing algorithm. The turn model of the XY routing algorithm is depicted in Figure 4.50. Only the packets from south and north are allowed

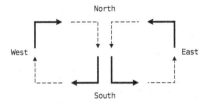

Figure 4.50 The turn model of the XY routing algorithm.

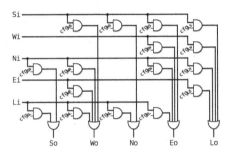

Figure 4.51 An optimized central module.

to change directions (dimensions), while the packets from west and east travel straight only. The corresponding turns are disabled and depicted in dashed lines.

An example of the optimized central module is shown in Figure 4.51. The structure remains the same as a normal crossbar as Figure 4.19, but the AND gates for those disabled turns are removed. Self-turns are also removed as it is normally disallowed to return a packet to its incoming direction. In total, nine out of 25 turns are removed in each central module. The area reduction in the whole 2-stage Clos switch is around 13.8% ∼ 25.7% when 2 ∼ 8 virtual circuits are implemented in each direction.

Thanks to the 2-stage structure, the 2-stage Clos scheduler shown in Figure 4.52 is much simpler than a 3-stage Clos scheduler (Figure 4.37). All the components for the OM requests *omr*, including the crossbars delivering *omr* (OMRICBs and OMR-CCBs) and the OM schedulers, are removed. Incoming requests are the *rt_r* signals from the XY routers in input buffers. The path allocation and

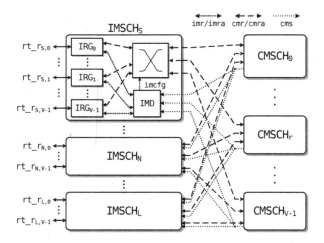

Figure 4.52   Scheduler for the 2-stage Clos switch.

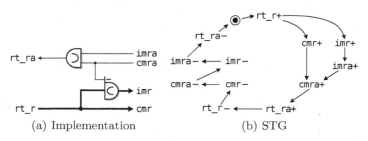

(a) Implementation   (b) STG

Figure 4.53   Input request generator in an SDM router.

release sequence is still controlled by the input request generator (IRG) connected to each input request. As shown in Figure 4.53, two rather than three requests are generated in each IRG: *imr* for the IM dispatcher (IMD) and *cmr* for the CM dispatcher (CMD). IMDs and CMDs dynamically reconfigure IMs and CMs using the asynchronous dispatching algorithm proposed in Section 4.3.2.2.

The modified input request generator in an SDM router is demonstrated in Figure 4.53. The incoming request *rt_r* is already coded in one-hot. It is directly forwarded to IMDs and CMDs. The C-elements ensure the STG shown in Figure 4.53b is followed during the path allocation and release process.

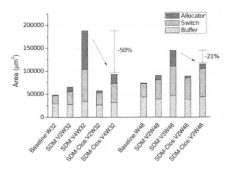

Figure 4.54   Router area.

The internal structures of IMDs and CMDs are basically the same as those described in Section 4.3.3.1. Thanks to the removal of disabled turns in CMs, the number of asymmetric C-elements in the request generate matrix in an IMD (Figure 4.39a) is significantly reduced in the IMDs for west and east inputs.

4.3.4.3 Performance Evaluation

Three routers were implemented for performance comparison: a baseline router (packet switched wormhole routers using neither VCs nor virtual circuits), an SDM router using a crossbar as the central switch and an SDM-Clos router using the 2-stage Clos switch. Described in gate-level SystemVerilog, all routers are laid out using the Synopsys design flow and a 0.13 μm standard cell library. Since most control circuits use speed-independent timing assumptions and data paths are implemented using multi-rail data encoding methods, no timing constraint is required to ensure correct circuit function in the back-end process. However, timing constraints are used, purely for the purpose of speed optimization. All implementations are iterated multiple times for the best speed performance without any timing or design rule violation.

Figure 4.54 reveals the area breakdown of routers with different numbers of virtual circuits (denoted by V) and port data widths (denoted by W). For the minimum area overhead, the input buffer in all routers has only one stage of buffers. It is shown that the differences in buffer area among routers with the same data width are

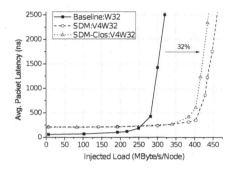

Figure 4.55   Packet transmission latency.

marginal compared to the differences due to switches and allocators. The switch area in SDM routers is approximately proportional
to the number of virtual circuits. The results also show that significant area overhead is introduced by the allocators in SDM routers.
Although various allocators lead to different area overhead, it is
generally true that the area increases faster than proportional to
the number of requests and resources. In the case of SDM:V4W32,
which has the largest number of virtual circuits, the allocator is
larger than the crossbar.

Using the 2-stage Clos switches significantly reduces the area of
both switches and allocators when more than two virtual circuits
are implemented. Compared with SDM:V4W32, SDM-Clos:V4W32
saves around 41% area in switches and 76% area in allocators (50%
of the total area). When two virtual circuits are used, the area
reduction of Clos switches is marginal.

Several 8×8 mesh networks have been built. Random uniform
traffic is injected into the network by the processing element connected to each router. Packets, containing 64-byte payloads, are
generated by processing elements in a Poisson process. Figure 4.55
shows the average packet transmission latency with various load
injection rates. It is shown that virtual circuits improve the saturation throughput significantly at a cost of long transmission latency.
Since a virtual circuit takes only a portion of the total data width,
packets are serialized during transmission, which causes the extra
latency. It is also shown that the throughput reduction led by the

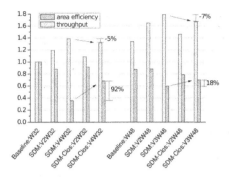

Figure 4.56 Network saturation throughput and area efficiency.

2-stage Clos switch is not significant. The periods of Baseline:W32, SDM:V4W32 and SDM-Clos:V4W32 routers at typical corner is around 2.2 ns, 2.8 ns, and 2.8 ns, respectively. The extra 0.6 ns in period is introduced by the central switches, which are large and complicated in SDM and SDM-Clos routers.

Figure 4.56 reveals the normalized saturation throughput and area efficiency of routers with data widths of 32 and 48 bits. The performance of Baseline:W32 is used as the baseline case for the normalization. The area efficiency is defined as saturation throughput divided by router area (Equation 4.39). Greater area efficiency means less area overhead for the same saturation throughput. As shown in the figure, all SDM routers improve the saturation throughput at a cost of low area efficiency. Using the 2-stage Clos switch compromises the throughput, but the area efficiency is boosted significantly in all the cases using more than two virtual circuits. If only two virtual circuits are used, the SDM routers using crossbars are the best choices.

The switching activities of the router at position (3,3) are recorded for power analysis. Figure 4.57 shows the energy breakdown of the routers when networks are saturated. The energy figures have been divided by the saturation throughput to directly reveal the energy consumption for every byte transmitted in the network. Most SDM routers show better energy efficiencies than baseline routers except for SDM:V4W32 and SDM-Clos:V3W48, whose switches consume too much energy. The energy breakdown

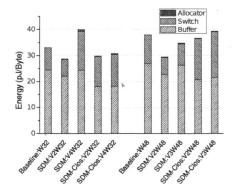

Figure 4.57   Energy consumption.

shows that using the 2-stage Clos switch increases the energy consumption of the switches, but the buffers consume less. This can be a benefit for the SDM-Clos routers using deep buffers as they may consume less energy than the SDM routers using crossbars.

In summary, using the 2-stage Clos switch (SDM-Clos) rather than crossbars (SDM) significantly reduces the area overhead of asynchronous SDM routers when more than two virtual circuits are used. As shown in the comparison with the 32-bit SDM router using four virtual circuits, the SDM-Clos router saves 41% area in switches and 76% area in allocators. The saturation throughput is slightly reduced due to the internal blocking of the 2-stage Clos switch but the area efficiency is improved. Using the 2-stage Clos switch increases the energy consumption of the switches, but the energy overhead of buffers is reduced. SDM-Clos routers may consume less energy than SDM routers when deep buffers are required.

CHAPTER 5

Fault-Tolerant Asynchronous Circuits

The design of more sophisticated electronic systems enabled by the advanced semiconductor manufacturing technology continuously stuffs more transistors and wires onto a single chip. Scaling effects, such as the reduced transistor dimensions, the decrease of critical charge[1], the increase of clock frequency and the increase of the power density, accelerate the occurrence of faults on circuit, intensify the frailty of electronic devices to environmental variations and then reduce the lifetime of chips [18, 56].

Fault-tolerance becomes an essential design objective for critical digital systems, especially those in highly specialized fields. It has been extensively studied in synchronous NoCs but rarely in asynchronous ones, such as the QDI NoCs investigated by this book. Without a global timing reference, faults on QDI circuits not only cause data errors but also stall the handshake process, which consequently causes physical-layer deadlock. It is found that even a transient fault can disrupt the handshake process and deadlock the network. This fault-caused physical-layer deadlock presents a new challenge especially for fault-tolerant asynchronous NoCs.

---

[1]Critical charge, Q_{crit}, refers to the minimum charge that differentiates the state of a node, i.e. 1 and 0 [147].

DOI: 10.1201/9781003284789-5

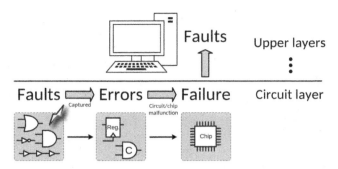

Figure 5.1   Relationship between *fault, error* and *failure.*

5.1   FAULT CLASSIFICATION

A computer system can be abstracted into multiple layers. A fault in a computer system denotes the malfunction of a component in one certain layer. It could be a software fault happening in applications or operating systems. It could also be a hardware fault due to radiation or wear-out faults leading to the malfunction of a silicon chip [37, 56]. The faults investigated in this book refer to the malfunction of integrated circuits.

Figure 5.1 illustrates the relationship between the three terms commonly used in fault-tolerance literature: *fault, error* and *failure* [162]. *Errors* are the manifestation of *faults*. In integrated circuits, a *fault* becomes an *error* only when it is captured by a memory component, such as a C-element in asynchronous circuits. If a *fault* occurs but is masked during its propagation, it would not be captured by any memory components and no *error* would be caused. For those captured *errors*, they may cause circuit malfunction or alter some chip outputs if they are not corrected. These then become circuit *failures* that may cause faults in upper layers of a computer system (such as the operating system level or the application software level). Detection and correction in upper layers are normally more complex and expensive than in lower layers. Therefore, it is required to protect all levels of a computer system, from the bottom circuit implementation to the user level software applications, using a multi-layered fault-tolerant architecture capable of handling different faulty scenarios [259]. This book concentrates on

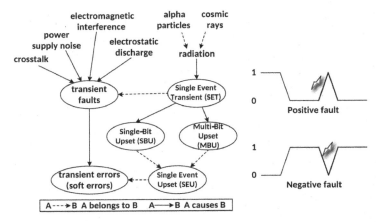

Figure 5.2   Sources of transient faults [19, 56, 111, 155, 215].

the fault tolerance in the circuit level, which tries to reduce circuit *errors* and prevent circuit *failures* from occurring.

Different faults may occur on gates or wires during data transmission and cause bit-flips on some signals. According to their duration, *faults* can be classified into two categories, *transient* faults and *permanent* faults [56], while *intermittent* faults are sometimes counted as a third category.

5.1.1   Transient Faults

The sensitivity of electronic devices to environmental variations has been significantly increased due to the shrinking transistor dimensions, the increasing clock frequency, the increasing density of integrated circuits and the decreasing critical charge. The increased sensitivity then leads to extra transient faults [18, 56]. As Figure 5.2 shows, transient faults can be provoked by a number of sources, including noise (such as crosstalk and power supply noise [215]), electromagnetic interference (EMI), electrostatic discharge [56] and radiation (including alpha particles and high energy cosmic rays like neutrons [111]). The typical outcome caused by a transient fault is a bit-flip, also known as a *glitch*, which can be either positive or negative. A *glitch* usually lasts for a short period and causes a *soft* error when it is captured by memory components. *Soft* errors are non-permanent and non-recurring.

Transient faults caused by radiation have been widely studied in the literature due to their unpredictable nature and increasing occurrence [111, 147, 151]. Two leading sources of radiation are alpha particles and high energy cosmic rays (mainly neutrons), which are produced by the radioactive decay of isotopes in device materials and space, respectively [111, 147]. The first reported incidence of an electronic device malfunction caused by cosmic rays happened in 1975 when anomalies emerged in communication satellites [26, 111]. In 1978, alpha particle induced soft errors were also observed at ground level [146]. After that, widespread of evidence of soft errors was found [20, 41, 111, 151, 180, 238]. Since the semiconductor geometry shrinks, the possibility that neutron and alpha particle strikes cause bit-flips in a cell significantly increases, leading to an increasing *soft error rate* (SER) [37, 111] threatening to break current digital systems. It has been reported that the SER per logic state bit roughly increases 8% by each technology generation [95].

The effect of a radiation event is commonly termed *single event effect* (SEE) [19, 100]. As shown in Figure 5.3, a strike of particles on silicon devices can generate a cloud of electron-hole pairs that allow a current flow. This may be evident as a transient

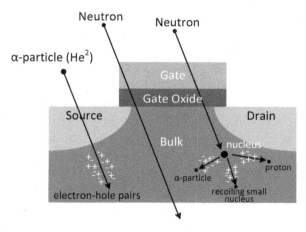

Figure 5.3   Transient faults caused by ionizing radiation.

voltage change, which can flip bit(s) in memory. This transient voltage fluctuation at a logic node is namely a *single event transient* (SET) [100, 118, 155]. A SET propagates in combinational logic and becomes a *single event upset* (SEU) [100] when it is captured by a memory component. SEUs are *soft* errors because they are random, transient and non-recurring [162]. An SEU usually lasts about 100 ps [111] and affects only one bit, which is also termed as a *single-bit upset* (SBU) [19]. If the radiation event is of high energy, a *multi-bit upset* (MBU) may be caused [19] as multiple bits flip (or *multiple cell upset* (MCU) in static or dynamic random access memories (SRAMs/DRAMs) [125]). The relations of these terms are illustrated in Figure 5.2. For simplicity, this book would not further differentiate these terms for various usage scenarios but uses *transient faults* and *transient errors* as the unified names for studying the impact and behavior of faults.

5.1.2 Permanent Faults

Permanent faults (or hard faults) can be classified into *manufacturing defects* and *operational hard faults* according to their time of occurrence. Manufacturing defects are introduced during the chip manufacturing process and normally contribute to the yield loss of chips [40]. *Defect-tolerance* techniques are usually adopted to enhance the chip yield [117, 154, 239]. With the improvement of semiconductor manufacturing techniques, this kind of permanent faults decrease [56].

The aging effect of modern chips is accelerated due to the increasing power density, the high temperature and the scaling effect in general. It has a sustained negative impact on the lifetime of the chips supposed to be working for long terms [233, 266]. Consequently, electronic systems become more susceptible to permanent faults than before because permanent faults can happen at runtime with the aging process, leading to *operational hard faults* [40, 123]. Figure 5.4 shows the possible sources of permanent faults [37, 150, 183, 240]. The two dominant factors causing operational hard faults are electromigration and time dependent dielectric breakdown (TDDB) [40, 150, 233].

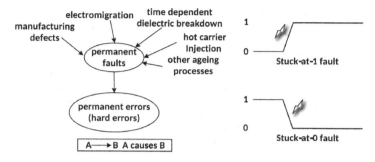

Figure 5.4   Sources of permanent faults [37, 150, 183, 240].

Electromigration happens when metal atoms migrate over time due to current flow. This type of migration will cause an accumulation and depletion of the metal, which may create hillocks or voids in wires. When the size of these hillocks or voids increase to a critical size, permanent faults appear in the form of open or short circuits [183, 235, 247]. A delay fault may happen before an open fault due to increased resistance [56].

Time-dependent dielectric breakdown (TDDB) starts with manufacturing imperfections in a gate oxide and is triggered by the aging process [40]. Imperfections produce electron *traps* in the oxide which then accumulates over time due to the continuous electric field stress and electron tunneling [134, 150]. The trapped electrons may eventually build up a conductive path between the gate and the bulk of the device, leading to a gate oxide breakdown and causing bit-flips or delays as the result. In some cases, manufacturing imperfections are so tiny that they cannot be detected during the initial test process or by *defect-tolerance* techniques [117, 154, 239] but exaggerate over a long period before becoming operational hard faults [123].

Permanent faults in this book refer to the operational hard faults without further classification. Once permanent errors occur, they exist for the remaining life of the circuits, bringing lifetime reliability problems. This may lead to a system failure or chips being discarded. For critical devices that supposed to work reliably for a long period, to keep them working, even with some performance loss in the presence of faults, is with significant importance. This leads to a strong demand for runtime permanent-fault-tolerant systems [40].

The gate-level stuck-at fault model, which has been widely accepted in the semiconductor industry, is employed by this book to study the behavior of permanent faults [5, 137]. According to the definition of the stuck-at model, the state of a faulty wire — which can be a gate input/output or a long interconnect — is either stuck-at-0 or stuck-at-1 (Figure 5.4). All the details of underlying fault behavior are masked in this model, which makes it easy to be used in analyzing the impact of permanently faulty circuits.

5.1.3 Intermittent Faults

The wear-out of transistors and interconnects is a slow process. Before becoming permanent faults, the timing of the related circuits are the first to be affected. The timing of the fault-related combinational circuits begins to violate their timing requirements, leading to delay faults [222]. Gradually, these delay faults become transient faults, intermittent faults (frequent transient faults on the some location) and finally permanent faults [56]. It has been reported that some of the DI and QDI circuits can tolerate some of the delay faults [231]. According to their duration or functional impact, intermittent faults can be regarded as either transient or permanent faults during the fault management process.

5.2 FAULT-TOLERANT TECHNIQUES

5.2.1 Masking Factors

A transient fault becomes a transient error only when it is captured by a memory component. If a fault goes undetected, no error is caused. In common combinational logic, three intrinsic masking factors could prevent transient faults from being captured [111, 118].

- *Logical masking*: Assume a logic gate with multiple inputs locates on the propagation path of a fault. During the whole duration of the fault, the output of the gate is not decided by the faulty input. The fault is therefore masked as it has no impact on the output of the logic gate and all circuit afterwards.

- *Electrical masking*: In the process for a transient fault propagating on a combinational path, the amplitude of the fault generated pulse gradually reduces. If the amplitude is sufficiently reduced before reaching the final memory component, it becomes an attenuated SET which would not be captured but only prolongs the transition time of affected signals.

- *Temporal masking*: A transient fault reaches a memory component (such as a flip-flop) with a pulse strong enough to be captured but not at the clock edge or the latching window of the final memory component. This fault is still not captured and no error is caused.

5.2.2 Redundancy Techniques

Although many faults might be masked during their propagation [111], fault-tolerant measures are still required to create a more secure environment considering the increasing occurrence of faults in the current sub-micron era. The most utilized fault-tolerant measure is to induce redundancy into the circuit design. Traditional redundancy techniques include physical, temporal and information redundancy [162, 229]:

- *Physical* (or *spatial*) redundancy achieves fault-tolerance by replicating hardware. A well-known physical redundancy technique is the triple modular redundancy (TMR) method [229], which adds two replicas of the original circuits. All the three copies of circuits are driven by the same input and the output is generated by a majority voter. A single error can be detected and masked by the voter as it may affect only one output. TMR is a strong method against SBUs but induces significant area overhead of at least 200% along with a tripled energy consumption.

- *Temporal* (or *time*) redundancy achieves fault-tolerance by performing operations multiple times. Errors can be found and corrected by comparing multiple results. Extra hardware is required to store the previous results. Due to the repeated operation, the consumed power will be multiplied as well as the latency, which constrains the circuit performance. This method is unsuitable for handling permanent faults because a permanent fault will constantly influence all results no matter how many times an operation is repeated.

- *Information* redundancy achieves fault-tolerance by introducing redundancy in the data being transmitted and calculated. It has been widely used to protect interconnection and memory. Extra check bits are added to the original data word, constructing an error detecting code or error correcting code, where faulty bits can be detected or corrected [93, 162]. The error detection and correction capability is determined by the minimum Hamming distance of the valid code words, which is the number of bit positions that any two code words differ on [162, 229]. Taking two code words $A = 0010$ and $B = 0011$ for example, their Hamming distance is one since they differ on only one bit. If $B = 0100$, the Hamming distance becomes two. Given a coding space, its Hamming distance (d) is defined as the minimum Hamming distance of any two valid code words. The Hamming distance of all 1-of-n code words is two $(d = 2)$. An error detecting/correcting code can detect up to $d - 1$ bit errors and correct up to $\lfloor (d - 1)/2 \rfloor$ bit errors [229].

The use of an error detecting/correcting code belongs to forward error recovery processes [229], where faults or errors are detected/-corrected as the data word progresses. The flow of data is therefore uninterrupted in the presence of a correctable fault. As error detection and correction circuits usually lie on the critical paths, they induce a slight performance penalty even when no errors happen. Additional performance loss might be introduced when errors actually happen and are corrected. Alternatively, the error correction can be done in a backward error recovery process [229] where data redundancy is used only to detect but not correct faults. Before sending any data, the fault-free copy is always retained as a recovery. When faults are detected at the receiver end, a retransmission of the retained copy is scheduled. When the overall data error rate is low, the backward error recovery shows better performance than the forward error recovery thanks to the avoided overhead on error correction and marginal overhead on transmission (detection is always cheaper than correction). However, in a fault-prone environment where data error rate is high, the backward error recovery suffers from significant throughput loss due to frequent retransmissions. If multiple data are allowed to be transmitted concurrently, the extra storage needed for retaining the fault-free data may introduce a large area overhead. In addition, retransmissions cannot resolve permanent faults. If a fault destroys the handshake process in asynchronous circuits, the local faulty handshake signals cannot be simply recovered by using retransmission. Therefore, this book concentrates on the techniques used in the forward error recovery process.

5.3 IMPACT OF TRANSIENT FAULTS ON QDI PIPELINES

Generally speaking, a router in a NoC acts as a switch which directs traffic from inputs to outputs according to specific routing and flow control method. Buffers are usually inserted on the path between input and output ports to support the chosen flow control and improve network performance. As a result, the data path inside a router can be modeled as a pipeline where different buffers construct pipeline stages, as depicted by Figure 5.5. As stated in Section 2.2, the simple 4-phase 1-of-n asynchronous protocol is chosen to implement the QDI NoC so that almost all data paths are

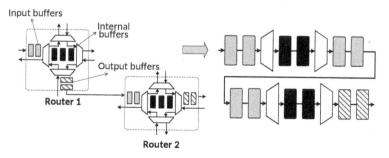

Figure 5.5   Pipelined NoC data path.

built by 4-phase 1-of-n QDI pipelines. A pipeline may comprise one or more parallel 1-of-n channels, as shown in Figure 2.8.

5.3.1 Faults on Synchronous and QDI Pipelines

Faults may happen on any gates and wires of a circuit at any time. In the presence of transient faults, QDI pipelines behave differently from synchronous ones due to their clockless nature. A fundamental difference between QDI and synchronous circuits is the timing reference of data words.

In synchronous circuits, the global clock signal acts as a timing reference controlling the data transmission. Each bit of a data word typically retaining its value for a period agreed between the transmitter and the receiver. Faults are able to corrupt the *value* of symbols but have no impact on the length of the period. Therefore, the value of a received faulty symbol can be used to analyze the fault type [229], locate the fault position and even correct errors.

QDI circuits have no such timing reference. The validity state of a data is implicitly encoded within the data word, whose transmission locally governed by the handshake protocol depending on the correct encoding of data. As a result, corrupted data words caused by faults can disorder the local control logic and then paralyze the data transmission. In other words, faults on QDI pipelines may produce fake data-validity or remove the correct data-validity, resulting in erroneous data insertions or data removals. A physical-layer deadlock could happen if the handshake process stalls due to a fault. As described in Section 5.4.2, even a transient fault can deadlock a QDI pipeline, which is a new challenge that has long been ignored by the asynchronous community.

This deadlock is harmful to the circuit function as long as QDI pipelines are used anywhere in a network. As an example, an asynchronous NoC can be used to construct a GALS system [119]. Redundant information can be added in the synchronous domain and transmitted through the asynchronous network. Errors are expected to be corrected and error-free when entering the network and arriving at the destination [48, 199]. This model saves lots of design overhead for the whole system, but the real risk is that the destination may never receive the packet due to a

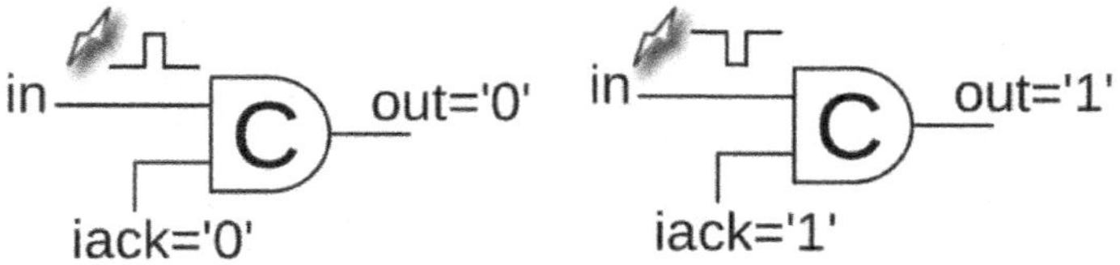

(a) Masked positive fault   (b) Masked negative fault

Figure 5.6   Transient faults masked by C-elements.

fault-caused physical-layer deadlock. Conventional fault-tolerant techniques used in synchronous circuits cannot work in QDI pipelines. It is necessary to provide special fault-tolerance techniques dedicated for the protection of asynchronous interconnects.

Not every transient fault causes an error. Some transient faults are masked automatically during their propagation by intrinsic masking factors of the circuit [111]. However, the three aforementioned conventional masking factors introduced in Section 5.2.1 which determine whether a transient fault would be captured as an error, are not fully compatible with QDI circuits. Temporal masking is largely incompatible with QDI circuits because there is no clock. Instead of making incoming data arrive at the memory component before the clock-triggered latching-window, the memory component in QDI circuits (such as a C-element) usually enters the latching-ready state before the arrival of incoming data. Electrical masking is common for long interconnects in both synchronous and asynchronous circuits.

Logical masking plays an important role in asynchronous circuits. The use of C-elements, which are the most fundamental and important cells in asynchronous circuits, actually enriches the concept of logical masking. A C-element outputs 1 or 0 if both of its inputs are 1s or 0s; otherwise, it keeps its previous output. As shown in Figure 5.6, when *iack* is 0, a positive glitch at the other input of the 2-input C-element is masked. Similarly, when *iack* is 1, a negative glitch at the other input is masked. Only when a glitch at the input *in* flips to the same level with *iack*, the fault would be latched. However, such a fault might still be tolerated depending on the correct input and the timing of the circuit:

- *Premature firing*: As shown in Figure 5.7a, if the flipped output of the affected C-element is not quick enough to withdraw

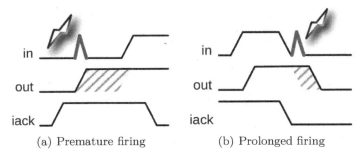

(a) Premature firing   (b) Prolonged firing

Figure 5.7   Premature and prolonged firing of a C-element due to a fault.

iack as the correct input signal arrives soon after the glitch, this fault actually produces a premature firing of the output. Instead of causing an error in the QDI circuit, this type of fault masking actually reduces the latency of this particular event.

- *Prolonged firing*: Similarly, a fault can prolong a firing if it happens soon after the correct input and with the same level, as shown in Figure 5.7b shows. Since *iack* does not rise before the fault caused glitch, the fault has no impact on the function but prolongs the timing.

If a fault is not masked, it would incur an erroneous level change on *iack* which then leads to significant impact on the logic function of the circuit, including deadlock the whole circuit. Therefore, a key issue faced by QDI pipelines is to prevent transient faults from being incorrectly latched and then disturbing the handshake process.

5.3.2   Impact Modeling of Transient Faults

A fault model is built to analyze the impact of a 1-bit transient fault on QDI pipelines. Figure 5.8 presents a single-symbol 4-phase 1-of-n pipeline model with two successive stages. The handshake between the two adjacent pipelines stages forms a loop, including a forward data path and a backward acknowledge path. A transient

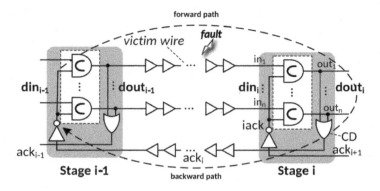

Figure 5.8   Two-stage pipeline model with one 1-of-n channel.

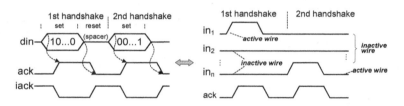

Figure 5.9   Fault-free 4-phase handshake process.

fault can happen on any gate or wire of the QDI pipeline, including pipeline stages (the asynchronous latch built from C-elements and the completion detector (CD)), the *data* wires and the *ack* wire. If the fault is not masked, the affected wire becomes a *victim* wire as depicted in Figure 5.8. Figure 5.9 models the 4-phase handshake process corresponding to the pipeline segment in Figure 5.8. In one 1-of-n channel, the data wire that should carry the correct 1 in the normal case is defined as the *active* wire, while the other data wires are *inactive* in the current handshake period. The *iack* is the inverted *ack* signal used to drive the preceding pipeline stage. To analyze all faulty occasions, the proposed fault model divides one handshake period into two intervals according to logical level of *iack*.

5.3.2.1 *Faults on Data with Positive Ack*

When *iack* is high, the QDI pipeline (and the C-element latch) is susceptible to positive data faults. Both active and inactive wires

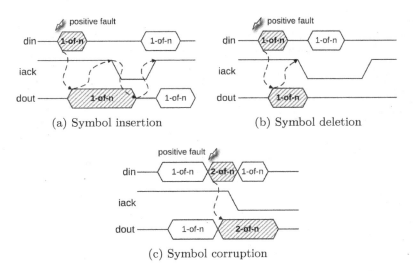

(a) Symbol insertion (b) Symbol deletion

(c) Symbol corruption

Figure 5.10   Transient faults happen when *iack* is high.

can be the victim, leading to an invalid 1-of-n or a 2-of-n code insertion.

- *Invalid 1-of-n code insertion* happens when a positive fault on an inactive wire is latched and flips the output before the arrival of the valid code word. It leads to an early drop of *iack*. As shown in Figure 5.10a, if the valid code word comes so late that a full reset phase of the invalid code has completed, the invalid 1-of-n code is *inserted* into the original code sequence. Otherwise, if the following valid code overlaps with the reset phase (*iack*−) from the inserted invalid code, as Figure 5.10b depicts, this original valid code may be *deleted* from the data sequence as the negative *iack* caused by the invalid code will block it from being latched. A positive fault on the *active* wire of the 1-of-n channel may lead to either the case shown in Figure 5.10a or the case shown in Figure 5.10b when the fault makes *iack* go low earlier than the arrival of the valid data. The major difference is whether a wrong code word is inserted. The case shown in Figure 5.10b does not insert a new code word. It has no effect on the handshake process and erroneous code word might be corrected later. The case

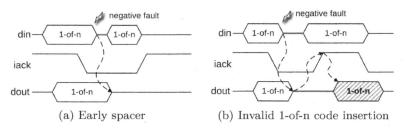

(a) Early spacer   (b) Invalid 1-of-n code insertion

Figure 5.11   Transient faults happen when *iack* is low.

shown in Figure 5.10a is more serious as a new (and wrong) code word is inserted. This case can also taken as an invalid spacer insertion.

- *Invalid 2-of-n code insertion*: As shown in Figure 5.10c, a positive fault on one of the inactive wires may coincide with the transition of the active wire, resulting in an invalid 2-of-n code at the output.

5.3.2.2   Faults on Data with Negative Ack

When *iack* is low, all positive data faults are masked and the pipeline is only vulnerable to negative faults happening on the only active wire.

- *Early spacer* (not an error): A negative fault on the active data wire may cause an early spacer to be latched (Figure 5.11a), which is naturally tolerated by QDI pipelines in most circumstances.

- *Invalid 1-of-n code insertion*: A negative fault may lead to a premature reset phase. As shown in Figure 5.11b, the negative fault on the active data wire causes an early spacer and a premature reset on *iack*. If the reset phase is short and the original data remains active when the transient fault finishes and *iack* returns 1, a copy of the original data is inserted as a new code word, leading to an code insertion error.

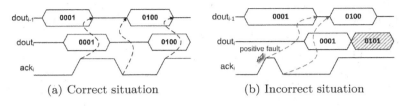

(a) Correct situation   (b) Incorrect situation

Figure 5.12   Transient faults on acknowledge wires.

5.3.2.3   Faults on Completion Detector and Ack

In addition to the data wires used for data transmission, acknowledge (ack) signals are equally critical to the handshake process. Although the number of ack wires is normally far lower than the number of data wires, faults on ack wires summarily cause complex faulty behavior as well. Unfortunately, the protection of acknowledge wires has been ignored by many existing fault-tolerant designs [199].

An example is shown in Figure 5.12 where $dout_{i-1}$ and $dout_i$ are outputs of *Stage $i - 1$* and *Stage i*, respectively; ack_i is the acknowledge signal from *Stage i* to *Stage $i - 1$*. Figure 5.12a shows the waveform when these signals operate correctly. Figure 5.12b then depicts a faulty situation where a positive fault happens on ack_i, mistakenly indicating that a valid code has been latched by *Stage i*. Consequently, *Stage $i - 1$* is reset due to this fault. When the transient fault disappears, *Stage $i - 1$* starts a new transmission of 0100, which may augment the first data word and lead to an invalid 2-of-n code insertion of 0101.

5.3.2.4   Physical-Layer Deadlock

Based on these analysis, it can be found that a transient fault could cause symbol *insertion, deletion* and *corruption* on a 1-of-n channel, significantly disordering the original symbol sequence. In a wide QDI pipeline comprising multiple parallel 1-of-n channels, multiple symbol sequences are transmitted simultaneously through the multiple parallel channels but are still synchronized at various places (the CD of each pipeline stage as shown in Figure 2.8) to retain the integrity of the transmitted data. If there is an extra (or a missing) symbol on one of the multiple parallel channels, this synchronization may fail and wait indefinitely. Consequently, the data transmission in the whole pipeline is stalled and cannot recover by itself. This kind of indefinite stall is termed a *physical-layer* deadlock since it breaks the handshake protocol relied by the physical layer. The behavior of this deadlock caused by transient faults has long been neglected by the asynchronous community besides some early explorations [216]. Both the physical-layer deadlock caused by transient faults (analyzed in this section) and by permanent faults (which stall the handshake permanently) will be thoroughly discussed in the next Section 5.4.

In conclusion, transient faults on QDI pipelines may cause symbol insertion (a 1-of-n code is inserted to the original data sequence), deletion (the original code is removed from the data sequence) and corruption (a 1-of-n code is corrupted into an invalid m-of-n code). Even worse, a physical-layer deadlock may occur where the handshake process is stalled by these faults.

5.4 DEADLOCK MODELING

Both transient and permanent faults can stall the handshake process, leading to a *fault-caused physical-layer deadlock*. This type of deadlock is a new challenge encountered by the asynchronous community. It asserts more serious impacts on QDI NoCs than pure data errors in packets, since it happens in the physical layer and cannot be solved by existing network-layer deadlock management techniques (Section 3.1.4.2). In a deadlocked state, most existing fault-tolerant techniques proposed for synchronous circuits fail to work [93, 229]. Even most of the existing fault-tolerant QDI designs would be deadlocked in the presence of these faults and fail to work as well [48, 106, 199, 264]. To study the behavior of the QDI pipelines deadlocked by different faults, a model of these faulty pipeline is constructed. With the help of this model, faults can be detected and recovered from.

A linear pipeline with d pipeline stages can be divided into $(d-1)$ *segments* $(d \geq 2)$. A segment begins and ends with contiguous half-buffer latches, as demonstrated in Figure 5.13. *Stage* i+1 $(1 \leq i < d)$ is counted as a part of the segment S_i. The direct result

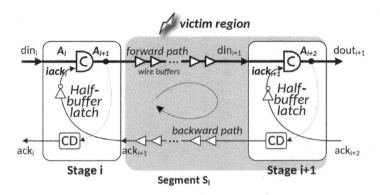

Figure 5.13   A QDI pipeline model divided into *segments*.

of a fault on the forward data path of a segment (S_i) may be a faulty input (din_{i+1}) to the half-buffer latch of the second stage (*Stage* i+1), which captures the faulty data and allows it to further affect the *ack* signal fed back to the preceding stage (*Stage* i). This fault on the forwarding *data* wires and the capturing asynchronous latches is termed a *Data* fault. On the backward *ack* path, including the completion detector (CD) and the *ack* wire, the direct fault impact may be a faulty *ack* signal (ack_{i+1}) to the preceding stage. This kind of faults are called *Ack* faults.

Segment is used as the basic unit to study the fault impact (the grey *victim* region in Figure 5.13). *Stage* i is termed the *pre-fault* stage, while *Stage* i+1 is the *post-fault* one. The proposed fault model is based on the following assumptions and rules:

- Although multi-bit faults could happen in practice, only a 1-bit fault is considered since it is enough to deadlock a QDI pipeline.

- No matter where a fault happens on the forwarding data path, either on the *latch input* or inside the *latch*, it is a *Data* fault to the current pipeline stage as long as the faulty data is captured by its latches.

- If a fault occurs on wires connecting the output of latches and the CD, it is an *Ack* fault because the faulty data is not captured by the latches but affects only the CD.

- If a fault happens at the *stage output* of the pipeline stage, it indicates that this fault neither gets stored by the current latch nor goes to the CD. This is a *Data* fault to the next pipeline stage.

5.4.1 Deadlock Caused by Permanent Faults

Since QDI asynchronous circuits are event-driven and controlled by handshake protocols, it is obvious that a permanent stuck-at fault will halt the handshake process, resulting a *physical-layer* deadlock in addition to the corruption of the data transmission.

In synchronous circuits, permanent faults typically cause consecutive data errors, as long as the clock tree stays intact and the circuit continues working under the control of the clock. It is therefore possible to detect the fault using accumulated history statistics of the circuit, i.e. *error syndromes* which are usually obtained by using transient-fault-tolerant techniques [130]. If the collected error syndromes satisfy specific patterns or some time-out conditions, the fault is taken as permanent and the recovery process is invoked; otherwise, it is transient or intermittent [78, 130, 131].

The situation is different in QDI circuits. Most existing transient-fault-tolerant QDI designs [48, 106, 199, 263] would still be deadlocked when a permanent fault happens. The physical-layer deadlock prohibits error syndromes from being collected by the upper layer, failing all traditional fault-detection techniques [78, 130, 131]. Furthermore, this physical-layer deadlock may reserve a sequence of network resources in a QDI NoC, which consequently leads to extended upper-layer deadlocks of the network, dramatically reducing the network performance and potentially paralyzing the whole network eventually. This section models the deadlocked QDI pipeline to find common deadlock patterns with which the permanent fault can be detected and located.

In a 4-phase, 1-of-n QDI pipeline, data are encoded as delay-insensitive (DI) symbols which are either *complete* or *incomplete*. Incomplete data exist between a complete data word and a spacer. According to the state transition in a pipeline stage (Figure 2.9), Figure 5.14 illustrates a possible transient state of a 6-stage pipeline without faults. The consequence of a permanent fault on segment

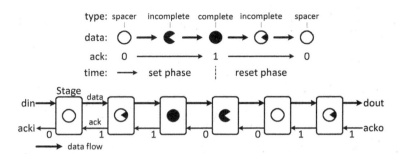

Figure 5.14 One possible transient state of the pipeline without faults.

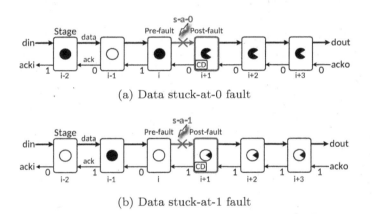

(a) Data stuck-at-0 fault

(b) Data stuck-at-1 fault

Figure 5.15 Deadlocked pipelines due to stuck-at faults on the forward data path.

S_i of a 4-phase, 1-of-n QDI pipeline can be classified into following four classes:

- *Data stuck-at-0*: This type of faults are caused by a stuck-at-0 fault on the forward data wire or inside the asynchronous latch. As shown in Figure 5.15a, an input to the asynchronous latch, such as the din_{i+1} in Figure 5.13, can get stuck at 0 and prevents a valid 1 from arriving at the post-fault stage (*Stage i + 1*). As a result, all pipeline stages downstream of the fault are stuck at the *set* phase with an incomplete data word and keep waiting for the lost 1. Their *ack* signals are all 0s awaiting a complete data word.

- *Data stuck-at-1*: This type of faults happen when a stuck-at-1 fault strikes on the forward data wire or the latch. As shown in Figure 5.15b, the input to the asynchronous latch of the post-fault *Stage i + 1* gets stuck at 1 and prevents all pipeline stages downstream of the fault from being reset because they keep holding the incomplete data word with the invalid 1. As a result, all their *ack* signals are stuck at 1s.

- *Ack stuck-at-0*: This type of faults are caused by a permanent stuck-at-0 fault striking on the backward *ack* wire as demonstrated in Figure 5.16a or the CD as depicted in Figure 5.16b, both of which lead to the *ack* signal (ack_{i+1}) to the preceding pipeline stage (*Stage i*) being stuck at 0. As a result, *Stage i* may hold either a complete data word if the faulty *ack* arrives at the preceding stage when it is in the *set* phase, or an incomplete data word if the preceding stage is resetting (the faulty *ack* stalls the *reset* operation). Therefore, the pre-fault stage and all pipeline stages downstream of the fault cannot

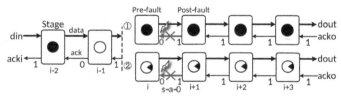

(a) Ack stuck-at-0 fault on the *ack* wire

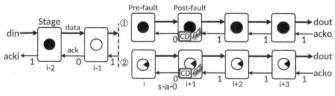

(b) Ack stuck-at-0 fault on the CD

Figure 5.16   Deadlocked pipelines due to stuck-at-0 faults on CD or *ack* wires.

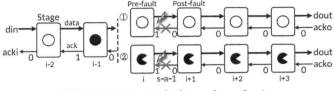

(a) Ack stuck-at-1 fault on the *ack* wire

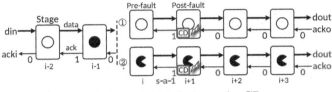

(b) Ack stuck-at-1 fault on the CD

Figure 5.17   Deadlocked pipelines due to stuck-at-1 faults on CD or *ack* wires.

be fully reset. Their *ack* signals are all 1s. As for the *ack* signal fed back to the pre-fault *Stage i*, it could be either 1 or 0 depending on where the fault is located.

- *Ack stuck-at-1*: This type of faults are caused by a permanent stuck-at-1 fault striking on the backward *ack* wire as demonstrated in Figure 5.17a or the CD as depicted in Figure 5.17b, both of which lead to the *ack* signal (ack_{i+1}) to the preceding pipeline stage (*Stage i*) being stuck at 1. As a result, incoming 1s or 1-of-n symbols to the pre-fault stage cannot be latched. The pre-fault stage and all pipeline stages downstream of the fault may hold a spacer or an incomplete data word, effectively stuck at the *set* phase with their *ack*s holding 0s.

For all the above cases, since pipeline stages before the pre-fault stage are fault-free, they would hold fault-free (complete) data words and spacers alternately according to the 4-phase handshake protocol, leading to alternate *ack* signal states [231], as shown in Figure 5.15, 5.16 and 5.17. It can be concluded that, all the above cases share the same deadlock pattern defined in Theorem 1, which is the key to detecting permanent faults in QDI pipelines.

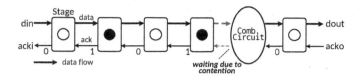

Figure 5.18   Blocked data flow without faults.

Theorem 1. *Pattern of the fault-caused physical-layer deadlock: The physical-layer deadlock caused by a permanent fault on a 4-phase 1-of-n QDI pipeline leads to a steady state where all pipeline stages downstream of the fault have the same ack while the ack signals of the upstream stages are alternately valued.*

It should be noticed that the data transmission through some pipeline stages may take a long time due to traffic contention in QDI NoCs applied with a high workload. As a result, the packet transmission is stalled for some time. In this scenario, all stalled pipeline stages store fault-free data. According to 4-phase handshake protocols, complete data words and spacers are stored alternately in this stalled packet path (Figure 5.18), which is different from the deadlock pattern caused by faults (Figure 5.15 ∼ 5.17). This difference in pattern can be used in QDI NoCs to differentiate the fault-caused physical-layer deadlock from both the network-layer deadlock and simply a network contention, as described in Chapter 7.

5.4.2 Deadlock Caused by Transient Faults

As mentioned in Section 5.3.2.4, a transient fault may insert or delete a symbol from a 1-of-n channel, stall the handshake process and deadlock the N-symbol wide QDI pipeline ($N > 1$). Such issue has barely been studied. The occurrence of this deadlock is more complicated than the one due to a permanent fault. This section will study the behavior of a transient fault stalling the 4-phase handshake process and the resulting deadlock patterns, which can be used to detect faults and diagnose the type of faults.

For an N-symbol 4-phase 1-of-n QDI pipeline, the input data to a pipeline stage can be expressed by using *active* signals (Figure 5.19) transmitting on the *active* wires belonging to the N 1-of-n

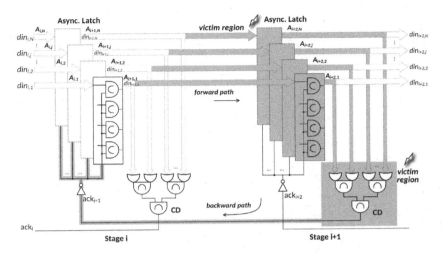

Figure 5.19   Pipeline model for transient faults.

channels (Section 5.3.2). Accordingly, the input data din_i to *Stage i* can be expressed as $\{A_{i,1}, A_{i,2} \cdots A_{i,N}\}$ where $1 \leq i \leq d$. $A_{i,j}$ represents the jth output active wire from the $(i\text{-}1)$th pipeline stage, as Figure 5.19 shows. Similarly, we can describe the state of a pipeline *segment* by using all its input and output active wires, such as using $(\{A_{i,1} \cdots A_{i,N}\}, ack_i, \{A_{i+1,1} \cdots A_{i+1,N}\}, ack_{i+1})$ to denote the state S_i for the *segment* from *Stage i* to *Stage i + 1*. The initial state after reset is $(\{0 \cdots 0\}, 0, \{0 \cdots 0\}, 0)$.

The production rule set (PRS) for basic logic gates [141] is employed to describe the behavior of a *segment*. A production rule with a form of $A \wedge B \longrightarrow C \uparrow, D \downarrow$ is equivalent to $A \wedge B \longrightarrow C \uparrow$ and $A \wedge B \longrightarrow D \downarrow$, meaning that if both A and B are *true*, the assignments $C \uparrow$ and $D \downarrow$ are fired. The firing of $C \uparrow$ and $D \downarrow$ is independent and with no order in timing. According to the 4-phase handshake protocol, the PRS related to an N-word pipeline segment S_i $(1 \leq j \leq N)$ is shown as follows.

For *segment* S_i:

$$A_{i,j} \wedge \neg ack_{i+1} \longrightarrow A_{i+1,j} \uparrow \tag{5.1}$$

$$A_{i+1,1} \wedge \cdots \wedge A_{i+1,j} \cdots \wedge A_{i+1,N} \longrightarrow ack_i \uparrow \tag{5.2}$$

$$\neg A_{i,j} \wedge ack_{i+1} \longrightarrow A_{i+1,j} \downarrow \tag{5.3}$$

$$\neg A_{i+1,1} \wedge \cdots \wedge \neg A_{i,+1j} \cdots \wedge \neg A_{i,N} \longrightarrow ack_i \downarrow \tag{5.4}$$

Left of *Stage i*:

$$ack_i \longrightarrow A_{i,j} \downarrow \tag{5.5}$$

$$\neg ack_i \longrightarrow A_{i,j} \uparrow \tag{5.6}$$

Right of *Stage i + 1*:

$$A_{i+2,1} \wedge \cdots \wedge A_{i+2,j} \cdots \wedge A_{i+2,N} \longrightarrow ack_{i+2} \uparrow \tag{5.7}$$

$$\neg A_{i+2,1} \wedge \cdots \wedge \neg A_{i+2,j} \cdots \wedge \neg A_{i+2,N} \longrightarrow ack_{i+2} \downarrow \tag{5.8}$$

Therefore, if the 4-phase handshake process is broken due to a fault-caused physical-layer deadlock, none of the above rules should be fired any more. The pipeline gets stuck at a *stable* state without any signal transitions. Considering the deadlock state of a pipeline *segment* S_i containing *Stage i* and *Stage i + 1* (Figure 5.19), its victim region comprises a *forward* data path, including the input data wires for the asynchronous latch of the post-fault *Stage* i+1, and a *backward ack* path, including the CD of the post-fault *Stage i + 1* and the *ack* wire (ack_{i+1}) back to the pre-fault *Stage i*. The input active wire ($A_{i,j}$) to the pre-fault stage and *ack* wire (ack_i) from the pre-fault stage are out of the victim region and thus they are fault-free. Theorem 2 can be thus inferred in a deadlocked state:

Theorem 2. *In a deadlocked 4-phase QDI pipeline, the two contiguous ack signals from and to the pre-fault pipeline stage are complementary.*

Proof. It is assumed that the two contiguous *ack* signals from and to the pre-fault *Stage i*, ack_i and ack_{i+1}, are equal in a deadlock state. Consequently, (ack_i, ack_{i+1}) gets stuck either at (11) or (00).

Assuming (ack_i, ack_{i+1}) gets stuck at (11): As ack_i is stuck at 1, $\{A_{i,1} \cdots A_{i,N}\}$ is stuck at $\{0 \cdots 0\}$ according to Equation 5.5. The low $A_{i,j}$ and the high ack_{i+1} causes a low $A_{i+1,j}$ using Equation 5.3, which then leads a low ack_i according to Equation 5.4 and generate a contradiction to the assumption.

Assuming (ack_i, ack_{i+1}) gets stuck at (00): As ack_i is stuck at 0, $\{A_{i,1} \cdots A_{i,N}\}$ is stuck at $\{1 \cdots 1\}$ according to Equation 5.6. The high $A_{i,j}$ and the low ack_{i+1} causes a high $A_{i+1,j}$ using Equation 5.1, which then leads to a high ack_i according to Equation 5.2 and generates a contradiction to the assumption.

Therefore, ack_i and ack_{i+1}, which are the two contiguous ack signals from and to the pre-fault pipeline *Stage i*, are complementary in a deadlocked state. In other words, the *segment* state $(\{A_{i,1} \cdots A_{i,N}\}, ack_i, ack_{i+1})$ should get stuck at either $(\{1 \cdots 1\}, 0, 1)$ or $(\{0 \cdots 0\}, 1, 0)$ when the physical-layer deadlock happens. □

Theorem 3. *A transient fault happening on a single-symbol 4-phase 1-of-n QDI pipeline can cause symbol insertion, deletion and corruption, but not a physical-layer deadlock in the current segment.*

Proof. It has been shown that a transient fault could cause symbol insertion, deletion and corruption in a single-symbol 4-phase 1-of-n QDI pipeline [106, 264] (Section 5.3.2); therefore, it is required to prove only that a transient fault cannot deadlock a single-symbol 1-of-n pipeline. Mathematical deduction is employed to prove the theorem in a formal way. The *segment* state of a single-symbol pipeline *segment* is indicated by $S_i = (A_i, ack_i, A_{i+1}, ack_{i+1})$. According to Theorem 2, (ack_i, ack_{i+1}) should get stuck at either (01) or (10) if deadlock happens.

Assuming (ack_i, ack_{i+1}) gets stuck at (01): The statement that ack_i being stuck at 0 is true if and only if A_{i+1} is stuck 0 according to Equation 5.4. The ack_{i+1} gets stuck at 1 if and only if A_{i+2} is 1 according to Equation 5.2, so that ack_{i+2} is high according to Equation 5.7. As described by Equation 5.3 and Equation 5.4, the low A_{i+1} and the high ack_{i+2} result in a low A_{i+2}, leading to a low ack_{i+1}, which contradicts to the assumption that ack_{i+1} gets stuck at 1.

Assuming (ack_i, ack_{i+1}) gets stuck at (10): Similarly, the assumption that ack_i is stuck at 1 is true if and only if A_{i+1} keeps high according to Equation 5.2. ack_{i+1} is 0 if and only if A_{i+2} is low according to Equation 5.4, so that ack_{i+2} is low according to Equation 5.8. As described by Equation 5.1 and Equation 5.2, the high A_{i+1} and low ack_{i+2} result a high ack_{i+1}, which contradicts to the assumption that ack_{i+1} gets stuck at 0.

Therefore, (ack_i, ack_{i+1}) cannot get stuck at neither (10) nor (01). In other words, a transient fault cannot deadlock a single-symbol 4-phase 1-of-n QDI pipeline. □

It should be noted that the symbol insertion and deletion may cause synchronization failure at a higher level (the data link layer [241]) where the data sequence in this 1-of-n channel needs to be synchronized with the data in other channels. Due to the unmatched number of symbols, these independent and parallel channels cannot be correctly synchronized at some points, potentially leading to deadlock at the data link layer [124]. However, this is not the type of deadlock discussed in this book and could be handled using traditional deadlock recovery methods.

In a multi-symbol pipeline, multiple 1-of-n channels are synchronized at each pipeline stage using a multi-input C-element connected to their CDs (Figure 5.19), which is different from a single-word pipeline where the CD is an OR-gate. To be more specific, there are two kinds of synchronization points in a multi-symbol pipeline. One is the asynchronous latch which synchronizes the forward and backward paths (denoted by Equation 5.1 and Equation 5.3) and outputs the latched data (A_i). The other is the CD that synchronizes multiple parallel forwarding 1-of-n channels (denoted by Equation 5.2 and Equation 5.4) and meanwhile generates the backward (ack_i). The introduction of the synchronization point at the CD makes the multi-symbol pipeline different from the single-symbol one when considering the impact of a transient fault.

Theorem 4. *A transient fault can cause a physical-layer deadlock in a multi-symbol 4-phase 1-of-n QDI pipeline.*

Proof. This theorem has been discussed by [216], where an instance was used to explain the deadlock process without any validation while the management techniques were not studied. It is difficult to prove this statement by just studying one case of the many deadlock scenarios without any further exploration. Here, we derive this theorem in a formal way step by step. By doing this, deadlock patterns can be abstracted to support the deadlock management methods proposed in Chapter 7 and 8. This proof is new and one of the major contributions of this book. It provides a new way of arguing about how to handle this deadlock issue in QDI NoCs or asynchronous circuits in general.

According to Theorem 2, *segment* state $(\{A_{i,1} \cdots A_{i,N}\}, ack_i, ack_{i+1})$ should get stuck at either $(\{1 \cdots 1\}, 0, 1)$ or $(\{0 \cdots 0\}, 1, 0)$ when a physical-layer deadlock happens.

We first prove that $(\{A_{i,1} \cdots A_{i,N}\}, ack_i, ack_{i+1})$ can be stuck at $(\{1 \cdots 1\}, 0, 1)$ in a deadlock state. In this case, whether the N input active signals of the pre-fault stage, $(A_{i,1} \cdots A_{i,N})$, are latched by *Stage i* depends on the time when ack_{i+1} goes high. The output active signals of the pre-fault *Stage i*, $(A_{i+1,1} \cdots A_{i+1,N})$, may have three different combinations of logic values:

- $\{A_{i+1,1} \cdots A_{i+1,N}\}$ *are stuck at* $\{1 \cdots 1\}$: In this case, all active signals to the pre-fault *Stage i* are latched and output. Consequently, ack_i should be high according to Equation 5.2, which however contradicts to the precondition that ack_i is stuck at 0.

- $\{A_{i+1,1} \cdots A_{i+1,N}\}$ *are stuck at* $\{0 \cdots 0\}$: In this case, none of the input active signals gets latched and output by *Stage i*, denoting that Equation 5.1 is not fired. It means when the new data word arrives at the *Stage i*, the ack_{i+1} signal fed back to *Stage i* is high. This violates the precondition in a 1-bit transient fault environment where ack_{i+1} cannot remain high.

- $\{A_{i+1,1} \cdots A_{i+1,N}\}$ *are stuck at neither all 0s nor all 1s*: Since this is the only combinations of logic values left, it is the only possible case for a deadlocked pipeline.

As Figure 5.19 shows, a transient fault in the victim region of *segment* S_i may happen on either the forward data path (including input data wires to the post-fault *Stage i + 1* and the asynchronous latch of *Stage i + 1*), resulting in a faulty $A_{i+2,f}$ where $1 \leq f \leq N$, or the backward *ack* path (including the CD of the post-fault *Stage i + 1* and the backward *ack* wire to the pre-fault *Stage i*), resulting in a faulty ack_{i+1}. The following proofs are divided into two cases: The 1-bit transient fault locates on the *forward data path* or on the *backward ack path*.

The 1-bit transient fault locates on the forward data path. As derived by the early part of this proof, $\{A_{i+1,1} \cdots A_{i+1,N}\}$ are neither all 0s nor all 1s in the final deadlock state. For the ack_{i+1} to be stuck at 1, Equation 5.1 and Equation 5.2 must have been fired, but Equation 5.3 and Equation 5.4 are not. The only possible scenario is that a 1-bit positive transient fault leads to a faulty active signal, $A'_{i+2,f}$, at the output of the post-fault *Stage i + 1*. This faulty signal is latched by the CD along with other fault-free active signals, resulting a high ack_{i+1} according to Equation 5.2. It then traverses through the fth 1-of-n channel to the destination with other fault-free symbols, resulting in high ack signals at all succeeding pipeline stages. Meanwhile, the fault-free $A_{i,f}$ arrives at the pre-fault *Stage i* after ack_{i+1} goes high, preventing the complete data word from being latched. As a result, ack_i keeps low, which prevents this complete data ($\{A_{i,1} \cdots A_{i,N}\} = \{1 \cdots 1\}$) to the pre-fault stage from being withdrawn according to Equation 5.6, resulting a physical-layer deadlock.

After this positive transient fault disappears, the faulty active signal $A_{i+2,f}$ resets to 0 and such 0 traverses through all pipeline stages downstream of the fault. However, the disappearance of this fault will not trigger Equation 5.3 and Equation 5.4 because the other fault-free active signals to the CD remain high. The ack_{i+1} will still be stuck at 1, preventing the complete data word from being latched by the pre-fault stage.

Figure 5.20 illustrates an example where a positive transient fault on the forward data path (the shaded victim region) deadlocks the N-symbol 1-of-4 pipeline. All the 1-of-4 symbols except for the delayed one on the second channel have been latched by *Stage i* at time $t1$, and output to the succeeding pipeline stages. At $t2$, a faulty $A_{i+2,2}$ appears because a positive transient fault strikes either directly on $A_{i+2,2}$ or on the second channel of the forward path, which creates a faulty $A_{i+1,2}$ later latched by *Stage i+1*. This $A_{i+2,2}$ triggers the CD of the post-fault *Stage i+1*, leading to a high ack_{i+1} preventing the later coming $A_{i,2}$ from being latched by the pre-fault *Stage i*. After the fault disappears at time $t3$, all stages downstream of the fault and the pre-fault stage keep holding the incomplete data word with a *spacer* on the second channel. Their ack signals are all stuck at 1s while the pipeline stages before the

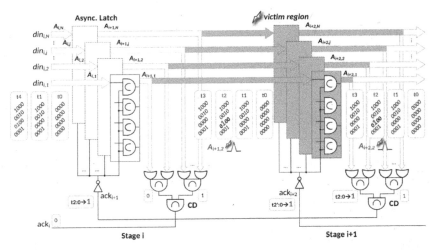

Figure 5.20 A positive transient fault on the forward path of the pipeline.

pre-fault stage hold fault-free data following a "complete data → spacer → complete word → spacer" pattern and their *ack* signals are alternately valued.

In this deadlock state, the input to the pre-fault *Stage i* is a complete data word, while all pipeline stages downstream of the fault (including the post-fault *Stage i + 1*) hold an *incomplete* data word. Under the precondition that only a 1-bit transient fault happens, this incomplete word needs one more 1-of-n symbol to become *complete*, which is named as an *almost-full* data word. The deadlock state of the *segment S_i* can be expressed as Equation 5.9.

$$(\{A_{i,1} \cdots A_{i,N}\}, ack_i, \{\cdots A_{i+1,f-1}A_{i+1,f}A_{i+1,f+1}\cdots\}, ack_{i+1})$$
$$= (\{1\cdots1\}, 0, \{\cdots101\cdots\}, 1)$$

$$(5.9)$$

The 1-bit transient fault is on the backward ack path. A positive transient fault on the backward *ack* path could cause a persistent high ack_{i+1} directly. If ack_{i+1} goes high before data symbols arrive at the pre-fault *Stage i*, the later coming symbols cannot be latched. This leads to a permanently low ack_i as Equation 5.1 and Equation 5.2 fail to fire. At the post-fault *Stage i + 1*, this fault should

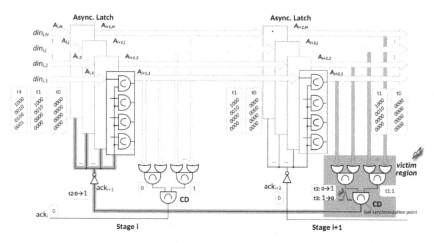

Figure 5.21 A positive transient fault on the backward path of the pipeline.

happen before the *last synchronization point* at the backward path (which is the C-element at the root of the CD tree in Figure 5.21) so that the backward ack_{i+1} is permanently high even after the disappearance of the fault. The 1-bit positive transient fault causes a fake event triggering the CD high along with other normal events, which is equivalent to the firing of Equation 5.2. Since the other inputs to the synchronization point of the CD are still high, ack_{i+1} stays high permanently even after the disappearance of the fault, preventing the later coming fault-free data symbols from being latched by the pre-fault stage. The low ack_i prevents the incoming data word to the pre-fault stage from being reset. A physical-layer deadlock is produced as the handshake protocol is stalled.

Figure 5.21 illustrates an example that a 1-bit positive transient fault locating on the CD of the post-fault *Stage $i+1$* deadlocks the N-symbol 1-of-4 pipeline. At time $t1$, all 1-of-4 symbols except for the symbols on the first and second 1-of-4 channels have been latched by *Stage i* and output to all following stages. At time $t2$, a positive fault happens on the CD of *Stage $i + 1$*, leading to a high ack_{i+1} to the pre-fault *Stage i* preventing the later coming symbols on the first and second channels from being latched (ack_i remains low). After the fault disappears at time $t3$, ack_{i+1} remains high because the other input(s) to the last C-element is (are) high, resulting a physical-layer deadlock as the handshake is permanently stalled.

In this deadlock state, the input to the pre-fault *Stage i* is a fault-free complete data word. All pipeline stages before the pre-fault *Stage i* hold fault-free data following a "complete data → spacer → complete data → spacer" pattern, with alternately valued *ack* signals. Pipeline stages after the fault and the pre-fault stage hold the same incomplete data. Compared with the deadlock state caused by a transient fault on the forward path, the deadlock state caused by a transient fault on the backward *ack* path holds the following differences:

- It is not necessary that the incomplete data held by the pre-fault stage and stages downstream of the fault are *almost-full* word.

- Pipeline stages downstream of the post-fault stage have the same *ack* signals while the post-fault stage has a complementary *ack* signal.

The above proof is also compatible with the case where the *segment* state $(\{A_{i,1}, \cdots, A_{i,N}\}, ack_i, ack_{i+1})$ gets stuck at $(\{0 \cdots 0\}, 1, 0)$. A negative transient fault on the forward data path will cause an *almost-empty* data, which contains only one 1-of-n symbol while the others are spacers. This *almost-empty* data word is latched by the pre-fault stage and transmitted to all pipeline stages downstream of the fault. They all have the same *ack* signals. Pipeline stages before the pre-fault stage hold a fault-free data stream with alternately valued *ack* signals. The deadlock state of the victim *segment* can be expressed by Equation 5.10. If the negative transient fault happens on the backward *ack* path (or the CD), it could deadlock the pipeline as well while the incomplete word latched by pipeline stages downstream of the fault are not necessary to be *almost-empty*.

$$(\{A_{i,1} \cdots A_{i,N}\}, ack_i, \{\cdots A_{i+1,f-1}A_{i+1,f}A_{i+1,f+1} \cdots\}, ack_{i+1})$$
$$= (\{0 \cdots 0\}, 1, \{\cdots 010 \cdots\}, 0)$$

$$(5.10)$$

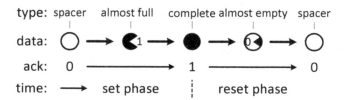

Figure 5.22   State transitions of a 4-phase pipeline stage with the extended sub-states.

Therefore, it can be concluded that a transient fault could deadlock a multi-symbol 4-phase 1-of-n QDI pipeline. This proof can be extended to m-of-n ($2 \leq m < n$) pipelines to demonstrate that they can be deadlocked by a transient fault as well. □

5.4.3   Deadlock Analysis

For an N-symbol wide 4-phase 1-of-n QDI pipeline, the pipeline stage stays in the three states at any of the time, including *complete*, *incomplete* and *spacer*, as described in Section 2.4.2. In this section, we restate these states using ($\mathbb{A} = \{A_i | 1 \leq i \leq N\}$) to represent the different data words in certain states and further extend the *incomplete* state with two more sub-states: *almost-full* and *almost-empty*. Figure 5.22 illustrates an updated state transition graph based on Figure 2.9 and Figure 5.14. The extended sub-states, *almost-full* and *almost-empty*, are used as the intermediate states between *spacers* and complete data words.

Here is a summary of the states:

- *complete* ($\mathbb{A}_{complete}$): All elements are 1s.

- *incomplete* ($\mathbb{A}_{incomplete}$): This is the intermediate state between a spacer and a complete data word where some of the N elements are 1s the others are 0s. When there is only one element holds a different value with others, we can define two specialized sub-states:

  - *almost-full* ($\mathbb{A}_{almost\_full}$): All elements are 1s except for one holding a 0.

- *almost-empty* ($\mathbb{A}_{\text{almost\_empty}}$): All elements are 0s except for one holding a 1.

- *spacer* ($\mathbb{A}_{\text{spacer}}$): All elements are 0s.

It can be concluded from Theorem 4 that possible deadlock states of an N-symbol 4-phase QDI pipeline caused by a transient fault can be classified into two categories according to the fault position:

- If a transient fault on the forward data path deadlocks the pipeline, the pre-fault stage and all pipeline stages downstream of the fault keep the same *almost-full* or *almost-empty* state, while pipeline stages before the pre-fault stage hold a fault-free data stream. As a result, any two contiguous *ack* signals after the fault are the same while the *ack* signals before the fault are alternately valued. Equation 5.11 and Equation 5.12 present the concluded expression of the deadlocked pipeline *segment* with the corresponding examples shown in Figure 5.23a and 5.23b.

$$(\mathbb{A}_i, ack_i, \mathbb{A}_{i+1}, ack_{i+1}) = (\mathbb{A}_{i,\text{complete}}, 0, \mathbb{A}_{i+1,\text{almost\_full}}, 1) \tag{5.11}$$

$$(\mathbb{A}_i, ack_i, \mathbb{A}_{i+1}, ack_{i+1}) = (\mathbb{A}_{i,\text{spacer}}, 1, \mathbb{A}_{i+1,\text{almost\_empty}}, 0) \tag{5.12}$$

- If a transient fault on the backward *ack* path (before the last *synchronization point*, which is the root of the CD tree at the post-fault stage in Figure 5.21) deadlocks the pipeline, the pre-fault stage and all pipeline stages downstream of the fault keep holding the same incomplete data word, while the preceding pipeline stages hold the fault-free data stream. As a result, any two contiguous *ack* signals after the post-fault stage are the same while the *ack* signals before the faulty CD are alternately valued. Equation 5.13 and Equation 5.14 present the expression of the deadlocked pipeline *segment* with the corresponding examples shown in Figure 5.23c and Figure 5.23d.

$$(\mathbb{A}_i, ack_i, \mathbb{A}_{i+1}, ack_{i+1}) = (\mathbb{A}_{i,\text{complete}}, 0, \mathbb{A}_{i+1,\text{incomplete}}, 1) \tag{5.13}$$

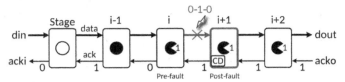

(a) A positive fault on forward data path

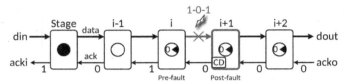

(b) A negative fault on forward data path

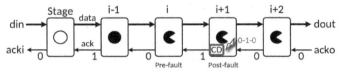

(c) A positive fault on backward ack path

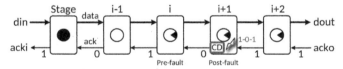

(d) A negative fault on backward ack path

Figure 5.23 Deadlocked pipelines caused by transient faults.

$$(\mathbb{A}_i, ack_i, \mathbb{A}_{i+1}, ack_{i+1}) = (\mathbb{A}_{i,\text{spacer}}, 1, \mathbb{A}_{i+1,\text{incomplete}}, 0) \tag{5.14}$$

It can also be concluded from Theorem 4 that a long enough time difference between the two slowest 1-of-n channels is necessary to the production of this physical-layer deadlock [216]. T_{skew} is used to denote the data skew between the two slowest parallel 1-of-n channels. The loop latency T_{loop} between two adjacent pipeline stages can be expressed as Equation 5.15 where T_{forward} and T_{backward} represent the propagation delays of the forward *data* and the backward *ack* signals, respectively. T_{forward} and T_{backward} can be expressed as Equation 5.16 and Equation 5.17 where t_{latch},

t_{CD}, t_{data} and t_{ack} are propagation delays of the asynchronous latch, the CD, *data* wires and the *ack* wire, respectively. To ensure that a 1-bit transient fault could deadlock the pipeline, Equation 5.18 should be satisfied as the precondition and the fault happens on the slowest channel.

$$T_{\text{loop}} = T_{\text{forward}} + T_{\text{backward}} \qquad (5.15)$$

$$T_{\text{forward}} = 2t_{\text{latch}} + t_{\text{data}} \qquad (5.16)$$

$$T_{\text{backward}} = t_{\text{CD}} + t_{\text{ack}} \qquad (5.17)$$

$$T_{\text{skew}} > T_{\text{loop}} \qquad (5.18)$$

This data skew or the time difference of data transmission between 1-of-n channels of a pipeline can be long because of a number of factors [15, 42, 203]. Along with the increasing size and function of a chip, on-chip wiring delay is having an increasing impact on the chip performance [203]. The geometry, design constraints and manufacturing variations can cause significant data skew between different link wires [15, 42], which becomes common as the semiconductor technology continuing to scale. The resulting data skew gradually approaches the time of transmitting multiple bits. It is even worse if considering the augmented effect due to the long distance. Besides these internal factors to the circuit itself, external parameter variations, such as crosstalk [172], worn-out wires or transistors with the aging process [56], and electromagnetic interference (EMI) [116] are able to introduce data skew between the large amount of on-chip interconnects as well. Therefore, if the data skew is common in a multi-symbol channel and the time difference between the two slowest 1-of-n channels is longer than the loop latency, Equation 5.18 is possible to be satisfied and the possibility that transient faults on the asynchronous pipeline cause a deadlock significantly increases. As a result, large-scale QDI NoCs are becoming extra sensitive to a physical-layer deadlock caused by transient faults. If data errors can be corrected in different network layers, or even at the interface to synchronous circuits, the well-studied conventional fault-tolerant techniques can be utilized in the synchronous domain of a GALS system. However, a fault-caused physical-layer deadlock can easily fail the whole system if it is without proper protection inside the asynchronous network. Therefore, it is essential to use extra fault-tolerant techniques in the asynchronous network to reduce the fault impact (Chapter 6), and also manage the physical-layer deadlock caused by different faults (Chapter 7 and 8).

Comparing the patterns of a physical-layer deadlock caused by a permanent and a physical-layer deadlock caused by a transient fault (Figure 5.15 ∼ 5.17 and Figure 5.23), it can be found that these faults cause the same deadlock patterns which can be described as:

1. No transitions are detected on the pipeline;

2. All pipeline stages downstream of the fault have the same *ack*, while the *ack* signals in pipeline stages upstream of fault are alternately valued.

Therefore, Theorem 1 can be extended to transient faults, which is the key to detecting the fault caused physical-layer deadlock.

5.5 RELATED WORK

Fault-tolerance is a well-studied topic in synchronous circuits and NoCs [201]. As discussed before, event-driven asynchronous circuits manifest much more complicated faulty scenarios than their synchronous counterparts. Several techniques have been proposed in the literature to protect asynchronous circuits or interconnection from transient faults, but the tolerance of permanent faults and the management of the fault-caused physical-layer deadlocks in asynchronous circuits have rarely been studied. This section introduces several representatives fault-tolerant techniques, as a way to demonstrate the state-of-the-art work related to this research area.

5.5.1 Tolerating Transient Faults

Section 5.2.2 has discussed the different redundancy techniques [78, 93, 130] potentially capable of dynamically detecting (transient) faults. Information redundancy techniques, or fault-tolerant codes [229], are important concepts in the field of fault-tolerance. Since Delay-Insensitive (DI) codes, which implicitly include timing information, are used to build data channels in QDI asynchronous circuits, information redundancy techniques should be adopted by DI codes in QDI circuits to obtain both timing-robustness and fault-tolerance.

5.5.1.1 Information Redundancy

Systematic codes [2] (Section 6.1.3), such as parity check codes and Hamming codes [93], have been widely used for fault-tolerance purposes [78, 130, 131, 199, 259]. Encoding them into DI codes for QDI interconnection may result in low coding efficiency [199, 264]. Among existing asynchronous designs, information redundancy techniques are often used to provide fault-tolerance in bundled-data rather than QDI designs [126, 130, 131].

The first paper that systematically addressed transient faults in 4-phase DI codes during transmission was presented by Cheng and Ho [48]. An unordered systematic code using a parity check code was proposed to correct 1-bit errors and detect completion simultaneously on 4-phase asynchronous links. Two error models were proposed, the first of which assumes only unidirectional errors (either $0 \rightarrow 1$ or $1 \rightarrow 0$) could happen. For the $1 \rightarrow 0$ error model, t 1s will be missing at the receiver if at most t errors can happen during the transmission, requiring a t-error correcting DI code to correct these errors. For the $0 \rightarrow 1$ model, where each error could contribute to two errors at the receiver side, a $2t$-error correcting code is required under the assumption of up to t transmission errors. In the reset phase of the 4-phase handshake process, where the transmission wires may not be reset to 0s due to either an unexpected and arbitrarily long delay or permanent faults, a bounded delay model is used in these error models to constrain the reset time, which unfortunately means it cannot be used in a QDI design. Taking the $1 \rightarrow 0$ case for example (Figure 5.24), the information bits, I, are first encoded into a DI code word I^{EC} at the sender. The DI code has a weight of n (n 1s) and supports a t-error correction capability. t errors may occur and remove t 1s during the transmission. By detecting $n - t$ 1s at the receiver side, all errors can be corrected and then the original information bits are decoded. Since the data are not protected during their transmission

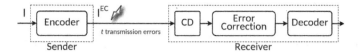

Figure 5.24 Error-correcting model proposed by Cheng and Ho [48].

in the asynchronous interconnects, symbol insertion, deletion, corruption or even a fault-caused physical-layer deadlock can happen. Obviously, the deadlock can paralyze the whole communication. No hardware implementation was disclosed.

Similarly, a parity check was used in a QDI communication design [199] to implement the error detection and correction. Taking a 8-bit binary vector 01011100 for example, it is equivalent to a data word with four 1-of-4 code words (0010, 0010, 1000 and 0001). The produced parity bits at the sender are $0010 \oplus 0010 \oplus 1000 \oplus 0001 \rightarrow$ 1001, which are further transformed to two 1-of-4 code words 0100 and 0010 before transmission. At the receiver end, parity bits are regenerated and compared with the transmitted ones through the XOR operation. The location of the faulty bit, if any, can be detected and then corrected. However, this method can resolve only symbol corruption on data wires. The error correction scheme would fail if the transmitted parity bits are faulty. The design requires the faulty data to be transmitted all over to the destination because the interconnection itself is not protected; therefore, the achieved fault-tolerance is limited. The added redundancy incurs area overhead only to network interfaces, which is around 11.6%. The overall network speed is reduced by 8.1%.

Another unordered systematic code named Zero-Sum [2, 3] was proposed to protect 4-phase asynchronous links. As depicted in Figure 5.25a, each bit position of a Zero-Sum code is assigned an index. Check bits are indexed by powers of two while indices of data bits occupy the remaining consecutive position. The check word is a binary representation of the sum of the indices of data bits whose values are 0s. Figure 5.25b presents a Zero-Sum communication system. The check word is generated by the sender and then transmitted to the receiver with the data word. Once a valid code word is detected by the CD of the receiver, the error correction unit

indices	data word		check bits			
	5	3	8	4	2	1
	0	0	1	0	0	0
	0	1	0	1	0	1
	1	0	0	0	1	1
	1	1	0	0	0	0

(a) Zero-Sum code with 2 data bits

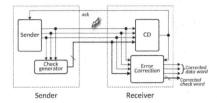

(b) Protected communication

Figure 5.25   Zero-Sum codes [3].

recalculates the check field C' and compares it with the incoming check word C. If their absolute difference $|C - C'|$ is zero, no error occurs. Otherwise, the value of $|C - C'|$ represents the index of the erroneous bit. To ensure forward progress, a time-out mechanism is used to force a data word to be corrected and latched by the receiver if its arrival cannot be detected by CD. Obviously, this is a violation of the QDI assumption. By a further check of the codes, it can be found that a 1-bit fault could mislead the error corrector to decode a wrong code word. Assuming that a transient fault mutates the data word 10 into 11 during its transmission while the transmission of its check word 0011 is delayed (Figure 5.25a), the erroneous "110000" will be incorrectly regarded as a valid code without error correction, even if the check word later arrives at the receiver. Some extensions [3] have been proposed to improve the error detection and correction capability but most of the aforementioned problems remain with a even larger hardware overhead.

Lechner et al. [127] studied the general fault-tolerance properties of DI codes and proposed methods for improving the fault resilience of 4-phase DI asynchronous communication links. In DI or QDI communication systems, signal transitions on long wires may appear at any time and in any order at the receiver because there is no timing assumption to guard the delay of signals. In a faulty environment, rising transitions caused by faults can make an intermediate transmission state of a DI code into a complete data word latched by the receiver. Taking a 2-of-4 code 0011 for example, one possible intermediate transmission state could be 0001, which can be mutated into 1001 by a positive fault and further be mistaken into a valid 2-of-4 code at the receiver. Resilient sub-codes can be built from the original DI codes to avoid this issue. To better understand this issue, let us say that two code words $x = (x_{n-1}, x_{n-2}, \cdots, x_0)$ and $y = (y_{n-1}, y_{n-2}, \cdots, y_0)$ *overlap* at bit position i if both x_i and y_i are equal to 1. If the number of non-overlapped 1s in the two code words is larger than f, it can be inferred that f faulty bits cannot erroneously convert an incomplete code word into a complete one. Resilient sub-codes are a set of DI code words where any two of the code words satisfy this condition. For example, 0011 and 1100 are two resilient sub-code words of 2-of-4 codes tolerating one bit transient fault. 10010 and 01100 are two sub-code words of 2-of-5 codes tolerating two bits transient faults.

The above resilient sub-codes are immune to a specific number of transient faults and neither detection nor correction is required. The price is the extremely poor coding efficiency due to the sparse use of code space. To improve the coding efficiency, a two-step data-encoding method was proposed [127]: at the sender, an error detection coding method first adds enough bit redundancy to the original data, which is then encoded into DI codes transmitting to the receiver. To achieve an f-bit fault-tolerance capability, the mapping between the error detection codes and the DI codes must ensure that f transient faults on the transmitted DI codes will cause at most f-bit errors on the decoded error detection codes, which can be then detected. Producing this mapping requires complex processes in searching a graph. No hardware detail is disclosed.

In addition, a self-timed bundled-data link is able to tolerate transient and permanent faults by combining multiple fault-tolerant methods [130, 131], such as applying Hamming coding and interleaving for detecting transient faults and then use retransmission to correct errors. The extra de-interleaving and Hamming decoding process introduces a large area overhead while breaks the QDI assumption. Nevertheless, Lechner et al. [126] proposed a robust asynchronous interfacing scheme for GALS systems. The interface performs a transformation between bundled-data and dual-rail encoding. Parity bits are employed to achieve error-correction. Delay elements are used to guarantee the correct operation of the code

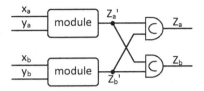

Figure 5.26   Double-checking protection [106].

generator, error detection and error correction. Unfortunately this is no longer a QDI design.

5.5.1.2   Physical and Other Redundancy

Many physical and temporal techniques have been proposed to provide fault-tolerance for asynchronous circuits and on-chip communication. As for QDI designs, Jang et al. [105, 106] proposed a physical-redundant double-checking technique which tolerates 1-bit or even some multi-bit faults. As Figure 5.26 shows, no matter it is a basic logic gate or a combinations circuit, all modules are duplicated. The variables (x_a, x_b), (y_a, y_b) and (Z_a, Z_b) are copies of the variable x, y and Z, respectively. A transient fault on inputs may result in a glitch on one of the *check-in* variables (Z'_a, Z'_b), which can be filtered by the double-checking C-elements. Two extra weak C-elements are added to the two double-checking C-elements respectively to tolerate accumulated soft errors (or multiple-event upsets). The main difference from other communication-enteric fault-tolerant techniques is that it can be used to build computational circuits. Compared with an unprotected QDI circuit, the area of the double-checking protected one is enlarged by a factor of between two and three, and the throughput is reduced between 40% and 50%. This double-checking technique has also been used in several other fault-tolerant asynchronous designs [8, 103, 135].

Similar to the double-checking technique [106], Almukhaizim et al. [8] proposed replication-based soft-error-tolerant solutions for asynchronous burst-mode machines (ABMM). To alleviate the large area overhead due to a pure duplication of the original circuit ($\geq 100\%$ of the cost), ABMM investigated a trade-off between the area overhead and the error reduction. Three partial duplication options were explored to protect sensitive gates or blocks, requiring 87%, 60% and 50% of its cost while providing 68%, 47% and 24% of its transient-error tolerance, respectively.

Monnet et al. studied the sensitivity of QDI circuits to transient faults [156, 157, 159] and proposed a rail synchronization technique between multiple parallel channels to filter glitches [158, 159]. Compared to the duplication-based techniques proposed by Jang et al. [106] and Almukhaizim et al. [8], duplication is avoided with significantly reduced area overhead. In this design, the synchronization between two channels ensures that data symbols cannot be latched in one channel without the presence of valid data symbols in the other one, which effectively filters most transient faults at the synchronization point. When there is only one circuit lack of a redundant channel to be synchronized with, a redundant control circuit is required to synchronize the original channel. A delay line is still used compromising the QDI assumption. Some minor timing assumptions are also required between synchronized channels. Some faulty scenarios (such as a 1-of-2 code 01 changed to a faulty 10) cannot be resolved. The design might still suffer from the fault-caused deadlock. The incurred area overhead depends highly on the circuit architecture to be hardened. A hardened asynchronous data encryption standard (DES) crypto-processor is 7.7% larger and 18% slower than the unhardened one. A robust C-element latch scheme using a similar synchronization technique was proposed in [83] but also requires a number of timing assumptions.

A duplication and recalculation technique was proposed [79, 80] for 2-phase 1-of-2 QDI circuits. The original channel is duplicated, and a checker is used to detects errors by sampling both the data from the original pipeline stage and the replica. Data transmission will be stalled until a fault-free result is successfully recalculated by the preceding combinational circuit. A cross-coupling technique was proposed to ensure that the circuit will not proceed to the next state until the error is resolved. The register transfer level (RTL) simulation demonstrated that the proposed techniques can tolerate data errors but will fail in the presence of physical-layer deadlock.

Julai et al. [110] proposed a fault-tolerant latch architecture which duplicates the original data rail so that XOR gates

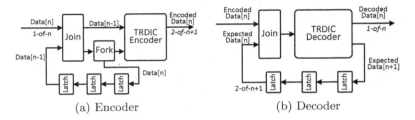

(a) Encoder   (b) Decoder

Figure 5.27   TRDIC communication system.

can compare the two supposed to be identical rails and detect faults. Similar to the Razor flip-flop technique [74] for synchronous pipelines, a shadow latch controlled by a delayed clock is added to support the error correction. A multiplexer at the output will choose either the main or the duplicated latch as the output if no faults are detected or use the shadow latch if faults are detected. As several timing assumptions are required in the latch control circuit, the design is not QDI.

Temporal redundancy has been used to tolerate transient faults on 1-of-n QDI pipelines. As shown by Figure 5.27a, the temporally redundant delay insensitive code (TRDIC) system [199] converts 1-of-n DI codes to 2-of-n+1 codes at the sender, which are then transmitted by the QDI data links. The conversion from 1-of-n to 2-of-$(n + 1)$ code can be easily implemented using a bitwise OR operation between the previous and the current 1-of-n code words while the most significant bit indicates whether the two consecutive code words are equal. In this way, two code words are transmitted inside the 2-of-$(n + 1)$ code word for each transmission and every code word is transmitted twice. At the receiver end (Figure 5.27b), a similar feedback loop of asynchronous latches is used to store the code word previously being transmitted, which is also the next data to be expected. This structure allows a detector to filter transient faults by comparing the incoming code word with the copy stored in the feedback loop because only one of them would be corrupted by a transient fault. Double checkers built from C-elements [106] are used in the receiver to filter transient faults. Without including the cost of TRDIC encoder and decoder, the area of a protected 2-of-5 pipeline is around three times larger than unprotected 1-of-4 pipeline. The throughput also decreases by 20%. The hardware cost is even higher if the rather complex decoding and encoding components are considered. As mentioned by the authors, some transient faults cannot be tolerated with the simple double checker, such as an insertion of a valid code word. A three-stage trellis structure was used in an extended version to improve fault-tolerance [199]. No implementation details were given but the area and speed overhead is expected to increase further.

Ogg et al. [176] proposed a technique which utilizes the phase relationship between multiple 1-of-2 data symbols and a redundant reference symbol to achieve the transient resilience of asynchronous links. The generation of the reference symbol follows the sequence of 00 → 01 → 11 → 10. If a data symbol is the same as the reference, they are *in-phase* and a bit of 0 is decoded. If a data symbol is complementary to the reference, it is 180° *out-of-phase* and a bit of 1 is decoded. A data symbol satisfying other phase relationships (±90°) will not be latched. However, this technique is time-dependent because wire delays can violate the normal phase relationship between the data and reference symbol. A faulty data symbol satisfying the phase relationship can be decoded into an incorrect value. For example, to transmit a bit 0 when the reference symbol is 01, the received data symbol should be 01 in the normal case. Any faults changing the data to 11 or 00 will not be latched or decoded, but a temporarily faulty 10 occurring before the correct data symbol will be incorrectly latched and decoded into 1. Consequently, it is not a QDI design.

Regarding the QDI circuits adopting the null convention logic (NCL) [231], Kuang et al. studied the fault-tolerance of NCL circuits and argued that reducing the sensitivity duration of the NCL logic to glitches could significantly suppress the rate of soft errors [120]. As an extension to the original work [121], a Schmitt trigger [207] implemented at transistor level was used to prevent most glitches from being captured by latches and becoming transient errors. In addition, extra latches along with detection and reset circuits were added to protect combinational blocks. When erroneous transitions are detected, the reset circuits clear the combinational circuits. However, these redundant circuits were assumed to be fault-free without any protection. Delay elements were used to mitigate some fault scenarios, compromising the timing-robustness feature of the circuits. Mosaffa et al. [161] proposed techniques to improve the robustness of NCL gates to transient faults by building robust threshold gates at transistor level, without being sensitive to transistor sizing and load capacitance. These robust threshold gates were later used in a macro synchronous micro asynchronous pipeline proposed by Lodhi et al. [135] to achieve fault-tolerance.

Bainbridge et al. proposed a series of techniques [14] to protect QDI pipelines from transient faults, which can be classified into three categories: preventing a glitch from causing an effect, mapping the consequences of a glitch onto a different consequence that is easier to detect or recover from and reducing the window of sensitivity to a glitch. However, none of them is robust enough to qualify as fault-immune. The transient-fault effects on different kinds of implementations of C-elements have been evaluated by means of fault-injection simulations at transistor level [17].

Although the above techniques seem promising, they cannot be easily migrated to protect QDI links or the large number of existing QDI NoCs without modifying most of the original circuit or compromising the timing-robustness. It can be summarized from the above techniques that the fault-tolerance and timing-robustness are difficult to achieve at the same time. Many existing techniques improve the circuit robustness but do not qualify as fault-immune. A trade-off should usually be made between the incurred overhead and the achieved fault-tolerance capability, so that a flexible protection strategy depending on the practical design requirement is extremely valuable. Chapter 6 will propose a general fault-tolerant coding scheme to protect QDI interconnects from transient faults according to the fault-tolerance requirement while keeping the timing-robustness, providing a flexible way to enhance the fault-tolerance of QDI links or NoCs.

5.5.2 Management for Permanent Faults and Deadlocks

5.5.2.1 Conventional Techniques

Transient faults may corrupt the on-chip data transmission, which can be either detected or corrected on-the-fly so that no further recovery operation is required. If the fault is detected but not

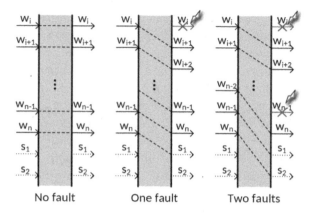

Figure 5.28 Spare wire replacement example.

corrected, end-to-end retransmission is a popular way to avoid packet loss in NoCs. However, it works only for transient faults while fail to protect the network from permanent faults.

As for permanent faults, they can be checked off-line using self-test mechanisms, such as scan chains [245], or detected on-line by searching for persistent errors using fault-tolerant coding schemes [78, 130, 131]. As discussed in Section 5.4.1, if the collected error syndromes satisfy specific patterns or some time-out conditions, the fault is taken as permanent and the recovery process starts. Although permanent faults cannot be eliminated, a network may survive with redundant or reduced resources, which is important to critical digital equipment. Based on the assumption that the permanent fault has been detected and located, many recovery techniques have been proposed [201], including spare wire replacement [130, 131, 260], splitting transmission [130, 260, 265] and fault-tolerant routings [78, 103, 204].

Spare wire replacement [130, 131, 260] is a physical-redundant technique substituting extra wires for faulty ones, whereas in the normal case, these spare wires are unused. Figure 5.28 illustrates the function of the reconfiguration unit implementing the switching between faulty and spare wires. If the output wire w_i is defective in the one-fault case, all input wires numbered no less than i will be redirected to new outputs numbered with an increment of one. The two-fault case is also depicted in Figure 5.28. Complicated control circuits are usually required to implement the wire switching. Splitting transmission [130, 260, 265] divides a physical link as all the flits transmitted on it into multiple corresponding groups. When one group is diagnosed as defective, the corresponding group is discarded while the other groups still work. As a result, transmission of a flit is split into two transmissions: parts on the functional groups are transmitted as normal while the part supposed to be transmitted on discarded group will be delivered by a second transmission on other functional groups. Data packets are disassembled at the transmitter side and reassembled at the receiver side to obtain the original data in a faulty environment. The size of the grouping is a important parameter. Dividing links into a large number of narrow groups provides higher bandwidth and throughput than a small number of wide groups in the presence of faults, but incurs more complicated control logic, consuming significant area and power. As the group size increases, the network throughput decreases as more wires are abandoned in case of a faulty wire but the complexity of the control logic decreases as well.

Note that splitting the transmission, which dynamically configures the link for one flit when a link wire is found defective, is different from the spatial division multiplexing (SDM, Section 4.2) which divides one link physically into multiple independent sub-links for different packets. Splitting transmission is a network layer or data link layer technique. When a link wire is found defective, the following flits should be disassembled to fit the remaining width of the link and reassembled after passing the link. Differently, the SDM applied in this research is a physical-layer technique which provides multiple narrow physical channels on each link. The flit width is adjusted to the width of each sub-link before a packet enters the network so that no disassembly or assembly operation is required inside the network even if a permanent fault removes a sub-link.

Fault-tolerant routing algorithms have also been widely used to recover the network function in the network layer [63, 78, 103, 204, 265]. It will detour the faulty links by choosing alternative and healthy links to carry data. A defective router can also be bypassed if it is identified. However, fault-tolerant routing algorithms by themselves cannot manage a fault-caused deadlock in the lower physical layer.

As an example, Lehtonen et al. [130] implemented the detection and position of permanent faults on an asynchronous bundled-data NoC by decoding error syndromes collected by fault-tolerant coding. Using Hamming codes [93], a number of equivalent syndromes indicate a permanent fault, otherwise, the fault is transient that can be corrected using retransmissions. Spare wires and half-splitting transmission were employed to bypass permanent faults. However, this bundled-data design is similar to a synchronous network rather than QDI.

The later work of Lehtonen et al. proposed an in-line test method to detect permanent faults in synchronous on-chip interconnects [131]. A test pattern generator at the sender injects test vectors to each adjacent pair of link wires periodically. An error detection unit at the receiver can tell whether a permanent fault happens by checking the received test outputs against specific patterns. This in-line test method was later used in a transient and permanent faults co-management synchronous NoC [260] to detect permanent faults. Another detection method using Hamming codes was also proposed in [131]. When one or multiple faults are detected by the fault-tolerant coding scheme, retransmissions are requested to transmit data through suspicious wires. If collected error syndromes satisfy specific patterns, faults are taken as permanent and the recovery process is launched; otherwise, the faults are transient. Spare wires are used to recover from permanent faults.

Feng et al. proposed an on-line fault diagnosis mechanism for synchronous NoCs [78]. Transient faults are detected and corrected using Hamming codes. At the receiver, a 1-bit error will be directly corrected no matter what type of fault causes it. If a 2-bit error is detected, a retransmission is requested. If the same 2-bit error happens again in the re-transmitted packet, the router enters a test mode and a group of test vectors are transmitted through the suspicious link multiple times. By checking the correctness of the received test vectors, permanent faults can be diagnosed. A fault-tolerant routing algorithm was proposed to bypass defective links.

It should be noted that, the above conventional detection and recovery techniques for synchronous circuits or NoCs cannot directly work for deadlocked asynchronous NoCs. In a deadlocked state, conventional techniques relying on fault-tolerant codes on longer work because the transmission of error syndromes is also stuck by the deadlock, making it impossible to detect and locate the faulty component. In terms of the network recovery, the aforementioned recovery techniques (spare wire replacement, splitting transmission and fault-tolerant routings) try to restore the network function in the data link layer or network layer (Chapter 3.1.1). They cannot be used to resolve the fault-caused deadlock occurring in the lower physical layer. Only after the physical-layer deadlock (or the broken handshake protocol) is resolved, can the traditional network recovery techniques be employed to further recover the function of the network. Therefore, new and effective detection and recovery techniques targeting on the fault-caused physical-layer deadlock are crucial for asynchronous NoC to work properly because both transient and permanent faults can deadlock the NoC.

5.5.2.2 Fault-Caused Physical-Layer Deadlocks

Existing research on permanent faults is mostly on synchronous circuits or NoCs [201]. There is rarely research on the management of permanent faults in QDI NoCs. This chapter has demonstrated that both transient and permanent faults can break the handshake protocol and cause physical-layer deadlocks, which is fatal to the network. Therefore, the task of tolerating a permanent or transient fault is transferred to the detection and recovery of the physical-layer deadlock. It is straightforward that a permanent fault could deadlock a QDI circuit, which has been studied in numerous existing researches [64, 99, 106, 142] but not under the context of NoCs. The statement that a transient fault could stall the handshake process was mentioned in [105, 124, 216] without further exploration. In a deadlocked state, traditional information redundancy [3, 48, 264] or duplication-based [106, 159] fault-tolerant techniques fail to work as the underlying circuits are stalled.

To detect the fault in asynchronous circuits, concurrent error detection (CED) or self-checking techniques have been proposed to provide a circuit with the capability to monitor its own function and report potential deviations from correct functionality [250]. Rennels and Kim [202] studied the CED in asynchronous differential cascade voltage switch logic (DCVSL). Fault effects on different DCVSL elements were investigated. A checker using a time-out counter was added to the outputs of the original circuits to signal errors. The fault-caused deadlock caused by stuck-at faults can be detected using the time-out mechanism. Traditionally, duplication-based CED techniques have been proposed to detect faults in synchronous circuits. Verdel and Makris [250] pointed out that the difficulty in duplication-based CED for asynchronous circuits is the lack of a global synchronization mechanism (i.e. the clock) so that it is unclear when the outputs of the original and the replica circuit are expected to match. A comparator circuit attached to two identical D-elements was proposed with a comparison synchronizer. A custom delay line defines a time window. If the outputs of the original and the replica circuits are the same in the window, the circuits are operating correctly. Otherwise, either of the circuits is operating too fast (a premature firing) or too slowly (or a halt in the presence of stuck-at faults). Extra circuits are required to determine the different fault effects. Applying a fault-tolerant coding scheme [70] and duplication, Hyde and Russell [101] proposed a CED architecture for a bundled-data processors. 12% area overhead was caused by the CED technique while a fault coverage of 98.5% of all unidirectional errors was achieved. Significant delay assumptions are required in the design of the asynchronous CED processors. David et al. [64] studied the detection of a stuck-at permanent fault on asynchronous circuits and proposed self-checking designs which either stop operating or produce illegal outputs when faults happen. The halt condition can be detected using a simple watchdog timer. Mathematical proofs were given in details while the fault detection circuits were not provided. The self-checking property of asynchronous circuits with respect to permanent faults was also studied in several publications [184, 193, 256].

With respect to asynchronous NoCs, Tran et al. [244, 245] proposed a design-for-test (DFT) architecture to improve the testability of an asynchronous NoC, which is illustrated in Figure 5.29. Each asynchronous router is surrounded by a test wrapper controlled by a local control module. A 2-bit configuration chain is built to connect serially the wrapper control modules of all routers

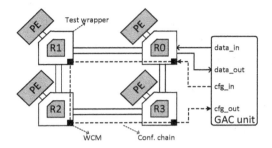

Figure 5.29   The DFT protected ANOC.

so that test vectors can be inserted to the network and test results can be achieved. The whole test process is controlled by a generator-analyzer-controller (GAC) unit. Using the single stuck-at fault model, the proposed test approach can achieve 99.86% test coverage. The area of a test wrapper is 32.7% of the router area. Considering the whole chip, the incurred area overhead is about $3 \sim 5\%$ of the chip area depending on the chip size. Since no redundant circuits are applied on the critical path of the router, the handshaking loop between the input and output of the router, the network throughput suffers no degradation from the DFT implementation.

Shi [216, 217] investigated the fault sensitivity of C-elements, and both the 4-phase and the 2-phase pipelines. The fault-tolerance of an asynchronous interface circuit between the 4-phase, 3-of-6 on-chip link and the 2-phase, 2-of-7 off-chip link was researched. The interface implements the protocol transformation between the two asynchronous domains, where transient faults can also cause deadlocks. Several methods were proposed to reduce or eliminate the deadlock, including a novel phase-insensitive 2-phase to 4-phase converter, a priority arbiter for reliable code conversion and a scheme that allows independent resetting of the transmitter and receiver to clear deadlocks. In some cases, an over-length packet due to faults may arrive and occupy all available buffer space, which can be detected using flit counters. The results show a reduction in deadlocks with 4% larger area compared with the baseline.

Peng and Manohar [189–191] proposed a failure-detection technique for QDI circuits which can achieve *fail-stop* with respect to

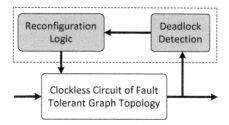

Figure 5.30 A reconfigurable self-healing asynchronous circuit [189].

both transient and permanent faults. It utilizes the deadlock behavior in the faulty circuit to realize the fault detection and online recovery. Instead of comparing the results from redundant computations or using extra modules to detect the fault, the design simply lets the QDI circuit stall in the presence of any faults, resulting in a *deadlock*. This deadlock is then discovered using a detector, as shown in Figure 5.30. Controlled by a timer (internally implemented by delay lines), the deadlock detector keeps monitoring the handshake activities of the data channel. Whenever a transition occurs on the data channel, it triggers a recounting of the timer. If no new transition or changes of the protocol state for a long time, the detector assumes that the circuit has deadlocked. In this scenario, a self-reconfiguration logic implemented using synchronous circuits would try to cover the circuit. It uses the time-out signal from the deadlock detector as the clock signal and try all possible valid configurations in the hope to find a workable one. To support multiple configurations, each module of the system should be built on a fault-tolerant graph (Figure 5.30) with spare resources corresponding to different configurations. Thus, the whole system achieves self-checking and self-healing. The *fail-stop* augmentation logic increases the hardware cost of asynchronous adders by 92%, which is close to the price of duplication. The circuit speed is reduced by around 30%. For the weak-condition half buffer, the *fail-stop* increases the area by 200%, while the speed decreases by 36%. The overhead of the deadlock detector and the reconfiguration logic was not given. In addition, many custom delay lines are required inside the deadlock detector to detect different signal transitions. The proposed technique is not easy to be implemented using standard cells.

Imai and Yoneda [103, 258] proposed a time-out detection and a recovery mechanism in a self-timed NoC using QDI inter-router links. A delay line is used to detect the abnormal data skew among the data wires of the same pipeline stage, so that a lost data bit due to a permanent fault can be detected. However, this method does not work in a pure QDI NoC. Since self-timed bundled-data pipelines are used inside the router and they do not latch incomplete data words, the fault-caused partial or incomplete data (which leads to the large skew) is isolated in one inter-router link only, which can be detected by the time-out mechanism and reported. However, in a pure QDI NoC, this faulty incomplete data word will propagate to all pipeline stages downstream of the fault. As a result, all the downstream stages are timed out and multiple faults are reported. The fault position cannot be located. This issue also lies in most of the above aforementioned fault detection techniques. These methods cannot be used easily in QDI NoCs and they cannot locate the faulty component [190]. As a result, an expensive system reboot may be used to eliminate the deadlock and recover the network after the system deadlock is detected. For a permanent fault, even the system reboot cannot restore the system. A fine-grained recovery mechanism was proposed [103, 258] though it was not implemented in the final chip: incoming flits to the faulty link are immediately accepted and acknowledged while a pseudo tail, generated at the end of the faulty link, releases all occupied channels along the deadlocked path. It was designed for an asynchronous NoC with self-timed bundled-data asynchronous routers and level encoded dual rail (LEDR) encoded inter-router links, which cannot work in a QDI NoC. Fault-tolerant routing was further used to recover the network function.

It can be summarized that, the self-checking or fail-stop feature of asynchronous circuits in the presence of faults has been studied to detect faults or the *deadlock*. Time-out mechanisms have been proposed to provide a time reference for the fault detection though most early studies did not present any implementation details. An asynchronous circuit can even be forced to *deadlock* in the presence of faults to enable the fault detection. However, most of these techniques target on specific circuits and cannot work in QDI NoCs. In a QDI NoC, a fault can break the handshake protocol, resulting in a long, deadlocked packet path (Figure 1.1b). In this case, most above techniques [103, 244, 245, 258] may report multiple deadlocks along the whole packet path so that it is difficult to locate the fault position. As all network resources on this packet path cannot be allocated to other fault-free packets, the fault-caused physical-layer deadlock may cause packet stalls spreading over the whole network, where the physical-layer and the network-layer deadlocks may co-exist, making the fault or deadlock detection more difficult. The recovery of this deadlocked network is difficult since the handshake protocol is broken in the physical layer and the faulty packet path is stalled. In terms of network recovery, a system reboot can release all deadlocked and fault-free network nodes, but the whole process can be too expensive for a critical system. Obviously, this reboot is not allowed in some cases [7]. The aforementioned traditional fault recovery techniques targets recovering the network function in the data link or network layer, but they cannot resolve the physical-layer deadlocks. Therefore, it is necessary to propose an on-line deadlock detection technique to isolate the faulty component in QDI NoCs, so that further custom fine-grained operations can be used to recover the deadlocked NoC at runtime according to the employed asynchronous and network protocols, without disturbing other fault-free components too much.

5.6 GENERAL DEADLOCK MANAGEMENT STRATEGY

It has been discussed in Section 3.1.4.2 that deadlock avoidance and deadlock recovery techniques can be used in NoCs to deal with network-layer deadlock. Since the physical-layer deadlock invalidates the avoidance techniques implemented in the network layer, recovery techniques should be employed to manage fault-caused physical-layer deadlocks. The management of the physical-layer deadlock can be divided into two phases: *detection* and *recovery*. When both permanent and transient faults are considered, *fault diagnosis* is required after the deadlock detection to diagnose the fault type so that different recovery methods can be used to recover the network.

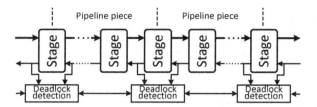

Figure 5.31   Protected pipeline pieces with deadlock detection circuits.

- *Deadlock detection* phase, during which the fault-caused physical-layer deadlock should be precisely located and differentiated from a network-layer deadlock or a temporary stall due to congestion.

- *Fault diagnosis* phase, during which the fault type is diagnosed when both transient and permanent faults are considered.

- *Deadlock recovery* phase, during which the deadlock should be removed first. If this deadlock is caused by a permanent fault, defective components should be isolated and the network continues working. As for the deadlock caused by a transient (or intermittent) fault, the isolated component should be salvaged for a reuse.

Figure 5.31 presents a long QDI pipeline model cut into multiple small sections, each of which contains multiple pipeline stages. By adding detection circuits to the two terminal stages of a pipeline piece to monitor their activities and check their *ack* signals, the fault-caused physical-layer deadlock can be detected and differentiated from the others (including the network-layer deadlock or temporary stall due to congestion). Under the assumption of a 1-bit fault each time, only one pipeline piece could satisfy the deadlock pattern mentioned in Theorem 1 so that the fault position can be precisely located. A time-out mechanism can be applied in the detection circuits to monitor the switching activity of each pipeline piece. If no switching activities are detected for a long period and the *ack* sequence satisfies the deadlock pattern in Theorem 1, the faulty pipeline piece is found. The detected fault can be transient or permanent. If both transient and permanent faults are considered, the fault type should be diagnosed first and then different recovery methods are used. More details will be discussed in the following chapters.

CHAPTER 6

Fault-Tolerant Coding

As an important issue in the design of asynchronous NoCs, the large number of long inter-router link wires, which are exposed to various environmental noises and fault sources, are susceptible to delay variations and transient faults [14]. QDI circuits [231] are a family of asynchronous circuits that tolerate all delay variations but they are vulnerable to faults. Occasionally, an erroneous signal transition may be accepted as a valid signal, producing a fault in QDI circuits. Fault-tolerant codes [229], which are important concepts in the field of fault-tolerance, have been widely used to protect interconnection communications. Coding performs an important role in QDI asynchronous circuits as well where DI codes are used to build data channels, achieving timing-robustness.

This chapter presents a novel DI redundant check (DIRC) coding scheme to protect QDI links from transient faults. The DIRC coding scheme tolerates all 1-bit transient faults and some multi-bit transient faults. It can be easily adopted in all existing 1-of-n QDI pipelines to provide fault-tolerance. The resulting DIRC pipeline, with different construction patterns, can provide flexible fault-tolerance for a QDI communication infrastructure with a moderate and reasonable hardware overhead. Another fault-tolerant technique, redundant protection of acknowledge wires (RPA), is also proposed to protect the acknowledge wires from transient faults, which has extremely low area overhead and can be used independently of DIRC. Detailed experimental results are provided to demonstrate the implementation overhead.

6.1 COMPARISON WITH RELATED WORK

In a GALS system [119], the on-chip communication fabric is provided by asynchronous or QDI NoCs. Its fault-tolerance can be achieved through different ways of protection. The end-to-end protection, which adds redundant information when data or packets enter into the network, and then detects and corrects errors where data leave the network, can provide fault-tolerance capability for the asynchronous network with little disturbance. In other words, fault-tolerant encodings [229], for example, can be used at the network interface to encode the original data into error detecting or correcting codes. These codes are then translated to DI codes required by the asynchronous NoC and sent across the network. During the data transmission, no error detection and correction is required. When data leave the network and pass the network interface again, these DI symbols are translated back to the usual binary data so that the erroneous data can be detected or corrected, depending on the fault-tolerance capability of the applied error detecting and correcting coding schemes.

In this way, the error detecting and correcting operations are executed in the synchronous domain, rather than the asynchronous domain of the network. The asynchronous network is rarely disturbed and it is only responsible for delivering packets. This method has been proposed and utilized in several existing asynchronous interconnections [48, 198], which demonstrated that managing errors in the synchronous domain can be cheaper and more effective than that in the asynchronous domain. However, this end-to-end protection has a limitation which cannot be ignored. Without protection inside the network or the asynchronous domain, a transient fault can insert, delete or corrupt a DI symbol, which brings difficulty to the synchronization at some places of the network [124]. More seriously, a transient fault is possible to break the handshake and cause a physical-layer deadlock. As a result, the destination node or the receiver may never receive a data packet. This fault-caused physical-layer deadlock can cause large amount of packet loss, in which case the end-to-end error detection or correction cannot work. Therefore, it is necessary to add fault-tolerance to protect the large number of long asynchronous interconnects inside the asynchronous domain, so as to significantly decrease the impact of faults on the network.

Many fault-tolerant techniques [126, 130, 176] have been proposed to protect asynchronous circuits but they cannot be easily used to protect QDI communications. Some duplication-based circuit redundancy techniques [8, 106, 159] are efficient to protect computation-centric QDI circuits, but they may not be suitable for communication-centric systems which may have a large number of long wires, making the duplication expensive. Codes play an important role in both asynchronous and fault-tolerance fields. Information redundancy techniques, or fault-tolerant codes, are attractive to fault-tolerant asynchronous designs. They are promising candidates to protect on-chip communication. Several fault-tolerant codes were proposed but none of them can be easily used in QDI interconnects [3, 127, 199]. Their QDI implementation may be difficult, require much design effort, or lead to a large hardware overhead. This chapter focuses on providing fault-tolerance for QDI interconnects with code redundancy while keeping the timing-robust nature of QDI circuits.

6.1.1 Non-QDI Designs

For code redundancy techniques, an unordered systematic code [48] using parity check codes can correct 1-bit error and detect completion simultaneously on 4-phase asynchronous links. Using several fault-tolerant methods [130], a self-timed bundled-data link is able to tolerate transient and permanent errors but introduces large area overhead due to the extra de-interleaving and Hamming decoding processes. Another unordered systematic code named Zero-Sum [2, 3] provides both 1-bit error correction and 2-bit error detection for asynchronous links. Its extensions [3] provide more fault-tolerance with the price of a larger hardware overhead. A time-out mechanism is required to constrain the bit arrival intervals.

For circuit redundancy technique, Ogg et al. [176] proposed a technique utilizing the phase relationships between data symbols and a redundant reference symbol to achieve transient-fault-tolerance. An asynchronous interfacing scheme using parity check codes has been proposed for GALS systems [126]. Triple modular redundancy (TMR) has been used in a GALS system to achieve fault-tolerance [128].

Although these techniques seem promising, none of them can be easily used in QDI interconnects.

6.1.2 QDI Designs

As for QDI designs, Bainbridge et al. [14] proposed a series of fault-tolerant techniques which improve the robustness of the circuits but not enough for achieving fault-immunity. Jang et al. [106] proposed a duplicated double-checking technique which tolerates 1-bit faults and some multi-bit faults. The fault-tolerant buffer using this technique is three times larger and runs twice slower than the normal one. Some circuit redundancy techniques [8, 159] can also be used in QDI circuits but their duplication is area-consuming.

In addition, Pontes et al. [198, 199] used temporal redundancy to tolerate transient faults on 1-of-n QDI pipelines. Peng and Manohar [190] proposed a failure-detection technique for pipelined QDI circuits which can achieve fail-stop with respect to permanent and transient errors. Kuang et al. [120] studied the fault-tolerance of Null convention logic QDI circuits.

6.1.3 Unordered and Systematic Codes

Two important code categories in the fault-tolerance field are *unordered* and *systematic* codes. The mathematical definition of *unordered* codes is given below:

Definition 1 (Unordered codes [33, 38]). *: Let us consider two code words* $X = (x_0, x_1, \cdots, x_{n-1})$ *and* $Y = (y_0, y_1, \cdots, y_{n-1})$ *with the same length n. We define X is contained in Y when* $X \cap Y = X$ *(for all* $i \in [0, n-1]$ *where* $x_i = 1$*, the corresponding* $y_i = 1$*). If no one is contained by the other,* $X \neq X \cap Y \neq Y$*, the two code words are unordered. When any pair of code words in a coding scheme are unordered, the coding scheme itself is unordered. Data words encoded by such a coding scheme are unordered codes.*

Taking the three code words $a = 011, b = 001, c = 100$ for example, a and b are not unordered because b is contained in a, while the other two pairs (a and c, b and c) are unordered. This

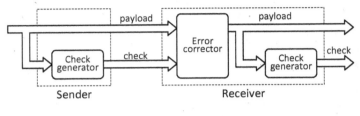

(a) Systematic codes

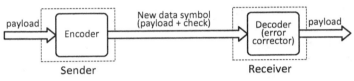

(b) Non-systematic codes

Figure 6.1 Implementation of systematic and non-systematic codes.

unordered feature ensures that valid data words in an unordered coding scheme are separated, which is a desirable feature widely utilized in DI communication [48]. Thus, DI codes are also known as unordered codes [251]. Extensively used unordered codes or DI codes are 1-of-n and m-of-n codes (Section 2.3.1). The unordered coding supports the detection of all unidirectional errors (both $0 \rightarrow 1$ and $1 \rightarrow 0$) in a data word [38]. Take a 1-of-2 code 01 as an example. Assuming it is mutated into 11 during its transmission, 11 is an invalid symbol and can be easily detected with a full symbol test [14].

Fault-tolerant codes can be classified into *systematic* and *non-systematic* codes according to their manner of construction. A systematic code [2] comprises two fields: an information field and a check field. The information field contains the original data payload while the check field is generated from the data and can be used to recover the original data when errors occur. Figure 6.1a presents an example of transmitting a systematic code. Since a systematic code is separable, the overhead of encoding and decoding processes incur moderate performance overhead [2, 108]. The main overhead comes from the check generator on the sender side and the error corrector on the receiver side.

Comparatively, non-systematic codes are inseparable codes because there is only one field for the encoded data, as shown in Figure 6.1b. Since the payload and the check bits are inseparable, an area-consuming decoder with error correction functionality on the receiver side is usually required.

Therefore, applying DI encoding to all parts of systematic codes, including both the information and check fields, allows them to be transmitted in parallel, avoids affecting the critical path by the encoding and decoding process and simplifies the design of completion detection. If non-systematic codes are used, the resulting non-systematic DI codes may use more but smaller completion detectors [2], but with a high overhead from the special encoder and decoder. All m-of-n codes are non-systematic codes when $n > m > 1$ [12].

6.2 DIRC CODING SCHEME

This section proposes a new fault-tolerant coding scheme to provide a flexible and efficient protection for QDI links. As one of the simplest asynchronous protocols, the 4-phase 1-of-n handshake protocols have been widely used in existing asynchronous (or QDI) NoCs [11, 75, 223, 244]. The proposed fault-tolerant codes are based on the 4-phase 1-of-n protocols so that they can be easily used in numerous existing asynchronous designs to protect QDI links.

The basic idea of the proposed fault-tolerant codes is simple: Assuming we apply a new systematic coding scheme on two code words x and y, the original code words are copied to the information field while the check field can be easily produced by *adding* them together. In other words, the check word $c = x + y$.

If either one of the code words, x or y, is incorrect during the transmission, the faulty one can be corrected by *subtracting* the other fault-free one from the check word. A faulty check word can be thrown away if it is not needed at the receiver or regenerated by adding x_0 and x_1. This process can be extended to the case of protecting multiple code words in the information field. It is simple and useful. Parity checking [229] belongs to this kind of method, whose process of generating the *parity* bit from the other data bits is effectively an *addition* operation. At the receiver, a fault can be detected by comparing the regenerated and the old parity bit, which is similar to the *subtraction* operation.

This chapter applies the above process to the widely used DI 1-of-n codes, achieving a new delay-insensitive redundant check (DIRC) coding scheme which provides fault-tolerance while retaining the original timing-robustness.

6.2.1 Arithmetic Rules

Before diving into the details of DIRC, let us first discuss the set of arithmetic rules used in the coding scheme for correcting transmitting errors.

6.2.1.1 Rules for 1-of-n Codes

Let x be an integer less than n $(0 \leq x < n)$. Its 1-of-n code representation is an n-bit vector $D^n(x)$ where the $(x+1)$th bit is high. For example, $D^4(2) = 0100$ and $D^4(0) = 0001$. The basic arithmetic rules for calculating two integer a and b using 1-of-n codes are defined as follows:

$$D^n(a) = D^n(a \bmod n) \tag{6.1}$$

$$-D^n(a) = D^n(-a) = D^n(-a \bmod n) = D^n(n-a) \tag{6.2}$$

$$D^n(a) + D^n(b) = D^n((a+b) \bmod n) \tag{6.3}$$

6.2.1.2 Rules for m-of-n Codes

Extending the arithmetic rules of 1-of-n codes to general m-of-n codes which have m 1s, a position set $A^m = (a_0, a_1, \cdots, a_{m-1})$ $(1 \leq m \leq n)$ is defined to denote positions of the m 1s in an m-of-n code. Let $D^n(A^m)$ be an m-of-n code. Equation 6.4 is used to construct an m-of-n code from m 1-of-n codes.

$$
\begin{aligned}
D^n(A^m) &= D^n(a_0, a_1, \cdots, a_{m-1}) \\
&= \bigcup_{i=0}^{m-1} D^n(a_i) \\
&= D^n(a_0) \cup D^n(a_1) \cup \cdots \cup D^n(a_{m-1})
\end{aligned} \tag{6.4}
$$

Taking a 2-of-4 code 1100 for example, it can be considered as a union of two 1-of-4 codes $D^4(2)$ and $D^4(3)$. Consequently, both $D^4(3,2)$ and $D^4(2,3)$ denote 1100. The extended arithmetic rules of m-of-n codes are shown in Equation 6.5 and Equation 6.6, which are unions of multiple 1-of-n operations.

$$
\begin{aligned}
-D^n(A^m) &= -\bigcup_{i=0}^{m-1} D^n(a_i) = \bigcup_{i=0}^{m-1} [-D^n(a_i)] \\
&= \bigcup_{i=0}^{m-1} D^n(-a_i)
\end{aligned}
\tag{6.5}
$$

$$
\begin{aligned}
D^n(A^m) + D^n(B^{m'}) &= \bigcup_{i=0}^{m-1} D^n(a_i) + \bigcup_{j=0}^{m'-1} D^n(b_j) \\
&= \bigcup_{j=0}^{m'-1} \bigcup_{i=0}^{m-1} D^n(a_i + b_j)
\end{aligned}
\tag{6.6}
$$

Taking a 1-of-4 code $D^4(3)$ and a 2-of-4 code $D^4(3,2)$ for example, we have:

$$
\begin{aligned}
-D^4(3,2) &= -[D^4(3) \cup D^4(2)] = D^4(-3) \cup D^4(-2) \\
&= 0010 \cup 0100 = 0110, \\
D^4(3) + D^4(3,2) &= [D^4(3) + D^4(3)] \cup [D^4(3) + D^4(2)] \\
&= D^4(1,2) = 0110.
\end{aligned}
$$

6.2.2 Delay-Insensitive Redundant Check Codes

Using the arithmetic rules of 1-of-n codes introduced in Section 6.2.1, the definition of DIRC codes is given below:

Definition 2 (DIRC Codes). *Let $X = (x_0, x_1, \cdots, x_{CN-1})$ ($CN \geq 2$) be a data vector containing CN 1-of-n code words as the payload. A check word c is generated from X using a 1-of-n accumulator which adds up all the CN code words. By concatenating the check word to the end of the original data vector, a DIRC code word $(x_0, x_1, \cdots, x_{CN-1}, c)$ containing $(CN + 1)$ 1-of-n code words, including the 1-of-n check word c.*

It can be found that the DIRC code is systematic (Figure 6.2): The information field contains the original 1-of-n data payload, while the check field is a single 1-of-n check word. This systematic

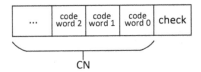

Figure 6.2   A systematic DIRC code.

feature allows the CD to be easily expanded to detect the completion including the check word. Since the transmitted DI codes are not changed, this coding scheme can be easily applied to the large quantity of existing 1-of-n asynchronous designs, providing fault-tolerance without significantly effecting the original circuit structure.

6.2.3   Check Generation and Error Correction

The check word generation process of DIRC, $f(X)$, is defined as Equation 6.7:

$$c = f(X) = \sum_{f=0}^{CN-1} x_f = x_0 + x_1 + \cdots + x_{CN-1} \qquad (6.7)$$

If any one of the code words x_f in a DIRC code word $(x_0, x_1, \cdots, x_{CN-1}, c)$ is corrupted by a fault during the transmission, the likely correct one x'_f can be regenerated at the receiver end. For simplicity, we denote $X_{\neq f}$ to be the received DIRC code word without the corrupted 1-of-n code word x_f:

$$X_{\neq f} = (x_0, \cdots, x_{f-1}, x_{f+1}, \cdots, x_{CN-1}, c) \qquad (6.8)$$

The correct x'_f can then be calculated by applying $X_{\neq f}$ to the error correction process $g(X_{\neq f})$ as described by Equation 6.9:

$$x'_f = g(X_{\neq f}) = c - \sum_{i=0, i \neq f}^{CN-1} x_i = -\left(-c + \sum_{i=0, i \neq f}^{CN-1} x_i \right) \qquad (6.9)$$

In Equation 6.9, subtraction has been transformed to addition so that both the check generation and error correction processes

Table 6.1   DIRC for 1-of-2 codes.

x_0	x_1	c
01	01	01
	10	10
10	01	10
	10	01

Table 6.2   DIRC for 1-of-3 codes.

x_0	x_1	c
001	001	001
	010	010
	100	100
010	001	010
	010	100
	100	001
100	001	100
	010	001
	100	010

can be implemented using the same addition unit as described in Section 6.3. Table 6.1~6.3 give some examples of the DIRC coding scheme for 1-of-n codes with $CN = 2$. The $CN > 2$ cases can be derived from Equation 6.7 and Equation 6.9. Figure 6.3 demonstrates one implementation of a DIRC channel where the check word is generated at the sender while the error correction operation is conducted by the receiver.

6.2.4   Error Filtering

For a code word x_i $(0 \leq i < CN)$ in a DIRC code $(x_0, x_1, \cdots, x_{CN-1}, c)$, the regenerated data word x_i' at the receiver is equal with x_i if no fault occurs. Under the assumption of a 1-bit transient fault, either x_i or x_i' may be altered by a fault but not

Table 6.3   DIRC for 1-of-4 codes.

x_0	x_1	c
0001	0001	0001
	0010	0010
	0100	0100
	1000	1000
0010	0001	0010
	0010	0100
	0100	1000
	1000	0001
0100	0001	0100
	0010	0000
	0100	0001
	1000	0010
1000	0001	1000
	0010	0001
	0100	0010
	1000	0100

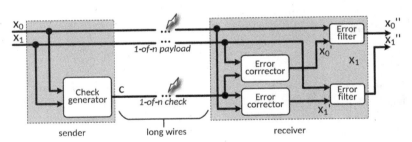

Figure 6.3   Example of a DIRC channel ($CN{=}2$).

both. To obtain the error-free data word x_i'', an error filter $h(x_i, x_i')$ is defined in Equation 6.10:

$$x_i'' = h(x_i, x_i') = x_i \ \& \ x_i' = x_i \ \& \ g(X_{\neq i}) \qquad (6.10)$$

where "&" denotes the logical operation of a C-element rather than a traditional AND operation. If a transient fault happens on one code word x_i during the transmission, it may erase the valid 1 (negative fault) or create a faulty 1 (positive fault) in this 1-of-n code for a while, but eventually the transient fault will disappear. This fault can be filtered using Equation 6.10 because x_i' is a 1-of-n code calculated from the other fault-free codes $X_{\neq i}$. The fault will only create a temporary 01 or 10 to the two-input C-element filter, which will not change the output. Otherwise, if the transient fault happens on the other code words, leading to a temporarily faulty $X_{\neq i}$, the fault-free 1-of-n code x_i is able to filter the faulty bit in the regenerated x_i' as well to ensure the eventual output x_i'' equals x_i. In other words, the C-element implemented & function effectively force the receiver to wait until the fault to fade away if a transient fault corrupt code word is detected. Consequently, the error-free DIRC code word can be obtained as $X'' = (x_0'', x_1'', \cdots, x_{CN-1}'')$.

Taking two 1-of-4 code words x_0 (0010) and x_1 (1000) for example, the check word c is 0001. Assuming a positive transient fault converts x_0 to the faulty 1010, the regenerated x_0' and x_1' are 0010 and 1010 respectively. For x_1', the first 1 from the right is generated from the invalid 1 in the faulty x_0 which can be filtered by using C-elements. Using Equation 6.10, the correct x_0'' and x_1'' are obtained:

$$x_0'' = x_0 \ \& \ x_0' = 0010$$
$$x_1'' = x_1 \ \& \ x_1' = 1000$$

If the check word is faulty while the incoming data words are error-free, both regenerated data words will be erroneous. These errors can also be filtered by the C-elements.

Considering the impact of a transient fault on the long data wires between the sender and the receiver (Figure 6.3), a transient fault may corrupt a 1-of-n code word and convert it into a 2-of-n one (symbol corruption), making one of the operands of Equation 6.10 2-of-n. The faulty 1 will be filtered out by the C-element. The other fault scenarios, including the symbol insertion, deletion and the fault-caused physical-layer deadlock, have a requirement on the data skew (the time difference) between parallel 1-of-n channels. Their probability of occurrence is significantly reduced since the error filter of each DIRC pipeline stage creates one synchronization

Table 6.4   Comparison of different fault-tolerant codes.

Codes	Unordered	Systematic	1-of-n	QDI
Hamming [93]	No	Yes	No	No
Blaum [33]	Yes	Yes	No	Unknown
Cheng and Ho [48]	Yes	Yes	No	No
Zero-Sum [3]	Yes	Yes	No	No
TRDIC [198, 199]	Yes	No	Yes	Yes
DIRC	Yes	Yes	Yes	Yes

point on the forward data path, which synchronizes these parallel 1-of-n data channels (including the $CN+1$ channels for transmitting a DIRC code) at each DIRC pipeline stage, reducing the possibility of the long data skew happening inside a DIRC channel.

It can be concluded that all 1-bit transient faults on 4-phase QDI interconnects can be tolerated by applying DIRC to all 1-of-n code words. The proposed DIRC coding scheme can also tolerate some multi-bit transient faults. If multi-bit, unidirectional transient faults happen in a single word while the other words of this DIRC code are fault-free, the faulty word can be corrected. Applying DIRC, the original data sequence cannot be easily disordered, and the harmful physical-layer deadlock becomes less likely to happen.

6.2.5   Code Evaluation

Table 6.4 summarizes the characteristics of the DIRC and several existing fault-tolerant codes. Since a large number of existing asynchronous designs [30, 75, 200, 244] use 1-of-n codes to encode data, the hardware support for 1-of-n implementation is also important. Among these coding schemes, the DIRC code is the only one which is unordered, systematic and can be implemented using QDI circuits.

It has been mentioned in Section 2.3 that coding efficiency can be measured by the code rate [12] as illustrated in Equation 2.1. Both code rates of the 1-of-2 and 1-of-4 codes are 0.50. Due to the use of DIRC, one extra check word is added for every CN 1-of-n data words. The code rate of the DIRC (R_{DIRC}) can be expressed as Equation 6.11. It is decreased by $\frac{1}{CN+1}$ compared with the code rate of the original 1-of-n code.

$$R_{\mathrm{DIRC}} = \frac{CN \cdot log_2 n}{n(CN+1)} \tag{6.11}$$

It can be inferred from Equation 6.11 that the code rate of the DIRC code increases with CN. In the worst-case of $CN = 2$, the code rates of 1-of-2 and 1-of-4 codes are both 0.33, which is 33.3% less than their original code rates. When CN increases to 5, the code rate reduction drops to only 16.7%. The code rates of most existing code redundancy techniques decrease further when applied to 1-of-n codes. For example, the code rate decreases to 40.0% when applying the parity check to 1-of-4 codes [198]. When applying the TRDIC code [199] by changing 1-of-n codes to 2-of-(n+1) codes to obtain fault-tolerance, the code rate decreases by 33.3% for 1-of-2 codes (from 0.50 to 0.33) and 20.0% for 1-of-4 codes (from 0.50 to 0.40), respectively.

6.3 IMPLEMENTATION OF DIRC PIPELINES

Figure 6.4 presents an implementation of a DIRC pipeline stage capable of transmitting one DIRC code (x_0, x_1, c) with two 1-of-n code words (CN=2). It includes 1-of-n adders, error filters, CDs and an acknowledge generator (AckGen).

6.3.1 1-of-n Adders and Error Filters

The check word generation and error correction processes can be implemented using QDI circuits. The key components are 1-of-n adders implementing the addition operation of 1-of-n (or m-of-n) codes. In Figure 6.4, the upper two adders are used to regenerate data words, while the bottom one is used to generate the check word. If no fault happens, the operands of the adder are all 1-of-n codes. When faults convert 1-of-n codes to erroneous m-of-n codes, the adder produces m-of-n codes as well, but those faulty bits will be filtered by the error filters.

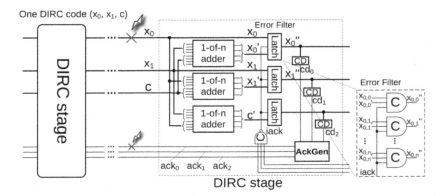

Figure 6.4 Implementation of a DIRC pipeline stage delivering two 1-of-n code words ($CN=2$).

The mathematical representation of a 1-of-n adder unit can be described by Equation 6.12:

$$s_i = \bigcup_{j=0}^{n-1} \left(a_j \ \& \ b_{(n+i-j) \bmod n} \right) \tag{6.12}$$

where a subscript denotes the index of a bit in the possibly m-of-n code words A $(a_0, a_1, \cdots, a_{n-1})$, B $(b_0, b_1, \cdots, b_{n-1})$ and S $(s_0, s_1, \cdots, s_{n-1})$. S is the sum of A and B.

Proof. According to Equation 6.6, we have:

$$s_i = 1 \iff \exists j, k \in [0, n) \ (((j+k) \bmod n = i) \wedge (a_j \ \& \ b_k = 1))$$

Therefore, we have Equation 6.12. □

Figure 6.5 shows a hardware implementation of a 1-of-2 and a 1-of-4 adders. Only C-elements and OR-gates are utilized to ensure the adder is QDI. Figure 6.6 shows the structures of 1-of-n adders when a adder has multiple operands (corresponding to different CN). It can be inferred that the 1-of-n adder is a modulo one which involves rotating a code by a distance specified by the other. The area of the adder approximately scales with n^2.

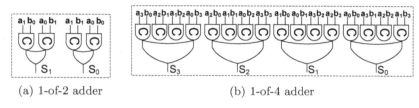

(a) 1-of-2 adder   (b) 1-of-4 adder

Figure 6.5   Implementation of 1-of-n adders.

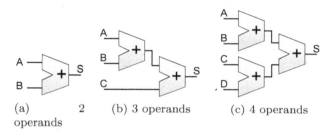

(a) 2 operands   (b) 3 operands   (c) 4 operands

Figure 6.6   Construction of 1-of-n adder trees with multiple operands.

During the error correction process, a negating operation of an m-of-n code is required in Equation 6.9. According to Equation 6.2 and Equation 6.5, the negation of a 1-of-n code $A = (a_0, \cdots, a_i, \cdots, a_{n-1})$ is merely a bit-reshuffle as described in Equation 6.13:

$$-A = (a_0, \cdots, a_{(n-i) \bmod n}, \cdots, a_1) \qquad (6.13)$$

The error filters described by Equation 6.10 are combined with pipeline latches to improve area and speed performance. The resulting 3-input C-element latch structure for data words is then used as depicted in Figure 6.4, while the asynchronous latch for check words is built from the normal 2-input C-elements.

6.3.2   Generation of Check Words

The most reliable way of generating the check word is to use the recovered data as shown in Figure 6.7, but the 1-of-n adder for the generation of check words is then added to the critical path of the

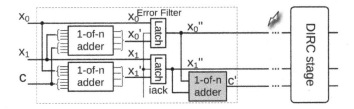

Figure 6.7 Generating the check word using recovered data words.

pipeline. In the actual hardware implementation of DIRC pipelines, the check word is generated from the incoming data words rather than the recovered data words, as shown in Figure 6.4. Consequently, the check word generation process and the error correction process run in parallel, which reduces the forward delay. The newly generated check word may be erroneous if the incoming data word is wrong. Since the wrong data words will be corrected and not propagated to the next stage, the check word would not be an issue as long as no fault occurs on the corrected data to the next pipeline stage. Under the assumption of a 1-bit transient fault, executing the error correction and check word generation processes in parallel is acceptable since the possibility of faults occurring on wires of adjacent stages is extremely low in practice. In an environment requiring especially high fault-tolerance instead of permanence, the implementation shown in Figure 6.7 can be employed with prolonged pipeline delay.

6.3.3 Redundant Protection of Acknowledge Wires

It has been described in Section 5.3 that *ack* signals are important for a reliable QDI pipeline. A new protection technique, namely redundant protection of acknowledge wires (RPA), is proposed to protect acknowledge wires from transient faults. As shown in Figure 6.8a, three C-elements are used to build an acknowledge generator (AckGen) which outputs three acknowledge signals: ack_0, ack_1 and ack_2. The three inputs of AckGen are cd_0, cd_1 and cd_2 which come directly from the completion detection circuit. The original CD of a pipeline stage, as shown in Figure 6.8b, can be easily

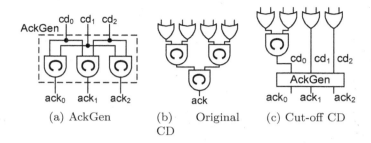

(a) AckGen   (b)   Original   (c) Cut-off CD
CD

Figure 6.8   Implementation of an acknowledge generator (Ack-Gen).

divided into three sub-CDs by cutting off the bottom one or two C-elements when the number of 1-of-n slices of a pipeline stage is at least three as depicted in Figure 6.8c. The generation of acknowledge signals is presented in Equation 6.14 where "&" denotes the logical operation of a two-input C-element. Finally, at the input side of the previous stage, an inverted 3-input C-element is used to generate the *iack* triggering the asynchronous latches (Figure 6.4).

$$
\begin{cases}
iack_0 = cd_0 \ \& \ cd_1 \\
iack_1 = cd_0 \ \& \ cd_2 \\
iack_2 = cd_1 \ \& \ cd_2 \\
iack = \neg(iack_0 \ \& \ iack_1 \ \& \ iack_2)
\end{cases}
\tag{6.14}
$$

It can be found that the *iack* flips only when cd_0, cd_1 and cd_2 are all set high or all reset low. Any one of the three acknowledge signals relies on two sub-CDs and any one sub-CD decides two acknowledge signals. This cross-related structure ensures that a 1-bit transient fault on any one of the acknowledge wires will always be masked. As shown in Figure 6.8, the area overhead brought by RPA is negligible compared with the large number of data latches because only one extra C-element is added to the original CD. This technique can be implemented independently of the DIRC coding scheme to protect acknowledge wires in all QDI pipelines.

6.3.4   Variants of DIRC Pipelines

DIRC and RPA can be easily used in existing 4-phase 1-of-n QDI pipelines to provide fault-tolerance with little modification.

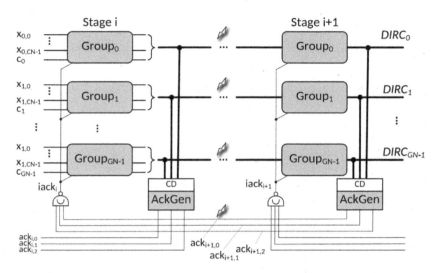

Figure 6.9   A DIRC QDI pipeline.

Figure 6.9 presents two contiguous stages of a DIRC pipeline. Assuming the unprotected basic QDI pipeline comprises N 1-of-n channel(s) where $N \geq 1$, all the N 1-of-n slices in a pipeline stage can be divided into GN groups ($GN \geq 1$). For pipelines with different widths, it can be protected with different levels of fault-tolerance using various schemes complying with the following rules:

- When $N = 1$, the original pipeline contains only one 1-of-n channel. Instead of using DIRC which requires at least two data words to generate a check word, the double-check technique [106] can be used to protect the pipeline from transient faults by duplicating the only 1-of-n channel.

- When $2 \leq N \leq 3$, DIRC can be used directly by adding a check word, resulting in a DIRC channel containing two or three data channels and one check channel ($GN = 1$).

- When $N = 4$, the four 1-of-n data channels can be either taken as one group which needs one extra check channel to

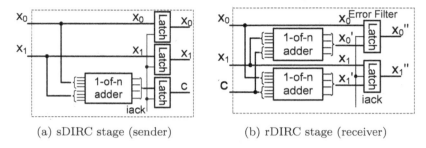

(a) sDIRC stage (sender)   (b) rDIRC stage (receiver)

Figure 6.10   Incomplete DIRC stages.

build a DIRC pipeline ($GN = 1$), or divided into two groups, each of which is added with one check channel ($GN = 2$).

- When $N > 4$, the N 1-of-n data channels can be divided into GN groups to build a DIRC pipeline. Different groups can have different numbers of data channels. For simplicity, in the following it is assumed that N 1-of-n channels are evenly divided into GN groups, each of which contains CN 1-of-n data channels so that $N = CN \cdot GN$. In the DIRC pipeline, one extra 1-of-n check word is added to each group to achieve fault-tolerance, resulting in a DIRC pipeline stage with $GN \cdot (CN + 1)$ slices. Each DIRC code contains CN code words and one check word.

In a DIRC pipeline, *complete* DIRC stages (Figure 6.4) are placed between a pair of *incomplete* DIRC stages, which are the sender and receiver denoted by sDIRC and rDIRC, respectively, as shown in Figure 6.10. The incomplete sDIRC stage generates the check words but omit the check of data words, requiring one 1-of-n adder as the check generator for each DIRC channel. The total number of adders is thus reduced to GN. The rDIRC stage corrects potential errors on the data words but omit the generation of check word, requiring N 1-of-n adders as error correctors for each channel. They are smaller than intermediate complete DIRC pipeline stages. The complete DIRC stage can correct errors and generate check words simultaneously, requiring a total of $(N + GN)$ 1-of-n adders.

6.3.4.1 Latency and Area

In QDI pipelines, the forward data path and the backward *ack* path between two contiguous pipeline stages form a loop (Figure 5.8) whose latency decides the saturation throughput of the pipeline. The loop latency is the sum of the latency of both the forward and the backward paths. The 1-of-n adders are the main contributor of the introduced latency overhead on the forward path. As shown in Figure 6.6, the depth of these adders is linear with $\log_2 CN$. CD is the main latency contributor on the backward *ack* path. As illustrated in Figure 6.8b, CD is normally implemented as a C-element tree while its latency scales approximately with $\log_2 N(1 + 1/CN)$ for a complete DIRC stage and $\log_2 N$ for an unprotected basic stage. A detailed latency analytical model will be presented in Section 6.4. It is found that the speed overhead of applying DIRC is less the 50% in many cases.

Considering the area overhead, 1-of-n adders are the main contributor: The area of a single adder unit increases with the code width n for the 1-of-n channel. It can be noticed from Figure 6.5 that the number of 2-input C-elements in the adder unit increases with n^2. The narrow 1-of-2 adder is much smaller than the 1-of-4 adder. The number of 1-of-n adders in a DIRC stage increases with CN as shown in Figure 6.6. The RPA introduced in Section 6.3.3 rarely brings any overhead. Therefore, it can be inferred that, to control the area overhead under a reasonable level brought by the DIRC code, a relatively narrow 1-of-n code should be used and the width of the DIRC code should be small as well, in which case the interconnects can get more fault-tolerance capability. Latency and area analytical models are built in Section 6.4 to evaluate of the DIRC implementation. Detailed experimental results are revealed in Section 6.5.

6.3.4.2 Different Construction Patterns

Since the DIRC code is systematic in that the original data words are transmitted transparently, it allows DIRC pipeline stages to be placed arbitrarily in an unprotected basic QDI pipeline as a way to protect some of the chosen but not all pipeline segments. According to the practical fault-tolerance requirement, the DIRC

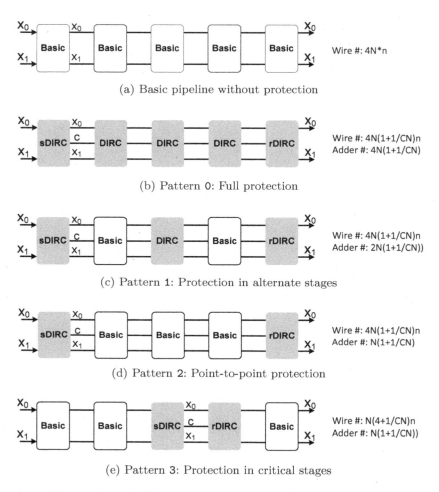

(a) Basic pipeline without protection

(b) Pattern 0: Full protection

(c) Pattern 1: Protection in alternate stages

(d) Pattern 2: Point-to-point protection

(e) Pattern 3: Protection in critical stages

Figure 6.11   Different construction of DIRC pipelines.

pipeline using different construction patterns can provide enough fault-tolerance for the communication infrastructure with a moderate and reasonable hardware overhead. This would make DIRC especially attractive to large-scale communication-enteric fabrics such as NoCs and buses.

As shown in Figure 6.11, DIRC and basic pipeline stages are mutually exchangeable. Arbitrary basic stages can be replaced with DIRC ones to strengthen their fault-tolerance. Figure 6.11a presents an unprotected basic pipeline with five stages. There are $4N \cdot n$ data wires between the first and the last pipeline stages. In Figure 6.11b, all pipeline stages are complete DIRC ones, providing a *full-protection* (pattern 0). This pattern makes the pipeline robust enough to tolerate all 1-bit transient faults between any contiguous pipeline stages but incurs a large area overhead. By adding one check channel to each DIRC group, the pipeline contains $N(1 + 1/CN)$ parallel 1-of-n channels. In total, there are $4N(1 + 1/CN)n$ data wires and $4N(1 + 1/CN)$ adders are added to each pipeline stage.

Since DIRC codes are systematic, it is allowed to place DIRC pipeline stages at discontinuous locations to reduce the area overhead. In a design, some parts may be critical or more susceptible to faults than other parts. In this case, DIRC stages can be used only for these parts to sufficiently protect the overall communication. As shown in Figure 6.11, DIRC stages can be placed using an arbitrary or specific pattern, including full protection (pattern 0 as in Figure 6.11b), protection in alternate stages (pattern 1 as in Figure 6.11c), point-to-point protection (pattern 2 as in Figure 6.11d) and protection in critical stages (pattern 3 as in Figure 6.11e). The protected pipeline segment starts from an sDIRC stage and ends with a rDIRC stage. Between the sDIRC and rDIRC stages, extra long wires are introduced for the redundant check words.

6.3.4.3 DIRC in Asynchronous NoCs

DIRC code is especially suitable for large-scale QDI NoCs due to its systematic and DI nature. A 3×3 mesh asynchronous NoC is illustrated in Figure 6.12a. Network interfaces (NIs) are used to connect synchronous IP cores to the asynchronous network. They implement the necessary transformation between the synchronous and asynchronous domains. The large number of long asynchronous links connecting routers are susceptible to transient faults. DIRC stages can be flexibly distributed in the network to protect on-chip communication. As an example, DIRC stages can be placed at the NIs as depicted in Figure 6.12a. In this scenario, the check word generation and the error correction operations are only executed when data passes NIs, providing an end-to-end protection. DIRC

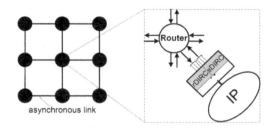

(a) Using DIRC stages at network interfaces

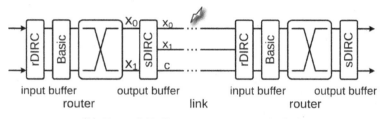

(b) Using DIRC to protect a specific link

Figure 6.12   DIRC applied to asynchronous NoCs.

can also protect specific links or routers. Figure 6.12b illustrates an example where a specific inter-router link is protected.

6.4   LATENCY AND AREA MODELS

The DIRC coding scheme has been proposed to protect QDI communication from transient faults. Applying DIRC codes and RPA for acknowledge wires, the resulting DIRC pipelines can be constructed in a flexible way to satisfy different fault-tolerance requirement. This section builds detailed latency and area analytical models to evaluate the hardware overhead of different DIRC pipelines with different construction patterns.

To make the following analytical models easy to follow, some constants and parameters used through out this section are listed below:

- **N and n:** An unprotected basic QDI pipeline contains N parallel 1-of-n channels.

- **CN**: The number of 1-of-n data words in one DIRC code word or the number of 1-of-n data channels in a DIRC channel.

- **GN**: The number of DIRC channels or the number of groups of data words after using DIRC. For simplicity, it is assumed that both CN and GN are integers and $N = CN \cdot GN$.

- **α**: Ratio of the area of 3-input to 2-input C-element.

- **β**: Ratio of the area of 2-input OR gate to C-element.

- **k**: Ratio of the area of long link wires (A_w) between two basic pipeline stages to the area of one basic asynchronous latch (A_{basic}).

6.4.1 Latency Analysis

The saturation throughput of a QDI pipeline is determined by the equivalent loop period of two contiguous pipeline stages where a forward data path and a backward *ack* path form a loop, as shown in Figure 5.8. A latency model is built to evaluate the speed overhead of DIRC pipelines. For simplicity, it is assumed that cell delays for positive and negative transitions are the same while the wire delay is zero. The loop latency T can be expressed by Equation 6.15, where t_{latch}, t_{CD} and t_{comb} are the propagation latency of an asynchronous latch, the CD and other combinational circuits, respectively. The equivalent period is approximated to $2T$.

$$T = 2t_{\text{latch}} + t_{\text{CD}} + t_{\text{comb}} \qquad (6.15)$$

Assume a basic pipeline stage (denoted by a subscript of "basic") contains N 1-of-n slices. According to the implementation shown in Figure 2.8, an asynchronous latch is built from 2-input C-elements whose propagation latency is t_{c2}. CD is a tree constructed by n-input OR-gates and 2-input C-elements. Its delay $t_{\text{CD,basic}}$ is determined by the propagation latency of an n-input OR-gate (t_{OR}) and the depth of the C-element tree $(\lceil \log_2 N \rceil)$. If the delay of the inverter used to invert the *ack* signal at the latch input is ignored, the loop latency of a basic pipeline T_{basic} can be estimated using the following parameters:

$$t_{\text{latch,basic}} = t_{c2} \quad t_{\text{CD,basic}} = t_{\text{OR}} + \lceil \log_2 N \rceil \cdot t_{c2} \quad t_{\text{comb,basic}} = 0$$

For a DIRC pipeline using both DIRC and RPA, as shown in Figure 6.4, 1-of-n adders are added to the data path. The asynchronous latch for data words uses 3-input C-elements instead of 2-input ones. The redundant check words increase the tree depth of the CD to $\lceil \log_2(N + GN) \rceil \approx \lceil \log_2 N \rceil + 1$. Using RPA does not change the depth of the tree but induces a delay of a 3-input C-element at the input side. Therefore, the loop latency of a DIRC pipeline T_{DIRC} can be estimated using Equation 6.16:

$$t_{\text{latch,DIRC}} = t_{c3} \quad t_{\text{comb,DIRC}} = t_{\text{adder}}$$
$$t_{\text{CD,DIRC}} \approx t_{\text{OR}} + (\lceil \log_2 N \rceil + 1)t_{c2} + t_{c3} \tag{6.16}$$

where t_{c3} and t_{adder} are the propagation latency of a 3-input C-element and a 1-of-n adder, respectively. t_{c3} and t_{c2} depend on the timing of the chosen cell library and the implementation of C-elements. Normally their delays are similar. According to the implementation of 1-of-n adders discussed in Section 6.3.1, t_{adder} can be estimated using Equation 6.17:

$$t_{\text{adder}} = \lceil \log_2 CN \rceil \cdot (t_{c2} + t_{\text{OR}}) \tag{6.17}$$

Therefore, the loop latency of a DIRC pipeline can be expressed by Equation 6.18:

$$T_{\text{DIRC}} = T_{\text{basic}} + (3t_{c3} - t_{c2}) + t_{\text{adder}} \tag{6.18}$$

It can be concluded that, when DIRC and RPA are both utilized, t_{adder} is the only variable in timing that determine the pipeline speed overhead as all other variables in Equation 6.18 are effectively constants. The propagation latency of the adder is proportional to $\lceil \log_2 CN \rceil$. Usually, the number of data channels in a DIRC code (CN) is far less than the total data channel number for a wide pipeline ($CN \ll N$). As analyzed in the next Section 6.4.2, a large CN could induce a large area overhead. The typical value of CN is normally 2 while the value of N depends on the link width and is usually much larger. Consequently, $t_{\text{adder}} \ll T_{\text{basic}}$. In this case, the loop latency of a DIRC pipeline, T_{DIRC} is generally less than $2T_{\text{basic}}$. In other words, applying DIRC on QDI pipelines introduces only less than 50% speed overhead comparing against the unprotected pipeline, which is actually a low speed overhead compared with other techniques.

6.4.2 Area Model for One Stage

DIRC keeps the original data words thanks to its systematic encoding scheme. The internal pipeline stages or combinational circuits between two DIRC stages can therefore access to the original data directly. This feature makes it possible to construct DIRC pipelines using different patterns, which provide designers with flexible choices. Since different DIRC pipeline patterns may have quite different area overhead, several area models are built to analyze the area overhead of DIRC pipelines.

An area model for a single pipeline stage is first built to analyze the area of different pipeline stages, including the basic unprotected (Figure 2.8), DIRC (Figure 6.4), sDIRC and rDIRC pipeline stages (Section 6.3.4, where sDIRC and rDIRC are incomplete DIRC pipeline stages used by the sender and the receiver, respectively, as shown in Figure 6.10). Since the area overhead introduced by the proposed RPA technique for the protection of acknowledge wires is rather marginal compared with the overhead caused by DIRC and the technique can be applied independently, this area model evaluates only the area overhead brought by applying DIRC without RPA.

The area of a single pipeline stage A can be expressed by Equation 6.19, where A_{latch}, A_{CD} and A_{comb} are the area of the asynchronous latch, the CD and other combinational circuits, respectively. Wire area is omitted in the evaluation for simplicity.

$$A = A_{\text{latch}} + A_{\text{CD}} + A_{\text{comb}} \tag{6.19}$$

For a basic unprotected 1-of-n pipeline delivering N data words, the area $A_{\text{latch,basic}}$ of the asynchronous latch built from 2-input C-elements can be estimated according to Equation 6.20, where A_{c2} is the area of a 2-input C-element. The area of the CD $A_{\text{CD,basic}}$

(whose internal structure is depicted in Figure 6.8b) can be approximated by Equation 6.21, where A_{OR} is the area of an n-input OR-gate. For the basic pipeline, $A_{comb,basic} = 0$ as there is no combinational logic between two pipeline stages. By ignoring the area of the inverter used to invert the ack signal as it is small, the overall area of a basic pipeline stage A_{basic} can be then estimated using Equation 6.22.

$$A_{\text{latch,basic}} = N \cdot n \cdot A_{c2} \tag{6.20}$$

$$A_{\text{CD,basic}} = N \cdot A_{\text{OR}} + (N-1) \cdot A_{c2} \approx N \cdot (A_{\text{OR}} + A_{c2}) \tag{6.21}$$

$$A_{\text{basic}} = A_{\text{latch,basic}} + A_{\text{CD,basic}} \tag{6.22}$$

When DIRC is applied to the basic pipeline, the N 1-of-n data channels are divided into GN groups, each of which contains CN 1-of-n data channels ($N = CN \cdot GN$) and one check channel. As a result, each DIRC stage contains ($N + GN$) slices. As described in Section 6.3.1, 3-input C-elements are used to latch the data words and 2-input C-elements are used to latch the check words in DIRC stages. The latch area $A_{\text{latch,DIRC}}$ can be estimated by Equation 6.23, where A_{c3} is the area of a 3-input C-element. The CD of a DIRC stage needs to detect ($N + GN$) 1-of-n codes. Its area $A_{\text{CD,DIRC}}$ can be estimated by Equation 6.24.

$$A_{\text{latch,DIRC}} = n(N \cdot A_{c3} + GN \cdot A_{c2}) = \left(\frac{A_{c3}}{A_{c2}} + \frac{1}{CN}\right) \cdot A_{\text{latch,basic}} \tag{6.23}$$

$$A_{\text{CD,DIRC}} = (N + GN)(A_{\text{OR}} + A_{c2}) - A_{c2} \approx \left(1 + \frac{1}{CN}\right) \cdot A_{\text{CD,basic}} \tag{6.24}$$

As shown in Figure 6.4, a complete DIRC stage has ($N + GN$) 1-of-n adders where N adders are used to regenerate data words and GN adders are used to generate check words. The area of a single 1-of-n adder unit A_a increases with n and can be estimated as Equation 6.25. When $CN > 2$, each adder becomes an adder tree containing ($CN - 1$) 1-of-n adder units as depicted in Figure 6.6. It is assumed that the area of the adders utilized to regenerate data words and produce check words is $A_{\text{adder,data}}$ (i.e. $A_{\text{comb,rDIRC}}$) and $A_{\text{adder,check}}$ (i.e. $A_{\text{comb,sDIRC}}$), respectively.

$A_{\text{adder,data}}$, and $A_{\text{adder,check}}$ can be expressed using Equation 6.26 and 6.27 while their sum is A_{adder} (i.e. $A_{\text{comb,DIRC}}$).

$$A_a = n^2 \cdot A_{c2} + n \cdot A_{\text{OR}} \tag{6.25}$$

$$A_{\text{comb,rDIRC}} = A_{\text{adder,data}} = N \cdot (CN - 1) \cdot A_a \tag{6.26}$$

$$A_{\text{comb,sDIRC}} = A_{\text{adder,check}} = N \cdot \left(1 - \frac{1}{CN}\right) \cdot A_a \tag{6.27}$$

$$A_{\text{comb,DIRC}} = A_{\text{adder}} = N \cdot \left(CN - \frac{1}{CN}\right) \cdot A_a \tag{6.28}$$

Assuming $A_{c3} = \alpha A_{c2}$ and $A_{\text{OR}} = \beta A_{c2}$, Equation 6.26 to 6.28 can be rewritten into Equation 6.29 to Equation 6.31. The area of a complete DIRC stage A_{DIRC} is depicted in Equation 6.32.

$$A_{\text{adder,data}} = (CN - 1)(n + \beta) \cdot A_{\text{latch,basic}} \tag{6.29}$$

$$A_{\text{adder,check}} = \left(1 - \frac{1}{CN}\right)(n + \beta) \cdot A_{\text{latch,basic}} \tag{6.30}$$

$$A_{\text{adder}} = \left(CN - \frac{1}{CN}\right)(n + \beta) \cdot A_{\text{latch,basic}} \tag{6.31}$$

$$\begin{aligned} A_{\text{DIRC}} = & \left(\alpha + \frac{1}{CN}\right) \cdot A_{\text{latch,basic}} + \left(1 + \frac{1}{CN}\right) \cdot A_{\text{CD,basic}} \\ & + \left(CN - \frac{1}{CN}\right)(n + \beta) \cdot A_{\text{latch,basic}} \end{aligned} \tag{6.32}$$

Comparing Equation 6.32 with Equation 6.22, it can be found that 1-of-n adders is the major contributor to the area overhead (the third term in Equation 6.32). According to Equation 6.25, the area of a single 1-of-n adder unit A_a increases along with n^2, so that 1-of-4 DIRC pipelines have larger area overhead than 1-of-2 ones with the same data width. For a 1-of-n DIRC pipeline stage with a fixed data width, A_{adder} increases approximately linearly with CN while the area overhead brought by the latch and CD decreases slightly according to Equation 6.32. As a result, the area of a DIRC stage increases with CN. Similarly, area of the incomplete DIRC stages, sDIRC and rDIRC, can be estimated using Equation 6.33 and 6.34.

$$\begin{aligned} A_{\text{sDIRC}} = & \left(1 + \frac{1}{CN}\right) \cdot A_{\text{latch,basic}} + \left(1 + \frac{1}{CN}\right) \cdot A_{\text{CD,basic}} \\ & + \left(1 - \frac{1}{CN}\right)(n + \beta) \cdot A_{\text{latch,basic}} \end{aligned} \tag{6.33}$$

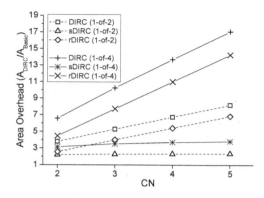

Figure 6.13 Area overhead estimation of a single pipeline stage.

$$A_{rDIRC} = \alpha A_{latch,basic} + A_{CD,basic} + (CN - 1)(n + \beta) \cdot A_{latch,basic}$$
$$(6.34)$$

According to their transistor counts [210], the area ratio of 3-input to 2-input C-element (α) and the area ratio of 2-input OR gate to 2-input C-element (β) can be estimated as:

$$\alpha \approx 1.25 \qquad \beta \approx 0.5$$

Figure 6.13 presents an estimation of the area overhead different DIRC pipeline stages with different configurations. The baseline is the area of basic pipeline stages. The Y-axis is the ratio of the area of DIRC (or sDIRC, rDIRC) stages to the area of the basic pipeline stages, measuring the area overhead. CN represents the number of data words in a DIRC code. As Figure 6.13 shows, for a complete 1-of-2 DIRC pipeline stage with $CN = 2$, the ratio A_{DIRC}/A_{basic} is approximately 3.8; when CN increases to 5, the ratio rises to 8.2. For a 1-of-4 DIRC pipeline stage, A_{DIRC}/A_{basic} is approximately 6.6 when $CN = 2$, and 17.0 when $CN = 5$. 1-of-4 pipeline stages have a steeper gradient compared with 1-of-2 ones. Consequently, if we consider only complete DIRC stages, applying DIRC to 1-of-2 pipeline with $CN = 2$ incurs the least area overhead. Compared with complete DIRC pipeline stages, the incomplete sDIRC and rDIRC stages incur less area overhead. The sDIRC stage has the lowest gradient with CN. The ratio A_{sDIRC}/A_{basic} increases slightly with a rising CN, from 2.2 to 2.3 for 1-of-2 pipelines and from 3.1 to 3.8 for 1-of-4 pipelines.

6.4.3 Models for Different Constructions

The area of a pipeline can be estimated as the total area of all pipeline stages and long wires. For the purpose of simplicity, it is assumed that all long inter-stage wires have the same area (short internal wires are ignored). A_{wire} is the area of $N \cdot n$ wires between two contiguous basic pipeline stages. When applied with DIRC, the number of wires increases to $N \cdot n \cdot (1 + 1/CN)$. Therefore, the wire area between two contiguous stages is $(1 + 1/CN) \cdot A_{\text{wire}}$ in a protected pipeline segment (*ack* wires are ignored due to their small number). The original basic pipeline stages between the sDIRC and rDIRC are expanded due to the check words. The area of an expanded basic pipeline stage (A_{eBasic}) can be estimated by Equation 6.35. The area of a whole pipeline (AP) can be estimated using Equation 6.36:

$$A_{\text{eBasic}} = \left(1 + \frac{1}{CN}\right) \cdot A_{\text{latch}} + A_{\text{CD,DIRC}} \approx \left(1 + \frac{1}{CN}\right) \cdot A_{\text{basic}}$$

(6.35)

$$AP \approx a A_{\text{basic}} + b A_{\text{eBasic}} + c A_{\text{sDIRC}} + d A_{\text{DIRC}} + e A_{\text{rDIRC}} + f A_{\text{wire}}$$
(6.36)

where a, b, c, d, e, f are constants for a specific pipeline.

Let us take the 5-stage pipeline as shown in Figure 6.11a as an example. The area of a basic pipeline AP_{basic} can be calculated using Equation 6.37:

$$AP_{\text{basic}} = 5 A_{\text{basic}} + 4 A_{\text{wire}}$$
(6.37)

If the pipeline is fully protected using three complete DIRC stages and two incomplete DIRC stages as shown in Figure 6.11b, the pipeline area $AP_{\text{DIRC,P0}}$ can be estimated by Equation 6.38:

$$AP_{\text{DIRC,P0}} = 3 A_{\text{DIRC}} + A_{\text{sDIRC}} + A_{\text{rDIRC}} + 4 \left(1 + \frac{1}{CN}\right) \cdot A_{\text{wire}}$$
(6.38)

When protection is applied on alternate stages as illustrated in Figure 6.11c, three DIRC stages are separated by two expanded basic stages. The area of this type of pipeline $AP_{DIRC,P1}$ is shown in Equation 6.39.

$$AP_{\text{DIRC,P1}} = 2A_{\text{eBasic}} + A_{\text{DIRC}} + A_{\text{sDIRC}} + A_{\text{rDIRC}} + 4\left(1 + \frac{1}{CN}\right) \cdot A_{\text{wire}}$$
(6.39)

The area of pipelines with point-to-point protection $AP_{DIRC,P2}$ as shown in Figure 6.11d and pipelines with protection on a critical-stage $AP_{DIRC,P3}$ as shown in Figure 6.11e can be estimated by Equation 6.40 and Equation 6.41, respectively:

$$AP_{\text{DIRC,P2}} = 3A_{\text{eBasic}} + A_{\text{sDIRC}} + A_{\text{rDIRC}} + 4\left(1 + \frac{1}{CN}\right) \cdot A_{\text{wire}}$$
(6.40)

$$AP_{\text{DIRC,P3}} = 3A_{\text{basic}} + A_{\text{sDIRC}} + A_{\text{rDIRC}} + \left(4 + \frac{1}{CN}\right) \cdot A_{\text{wire}}$$
(6.41)

To discuss the area overhead of a whole 5-stage pipeline, we consider two different assumptions on the wire area: $A_{\text{wire}} = 0$ or $A_{\text{wire}} > 0$.

- *The wire area is assumed to be zero* $(A_{\text{wire}} = 0)$:

  Using Equation 6.35 to Equation 6.41, the area overhead estimation of the pipelines using different patterns is summarized in Figure 6.14. The area of the basic pipeline is used as the baseline. The Y-axis represents the area overhead introduced by applying DIRC, which is the ratio of the area of DIRC pipelines to the corresponding basic pipelines $(AP_{\text{DIRC}}/AP_{\text{basic}})$. It can be found that, the area overhead increases approximately linearly with CN for all pipelines patterns. The pipeline protecting only the critical stages (pattern 3) brings the least redundant circuit and the smallest area overhead.

  As shown by the area estimation, DIRC pipelines using different construction patterns have a quite different area overhead. If DIRC is used to protect some specific or only the critical

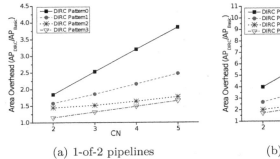
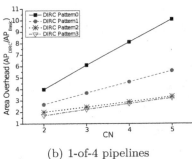

(a) 1-of-2 pipelines

(b) 1-of-4 pipelines

Figure 6.14 Area overhead of different pipelines (wire area $A_{\text{wire}} = 0$).

pipeline segments, the incurred area overhead is greatly decreased.

- *The wire area is non-zero* $(A_{\text{wire}} = kA_{\text{basic}}, k > 0)$:

  In practical pipelines, the data wires between two contiguous stages are usually long and occupy a lot of area due to the large number of inserted wire-buffers. Assuming that $A_{\text{wire}} = kA_{\text{basic}}$ where k is the ratio of the area of long wires to the area of a basic pipeline stage as shown by Equation 6.22. Its value can vary from design to design as it is decided by the practical circuit after fabrication. The area overhead of different pipelines is re-estimated using the previous model. The fully-protected DIRC pipeline (pattern 0), which has the largest area overhead than other pipelines, is first presented to analyze the effect of k on the worst-case area overhead, as revealed in Figure 6.15. For the fully-protected DIRC pipeline, the number of long wires between two contiguous DIRC stages is $N \cdot (1 + 1/CN) \cdot n$.

  In Figure 6.15, the Y-axis still denotes the area ratio $AP_{\text{DIRC}}/AP_{\text{basic}}$ as in Figure 6.14. 1-of-4 pipelines have a larger area overhead than 1-of-2 pipelines. The area overhead decreases with the growing k. In an extreme condition when wires consume a significantly larger area than pipeline stages, the ratio will approach to $(1 + 1/CN)$. A small k denotes that

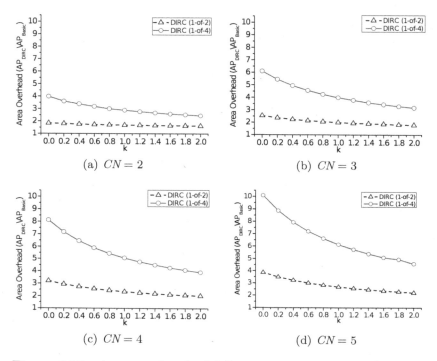

Figure 6.15   Area overhead of fully-protected pipelines ($A_{\text{wire}} = k A_{\text{basic}}$).

the pipeline stages are the main contributor of the whole area. Since the area of complete DIRC stages increases quickly with CN as shown in Figure 6.13, a small CN, such as $CN = 2$, is more acceptable than a larger one. Although the wire number can be reduced by increasing CN, the area of the whole pipeline still increases.

DIRC and basic pipeline stages are mutually exchangeable. Arbitrary basic stages can be replaced by DIRC ones to strengthen fault-tolerance. This feature permits designers to use DIRC flexibly according to the practical design requirement. If the pipeline is constructed using other patterns as depicted by Figure 6.11c to 6.11e, the area overhead can be further reduced. As an example, Figure 6.16 presents the area overhead of 1-of-2 pipelines using the

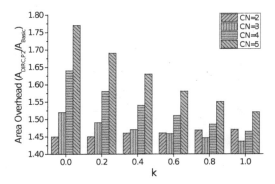

Figure 6.16 Area overhead of 1-of-2 pipelines (point-to-point protection).

point-to-point protection pattern (pattern 2 in Figure 6.11d). Since the area overhead of incomplete DIRC stages is lower than that of a complete DIRC stage (Figure 6.13), increasing CN may not lead to a very large area of pipeline stages but reduces the wire area a lot. As a result, the overall pipeline area can be reduced. Figure 6.16 shows cases where a large CN may reduce the area ratio, such as setting CN to 3 when $k \geq 0.6$. This feature provides flexible choices for designers to design a fault-tolerant system with an acceptable overhead according to their practical requirement.

6.5 EXPERIMENTAL RESULTS

To evaluate the hardware overhead of the proposed fault-tolerant techniques, a number of DIRC pipeline stages, as depicted in Figure 6.9, were implemented using the a 0.13 μm standard cell library and synthesized using the Synopsys design flow with default wire load models. Results were collected from post-synthesis gate-level netlists. Because this is a study of logic circuit design, the implementation technology is not with primary importance. An older but freely available library still provides useful results for relative comparisons of size and speed which should be good as guides across a range of fabrication processes. As a comparison, the unprotected basic pipeline stages, as shown in Figure 2.8, were also implemented. The experiments target evaluating the general performance and overhead of the proposed techniques, which can be achieved by comparing the protected and unprotected asynchronous pipelines.

Table 6.5 shows the detailed experimental results for the $CN = 2$ case, where CN is the number of 1-of-n codes in a DIRC word. The results include the area of a pipeline stage, forward delay, equivalent period and power consumption under different pipeline configurations. The area information was obtained from the synthesis report directly. After the post-synthesis netlists are annotated with gate latency, a SystemC model is used to arbitrarily insert ten extra pipeline stages on the QDI link (interconnection wiring with some existing periodic asynchronous buffers). This can represent a connection across a significant part of a chip where a fault is more likely to occur. In practice, the number of stages will depend on the particular application, but they can be inserted arbitrarily in an asynchronous pipeline. The logically more complex stages will tend to be slower than these simple repeaters and, for modeling purposes, it was assumed that the delay due to long wires could be factored into the delay of gates at layout time. To obtain the transmission delay and power information, millions of data were injected and transmitted through the ten-stage pipelines. The forward delay was measured by averaging the time that a data word traveling through an idle pipeline. By greedily injecting data words to the pipeline as long as the first stage can receive data (so that the asynchronous pipeline is saturated), the equivalent period can be obtained by counting the received data words at the output of the pipeline during a specific length of time. The power consumption was evaluated from the recorded signal transition activities.

6.5.1 Performance Evaluation

Since DIRC pipelines can be constructed using various patterns, the practical pipelines may have quite different areas. To provide a general evaluation, the area results of *complete* DIRC stages are presented to demonstrate the area overhead brought by the DIRC and RPA. Figure 6.17a compares the area of different pipeline stages, which increases with the growing of the data width. DIRC and RPA

Table 6.5 Experimental results of the basic and DIRC pipelines ($CN=2$).

Code	Data Width	GN	Unprotected Basic Piplines				DIRC Pipelines				$AP_{\mathrm{DIRC}}/AP_{\mathrm{basic}}$			
			Area (μm^2)	Delay (ns)	Period (ns)	Power (mW)	Area (μm^2)	Delay (ns)	Period (ns)	Power (mW)	Area	Delay	Period	Power
1-of-2	4	2	193	0.071	1.34	0.41	960	0.260	2.10	0.76	4.97	1.57	3.67	1.86
	8	4	400	0.071	1.80	0.60	1791	0.266	2.65	1.06	4.48	1.47	3.75	1.76
	16	8	822	0.075	2.18	1.03	3321	0.279	3.04	1.79	4.04	1.39	3.73	1.74
	32	16	1727	0.075	2.76	1.74	6482	0.278	3.54	2.99	3.75	1.28	3.70	1.71
	64	32	3227	0.075	2.97	3.04	12673	0.290	3.92	5.34	3.93	1.32	3.86	1.76
	128	64	6481	0.078	3.32	5.55	24204	0.294	4.25	9.28	3.73	1.28	3.80	1.67
1-of-4	4	1	176	0.075	1.19	0.30	1424	0.257	1.93	0.56	8.09	1.63	3.44	1.91
	8	2	365	0.075	1.64	0.45	2842	0.266	2.28	0.93	7.79	1.39	3.56	2.07
	16	4	738	0.074	1.90	0.76	5535	0.277	2.80	1.39	7.50	1.48	3.73	1.84
	32	8	1357	0.075	2.29	1.17	10958	0.278	3.23	2.33	8.08	1.41	3.70	2.00
	64	16	2745	0.075	2.72	1.99	21711	0.301	3.64	4.28	7.91	1.34	4.01	2.15
	128	32	5664	0.079	3.09	3.80	43478	0.317	4.37	7.76	7.68	1.41	4.00	2.04

introduce some area overhead due to the check generation and the error correction mechanisms. On average, the ratio $AP_{\mathrm{DIRC}}/AP_{\mathrm{basic}}$ is around 4.15 for 1-of-2 pipeline stages and 7.84 for 1-of-4 one, as shown in Figure 6.17b. The results are generally consistent with the area model proposed in Section 6.4. When the area of the large number of long wires is considered, the area ratio will decrease. In practical designs where the pipeline may be constructed using different patterns utilizing incomplete DIRC stages, the area overhead can be further reduced.

The forward delay of an asynchronous pipeline stage is the time needed by the data to traverse the asynchronous latch. Figure 6.17c shows that the average forward delay increases slightly with data width. On average, the forward delay of DIRC pipelines is 3.75 times the delay of basic pipelines. The fault-tolerant mechanism of the DIRC pipelines causes an extra delay (DIRC-Basic) which is only 0.21 ns on average for both 1-of-2 and 1-of-4 pipelines.

The equivalent period is an important factor that affects the maximum pipeline throughput as described in Section 6.3.4. Figure 6.17d shows that the period increases with the data width of a pipeline. Since the CD tree is one level shallower in 1-of-4 pipelines than that of 1-of-2 pipelines, 1-of-4 pipelines have relatively shorter periods with the same data width. In most cases, the equivalent period of the DIRC pipeline is less than 1.5 times of the basic pipeline, as revealed in Figure 6.5. The period of the 128-bit wide 1-of-2 DIRC pipeline is only 1.28 times the period of the basic pipeline. Compared with the fault-tolerant design proposed by Jang et al. [106], whose average speed is only half of the basic one without fault-tolerance, the speed overhead of DIRC pipelines is moderate and competitive.

Figure 6.17e shows the power consumption of different pipelines. The redundant circuit introduced by DIRC and RPA leads to extra transition activities. As demonstrated in Figure 6.17f, the power of the 1-of-2 DIRC pipelines is on average 1.75 times greater than basic pipelines, while for 1-of-4 pipelines the ratio is about 2 (Figure 6.17f).

To evaluate the effect of CN (the number of data words included in a DIRC code) on the hardware overhead of DIRC pipeline stages, a number of wide 1-of-2 pipeline stages (60-bit) are implemented

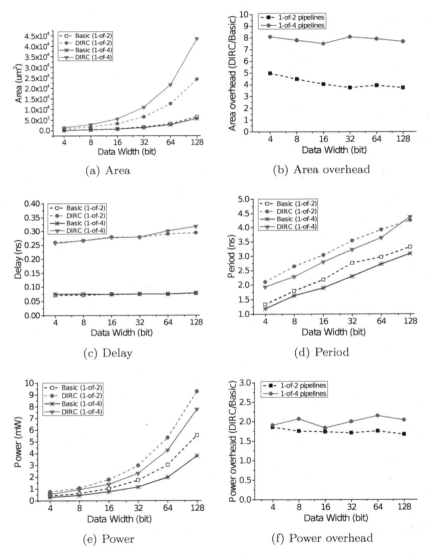

Figure 6.17 Comparison between basic and DIRC pipelines ($CN=2$).

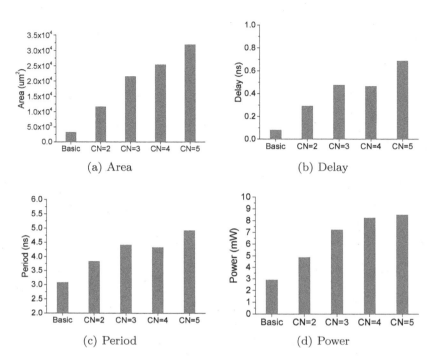

Figure 6.18   Comparison between the basic and DIRC pipelines with different *CN*.

and synthesized. Figure 6.18 compares the basic and the DIRC pipeline stages using different *CN*. It can be found that the area of a pipeline stage increases approximately linearly with *CN*. The forward delay increases as well because a larger *CN* leads to a deeper adder tree inserted into the data path. For the cases with *CN* = 3 and *CN* = 4 cases, the adder trees have the same depth (both are 2-level), but the *CN* = 3 case requires more asynchronous latches for the check words than the *CN* = 4 case, leading to a deeper CD tree. As a result, the speed of the DIRC stage with *CN* = 3 is a little bit slower than the stage with *CN* = 4, as revealed by Figure 6.18b and 6.18c. The power consumption also increases with *CN* due to the increased transition activities.

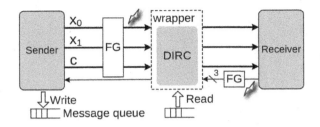

Figure 6.19   Test environment for DIRC pipelines.

6.5.2   Fault-Tolerance Evaluation

To evaluate the fault-tolerance capability of the whole scheme (DIRC+RPA), a SystemC test environment was built according to Figure 6.19. It included a sender, a receiver, a DIRC pipeline stage, fault generators (FGs) and a stage wrapper. The DIRC pipeline stage was a synthesized gate-level netlist while other parts are behavioral level SystemC models. The sender works as the incomplete sDIRC stage (DIRC stage at the sender with check generation functionality), producing random data and corresponding check words to the DIRC stage, while the receiver works as rDIRC stage (DIRC stage at the receiver with error correction functionality). FGs generate random faults on all wires including data wires (between the sender and the DIRC stage) and acknowledge wires (between the DIRC stage and the receiver). The stage wrapper checks the correctness of the output data and produces statistics. A shared message queue is used to store the error-free data being transmitted.

In this test environment, faults can be inserted on any wires at any time, which mimics a real environment where not only 1-bit faults, but also multi-bit faults may happen. Assuming that the occurrence of faults on a single wire is a Poisson process [206], the intervals between adjacent faults are randomized using an exponential distribution. Faults are inserted on different wires independently. The mean interval between faults is set to 1 μs, while the duration of faults is randomized using a uniform distribution between 10 ps and 2 ns. These create a more comprehensive and severe fault environment than most in existing literature [106, 176, 199].

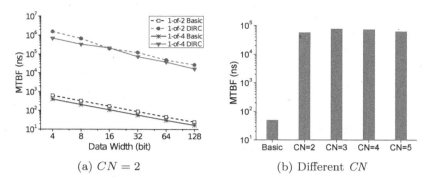

(a) $CN = 2$ (b) Different CN

Figure 6.20   Comparison of MTBF between the basic and DIRC pipelines.

Data are transmitted continuously using the maximum injection rate. In total, one million data packets were transmitted during the simulation.

The transient-fault-tolerance capability is evaluated by the mean time between failures (MTBF). Figure 6.20a illustrates the MTBFs of different pipelines with $CN = 2$. Since the increasing number of wires leads to a higher occurrence of faults, the MTBFs of all pipelines decrease with data width. When the data width is 4-bit, the MTBFs of the DIRC 1-of-2 and 1-of-4 pipelines are 2520 and 1748 times longer than the basic 1-of-2 and 1-of-4 pipelines, respectively. When the data width rises to 128-bit, the ratio becomes 1117 for 1-of-2 pipelines and 1012 for 1-of-4 pipelines. For the basic 1-of-4 pipeline with a data width of 128 bits, 174647 out of 730498 (24%) transient faults result in errors during simulation period, while only 222 out of 1420558 (0.016%) transient faults lead to errors when using DIRC and RPA. (Note that this test uses a multi-bit fault environment so that DIRC pipelines can make errors, while 1-bit transient faults are always fully tolerated.) The resulting MTBF for the basic pipeline is 16 ns while it is prolonged to 16561 ns for the DIRC pipeline. It indicates that the basic pipeline without protection can easily make errors while the fault-tolerance capability of DIRC pipeline increases thousands-fold.

For DIRC pipelines using different CN, Figure 6.20b compares their MTBFs with the MTBF of a wide 1-of-2 basic pipeline of 60 bits. It can be found that, under such a severe environment with multi-bit faults, the MTBFs of all DIRC pipelines are more than 1000 times longer than the basic pipeline. For the basic pipeline, 57067 out of 334679 (17%) faults result in errors while only 62 out of 553143 (0.011%) faults result in errors for the DIRC pipeline with $CN = 5$. This demonstrates that a more severe multi-bit fault environment may largely reduce the MTBF of pipelines (although this rarely happen). Most of the resulting errors can be filtered by using DIRC coding scheme. DIRC pipelines achieve thousands-fold increment of fault-tolerance capability compared with the unprotected basic pipelines.

6.5.3 Comparison with Related Work

Compared to the state-of-the-art work presented in Section 5.5, this implementation of the proposed DIRC coding scheme is QDI. Fault-tolerance is achieved without compromising the timing-robustness nature of QDI circuits. This is one of the major advantages of the DIRC coding scheme compared with most existing fault-tolerant asynchronous designs. Existing fault-tolerant coding schemes for asynchronous communications have already been summarized in Table 6.4. It can be found that, most fault-tolerant designs either protect non-QDI designs [126, 130, 131, 176], or obtain the fault-tolerance by sacrificing the timing-robustness nature of QDI pipelines, such as the fault-tolerant code in [48], Zero-Sum and its extensions in [2, 3], the rail synchronization technique in [158, 159], the fault-tolerant NCL designs in [121] and the fault-tolerant latch architecture in [110]). Some techniques can improve the robustness of QDI circuits but do not qualify as fault-immune [14, 135, 161]. Similar to the proposed DIRC techniques, the double-checking technique [105, 106], the duplication-based asynchronous burst-mode machines (ABMM) [8] and the temporally redundant delay insensitive code (TRDIC) system [199] can protect 4-phase 1-of-n QDI links from transient faults without losing their timing robustness. In addition to timing robustness and fault-tolerance, DIRC coding scheme has also the following advantages:

- DIRC coding scheme tolerates all 1-bit transient faults and some multi-bit transient faults. It can be easily implemented using standard cell libraries and adopted in existing 1-of-n QDI link designs to provide fault-tolerance.

- DIRC pipelines can be implemented in a flexible way using different construction patterns to achieve a flexible fault-tolerance capability with a moderate hardware overhead.

The area and performance overhead incurred by DIRC and RPA techniques has been demonstrated in Table 6.5. The throughput of the DIRC-protected pipeline decreases less than 50%, which is competitive compared with existing research [105, 106, 199]. A latency analytical model has been described in Section 6.4.1 to study the speed overhead, theoretically.

The area overhead of complete 1-of-4 DIRC stages can be as high as roughly 8× compared with unprotected ones. Even the area of a complete 1-of-2 DIRC pipeline stage can be around 4× larger than the basic one. Considering that the double-checking technique incurs an overhead between 2× and 3× [105, 106], using complete DIRC pipeline stages is quite area-consuming. A trade-off was made between the hardware overhead and the fault-tolerance capability in the duplication-based ABMM designs [8] where the function of the implemented circuit was considered. The incomplete duplication resulted in an area overhead less than 2×. This kind of trade-off between the fault-tolerance and the incurred hardware overhead is common and necessary in practical designs where the practical fault-tolerant requirement and the expected hardware overhead should be evaluated in the beginning. Table 6.5 has evaluated the implementation of *complete* DIRC pipelines, while it has been demonstrated that the protected QDI pipeline can be flexibly configured using different construction patterns as depicted in Figure 6.11. *Incomplete* DIRC pipeline stages, such as using sDIRC as the sender stage and rDIRC as the receiver stage, are used to replace complete ones at some segments to reduce hardware overhead. As an example shown in Figure 6.11d, a pair of sDIRC and rDIRC pipeline stages can protect a section of QDI pipelines. The area of a 32-bit 1-of-2 sDIRC and a rDIRC stage ($CN = 2$) is 3643 μm^2 and 4215 μm^2, which is around 2.1× and 2.4× larger than the basic one, respectively. This is competitive compared with the duplicated-based double-checking technique [105, 106] and the full-duplication ABMM design [8].

It should be noticed that these area results represent only the area of pipeline stages. No place and route was done so that the link wires between the stages were not considered. The double-checking or duplication-based techniques result in a full replica of the link while the DIRC coding scheme incurs only $1/CN$ of the link wires ($CN > 1$), avoiding the full duplication of the link. Taking the 32-bit 1-of-2 pipeline with a 64-wire-wide channel for an example, 128 wires are required when using the double-checking technique [105, 106]. For a DIRC pipeline with $CN = 2$, only 96 wires are needed. The overhead is only 50%. Therefore, when the wire area is considered, the area overhead incurred by DIRC is further reduced. As the area analytical model in Section 6.4.2 has shown, when wires consume significantly larger area than pipeline stages, the ratio of the area of protected pipelines to unprotected ones will approach to $(1+1/CN)$, which is 1.5 in the case of $CN = 2$. The fault-tolerant TRDIC coding system [199] avoids the full duplication of a link as well. However, without including the cost of TRDIC encoder and decoder, the area of a protected 2-of-5 pipeline is almost 3× larger than the unprotected 1-of-4 one. Although the cost of the TRDIC encoder and decoder was not given in the original research [199], they would incur extra cost.

The 1-of-n adders in DIRC pipeline stages are currently implemented using the delay-insensitive minterm synthesis (DIMS) approach [232] with standard cells, which is relatively expensive. Custom cells for asynchronous circuit [231] can be used to further reduce the hardware overhead. In addition, 1-of-4 DIRC pipelines are less area efficient that 1-of-2 ones due to the area-consuming 1-of-4 adders. The area of a 32-bit 1-of-4 sDIRC and rDIRC pipeline stage can still reach to 4457 μm^2 and 6837μm^2, which is around 3.3× and 5× larger than the basic one respectively. More details have been discussed in the area model in Section 6.4.2.

6.6 SUMMARY

This chapter proposed a new coding scheme that significantly improves the tolerance of 4-phase 1-of-n QDI links to transient faults, namely the delay-insensitive redundant check (DIRC) code [263]. The DIRC coding scheme tolerates all 1-bit transient faults and some multi-bit transient faults. Furthermore, it can easily be adopted in all existing 1-of-n QDI pipelines to provide fault-tolerance. Since the DIRC code is systematic, it allows DIRC pipeline stages to be placed arbitrarily in an unprotected QDI pipeline. In other words, the fault-tolerance protection can be applied selectively on the pipeline stages requiring high fault-tolerance level. According to the practical fault-tolerance requirement, the DIRC pipeline using different construction patterns can provide enough fault-tolerance for the communication infrastructure with a moderate and reasonable hardware overhead, making DIRC especially attractive to large-scale communication-centric fabrics such as NoCs and buses. DIRC is especially suitable for large-scale communication-centric designs. A new technique named Redundant Protection of Acknowledge wires (RPA) was also proposed to protect acknowledge wires. It can be used independently but causes little hardware overhead.

Detailed experimental results showed that the DIRC pipelines achieve thousands-fold improvement on the fault-tolerance capability even in a severe faulty environment. The hardware overhead of DIRC pipelines (using DIRC plus RPA) is moderate and can be further reduced using different construction patterns. In most cases, the DIRC pipeline is less than 1.5 times slower than the basic one, while the fault-tolerance is measured to be more than 1000 times stronger. However, in the presence of permanent faults, DIRC pipelines can still deadlock, which is life threatening to a QDI NoC. Without a full protection, data words transmitted in some pipeline stages are not protected, so that a transient fault can still deadlock the QDI pipeline though the possibility is lowered. The following chapters will discuss the management of the fault-caused physical-layer deadlocks in QDI NoCs.

CHAPTER 7

Deadlock Detection

It has been observed that faults could cause errors in QDI pipelines, which may destroy the handshake protocol and deadlock the communication, as previously analyzed in Section 5.4. When these faults occur in a QDI NoC, the situation could be complicated and severe. Data errors, or packet loss, can be managed through different network abstraction layers, but a deadlock can paralyze the whole network. This fault-caused deadlock happening in the physical layer is different from the usual network-layer one due to cyclic dependence of transmitting packets as described in Section 3.1.4.2, which cannot be resolved using conventional deadlock management techniques. As a solution, a general framework designed for QDI NoCs is proposed in this chapter to detect this fault-caused physical-layer deadlock caused by different faults and locate the faulty component, so that further operations can be taken to recover the network function (Chapter 8).

7.1 BASELINE QDI NOC

Before diving into the details of detecting the physical layer deadlock, let us recall the basics of QDI NoCs.

7.1.1 Network Principles

A 2D-mesh QDI asynchronous NoC was shown in Figure 3.12b, constructing a GALS system with synchronous IP cores attached [119]. Though a QDI NoC has many potential advantages over its synchronous counterpart due to its clockless nature, its area can be larger with complicated control logic, affecting the communication efficiency. Therefore, many existing QDI NoCs prefer simple and cheap network protocols [11, 75, 223, 244]; so does the baseline QDI NoC implemented in this book. Since the deadlock detection technique proposed in this chapter does not rely on the network topology, for simplicity of purpose a 2D-mesh is used as the backbone. To focus on fault-tolerance and study the effect of fault-caused deadlocks in the physical layer, the popular XY dimension-ordered routing (XY-DOR) is employed to avoid the traditional network-layer deadlocks [63]. Packets traverse the X-dimension first and then the Y-dimension, as depicted in Figure 3.11a.

Wormhole switching is employed in the baseline NoC because of its simple implementation and wide use in existing asynchronous NoC designs. According to the wormhole switching, data is transmitted in packets made of different types of flits, comprising a head flit, multiple body flits and a tail flit. The destination address is stored in the head flit, with which the routing request is generated to compete for the appropriate output port. Body flits carry the main data information. The tail flit is used to separate consecutive packets and release reserved network resources on the path built by the packet. The head flit leads the route and the remaining flits follow in a pipelined fashion, so that a packet with many flits may span multiple routers and links, reserving a long data path in the network. The network resources on this reserved path are gradually released in sequence along with the progress of the tail flit towards its destination.

7.1.2 Asynchronous Protocols

Routers and links of asynchronous NoCs can be implemented with different asynchronous protocols, including handshake protocols and data encoding methods. Among all the existing asynchronous NoCs using different protocols, only the NoCs using 4-phase, 1-of-n are QDI [11, 75, 223, 244], which can tolerate delay variations on both routers and links. The QDI NoC studied in this chapter also uses 4-phase, 1-of-n asynchronous protocol. A baseline QDI NoC is proposed as a design case to demonstrate the fault impact on QDI

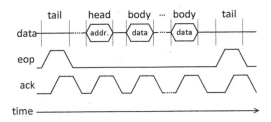

Figure 7.1   Flit sequence.

NoCs and how proposed fault-tolerant techniques can be used in real designs.

In the baseline NoC, data bits are grouped and encoded into multiple 1-of-n symbols, each of which can deliver $\log_2 n$ bits. The data channel of the network is broken down by every 2 bits, each of which is then delivered by a parallel 1-of-4 bus or sub-channel. The whole flit is accompanied by a single end-of-packet (*EoP*) indicator and a single acknowledge signal *ack*. The *EoP* flag indicates the tail of the packet, which separates consecutive packets so that no more flags are required to represent the head flit, simplifying the NoC design. In a fault-free environment, the head flit is defined as the first flit after system reset or the one after a tail flit. Figure 7.1 demonstrates the flit sequence under the 4-phase, 1-of-n protocol. A *spacer* is inserted between two consecutive 1-of-n symbols as the 4-phase handshake protocol requires, providing a *return-to-zero* phase. Therefore, the head and body flits, which are a group of 1-of-n symbols, are separated by *spacers*. A high *ack* wire notifies the successful acceptance of a complete flit or data word. For the last tail flit, without any payload, a high *EoP* signal indicates the end of the packet. As the tail flit progresses, network resources on the packet path previously reserved are released in sequence.

7.2   FAULT IMPACT ON DATA PATH

7.2.1   Fault Classifications

A router can be divided into the data path and control logic. The pipelined buffers at the input/output ports and the crossbar construct the data path through the router, while the control logic comprises a routing computation unit, a buffer controller and a switch allocator. Faults on NoCs can be classified into two types according to their locations, faults on the data path and faults on the control logic. Neither kind of faults has been thoroughly studied in existing QDI NoCs.

Faults on the control logic of a NoC can be harmful because they may produce wrong control signals, which then lead to erroneous network configuration and interrupt the normal flit flow. A direct way to protect the control logic of the NoC is using replication-based techniques [8, 106, 159], with which the temporary faulty behavior can be filtered and the permanently defective component can be replaced or bypassed [78, 260]. In addition, a large proportion of this kind of faults can be masked according the common masking factors. For example, the routing computation unit is used only when a head flit is being processed. Faults occur outside this window have no impact on the function as the route has already been configured and the result of this unit is ignored.

Compared with the faults on the control logic, faults on the data path are straightforward to analyze and likely to happen considering on the high-density data flow traveling through the network. All kinds of flits may be polluted by a fault during their transmission. As an example, the long inter-router links, which are usually routed on high metal layers, are prone to be affected by fault originated from the environment. Faults on these large number of wires are likely to be latched, causing different errors which are transmitted with the flit flow and affect the network. Assuming that the control logic has been protected [106], this chapter concentrates on studying the fault-tolerance of the data paths in a QDI NoC.

7.2.2 General Fault Impact

Before the detailed analysis of the fault-caused physical-layer deadlock, the general fault impact on NoCs (synchronous or asynchronous) is briefly introduced. Under the assumption that the control logic is fault-free, a fault may affect the traversal of a packet through a router, resulting different network behavior depending on the specific design. Figure 7.2 describes several typical faulty

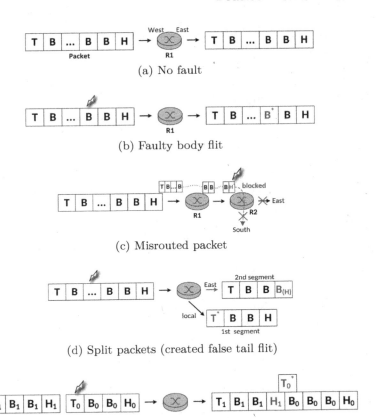

(a) No fault

(b) Faulty body flit

(c) Misrouted packet

(d) Split packets (created false tail flit)

(e) Assembled packets (erased tail flit)

Figure 7.2 · Several faulty scenarios of NoCs.

scenarios where Figure 7.2a shows the fault-free case where a flit-based packet traverse a router.

- As the most likely case, a fault may pollute one (or several) of the multiple body flits, as shown in Figure 7.2b. The faulty bit reaches the right destination and cause data errors, which can be corrected by the network layer using error correction codes [229].

- A fault on the head flit may change the destination address information and divert the packet to a wrong direction. Besides the possible packet loss, this kind of misrouting could cause forbidden turns in the network or blockage due to the undefined/unrecognized route or network edge, both of which may further cause a network-layer deadlock or livelock [63]. Figure 7.2c shows such an example where a head flit which was originally directed to the east output of router R2 encounters a fault during its transmission, producing a faulty routing request to the South. The faulty head flit is blocked in the west input buffer of R2 since the routing request is invalid under the employed turn model. These scenarios can be avoided by a careful redesign of the routing computation unit [226].

- Figure 7.2d presents a case where a long packet splits into two segments due to a fault created tail flit. The front segment goes to the right destination (local) eventually with severe data loss. If a head flit is identified by specific flag bits and those flag bits are not present in the body flit following the fake tail, the second segment may be jammed at the router input and occupies certain amount of network resources, which needs extra measures to deal with. If a head flit is simply defined as *the one following a tail flit*, the body flit following the fake tail will now be incorrectly interpreted as a header in this case, which may cause another corrupted packet to travel in an inappropriate direction (such as east as demonstrated in the example shown in Figure 7.2d).

- A tail flit may be removed by a fault during its transmission. If the head flit is defined as the one after the tail flit without extra indication flags, the head flit of the following packet is incorrectly taken as a body flit and traverses along the reserved path. Multiple packets could be assembled together, forming a long packet as shown in Figure 7.2e. Otherwise, the following packet may get blocked at the input which cannot be reallocated without being released first.

Table 7.1 summarizes the aforementioned impact exerted by faults. A fault may cause packet loss, misrouting, network-layer deadlock/livelock and different kinds of blockage in the network layer. Although permanent faults rarely happen compared with

Table 7.1   General fault impact on NoCs.

	H.1 No routing request is generated
Faults on the head flit	H.2 Misrouting (Incorrect routing request) (1) Packet loss (2) Livelock (network layer) (3) Deadlock (network layer)
Faults on body flits	B. Data errors
	T.1 No tail flit
Faults on the tail flit or a false tail flit	T.2 False tail flit (1) Split packet (2) Assembled packet

transient faults [56], they can remove signal bits completely and induce more severe results. Many techniques have been proposed in previous literature to deal with these traditional faulty scenarios [103, 260]. Different from these general fault effects listed in Table 7.1, faults on QDI NoCs could break the handshake protocol, leading to a fault-caused physical-layer deadlock. This kind of deadlock is the research target of this chapter.

7.3   DETECTING PERMANENT FAULT ON DATA PATH

As described in Section 3.1.1, the architecture of a NoC can be abstracted to the physical layer, the data link layer and the network layer in the bottom up order. A traditional network-layer deadlock occurs when the transmission of message results in a cyclic dependence. As discussed in Section 3.1.4.2, these deadlocks can be avoided by either providing enough network resources in the data link layer or using restricted routing algorithms in the network layer. Under a faulty environment, the network may behave erroneously due to fault caused errors, which exists in both synchronous and QDI NoCs, and is not with the direct interest of this chapter.

Unique to QDI NoCs, a fault could break the handshake process and cause a physical-layer deadlock, as illustrated in Section 5.4. This type of fault-caused physical-layer deadlock cannot be easily managed using traditional deadlock management techniques. Since

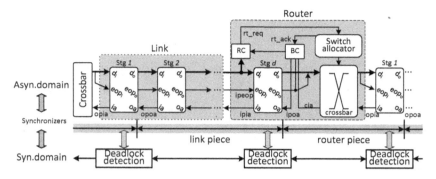

Figure 7.3   Protected pipeline pieces with deadlock detection circuits.

keeping the network working in the presence of faults, even with some packet loss or degradation of network performance, is essential for critical digital equipment, it is important to investigate the online deadlock detection and recovery mechanisms capable of handling the fault-caused physical-layer deadlock.

7.3.1   Data Path Partition

It has been demonstrated that the data path in a NoC typically includes inter-router links, input/output buffers and crossbars. Together, they form a long QDI pipeline. This pipelined *data* path can be flexibly partitioned in different pieces according to their different fault-tolerance requirement, as indicated in Section 5.6. Figure 7.3 presents one possible partition where the link (including its end router buffers) and router (crossbar) are separately protected within two pieces. Correspondingly, faults on the *data* path can be classified into *link* and *router* faults depending on their location.

A permanent fault on a link may corrupt the routing request and affect the router control logic, which can be captured in the *link* piece. A fault on the router piece of a previously reserved data path would cause data errors. A pair of deadlock detection circuits could be added to the ends of each piece (input/output buffers) to monitor its activities According to the general strategy to detect deadlocks as described in Section 5.6 and the summarized deadlock patterns according to Theorem 1, whether the monitored link/router piece is defective can be determined by checking if the following conditions are satisfied.

- No transition is detected on the pipeline piece for a *long* period. The pipeline piece must be one of the three scenarios: idle, temporarily blocked due to congestion, or deadlocked.

- The link piece (including the inter-router links and pipelined input/output buffers) and the router piece (the crossbar) show different deadlock patterns in the presence of a permanent fault.

  - *Link fault*: The *ack* signals at the output of the pre-fault router are alternately valued as the link is not idle. For the input of the post-fault router, all pipeline stages on the reserved path (by the packet under transmission) have the same *ack* (so that the blockage is not caused by either congestion or the network-layer deadlock where the *ack* should be alternately valued as well).

  - *Router fault*: A *data* path has been built by a packet through the router. The *ack* signals at the router input are alternately valued and the *ack* at its granted output has the same value.

7.3.2 Deadlock Caused by Permanent Link Fault

Faults may happen on any gates and wires of the links at any time, affecting the transmitting *data*, the end-of-packet (*EoP*) indicator or the *ack* signal. By considering all faulty scenarios, there are six types of permanent stuck-at (s-a) conditions: *data/EoP/ack* · s-a-1/0. They are possible to affect all the three types of flits (head, body and tail). Faults or faulty flits can transit to the input buffer and paralyze the normal router behavior. The control logic inside a router, including the routing computation unit and the buffer controller, samples the head and tail flits directly from the input buffer. They may get stuck at some specific states due to the permanent fault, which can be considered as a marker and used to detect and recover the fault. For an incoming packet, it is generally processed by a wormhole router sequentially through three

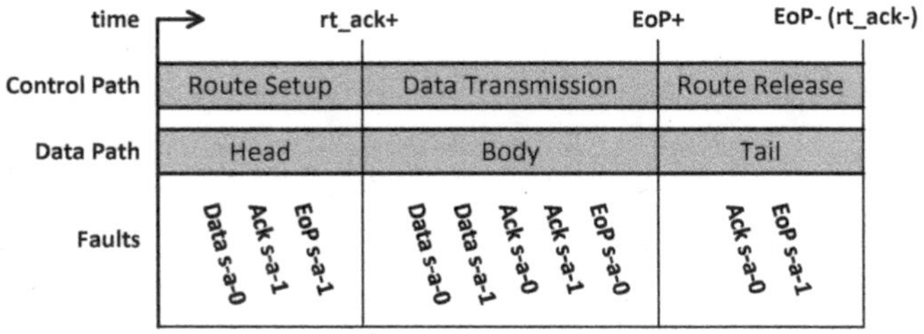

Figure 7.4 Router state transitions under permanent link faults.

states: *route setup*, *data transmission* and *route release*. As shown in Figure 7.4, the post-fault router could get deadlocked when a permanent faults occurs.

1. *Route setup*: For the data path, the head flit of an newly arrived packet ·is first stored into the router input buffer and gets blocked while waiting to be granted with an router output. For the control logic, the routing computation unit samples the address information from the head flit, generates a routing request and waits for the grant from the switch allocator. The following faults could happen in this state:

   - *Data s-a-0* fault: The address information is encoded into 1-of-n codes in the head flit. A *data s-a-0* fault may corrupt the 1 of a 1-of-n symbol into 0, effectively preventing a complete head flit from arriving.

   - *Ack s-a-1* fault: A high *ack* signal denotes the successful acceptance of a complete word, which then starts the *reset* phase when the received 1-of-n codes are gradually reset to spacers. An *ack s-a-1* fault would stop one or more codes from being reset, which then prevent the whole or part of the head flit from arriving at the front of the input buffer depending on the specific time of occurrence of the fault.

   - *Data s-a-1* or *ack s-a-0*: These two faults could prevent a flit from being fully reset, stalling the 4-phase handshake at the *set* phase. The address information might be accepted by the routing computation unit success-fully and a routing request is generated by later granted by the switch allocator. Note that, a *data s-a*-1 fault may create a 2-of-n code. It can be forced to be reduced into a 1-of-n code using a mutex element (ME, Figure 2.20). If the routing request generated from this head flit is invalid according to the turn model, it can be recog-nized by the routing computation unit and deliberately dropped [226]. Otherwise, this packet would be directed to a (either right or wrong) destination. In all scenar-ios, this post-fault router will get stuck at the next *data transmission* state when these two faults eventually take effect.

- *EoP s-a*-0: Although an *EoP s-a*-0 fault may occur, it will not manifest itself because *EoP* stays low during the whole *route setup* state.

- *EoP s-a*-1: This fault will create a fake tail flit in this state and lead to two possible outcomes: It may take pri-ority at the front of input buffer (causing to a high *ack* signal) and prevent the following head flit from arriv-ing. No routing request is generated. Otherwise, the fake tail flit *arrives late* and the incoming packet has already been granted an output. This fake tail flit then prema-turely forces the router into the *route release* state.

In summary, in the presence of a *data s-a*-0, *ack s-a*-1 or *EoP s-a*-1 fault, the post-fault router can get deadlocked at the *route setup* or *release* state. A complete head flit is not received by the post-fault router. No routing request is gen-erated or granted. The incoming packet is stalled at the front of the router input buffer.

2. *Data transmission*: The switch allocator has allocated an out-put to an incoming packet in this state, and the head and body flits are sequentially traversing through the router. All *data* and *ack* stuck-at faults can deadlock the reserved data path. They will cause data errors and break the handshake but not disturb the network protocol because a route has

been reserved and the control logic does not need to sample the data payload. Following is a detailed analysis of the possible faulty scenarios in this state:

- *Data s-a-0/1*: A *data s-a-0* fault can remove a 1-of-n symbol from a flit. A *data s-a-1* fault may create a 2-of-n symbol depending on the fault position. The erroneous 2-of-n symbol may traverse through the reserved path. When the fault-free 1 later gets reset, the faulty 1 remains and blocks the pipeline stage from accepting the next flit.

- *Ack s-a-0/1*: These two faults could prevent one flit from being reset or set, which then halt the handshake. Consequently, an incomplete packet might be received at the destination without a tail flit.

- *EoP s-a-0*: This fault would prevent the tail flit indicator from being latched. As a result, all routers downstream of the fault are stalled at the *data transmission* state.

- *EoP s-a-1*: A fake tail flit is created when an *EoP s-a-1* strikes. This fake tail flit then prematurely forces router to transit to the *route release* state.

3. *Route release*: In a baseline QDI NoC, the tail flit separates two consecutive packets. As illustrated in Figure 7.1, the head flit can simply be defined as the flit after the tail. In the end of the *data transmission* state, a high *EoP* indicator enables the *route release* state during which the withdrawal of the *EoP* signal is monitored by the buffer controller. After the *EoP* is reset, the buffer controller releases the reserved route inside the router. The router state goes back to *route setup* afterwards. Several faults can happen in this state:

- *Data s-a-0/1 and ack s-a-1*: These two faults can happen but exert no effect because they cannot prevent the resetting operation of the triggered *EoP* indicator. They would eventually paralyze the router in the *route setup* state of the next packet.

- *Ack s-a-*0 and *EoP s-a-*1: These two faults can prevent the *EoP* signal from resetting, which then blocks the state transition and produces a deadlock.

- *EoP s-a-*0: An *EoP s-a-*0 occurs in this state would prematurely complete the release operation. It may not affect the current packet but would later stall the next packet at the *data transmission* state.

Table 7.2 summarizes the impact of all types of permanent faults on the NoC data path. Note that the effect of stuck-at faults may not appear immediately but causes the post-fault router to be stuck in a specific state. A fault-caused physical layer deadlock manifests itself only when the router ends up in a state exhibiting a deadlock pattern as described in Table 7.2. In the baseline QDI NoC, *rt_ack* is the signal indicating if the switch allocator has granted an output to the input. The *EoP* indicator used by the buffer controller at the router input is denoted by the *ipeop* signal. Therefore, the data path may deadlock in all the three states: *route setup* with *rt_ack−*, *data transmission* with *rt_ack+* & *ipeop−* and *route release* with *rt_ack+* & *ipeop+*. In a deadlocked state, packet transmission is stalled and all control signals are steady, making it safe to sample control signals to locate the exact location of the fault.

7.3.3 Deadlock Patterns Due to Permanent Link Fault

If a permanent fault on the link piece deadlocks a reserved data path, the faulty data may traverse to the destination and affect other healthy routers and links downstream of the faulty link. By analyzing the fault scenarios just described in Section 7.3.2 and the deadlock model proposed in Section 5.4, the effect of stuck-at faults on the post-fault router can be categorized into the following three deadlock cases, as highlighted as the **pattern** column in Table 7.2. These cases can be checked by a pattern checker at each router input by sampling the values of some critical control signals as depicted in Figure 7.3, including two contiguous *ack* signals (*ipia* and *ipoa*), the *EoP* indicator (*ipeop*) and the grant indicator (*rt_ack*). By checking values of these signals when a router is stalled, it can

Table 7.2 Deadlocked states of a post-fault router.

Router State	Fault Type	Impact	Pattern	Boolean Expression
	$Data$ s-a-0	No request is granted. Pipeline stages downstream of the fault capture an incomplete flit and constantly wait for the lost valid 1.	①	`!rt_ack & !ipia & !ipoa`
Router Setup	Ack s-a-1	No request is granted. Pipeline stages downstream of the fault capture a spacer or an incomplete flit.		
	EoP s-a-1	No request is granted. The fake tail flit gets stuck at the front of the input buffer.	②	`!rt_ack & ipeop & !ipoa`
Data Transmission	All types except for EoP s-a-1	Request is granted. All pipeline stages store the same incomplete/complete flit or spacers.	③	`rt_ack & (ipia == ipoa)`
Route Release	Ack s-a-0 EoP s-a-1	Request is granted. All stages hold the tail flit, waiting for being reset.		

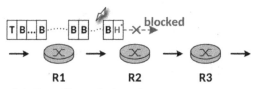

(a) Case ①: stalled at the *route setup* state

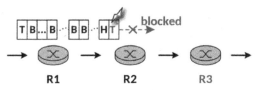

(b) Case ②: stalled at the *route setup* state

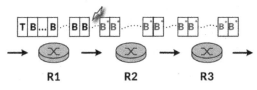

(c) Case ③: stalled at the *data transmission* or *route release* state

Figure 7.5   Patterns of deadlocked network due to a permanent link fault.

be determined if this router is on the *downstream* path of a faulty link.

Case ①: A *data s-a-0* or *ack s-a-1* fault in the *route setup* state will prevent the input buffer from receiving a complete head flit. Pipeline stages after the fault may hold spacers or the same incomplete flit, producing low *ack* signals (*ipia−* & *ipoa−*). As a result, no routing request is generated and granted (*rt_ack−*). This case can be indicated by boolean expression !*rt_ack* & !*ipia* & !*ipoa*. One of such example is shown in Figure 7.5a.

Case ②: An *EoP s-a-1* fault happening on an idle link at the *route setup* state creates a fake tail flit (*ipeop+*) which reaches the front of the input buffer and prevents it from receiving following packets. No routing request is generated or granted (rt_ack-). Such case can be denoted by boolean expression $!rt\_ack$ & $ipeop$ & $!ipoa$ with one example depicted in Figure 7.5b.

Case ③: As the most general scenario for all kinds of stuck-at faults in the *data transmission* and *route release* state, the routing request has been granted and body flits of a packet are traversing the router (rt_ack+). All pipeline stages downstream of the fault store the same incomplete/complete flit or spacers. Therefore, any two contiguous *ack* signals of two adjacent pipeline stages on the downstream path are equal. This case can be detected by boolean expression rt_ack & $ipia == ipoa$. One of such an example is illustrated in Figure 7.5c.

When the network is deadlocked, but none of three cases is satisfied, the router is not *downstream* of a faulty link. Network congestion and the network-layer deadlocks due to the cyclic dependence of transmitting packets can stall the packet transmission, but can be distinguished from a fault-caused deadlock using the boolean expressions provided by the three cases. This is because the stalled packet flits are fault-free. The *ack* signals of any two adjacent pipeline stages hold different values. None of the three deadlock cases is satisfied. In the next section, a detection mechanism will be proposed to detect this deadlock using a time-out mechanism and locate the position of the faulty link piece using these deadlock patterns.

7.3.4 Time-Out Detection Mechanism

A generic time-out method was mentioned in Section 5.6 to detect the fault-caused physical-layer deadlock on 4-phase, 1-of-n QDI pipelines. When it comes to a QDI NoC, this deadlock shows more patterns as discussed previously in Section 7.3.3. This section proposes a novel time-out strategy to detect the physical-layer deadlock due to a permanent link fault and locate the faulty link piece in QDI NoCs.

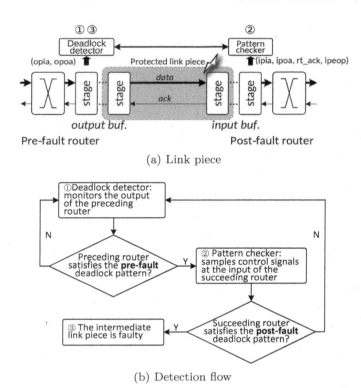

(a) Link piece

(b) Detection flow

Figure 7.6   Flow of detecting a deadlocked link piece.

To locate the faulty component or pipeline segment, deadlock detection circuits are put at the ends of each protected region, such as a link piece as shown in Figure 7.3. Therefore, the long pipelined data path in the network is cut into multiple segments, each of which is protected by a pair of detection circuits. *Only when a fault can be accurately located by these detectors, a fine-grained recovery mechanism can be implemented to precisely isolate the faulty component and resolve the network congestion led by the fault-caused physical-layer deadlock.* This type of runtime recovery avoids a system reboot, or a cold replacement of the whole (or a large part of the) system.

As demonstrated in Figure 7.6a, the protected link piece includes pipelined input/output buffers and the intermediate long link wires. To detect a potentially permanently faulty link, a pair

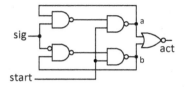

Figure 7.7 Transition detector [217].

of deadlock detection circuits are added to the output and input buffer of two adjacent routers to monitor the intermediate link. Figure 7.3 provides more details of the deadlock detection circuits, which add a deadlock detector at the input end of the pipelined link (*Stg* 1 at the output buffer of the preceding router) controlling another pattern checker at the link output end (*Stg d* at the end of the input buffer of the succeeding router). Figure 7.6b presents the general flow of detecting a deadlocked link piece:

1. The output buffer of the preceding router (or the input end of the link) is monitored by a deadlock detector. If the pre-fault deadlock pattern is satisfied as no transitions are detected and two contiguous *ack* signals are complementary, this router is recognized as upstream of a faulty link and starts enquiring the succeeding router.

2. The input buffer of the succeeding router (or the output end of the link) is monitored by a pattern checker. If no signal transitions are detected and anyone of the three post-fault deadlock patterns detailed in Section 7.3.3 is satisfied, this router is recognized as downstream of a faulty link.

3. After confirming both 1 and 2, the intermediate link piece is identified as faulty. Consequently, the two routers are recognized as the pre-fault and the post-fault routers respectively.

The key component in the deadlock detector is a transition detector (TD) monitoring the transition of certain signals as shown in Figure 7.7 [217]. The *start* is an active-high level-triggered enable signal. During the detection process (*start*+), a positive *act* denotes transitions are detected occurring on the monitored signal (*sig*).

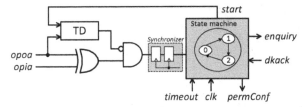

(a) Deadlock detector at router output

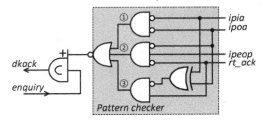

(b) Pattern checker at router input

Figure 7.8   Detection circuits protecting a link piece.

The reset of *start* causes *act* to reset to 0. The transition detector is used to determine if the monitored link is transmitting packets. If no transition is detected (*act−*) for a predefined long period, indicating either the link is idle or packets are stalled due to the network congestion or deadlock, *ack* sequences at the two ends of the link are checked against the deadlock patterns as defined by Theorem 1 in order to determine if this link is deadlocked by a fault. Note that this fault can be permanent, intermittent or even transient.

Figure 7.8 illustrates the detection circuits added to protect an inter-router link. Besides the redundant detection logic, two extra wires (*enquiry* and *dkack*) are added to each link to exchange the information between the output and input of each pair of routers. The whole deadlock detection process is controlled by a state machine inside the deadlock detector at each output port. Each router has a counter generating a *timeout* signal to control the state machine, so that the deadlock detector is a sync./async. hybrid circuit where the metastability could happen [86, 115]. In this design, detection circuits are assumed safe to sample asynchronous

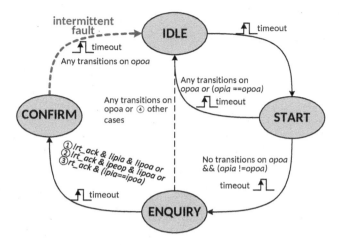

Figure 7.9   State machine used to detect defective link.

signals from the QDI pipeline if the links are monitored inactive for the predefined *long* timeout period. Synchronizers [86, 230] are added to the sync./async. interface to further reduce the possibility of metastability as depicted in Figure 7.8a. The state machine has four states: **IDLE**, **START**, **ENQUIRY** and **CONFIRM**, as shown in Figure 7.9. State transitions are enabled only by the *timeout* signal except when returning to **IDLE** from **ENQUIRY**. The meaning of each state and the transition between them are described as follows:

- **IDLE**: This is the default state after power-on or reset. At the beginning of the **IDLE** state, all flip-flops of the state machine being low. After a time-out period, the state machine transits to the **START** state, which can also be indicated by a high *start* signal.

- **START**: In this state, the transition detector in the deadlock detector is enabled to monitor the transition activities of the *ack* signal (*opoa*) at the output buffer of the preceding router (the input end of the link piece). At the end of the second time-out period, the deadlock detector either transits to **ENQUIRY** to check the succeeding input buffer (the output end of the link) if: (1) no transitions were detected during the second time-out period and (2) two contiguous *ack* signals at the output (*opia* and *opoa*) are complementary, satisfying the deadlock pattern of the pre-fault stage according to Theorem 1. Otherwise, the state goes back to **IDLE** because either the network is not congested as transitions are detected or the network is congested but not physically deadlocked as *opia* == *opoa*.

- **ENQUIRY**: In this state, the deadlock detector sends a *enquiry* signal to the output end of the protected link piece to interrogate about the deadlock pattern. The pattern checker samples three asynchronous signals from the headmost pipeline stage (*Stg d* in Figure 7.3) of the input buffer of the succeeding router. It should be reminded that in this state, the input end of the link has been taken as pre-fault in **START**. Therefore, if no transitions are detected and one of the three deadlock patterns summarized in Section 7.3.3 is found satisfied during the third time-out period, this router is confirmed as post-fault (indicated by an active-low *dkack*) and the link piece is recognized as faulty. In other words, the fault position is detected and located at the link. The state machine will transit to **CONFIRM** in the end of the third *timeout* (indicated by a high *permConf*). If the pattern checker fails to obtain the deadlock pattern (none of the three cases in Section 7.3.3 is matched) or transitions are detected, the state machine is reset to **IDLE** immediately.

- **CONFIRM**: This is the state indicating that a fault-caused physical-layer deadlock has been detected and the faulty link piece is located. The intermediate link between the pair of deadlock detection circuits is the defective one. For a permanent fault, the state machine will get stuck at this state to permanently block the faulty link. Different recovery methods can be further employed to recover the network function, which will be discussed in Chapter 8.

Considering a long lasting intermittent fault which behaves like a permanent one and is able to stall the packet transmission for a long time, a recovery mechanism is required to resume the usage of

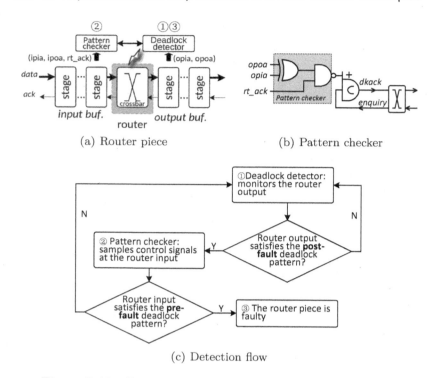

(a) Router piece

(b) Pattern checker

(c) Detection flow

Figure 7.10   Detection flow of a permanent router fault.

the previously blocked link when the long-lasting intermittent fault finally fades. A transition from **CONFIRM** to **IDLE** is added. The disappearance of the intermittent fault would bring back signal transitions on *data*, *eop* or *ack* wires, which then leads to the transition of the *ack* signal at the preceding router output buffer (*opoa*). This could be detected by the transition detector at the input end of the monitored link piece. Consequently, when the next *timeout* arrives, the state machine is reset to **IDLE** and the blocked link is resumed afterward. To some extent, this method can also be used to tackle permanent faults with floating values [5] as long as the fault deadlocks path reserved for a packet.

7.3.5 Detection of Permanent Router Fault

A fault may happen inside a router and deadlock the reserved data path as well. As shown in Figure 7.10a, the main component or

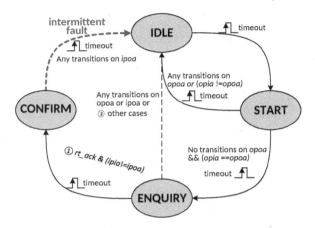

Figure 7.11 State machine used to detect defective router piece.

router logic on the *data* path is a crossbar connecting input to output ports. Similar to the detection circuits for faults on links, a pair of detection circuits is added before and after the crossbar to monitor activities of its input and output. A state machine is implemented in the deadlock detector at the output buffer of the router. The general detection flow is illustrated in Figure 7.10c. This flow is similar to the flow used to detect faulty links as shown in Figure 7.6b. The main difference is that, instead of interrogate a deadlock pattern checker at the input buffer of the downstream router, the deadlock detector at the router output interrogate the pattern checker at the input buffer of the same router, when a potential deadlock is detected in the **ENQUIRY** state. The internal structure of the pattern checker at the router input is depicted in Figure 7.10b, which is simpler than the one used for detecting link faults. The deadlock detection process for a permanent router fault is operated locally at one router.

Figure 7.11 depicts the state machine used for detect router faults, which is a slightly modified version of the one used for detect link faults as shown in Figure 7.9.

In the **START** state, the deadlock detector at the router output port checks if two contiguous *ack* signals are the same. If no signal transitions are detected and the two *ack* signals stay the same ($opia == opoa$) for a whole time-out period, the output buffer could potentially be downstream of a fault. In this case, the state machine transits to **ENQUIRY** at the end of the second time-out period to interrogate the router input. Otherwise, the state machine returns to **IDLE**.

In the **ENQUIRY** state, the pattern checker at the input port of the same router checks if two contiguous *ack* signals at the input are complementary. If no transitions are detected and the two *ack* signals are indeed different (*ipia!* = *ipoa*) during the third time-out period, the signal status does match with the pattern of ore-fault stages. Consequently, a permanent router fault is confirmed to be detected and the state machine transits to **CONFIRM**. It should be noted that a fault on the router logic will not exhibit if it is not on any reserved routes. Only when the fault happens on a path allocated for a packet (indicated by *rt_ack+* at the router input), would the fault be apparent and affect the network by deadlocking this reserved path.

It can be concluded that, no matter what the type of a fault is (permanent, intermittent or even transient), when the fault occurs on the network data path, breaks the handshake protocol and causes a physical-layer deadlock in the QDI NoC, it can be detected using the proposed deadlock detection techniques. Two to four time-out periods are required to locate the faulty component from the occurrence of the deadlock. The time-out period is normally predefined as a number of clock cycles. Since there is no requirement on the skew, jitter and frequency of the clock used by the deadlock detection, this clock can be easily obtained from the local synchronous IP cores or other clock sources. It is needed only to drive the state machine. A synchronizer [86, 230] is required between the synchronous detection circuit and the asynchronous router to reduce metastability, as depicted in Figure 7.8a. More technical issues will be discussed in Section 8.4.

7.4 HANDLING DEADLOCKS CAUSED BY DIFFERENT FAULTS

It has been pointed out in Section 5.4 that even a transient fault could break the handshake process and deadlock the QDI communication. Such type of deadlocks have rarely been studied before, not to mention their impact in the context of a QDI NoC. It is common that transient faults cause data errors. Most of these errors can be tolerated using the DIRC codes proposed in Chapter 6 or other fault-tolerance techniques [106, 159]. However, when a physical-layer deadlock is caused by a fault, such deadlock can significantly reduce the network performance and cannot be recovered using existing fault-tolerance techniques in the upper network-layer. The process of detecting a physical-deadlock due to a transient fault is the same as detecting a permanent fault according to the analysis in Section 5.4.3. The only difference is that the faulty component affected by a transient fault is still functional and can be reused rather than thrown away as for a permanent fault. Therefore, when both transient and permanent faults are considered, detecting the deadlock and diagnosing the fault type is crucial for the following recovery from the deadlock.

7.4.1 Fault Diagnosis

The characteristics of the physical-layer deadlock caused by different faults have been thoroughly studied in Section 5.4. A transient fault happening on the forward data path could deadlock an N-symbol-wide QDI pipeline as depicted in Figure 7.12, where the data word latched by pipeline stages downstream of the fault is either an *almost full* word with a positive *ack* or an *almost empty* word with a negative *ack* (described by Equation 5.11 and Equation 5.12 in Section 5.4.3). Comparably, a permanent fault on the forward data path (*data* stuck-at faults) could cause an *almost full* word with a negative *ack* as shown in Figure 5.15a or an *almost empty* word with a positive *ack* as shown in Figure 5.15b. This difference is summarized in Figure 7.13, which is the key to the diagnosis of the fault type. The region of the forward data path is defined in Figure 5.20. It should be noted that faults can also happen on the backward *ack* path. Pipeline stages downstream of the fault may store any kinds of data words. Diagnosis of the fault on the *backward* path is still an open question and left for future research. This section presents only the diagnosis of the fault on the forward data path.

Let us assume the link piece is protected according the mechanism depicted in Figure 7.3. Located at the last stage of the

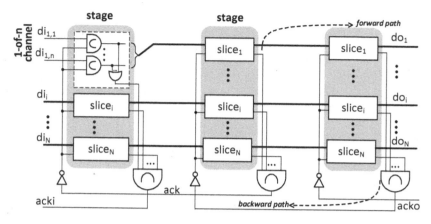

Figure 7.12 An N-symbol-wide 1-of-n pipeline.

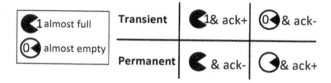

Figure 7.13 Deadlock pattern of pipeline stages downstream of the fault.

protected region ($Stg\ d$ at the router input), a fault diagnosis circuit takes the completion detection signal from the CD of each 1-of-n channel of the pipeline as its input. If the pipeline is N-symbols wide ($N>2$), the fault diagnosis circuit has N inputs denoted as $S_{CD}=\{cd_1,...cd_N\}$, where cd_i can be either 0 or 1. Let $Num(1)$ denote the number of 1s in S_{CD} and $Num(0)$ denotes the number of 0s. Under the assumption of a 1-bit fault on the forward data path, only one cd in S_{CD} could be different from the others in the deadlocked state. The output of the fault-diagnosis circuit is a boolean signal: a high value indicates the latched data word is *almost full* while low indicates *almost empty*. For simplicity, we name the output as *almost_full*. Consequently, the function of the diagnosis circuit can be described as:

- If $Num(1) > Num(0)$, *almost_full* $= 1$;

- If $Num(1) < Num(0)$, *almost_full* $= 0$.

Note that $Num(1)$ and $Num(0)$ are not allowed to be equal. The type of the latched data symbol can be determined by comparing $Num(0)$ and $Num(1)$ using the following rules:

- If $N = 1$, as discussed in Section 5.4, the pipeline can only be deadlocked by a permanent fault. Therefore, there is no need to differentiate the types of faults.

- If $N = 2$, one extra redundant check channel can be added to make the pipeline 3-symbols wide. The fault type can then be diagnosed using the rule for $N = 3$. In addition, this enables the usage of the proposed DIRC codes (Section 6.3.4) to tolerate the symbol corruption caused by transient faults.

- If $N = 3$, $almost\_full = cd_1cd_2 + cd_1cd_3 + cd_2cd_3$, which can be implemented by a majority voter circuit as shown in Figure 7.14a. For an $almost\ full$ symbol with two 1s in S_{CD}, $almost\_full$ is high. Similarly, a $almost\ empty$ symbol has two 0s in S_{CD} and $almost\_full$ is low.

- If $N \geq 4$, the diagnosis circuit can be implemented as a symmetric tree structure as shown in Figure 7.14b and 7.14c for the $N = 4$ and $N = 8$ cases respectively. It requires the N to be an even number. If N is odd, one extra 1-of-n channel shall be added with extra fault-tolerance [106, 264]. In general, $almost\_full = cd_1cd_2 + cd_3cd_4 + \cdots + cd_{N-1}cd_N$.

Figure 7.14b illustrates the diagnosis circuit for a 4-symbol-wide pipeline. Under the assumption of a 1-bit fault, at most one cd in S_{CD} could be different from the others. Since the data word in the deadlock state is either almost full or almost empty, if $almost\_full$ is low, the data word must be an almost empty word that $(N-1)$ 0s exist in S_{CD} $(Num(0) > Num(1))$. If the latched data word in the deadlock state is an almost full word, there are $(N-1)$ 1s in S_{CD} and $almost\_full$ is high. The data type is therefore diagnosed. Figure 7.14c presents an expanded diagnosis circuit for an 8-symbol pipeline.

Fault type is denoted by a 1-of-2 signal $ft\_type[1:0]$ whose default value is 00. When a deadlock is detected, it should be either 01 denoting a transient fault or b10 denoting a permanent fault. 11

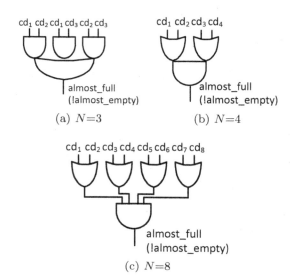

Figure 7.14 Fault diagnosis circuits for an N-symbol pipeline.

is invalid as it is assumed that the transient and permanent fault cannot happen and deadlock the same pipeline segment at the same time. According to Figure 7.13, the fault type can be decided using Equation 7.1:

$$ft\_type = \{(almost\_full \ \& \ !ack) \mid (almost\_empty \ \& \ ack),$$
$$((almost\_full \ \& \ ack) \mid almost\_empty \ \& \ !ack)\} \quad (7.1)$$

where $almost\_empty$ is the inverse of $almost\_full$. For example, if $S_{CD} = \{00010000\}$ where cd_4 from the fourth channel is affected by a fault. Using the diagnosis circuit, we know $almost\_full = 0$ ($almost\_empty = 1$). The fault type is then decided using Equation 7.1. Potentially, the proposed diagnosis circuit can be extended to the case of multi-bit faults.

7.4.2 Modified Time-Out Mechanism

The time-out mechanism proposed to detect the physical-layer deadlock caused by permanent faults can be modified to manage

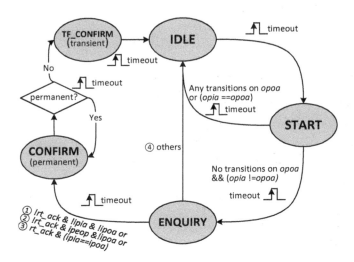

Figure 7.15   Modified state transition graph for transient and permanent faults.

both transient and permanent faults. This section uses the protection of the link piece to demonstrate the fault detection and diagnosis process.

Figure 7.15 illustrates the modified state machine controlled by a time-out mechanism. An extra state of **TF_CONFIRM** is introduced compared with the original one shown in Figure 7.9. For link faults, the fault diagnosis circuit is at the headmost pipeline stage of the protected link. In the end of the **ENQUIRY** state where the input of the succeeding router is interrogated about the deadlock pattern, the fault type (*ft_type*) information is reported to the deadlock detector at the other end of the link piece. Therefore, when the physical deadlock is detected or confirmed in **CONFIRM**, the deadlock detector knows that the fault type *ft_type* is either 01 or 10, indicating a transient or permanent fault. The fault is taken as a permanent one by default. The faulty link piece is blocked first and the recovery measures start, as described in Chapter 8.

If it is a permanent fault that deadlocks the link infinitely, the state machine will stay at **CONFIRM** to ensure the defective link is permanently blocked and bypassed; therefore, other healthy network components are not affected by it. If the fault is diagnosed as transient, the state machine transits to **TF_CONFIRM** to resume the operation of the previously blocked but healthy link after a fault recovery process, which normally finishes in one *time-out* period. One extra *time-out* period is further added between **TF_CONFIRM** and **IDLE**, allowing all necessary recovery processes (in neighboring routers) to finish.

It can be inferred that it needs two to four time-out periods to detect the deadlock from its occurrence, and four to six time-out periods in total to recover the network from the physical-layer deadlock caused by a transient fault. Compared with detection circuits for a permanent link fault as shown in Figure 7.8, one more wire is added between the two routers to carry the fault type information. As a result, a total of three redundant wires are added to each link to support the deadlock detection. By adding fault diagnosis circuits to the output buffer of a router, faults on the crossbar can also be diagnosed when they deadlock the built packet path. Together, most of the data paths in a NoC are protected.

7.5 SUMMARY

Permanent faults are likely to occur due to the aging process. A permanent fault is capable of breaking the asynchronous handshake protocol and causing to a physical-layer deadlock. This deadlock is different from the traditional network-layer one due to the cyclic dependence of packet transmissions [63]. It cannot be detected and recovered using traditional deadlock management techniques described in Section 5.5.2. This chapter thoroughly studied the fault impact on QDI NoC data paths and proposed a new time-out mechanism, which can be used to detect the fault and locate its position precisely as long as it causes a physical-layer deadlock. This chapter has also demonstrated the detection processes of a permanent link fault and a router fault, with which most data paths of a QDI NoC are protected.

A transient fault could also stall the handshake protocol, leading to a physical-layer deadlock, which is a newly found challenge for QDI NoCs. The faulty link can be detected using the same time-out mechanism proposed for permanent fault. When both transient and permanent faults are considered, a fault diagnosis method is proposed to differentiate transient fault caused deadlocks from the permanent ones, because they require different recovery methods. This fault diagnosis strategy utilizes the different deadlock patterns caused by transient and permanent faults on the forward data path, with which the fault type is then diagnosed. Correspondingly, an updated detection process has been proposed to handle both types of faults. The next step is to recover the network from a detected deadlock, which will be discussed in the next chapter.

CHAPTER 8

Deadlock Recovery

Using the detection techniques proposed in Chapter 7, the physical-layer deadlock caused by a fault can be detected and the faulty component can be located precisely. To recover from such a physical-layer deadlock, two processes are usually required: (1) *Deadlock removal*: eliminating the deadlock and releasing fault-free network resources and (2) *Faulty component isolation*: reconfiguring the network to ensure all its communication function is unhindered. Different recovery methods should be adopted depending on the types of faults. For transient faults, the temporarily faulty component should be reused after the deadlock is removed. For permanent faults, the defective component should be isolated forever to prevent it from affecting the network traffic in the future and deadlocking the network again.

This chapter proposes a fine-grained strategy to recover QDI NoCs from physical-layer deadlocks caused by link faults. The proposed *Drain & Release* techniques can recover the broken handshake process according to the specific state where the network is deadlocked, so as to release the deadlocked but fault-free network resources. To bypass the faulty component, spatial division multiplexing (SDM) [132, 223] is used to improve the network throughput while introduces the necessary redundancy of data paths. Along with the router input/output buffers, every inter-router link is physically divided into multiple sub-links. Since a single fault affects only one sub-link, this faulty sub-link can be blocked and prevented from being allocated to succeeding traffic. As other sub-links of the same link are still healthy, packets can be diverted to these healthy

DOI: 10.1201/9781003284789-8

sub-links and bypassing the faulty one. The network function remains with some loss in network throughput.

Router logic is complicated and vulnerable to faults as well. It is difficult to isolate one specific defective logic element without a full duplication. Based on the fault location information obtained from the proposed detection method described in Chapter 7, conventional network recovery techniques, such as fault-tolerant routings in the network layer, can be used to bypass the defective router as a way to resume the normal network communication. This chapter focuses on the recovery of a deadlocked NoC from faulty links.

8.1 DEADLOCK REMOVAL BY DRAIN AND RELEASE

A fault occurring on a link would stall a packet and divide the reserved path into an upstream and a downstream pipeline segments. A pair of *Drain & Release* techniques are proposed to free the deadlocked pipeline segments *upstream* and *downstream* of the faulty link, respectively. A similar method was proposed for a self-timed bundled-data asynchronous router [258] but it cannot work in a QDI NoC. Let us describe the *Drain* and the *Release* techniques according to the faulty scenario shown in Figure 8.1:

- *Drain*: By draining the fault-free flits from the *upstream* pipeline segment at the output of the pre-fault router, deadlocked network resources *upstream* of the fault can be reactivated;

- *Release*: By producing a fake tail flit at the input of the post-fault router and letting it go through the network along

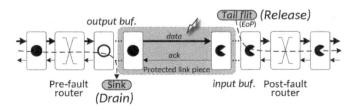

Figure 8.1   Deadlock removal using *Drain & Release*.

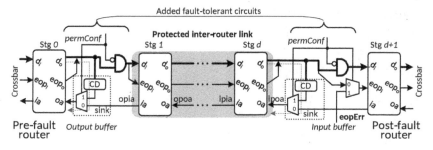

Figure 8.2 Modified input/output buffers for the support of deadlock recovery.

the reserved path of the fault-corrupted packet, deadlocked routers and links *downstream* of the fault would be released.

To support the *Drain & Release* technique, some modifications are made to the input/output buffers of two adjacent routers as demonstrated in Figure 8.2, where the intermediate link (the shaded area, including link wires and pipelined router buffers) is the protected region. Extra circuits are added before and after the protected link, respectively, to support deadlock recovery. Since the throughput of the QDI NoC is constrained by the loop latency through the crossbar, which is effectively the critical path, two more pipeline stages (*Stg* 0 and *Stg* $d+1$) are added to avoid potential timing impact on the critical path by the mentioned modification. Therefore, the support for network recovery from deadlocks should have very limited impact on the network throughput performance.

8.1.1 The Drain Operation

At the output of the pre-fault router, the *Drain* operation releases network resources *upstream* of the faulty link which hold fault-free flits. According to the 4-phase handshake protocol and the deadlock model described in Section 5.4, complete data symbols and spacers are distributed alternately along the upstream pipeline segment. Therefore, by using a *sink* at the start of the protected link piece which sends back an *ack* signal when detecting a complete data word, the data stream remaining in routers upstream of the faulty link will be drained at the output buffer of the pre-fault router. Along with the tail flit of the fault corrupted packet gradually traversing through the path, the allocated routers and links are released one after another. They can then be reused by other packets after the recovery process.

As depicted in Figure 8.2, the *sink* at the beginning of the link (router output buffer) comprises a CD and a multiplexer. When a recovery process is started by a positive *permConf* (generated by the deadlock detector as described in Section 7.3), the multiplexer replaces the *ack* signal to the preceding stage (*Stg* 0) with one generated by the local CD added by the sink. This effectively disconnects the data just after the CD and causes incoming *ack*s to be ignored. This added CD can reuse the one belonging to the preceding pipeline stage (*Stg* 0). An AND gate is also added on the forward data path to prevent the protected link from being polluted by the flits from the *upstream* routers during the *Drain* operation.

8.1.2 Buffer Controller at Router Input

Since the *upstream* pipeline segment of the fault holds fault-free data, the *Drain* operation can release the network resource along the reserved path by reusing the original tail flit. Unfortunately , the pipeline segment *downstream* of the faulty link may be polluted by the fault and it may never receive the tail flit. Therefore, clearing the faulty data remaining in the pipeline stages and producing a fake tail flit are two necessary operations to release the *downstream* network resources. These operations are executed at the input buffer of the post-fault router (output of the link). It was shown in Section 7.3.3 that the buffer controller (BC) at the input of the post-fault router, which controls the flit flow through the router, may get stalled at one specific deadlocked state. Since it is critical to get the BC running again depending on the deadlock state, extra circuits are added to the input buffer of each router to determine this deadlocked state of the BC and thus drive the recovery accordingly. Let us discuss the extra circuit added to BC before going deep into details of the recovery operation.

The internal structure of the BC is revealed in Figure 8.3a. It controls the packet transmitting process according to the wormhole switching [63] as described in Section 4.2.3.1. Its function can

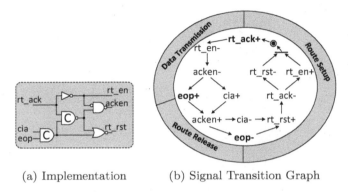

(a) Implementation   (b) Signal Transition Graph

Figure 8.3   Buffer controller at the router input.

be better illustrated using a STG (Section 2.5.1) as shown in Figure 8.3b, which is also surrounded by the corresponding state as described in the faulty model (Figure 7.4 in Section 7.3.2).

Initially the head flit of the arriving packet is blocked before the front pipeline stage of the input buffer (*Stg $d+1$* in Figure 8.2). The routing computation (RC) unit samples the destination address in the head flit and generates a routing request (*rt_req+*). If the requested output is busy, the requesting packet has to stay in the input buffer and waits to be granted by the switch allocator, which arbitrates the simultaneous routing requests coming from all inputs. The winner will be allocated an idle output port, indicated by *rt_ack+*, which effectively reserved a path for the requesting packet. Then, the RC unit is disabled (*rt_en−*) to stop further sampling the data path and the input buffer is activated (*acken−*) to allow the flit to traverse the crossbar. The data path enters the *data transmission* phase and waits for a tail flit indicating the end of the packet. When a tail flit is detected by the BC, as denoted by *eop+*, and is latched by the output buffer (*cia+*), the packet enters into the *route release* phase. In this phase, the BC blocks the input buffer by setting *acken+*, withdraws the tail flit (*eop−* and *cia−*) and resets the RC by raising *rt_rst+*, which then clears the old routing request (*rt_req−*). As a result, the allocated path inside this router is released, as denoted by *rt_ack−*. The input enables the RC unit to sample the data path (*rt_en+* and *rt_rst−*)

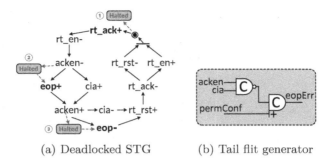

(a) Deadlocked STG   (b) Tail flit generator

Figure 8.4   Modified buffer controller for network recovery.

and starts waiting for the arrival of the next packet. This process strictly follows the wormhole switching.

8.1.3   The Release Operation

A permanent link fault may occur at any time, corrupt the head, body or tail flit of a packet, and deadlock the post-fault router or the buffer controller into a specific state. By analyzing the deadlocked state of the buffer controller and carefully resume the handshake process according to the deadlocked state, a fake tail flit can be generated locally at the input of the post-fault router and transmitted following the reserved path to release all the network resources downstream of the fault. This is the main idea behind the proposed *Release* operation.

According to the deadlock model described in Section 7.3, the input of a router may be deadlocked in one of the three states, *route setup, data transmission* and *route release,* as shown in Figure 8.3b. As shown in Figure 8.4a, the STG of the buffer controller at the input may halt before one of the three transitions, *rt_ack+, eop+* and *eop−,* which are also the deadlocked states. By reactivating the halted transition in this STG using some extra circuit, the buffer controller resume its function. The deadlock is then removed and the reserved network resources downstream of the faulty link obtain a chance to be released.

There are two possible scenarios that the input of a router may be deadlocked in the *route setup* state:

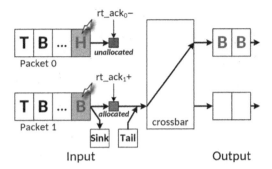

Figure 8.5   Abstracted release operation.

- A permanent fault may occur before or just when the head flit comes into the router. In this scenario, no routing request was generated due to the faulty (incomplete) head flit. As a result, the input of the post-fault router is deadlocked at the *route setup* phase. Since the switch allocator has not allocated any outputs to this incoming packet, such as the Packet 0 as depicted in Figure 8.5, this input buffer is the end of the deadlocked path and this post-fault router is the only one *downstream* of the fault. No further recovery operation is required.

- If a fault pollutes a packet which has been allocated a data path through the post-fault router, such as the Packet 1 in Figure 8.5, the input of the post-fault router is deadlocked either at the *data transmission* or at the *route release* phase, as shown in Figure 8.4a. The routing request has been granted by the switch allocator (rt_ack+). There may be multiple routers *downstream* of the fault staying deadlocked as no tail flit would ever arrive due to the fault. A fake tail is therefore generated by a tail generator circuit locally at the input of this post-fault router to release all the *downstream* routers.

Figure 8.4b depicts the implementation of this tail generator added to the buffer controller at the router input. To mimic the normal operation of real tail flit, the generation of this fake tail flit should follow the 4-phase handshake protocol and the flow control protocol. When a fault-caused deadlock is detected ($permConf+$), the tail generator produces a tail flag ($eopErr$), which is used to replace the original eop wire suppose to arrive at the front of the input buffer. Note that the replacement is safe since the pipeline has been confirmed to be deadlocked ($permConf+$). The cia is the ack signal fed back to the input buffer by the crossbar to acknowledge the capture of a complete flit (here is the fake tail flit) by the output. The signal $acken$ goes high when a tail flit is detected so that the reserved path through the crossbar can be released.

Now, let us discuss the scenarios when the input buffer controller is deadlocked in the *data transmission* and *route release* states:

- If the input is deadlocked at the *data transmission* state as denoted by $acken-$, the real tail flit would never reach the front of the input buffer ($Stg\ d + 1$ at the post-fault router input in Figure 8.2). As shown in Figure 8.2, the added AND gate at the input of the router ensures a low ack (cia) from the crossbar. Therefore, the tail generator would produce a high $eopErr$ which is then latched and transmitted to all the deadlocked stages downstream of the fault. In other words, this tail generator reactivates the transition of $eop+$ in the STG of the buffer controller (Figure 8.4a), which is equivalent to creating a tail flit. This fake tail flit will traverse through all *downstream* routers and release them one by another. This tail flit is withdrawn ($eopErr-$) when it is captured by the output as indicated by both $cia-$ and $acken+$.

- If the input is deadlocked at the *route release* state, the EoP wire remains high in all pipeline stages downstream of the fault and leads to a high cia. The buffer controller gets stuck at $acken+$ as shown in Figure 8.4a. Only spacers rather than data words are allowed to traverse the router as it keeps waiting for the withdrawal of the tail flit. When the permanent fault is confirmed ($permConf+$), the tail generator produces a low $eopErr$ at the router input, which mimic a withdrawal of the tail flit. This transition is then delivered cross this post-fault router to all downstream routers following the reserved path. This reactivates the transition of the buffer controller back to *eop−*. With the withdrawal of the tail flit (*eopErr−*), all deadlocked routers downstream of the fault are released sequentially.

For all the aforementioned scenarios, the input buffer of the post-fault router is halted at the *route setup* phase after the *Release* operation. It keeps waiting for a new head flit, but it will never come as the link is damaged in the case of a permanent fault. All the other fault-free routers and links *downstream* of the faulty link are released and resume to work. Until now, the fault-caused physical-layer deadlock has been resolved and the network is partially functional again. The next step is to isolate the defective link from the network to prevent it from being utilized and affecting the network, which can be implemented by using the SDM switching technique [132, 223] as previously proposed in Section 4.2.

8.2 FAULTY LINK ISOLATION BY USING SDM

For a system with permanent faults, the usual recovery method is to block the defective component and use redundancy to compensate for its function, which may incur a large hardware overhead. When it comes to NoCs, fault-tolerant adaptive routings [78, 103] could be used to bypass the defective link. The recovery method proposed in this research is based on the Spatial Division Multiplexing (SDM) [132, 223] which does not rely on any routing algorithms or duplication. Thus, the switch allocator of a SDM router may have a choice of sub-link for the output. If one sub-link is faulty, it is removed as a possible choice, reducing the link aggregate bandwidth but retaining the link.

8.2.1 Spatial Division Multiplexing

Figure 8.6a shows a w-bit link between two wormhole routers, which can carry a w-bit data unit per transmission. Alternatively, the link between two SDM routers can be physically divided into m sub-links, each of which transfers (w/m)-bit wide flits separately as shown in Figure 8.6b. The crossbar of a p-port SDM router becomes $pm \times pm$ (w/m)-bit wide [132]. In other words, an SDM link with m sub-links can transfer m flits of m different packets in parallel,

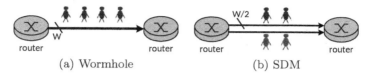

(a) Wormhole   (b) SDM

Figure 8.6   Link connections using wormhole and SDM.

but each requires a longer latency to reach its destination due to the narrowed bandwidth. From the point of view for the whole network, the performance of the SDM NoC is competitive with a network without SDM. SDM has been used to improve the network overall performance and it was proved that the SDM NoCs have advantages in energy consumption, area overhead and flexibility, as already discussed in Section 4.2.

Since a link is physically divided into multiple sub-links, a single fault will affect only one sub-link; the other sub-links of the same link can still be used to transfer packets to the same direction. This feature is inherent to SDM NoCs which supports the recovery from permanent faults. By reconfiguring the switch allocator of the SDM router to block the defective sub-link, following packets to the same output direction will go through fault-free sub-links and the network function is recovered.

It has been mentioned in Section 7.3 that, two redundant wires are added to each inter-router link to detect and locate a permanently faulty link. Adding network recovery, the fault or deadlock confirmation signal ($permConf$) generated at the deadlock detector of the pre-fault router output needs to be transmitted to the input of the post-fault router. Furthermore, since SDM divides every link into several physically independent sub-links, each sub-link requires its own deadlock detection and recovery techniques. Putting them altogether, three extra wires are added to each sub-link besides the extra redundant detection and recovery logic.

8.2.2   Switch Allocator Reconfiguration

As an example, Figure 8.7 illustrates a 5-port SDM router with each link divided into two sub-links. The input and output buffer in each port is correspondingly halved. The crossbar is increased to

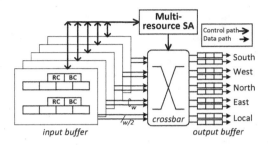

Figure 8.7   SDM router.

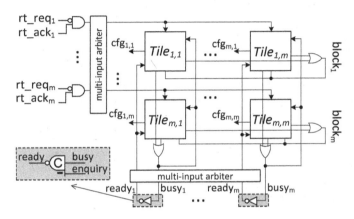

Figure 8.8   Multi-resource switch allocator [223].

10×10 one with $(w/2)$-bit wide ports [132]. To efficiently schedule packets through the crossbar, a multi-resource allocator is used to implement the switch allocator, which sequentially allocate the multiple output sub-links to requests from the multiple input sub-links.

Figure 8.8 shows the internal structure of a multi-resource arbiter [88], which is a key component of the multi-resource switch allocator. It is responsible to sequentially match multiple requests to the m resources (i.e. output sub-links). Two multi-input arbiters are used to select one routing request and one output sub-link, respectively, identifying the pair to be matched. The state of the output sub-link is indicated by a *ready* signal. A low *ready* indicates the output sub-link has been allocated to a request and is actively transmitting a packet. Only an idle output with a high *ready* can be granted to an incoming request.

Now, let us consider a NoC that might be deadlocked by a faulty link. By keeping the *ready* indication flag low, the faulty output sub-link is isolated from the network. One way to implement this isolation for a permanent faulty link is to ensure that, when the recovery process starts (or this deadlock is detected), the faulty link is "busy" and will never be "ready" (or idle) to use, so that this defective sub-link is isolated. To make this possible, the inverter shown in Figure 8.8 is replaced with an asymmetric C-element to generate the *ready* from the *busy* signal. In the detection circuits, a physical-layer deadlock can be confirmed only when the pre-fault router has allocated a packet to this faulty output sub-link (if this sub-link is idle and not transmitting any packets when the fault happens, it does not need to be recovered), so that the *busy* flag is high and *ready* is low. Using this asymmetric C-element, its minus input *enquiry* would keep *ready* to low permanently as it is set high when the sub-link was suspected to be deadlocked (the **ENQUIRY** state in Figure 7.9) and will never drop if the fault is confirmed, even after the reserved path is released by the *Drain* operation. Therefore, this added asymmetric C-element ensures that no packets will use the defective link ever again once it is confirmed. The succeeding packets requesting the same direction will be directed to other, fault-free non-busy sub-links. The function of the network remains with some performance loss.

8.3 RECOVERY FROM INTERMITTENT AND TRANSIENT FAULTS

As analyzed in Section 5.4, intermittent faults may happen and appear after some time. In terms of intermittent faults, transitions will be detected at the input/output of the post/pre-fault router when the fault disappears. The state machine of the deadlock detector would be reset to **IDLE** accordingly and withdraw the *enquiry* signal. This would unlock the added asymmetric C-element in the switch allocator as depicted in Figure 8.8. The blocked sub-link is then recovered and resume allocatable. This process has been depicted in Figure 7.9 with a dotted line. It should be noted that, one time-out period is required before recovering the blocked faulty sub-link to let the deadlock recovery operation finish so that the fault impact is cleared. Consequently, the time-out period should be at least longer than the packet transmission delay through a router when the intermittent fault is considered.

Transient faults can also break the handshake protocol and deadlock the QDI NoC. Differently from a permanent fault that leads to the isolation of the defective sub-link, a transient fault will not break a wire or gate. Therefore, the fault struck logic is still healthy and can be used again immediately. Some of the existing fault-tolerant techniques focusing on transient faults on QDI circuits [106, 264] can be used to avoid the occurrence of the deadlock, but the requirement is quite high as all pipeline stages should be continuously protected by extra circuits or duplication. This cost might be too expensive and make the method impractical. A system or chip reboot can eliminate the transient-fault-caused deadlock. This is expensive as well and may be not allowed in some critical equipment [7]. Therefore, it is beneficial to propose a fine-grained recovery mechanism for transient-fault-caused deadlock.

When SDM is utilized, a sub-link deadlocked by a transient fault is not defective and should be reused. When the state machine in the deadlock detection circuit goes to **CONFIRM** as shown in Figure 7.15, the deadlock is detected and the fault type is classified. The sub-link is initially regarded as permanently faulty by default. All recovery operations designed to dealing with a permanently faulty link, including the *Drain & Release* operations, and the blockage of the sub-link, proceed as normal and they are assumed to finish in one long time-out period. If the fault is transient, the state machine will transit to **TF_CONFIRM** after all the recovery operations finish, the blocked sub-link is reset and the link is resumed. Otherwise, the fault is permanent (**CONFIRM**) and the defective sub-link is blocked forever. Note that a transient is likely to disappear before the finish of the recovery operations. However, this sudden disappearance might affect the control circuit of the recovery operation and unexpectedly deadlock the circuit. Consequently, the faulty link is blocked until the finish of all the recovery operations for all types of faults.

According to Section 7.4.2, deadlock detection circuits require three wires for each sub-link (using SDM) when both transient and permanent link faults are considered. Adding the network recovery, the fault confirmation signal needs to be transmitted to the post-fault router to start the *Release* operation. As a result, four redundant wires are added to each sub-link to implement the network detection and recovery.

8.4   TECHNICAL ISSUES

In a QDI NoC, the fault-caused physical-layer deadlock deadlocks not only the network resource reserved by the packet directly affected by the deadlock but also all packets waiting the release of the deadlocked resources. The deadlock would gradually and eventually spread to the whole network, which would significantly decrease network performance until the whole network become literally useless. This is much more harmful than just data errors or packet loss. Chapter 7 and 8 proposed fault-tolerant techniques to detect the fault-caused physical-layer deadlock and then recover the network function. Redundant deadlock detection and recovery circuits are added to sample signals from the asynchronous NoC and control the flit flow during the recovery process, providing a complete fault-tolerant architecture.

It has been demonstrated that the fault-caused physical-layer deadlock can be accurately detected by a pair of detection circuits added to the network data path, including a deadlock detector and a pattern checker. When SDM is employed to support the network recovery from a link fault, each sub-link requires a pair of detection circuits. Two to four redundant wires are added to each link (or sub-link when SDM is used) to implement different scenarios of deadlock detection or recovery. Currently, these redundant circuits are not protected and the added circuit area could have a negative impact on the overall reliability of the chip. Given most runtime permanent faults are strongly related to the workload of the device [4, 35], it is reasonable to assume that the overall reliability against permanent faults largely increases through protecting the links since there are far fewer activities on these extra circuits compared with the usual router logic, especially when a long time-out period is used.

Different from permanent faults caused by the aging process, transient faults can happen randomly on the network. Their occurrence does not necessarily rely on signal activities. Considering the fault-tolerant designs proposed in this research, the state machine in the deadlock detector is critical and should be safe. Most of transient faults happening on detection circuits could be masked [111]. A transient fault may cause a wrong deadlock indication (*perm-Conf+*) and start the network recovery process. This could result data errors, which can be tolerated using other fault-tolerant techniques [106, 264]. The state machine controlling the detection and recovery process will keep running under the control of the clock and finally resets to the initial state as activities would be detected on the data wires. Another possible risk is that a transient-fault-caused physical-layer deadlock is mistakenly classified into a permanent one due to a transient fault on the signal indicating the fault type. Under the assumption of a 1-bit fault during a detection cycle, this cannot happen. Since the physical-layer deadlock caused by transient faults can paralyze the function of the whole network, using reasonable redundancy for deadlock detection and recovery could avoid system reboot and make the network more reliable. Some techniques such as scan chains [245] can be used to monitor and protect the behavior of these redundant circuits periodically. In addition, a fault or the deadlock recovery operation can destroy a transmitting packet, resulting in packet loss. Extra retransmission mechanisms should be employed to redeliver the lost packet. These are left as future work but are fairly conventional techniques.

Another technical issue is about the implementation of the synchronous deadlock detection circuits. The clock needs to drive only the state machine in deadlock detection circuits. There is no requirement on its skew, jitter and frequency. Different routers may use different clocks, producing different time-out periods. In fact, designers can use any clock sources in the NoC, such as the local clock from the synchronous processing element or a slow global clock. Also since every deadlock detector works independently, it can have its own counter to generate a *timeout* signal at arbitrary frequencies or share the counter (*timeout* as well) among arbitrary number of neighbors for area efficiency. The total latency T_{det} of detecting the fault that causes a physical-layer deadlock from the fault occurrence has two parts:

$$T_{\text{det}} = T_{\text{deadlock}} + T_{\text{report}} \tag{8.1}$$

where T_{deadlock} denotes the time to form a deadlock and T_{report} is delay of reporting or confirming this deadlock (at state **CONFIRM**, in Figure 7.9, 7.11 and 7.15). T_{deadlock} is out of control of the deadlock detection and recovery. It is short on a busy link or internal router path but infinite on an idle channel. Nevertheless, no damage is made if no deadlock is formed.

The latency reporting the confirmation of the fault-caused deadlock T_{report} is an important factor in evaluating the detection speed. The upper and lower bounds of T_{report} can be described as Equation 8.2:

$$2T_t \leq T_{\text{report}} \leq 4T_t \tag{8.2}$$

where T_t is the time-out period. The lower bound is achieved when the deadlock is formed just before the state machine in the detection circuits transits to **START**. The upper bound is reached when the deadlock occurs before **IDLE**. There is no strong constraint on the period of the clock (T_{clk}) and the time-out period (T_t). Obviously reducing T_t decreases the report latency T_{report}, but several issues should be considered:

- If only a permanent fault or only deadlock detection is considered, T_t should be larger than T_{clk} and the latency of transmitting one flit through one pipeline stage (usually several nanoseconds, to allow a stable sample from transition detectors).

- If the proposed network recovery technique is employed to deal with deadlocks caused by intermittent or transient faults, T_t should be long enough (at least longer than a packet transmission latency through a router) to ensure that all recovery operations are finished in one time-out period, so that the state machine can safely transit to the initial state **IDLE**. This case is employed in the implemented NoC.

As mentioned in Section 5.1.3, an intermittent fault can be taken as a long transient fault or a permanent fault depending its length. Both the intermittent and transient faults will disappear, so that the previously blocked faulty sub-link should be recovered to use after the default recovery process (for a permanent fault). Their recovery methods are different. An intermittent fault is assumed to disappear after the recovery process (if it disappears during the detection process, no deadlocks happen) and the resulting deadlock pattern is the same as the one caused by permanent faults, so that the resulting signal transition can be captured by the deadlock detector and recover the blocked sub-link after the default recovery process (Figure 7.9). Differently, a transient fault disappears during the deadlock detection process, which will not cause detectable transitions once the physical-layer deadlock has been formed, so that the faulty link is recovered only if the fault is diagnosed as transient after the deadlock detection (Figure 7.15).

In the implemented NoC with both deadlock detection and recovery, a long time-out period is employed. On one hand, it ensures the network function has enough time to recover after the deadlock detection; on the other hand, a long time-out period can reduce the possibility of the metastability caused by the sampling of asynchronous signals by synchronous circuits every one time-out period. Figure 8.9 shows the interface between the synchronous deadlock detection circuits and the asynchronous router. Transition detectors

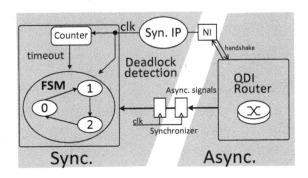

Figure 8.9   Interface between the detection circuits and the QDI NoC.

are enabled to monitor activities of some asynchronous signals from the second time-out period (the **START** state in Figure 7.9). If a transition is detected, the sampling stops and the state machine will be reset afterwards. Otherwise, asynchronous signals are sampled every one time-out period to check against the deadlock patterns, where the metastability could happen. The metastability possibility decreases after each long time-out since the asynchronous data path becomes more like to be deadlocked. A synchronizer [86, 230] is added between the synchronous detection circuit and the asynchronous router to further reduce the metastability effects. Therefore, it can be claimed that this asynchronous/synchronous interface design is highly robust against metastability.

This chapter presents the recovery of a link fault that causes a physical-layer deadlock. A fault on the router logic could also deadlock the NoC, which has been able to be detected to some extent, as described in Section 7.3.5. However, its recovery is difficult if no redundancy or spares are used. If a permanent fault is confirmed to be happening in a router, the usual way is using fault-tolerant routing algorithms to detour the whole router [103]. To tolerate transient faults in the router logic, error detection or correction is usually added to the router ports to correct transient faults on the fly so that no deadlock could happen [201]. The recovery of the network function from a router fault is left as future work. To our best knowledge, there is no previous publication which fully tolerates a permanently faulty link of QDI NoCs. The proposed detection and recovery techniques are novel and are the first time to solve the serious fault-caused physical-layer deadlock problems in QDI NoCs.

8.5 SUMMARY

It can be concluded that the network recovery from a fault-caused physical-layer deadlock can be easily implemented using the SDM switching technique. In terms of a permanently faulty sub-link, it is isolated so that all the following packets requesting the same direction will go through fault-free ones. Though this removal of the faulty sub-link leads to a moderate performance loss, it is acceptable for specific critical digital systems since keeping them working is important. Note that most redundant circuits are used to eliminate the deadlock and clean the flits remaining in the reserved fault-free network resources, such as in the *Drain & Release* operation, which is unavoidable for a fine-grained network recovery in QDI NoCs. A coarse-grained recovery strategy such like a system reboot does not need this process but it cannot locate the faulty component without further overhead such as built-in-self-test circuits [148]. The reconfiguration of the route connection is achieved by borrowing the internal circuit of the original the SDM router, which induces little area overhead. When a transient or intermittent link fault is also considered, the previously blocked sub-link can be reused again so that the network function is fully recovered.

These proposed recovery methods do not rely on any specific routings. Other traditional recovery techniques, such as fault-tolerant routings, can be further used to release the traffic pressure of the damaged link, avoiding making hot spots in the network and compensating for the performance loss, which is left as future work. In addition, the proposed fault detection and recovery techniques do not try to correct faults, so that packet loss is possible, which can be detected in a higher network layer. Using retransmission or other fault-tolerant techniques, the lost packet can be routed to the destination or recovered, which is outside the scope of this book and left as future work as well.

CHAPTER 9

Summary

NoCs are promising fabrics to provide scalable and efficient on-chip communication for large-scale many-core systems. They can be implemented using synchronous or asynchronous circuits. Most existing NoCs are built synchronously with a clock distribution network. Faults on synchronous NoCs typically cause data errors, which can be detected and corrected using conventional well-studied, fault-tolerant techniques. Asynchronous NoCs have many potential advantages over the synchronous ones due to their clockless feature, which are promising for the future large-scale multi-core systems. Faults occurring on asynchronous NoCs, however, can not only corrupt data, but disrupt the handshake process and cause physical-layer deadlocks. In a wormhole network, this deadlock may break or stall a transmitting packet. The broken or stalled packet may straddle multiple routers, which will cause more packet stalls. As a result, the deadlock spreads over the network and the network function is paralyzed. Due to the broken handshake protocol, this fault-caused, physical-layer deadlock is different from those due to the cyclic dependence of packet transmissions in the network layer, and cannot be handled using conventional deadlock management techniques. Resolving this deadlock in the physical-layer is mandatory to restore the network operation.

This book targets the design of high-performance and reliable asynchronous NoCs. It studies the impact of different faults on asynchronous circuits and NoCs, and presents thorough fault-tolerant solutions at the circuit level, including using fault-tolerant coding and managing the fault-caused destructive deadlocks. Optimizing techniques are researched to improve the throughput performance of asynchronous NoCs. To the best knowledge of the authors, this is the first thorough research on the fault-tolerance and fault-caused deadlock effect of QDI NoCs.

9.1 OVERALL REMARKS

This book demonstrates that both transient and permanent faults can cause physical-layer deadlocks, and produce different syndromes or patterns which help to differentiate physical-layer deadlocks from network-layer ones or temporary network congestion. Thus, the faulty component can be detected and located precisely. Meanwhile, these deadlock patterns often determine the fault type so that fault diagnosis circuits were implemented to tell which fault (transient or permanent) deadlocks the packet path. After the deadlock detection and diagnosis, the deadlocked network needs to be recovered.

A packet may be stalled or broken by a fault during its transmission across the asynchronous network. As a result, the reserved packet path is jammed with fault-free (upstream of the fault) and polluted (downstream of the fault) flits when the deadlock is detected. To restore the network operation, a *Drain&Release* mechanism is demonstrated which drains remaining flits in the deadlocked packet path and releases healthy network resources. Depending on the fault type, the faulty component (inter-router link in this research) should be either permanently blocked (for permanent faults) or reused (for transient faults). Spatial division multiplexing (SDM) provides a natural way to restore the network function from a permanently faulty link wire. By locking the faulty sub-link belonging to one physical link, the other healthy sub-links can still be used to transmit packets in the same direction. The deadlock network is recovered.

These proposed deadlock management techniques are essential to maintain the function of asynchronous NoCs in the presence of faults. Keeping the network running is essential even with some graceful performance degradation. It is demonstrated that, applying these fault-tolerant techniques to different baseline QDI NoCs may incur around 1.6%~8.5% area overhead and 2%~14% speed overhead. It is believed that, considering the largely enhanced fault-tolerance capability achieved by resolving the harmful deadlock issue, these accompanied penalties are moderate and acceptable in practical asynchronous NoC designs. The proposed fault-tolerant techniques in this book are feasible to protect asynchronous NoCs and provide a realistic fault-tolerance solution for future large-scale many-core SoCs.

As a complementary measure to enhance the reliability of asynchronous NoCs, the proposed systematic DIRC coding scheme can be flexibly employed to protect the large number of long link wires in QDI NoCs from transient faults, reducing the data error rate. The protected QDI interconnects achieve both timing-robustness and fault-tolerance. The incurred overhead varies depending on the construction manner. It is demonstrated that, the area of a complete DIRC pipeline stage can be around four times larger than the unprotected one, while the speed overhead can be less than 50%. If the area of link wires is considered and these wires consume significantly large area, the area overhead will approach to $(1/CN)$, which is 50% when $CN=2$ (CN denotes the number of 1-of-n data words in a DIRC code). The area-consuming 1-of-n adders can be designed in the transistor level to reduce the hardware overhead. A trade-off can be made between the achieved fault-tolerance capability and the hardware overhead according to the practical design requirement. Protecting links in only critical regions can further reduce the hardware cost.

It can be inferred from this book that, compared with synchronous NoCs where faults typically cause data errors, asynchronous or QDI NoCs are more vulnerable to faults since the possibly fault-caused physical-layer deadlocks can easily paralyze the network function. Besides permanent faults which can stall the handshake process, even a transient fault can deadlock the network, which is a new challenging topic deeply studied in this book. The occurrence of this kind of deadlock is indirectly due to the adaptability of asynchronous circuits to timing variations, though this timing-robustness is an attractive feature that synchronous circuits do not have. Therefore, it has to be admitted that, *from this deadlock point of view, without any fault-tolerant techniques, asynchronous NoCs are less reliable than conventional synchronous ones.*

Besides the fault-tolerance challenge studied in this book, it should also be kept in mind that, due to the additional circuits controlling the handshake process, asynchronous circuits often have drawbacks in area and speed in practical designs. As the leakage currents become a major contributor to the power consumption in nanoscale technologies, controlling the circuit area below a specific level is necessary for low-power designs [94]. The hardware cost incurred by the fault-tolerance should also be balanced. Meanwhile, the lack of mature electronic design automation (EDA) tools and design methodology makes it difficult to implement high-performance large-scale asynchronous circuits effectively, deterring the wide use of asynchronous designs in commercial fields [231]. However, as has been widely accepted by asynchronous circuit designers, asynchronous NoCs are promising for the future large-scale many-core Systems-on-Chip (SoCs) where distributing the global clock and the chip-level timing closure becomes increasingly difficult. The resulting globally asynchronous, locally synchronous (GALS) system achieves promising advantages over the synchronous counterparts, including the simplified chip-level timing closure, the decreased clock distribution network, the good support for modularity and design reuse and the independent frequency/-voltage control in different synchronous domains. The static power consumption can be reduced by adding power gating circuits [181] or using leakage control techniques [94] while the performance can be improved through carefully designing the asynchronous pipeline structure [53]. These all drive the research and usage of asynchronous circuits in implementing the future large-scale NoCs.

This book proposes a holistic, efficient, resilient and cost-effective solution to resolve the deadlock effect caused by faults, providing an opportunity for asynchronous NoCs to cater for the future on-chip interconnections requiring high reliability. The proposed fault-tolerant techniques can maintain the function of asynchronous NoCs in the presence of different faults, which is significant for critical electronic devices, since keeping them running is essential even with some performance degradation. In addition, though this book focuses on studying the fault-tolerance of asynchronous circuits or

NoCs, the trade-off between the achieved fault-tolerance capability and the incurred hardware cost is necessary and has been explored. Optimizing techniques have been proposed to further improve the network performance. Taking the proposed DIRC coding scheme protecting QDI links for example, the systematic feature of the DIRC codes makes it possible to place DIRC pipeline stages arbitrarily in an unprotected QDI pipeline, thus some certain pipeline segments can be protected. According to the practical fault-tolerance requirement, the DIRC pipeline using different construction patterns can provide required fault-tolerance with a moderate and reasonable hardware overhead. For the proposed deadlock management techniques, redundant circuits can be placed at a specific pipeline segment to monitor its activities, so as to detect the fault-caused deadlock and recover the network function. This general strategy allows designers to flexibly apply the deadlock management circuits to protect asynchronous NoC or general asynchronous pipelines from the fatal deadlock, while the hardware cost is under control.

Although the proposed fault-tolerant techniques are based on 4-phase, 1-of-n asynchronous protocols in this book, they provide a basic clue to correct data errors and resolve the destructive deadlock effect caused by different faults and can be generalized to provide protection for other types of QDI NoCs.

9.2 FUTURE WORK

Fault-tolerance is a concept over a whole system, which needs protection from multiple different layers to ensure all system functions are correct under a specific fault environment. The redundancy required by the fault-tolerance brings performance and hardware overhead. Thus, it is valuable to be aware of practical fault-tolerant requirement, and from a system view to achieve required fault-tolerance from different network layers with cost-effective designs. As an example, to protect QDI NoCs, the proposed techniques managing the fault-caused physical-layer deadlocks in this book are mandatory in the bottom circuit level to keep the network functioning. It is impossible to protect all components in a network. The relatively expensive point-to-point protection (DIRC) can be applied to some critical network region or components depending on the practical designs to filter a large portion of transient faults on-the-fly. These methods mainly protect the network from the bottom physical or data link layer. At higher layers, the same techniques employed in synchronous NoCs can still be used, such as resending corrupted packets, fault-tolerant routings, end-to-end protection [48, 103, 198], etc. to provide protection.

This book explores the fault-tolerance of asynchronous NoCs. There is still lots of work to do to provide full protection, including the metastability problem in asynchronous designs, precise fault diagnosis, the protection of the router control logic, the protection of the added redundant circuits for fault-tolerance, multi-layer protection and systematic fault-tolerance evaluation of NoCs, etc, which is left the future work.

Bibliography

[1] Adrijean Adriahantenaina, Hervé Charlery, Alain Greiner, Laurent Mortiez, and Cesar Albenes Zeferino. SPIN: A scalable, packet switched, on-chip micro-network. In *Proceedings of the Design, Automation & Test in Europe Conference & Exhibition*, pages 20070–20073, Washington, DC, USA, March 2003. IEEE Computer Society.

[2] Melinda Y. Agyekum, and Steven M. Nowick. An error-correcting unordered code and hardware support for robust asynchronous global communication. In *Proceedings of the Design, Automation & Test in Europe Conference & Exhibition*, pages 765–770. IEEE Computer Society, March 2010.

[3] Melinda Y. Agyekum, and Steven M. Nowick. Error-correcting unordered codes and hardware support for robust asynchronous global communication. *IEEE Transactions on Computer-Aided Design of Integrated Circuits and Systems*, 31(1):75–88, January 2012.

[4] Robert C. Aitken, Görschwin Fey, Zbigniew T. Kalbarczyk, Frank Reichenbach, and Matteo Sonza Reorda. Reliability analysis reloaded: How will we survive? In *Proceedings of the Design, Automation & Test in Europe Conference & Exhibition*, pages 358–367, 2013.

[5] Sami A. Al-Arian and Dharma P. Agrawal. Physical failures and fault models of CMOS circuits. *IEEE Transactions on Circuits and Systems*, 34(3):269–279, March 1987.

[6] Ra'ed Al-Dujaily, Terrence S. T. Mak, Fei Xia, Alexandre Yakovlev, and Maurizio Palesi. Run-time deadlock detection in networks-on-chip using coupled transitive closure

networks. In *Proceedings of the Design, Automation & Test in Europe Conference & Exhibition*, pages 497–502. IEEE, March 2011.

[7] Homa Alemzadeh, Ravishankar K. Iyer, Zbigniew Kalbarczyk, and Jai Raman. Analysis of safety-critical computer failures in medical devices. *IEEE Security & Privacy*, 11(4):14–26, July 2013.

[8] Sobeeh Almukhaizim, Feng Shi, Eric Love, and Yiorgos Makris. Soft-error tolerance and mitigation in asynchronous burst-mode circuits. *IEEE Transactions on Very Large Scale Integration (VLSI) Systems*, 17(7):869–882, 2009.

[9] Thomas E. Anderson, Susan S. Owicki, James B. Saxe, and Charles P. Thacker. High-speed switch scheduling for local-area networks. *ACM Transactions on Computer Systems*, 11(4):319–352, November 1993.

[10] J. L. Autran, D. Munteanu, S. Moindjie, T. Saad Saoud, S. Sauze, G. Gasiot, and P. Roche. ASTEP (2005–2015): Ten years of soft error and atmospheric radiation characterization on the Plateau de Bure. *Microelectronics Reliability*, 55(9-10):1506–1511, August 2015.

[11] John Bainbridge and Steve Furber. Chain: A delay-insensitive chip area interconnect. *IEEE Micro*, 22(5):16–23, 2002.

[12] John Bainbridge, Will Toms, Doug Edwards, and Steve Furber. Delay-insensitive, point-to-point interconnect using m-of-n codes. In *Proceedings of the IEEE International Symposium on Asynchronous Circuits and Systems*, pages 132–140. IEEE Computer Society, May 2003.

[13] William John Bainbridge. *Asynchronous system-on-chip interconnect*. PhD thesis, Department of Computer Science, the Faculty of Science & Engineering, the University of Manchester, March 2000. http://apt.cs.manchester.ac.uk/ftp/pub/apt/theses/bainbridge_phd.pdf.

[14] William John Bainbridge and Sean James Salisbury. Glitch sensitivity and defense of quasi delay-insensitive network-on-chip links. In *Proceedings of the IEEE International Symposium on Asynchronous Circuits and Systems*, pages 35–44. IEEE Computer Society, May 2009.

[15] Ramanatha V. Balakrishnan, and Desmond W. L. Young. System for reducing skew in the parallel transmission of multi-bit data slices, March 1992. US Patent 5,101,347.

[16] Arnab Banerjee and Simon W. Moore. Flow-aware allocation for on-chip networks. In *Proceedings of the International Symposium on Networks-on-Chips*, pages 183–192. IEEE Computer Society, May 2009.

[17] Rodrigo Possamai Bastos, Gilles Sicard, Fernanda Kastensmidt, Marc Renaudin, and Ricardo Reis. Evaluating transient-fault effects on traditional C-element's implementations. In *Proceedings of the IEEE International On-Line Testing Symposium*, pages 35–40, July 2010.

[18] Robert C. Baumann. Soft errors in advanced semiconductor devices-part I: The three radiation sources. *IEEE Transactions on Device and Materials Reliability*, 1(1):17–22, 2001.

[19] Robert C. Baumann. Radiation-induced soft errors in advanced semiconductor technologies. *IEEE Transactions on Device and Materials Reliability*, 5(3):305–316, 2005.

[20] Robert C. Baumann, Tim Hossain, Eric Smith, Shinya Murata, and Hideki Kitagawa. Boron as a primary source of radiation in high density DRAMs. In *Proceedings of the Symposium on VLSI Technology*, pages 81–82, June 1995.

[21] Edith Beigné, Fabien Clermidy, Sylvain Miermont, and Pascal Vivet. Dynamic voltage and frequency scaling architecture for units integration within a GALS NoC. In *Proceedings of the ACM/IEEE International Symposium On Networks-on-Chip*, pages 129–138. IEEE Computer Society, April 2008.

[22] Edith Beigné, Fabien Clermidy, Pascal Vivet, Alain Clouard, and Marc Renaudin. An asynchronous NOC architecture providing low latency service and its multi-level design framework. In *Proceedings of the IEEE International Symposium on Asynchronous Circuits and Systems*, pages 54–63. IEEE Computer Society, March 2005.

[23] Václav E. Beneš. On rearrangeable three-stage connecting networks. *Bell System Technical Journal*, 41(5):1481–1492, September 1962.

[24] Luca Benini and Giovanni De Micheli. Networks on chips: A new SoC paradigm. *IEEE Computer*, 35(1):70–78, 2002.

[25] Davide Bertozzi and Luca Benini. Xpipes: A network-on-chip architecture for gigascale systems-on-chip. *IEEE Circuits and Systems Magazine*, 4(2):18–31, 2004.

[26] D. Binder, E. C. Smith, and A. B. Holman. Satellite anomalies from galactic cosmic rays. *IEEE Transactions on Nuclear Science*, 22(6):2675–2680, December 1975.

[27] Tobias Bjerregaard, Shankar Mahadevan, Rasmus Grøndahl Olsen, and Jens Sparsø. An OCP compliant network adapter for GALS-based SoC design using the MANGO network-on-chip. In *Proceedings of the International Symposium on System-on-Chip*, pages 171–174. IEEE, November 2005.

[28] Tobias Bjerregaard and Jens Sparsø. A router architecture for connection-oriented service guarantees in the MANGO clockless network-on-chip. In *Proceedings of the Design, Automation & Test in Europe Conference & Exhibition*, pages 1226–1231. IEEE Computer Society, March 2005.

[29] Tobias Bjerregaard and Jens Sparsø. A scheduling discipline for latency and bandwidth guarantees in asynchronous network-on-chip. In *Proceedings of the International Symposium on Advanced Research in Asynchronous Circuits and Systems*, pages 34–43. IEEE Computer Society, March 2005.

[30] Tobias Bjerregaard and Jens Sparsø. Implementation of guaranteed services in the MANGO clockless network-on-chip. *IEE Proceedings — Computers and Digital Techniques*, 153(4):217–229, 2006.

[31] David Blaauw, Kaviraj Chopra, Ashish Srivastava, and Lou Scheffer. Statistical timing analysis: From basic principles to state of the art. *IEEE Transactions on Computer-Aided Design of Integrated Circuits and Systems*, 27(4):589–607, April 2008.

[32] Geoffrey Blake, Ronald Dreslinski, and Trevor Mudge. A survey of multicore processors. *IEEE Signal Processing Magazine*, 26(6):26–37, November 2009.

[33] Mario Blaum and Jehoshua Bruck. Unordered error-correcting codes and their applications. In *Proceedings of the International Symposium on Fault-Tolerant Computing*, pages 486–493, July 1992.

[34] Paul Bogdan and Radu Mărculescu. A theoretical framework for on-chip stochastic communication analysis. In *Proceedings of the International ICST Conference on Nano-Networks*, pages 1–5. IEEE, September 2006.

[35] Mark Bohr and Kaizad Mistry. Intel's revolutionary 22 nm transistor technology, May 2011. http://www. intel.com/content/www/us/en/silicon-innovations/ revolutionary-22nm-transistor-technology- presentation.html.

[36] Evgeny Bolotin, Israel Cidon, Ran Ginosar, and Avinoam Kolodny. Routing table minimization for irregular mesh NoCs. In *Proceedings of the Design, Automation & Test in Europe Conference & Exhibition*, pages 942–947. IEEE, April 2007.

[37] Shekhar Y. Borkar. Designing reliable systems from unreliable components: The challenges of transistor variability and degradation. *IEEE Micro*, 25(6):10–16, November 2005.

[38] Bella Bose. On unordered codes. *IEEE Transactions on Computers*, 40(2):125–131, 1991.

[39] W. R. Bottoms. A roadmap for heterogeneous integration in electronics, May 2015. `http://www.itrs2.net/itrs-reports.html`.

[40] Fred A. Bower, Daniel J. Sorin, and Sule Ozev. A mechanism for online diagnosis of hard faults in microprocessors. In *Proceedings of the Annual IEEE/ACM International Symposium on Microarchitecture*, pages 197–208. IEEE Computer Society, November 2005.

[41] P. D. Bradley and E. Normand. Single event upsets in implantable cardioverter defibrillators. *IEEE Transactions on Nuclear Science*, 45(6):2929–2940, 1998.

[42] John F. Bulzacchelli, Timothy O. Dickson, Frank D. Ferraiolo, Robert J. Reese, and Michael B. Spear. Calibration of multiple parallel data communications lines for high skew conditions, March 2014. US Patent 8,681,839.

[43] Alex Bystrov, David Kinniment, and Alex Yakovlev. Priority arbiters. In *Proceedings of the International Symposium on Asynchronous Circuits and Systems*, pages 128–137. IEEE Computer Society, 2000.

[44] Thomas J. Chaney and Charles E. Molnar. Anomalous behavior of synchronizer and arbiter circuits. *IEEE Transactions on Computers*, 22(4):421–422, April 1973.

[45] H. Jonathan Chao, Kung-Li Deng, and Zhigang Jing. PetaStar: A petabit photonic packet switch. *IEEE Journal on Selected Areas in Communications*, 21(7):1096–1112, September 2003.

[46] H. Jonathan Chao, Zhigang Jing, and Soung Y. Liew. Matching algorithms for three-stage bufferless Clos network switches. *IEEE Communications Magazine*, 41(10):46–54, October 2003.

[47] H. Jonathan Chao, Cheuk H. Lam, and Eiji Oki. *Broadband Packet Switching Technologies: A Practical Guide to ATM Switches and IP Routers*. John Wiley & Sons, Inc., 2001.

[48] Fu-Chiung Cheng and Shuen-Long Ho. Efficient systematic error-correcting codes for semi-delay-insensitive data transmission. In *Proceedings of the IEEE International Conference on Computer Design*, pages 24–29. IEEE Computer Society, September 2001.

[49] Jan Cheyns, Chris Develder, Erik Van Breusegem, Didier Colle, Filip De Turck, Paul Lagasse, Mario Pickavet, and Piet Demeester. Clos lives on in optical packet switching. *IEEE Communications Magazine*, 42(2):114–121, February 2004.

[50] Ge-Ming Chiu. The odd-even turn model for adaptive routing. *IEEE Transactions on Parallel and Distributed Systems*, 11(7):729–738, July 2000.

[51] Fabio M. Chiussi, Joseph G. Kneuer, and Vijay P. Kumar. Low-cost scalable switching solutions for broadband networking: The ATLANTA architecture and chipset. *IEEE Communications Magazine*, 35(12):44–53, December 1997.

[52] Tam-Anh Chu. *Synthesis of Self-Timed VLSI Circuits from Graph-Theoretic Specifications*. PhD thesis, Massachusetts Institute of Technology, 1987. https://dspace.mit.edu/handle/1721.1/14794.

[53] Fabien Clermidy, Christian Bernard, Romain Lemaire, Jerome Martin, Ivan Miro-Panades, Yvain Thonnart, Pascal Vivet, and Norbert Wehn. A 477mW NoC-based digital baseband for MIMO 4G SDR. In *Proceedings of the IEEE International Solid-State Circuits Conference*, pages 278–279. IEEE, February 2010.

[54] Charles Clos. A study of non-blocking switching networks. *Bell System Technical Journal*, 32(5):406–424, March 1953.

[55] Nicola Concer, Luciano Bononi, Michael Soulié, and Riccardo Locatelli. CTC: An end-to-end flow control protocol

for multi-core systems-on-chip. In *Proceedings of the International Symposium on Networks-on-Chips*, pages 193–202. IEEE Computer Society, May 2009.

[56] Cristian Constantinescu. Trends and challenges in VLSI circuit reliability. *IEEE Micro*, 23(4):14–19, 2003.

[57] Jordi Cortadella, Michael Kishinevsky, Alex Kondratyev, Luciano Lavagno, and Alex Yakovlev. Petrify: A tool for manipulating concurrent specifications and synthesis of asynchronous controllers. *IEICE Transactions on Information and Systems*, E80-D(3):315–325, 1997.

[58] William J. Dally. Virtual-channel flow control. *IEEE Transactions on Parallel and Distributed Systems*, 3(2):194–205, March 1992.

[59] William J. Dally and Hiromichi Aoki. Deadlock-free adaptive routing in multicomputer networks using virtual channels. *IEEE Transactions on Parallel and Distributed Systems*, 4(4):466–475, April 1993.

[60] William J. Dally and Charles L. Seitz. The torus routing chip. *Distributed Computing*, 1(4):187–196, December 1986.

[61] William J. Dally and Charles L. Seitz. Deadlock-free message routing in multiprocessor interconnection networks. *IEEE Transactions on Computers*, C-36(5):547–553, 1987.

[62] William J. Dally and Brian Towles. Route packets, not wires: On-chip interconnection networks. In *Proceedings of the Design Automation Conference*, pages 684–689. IEEE, ACM, 2001.

[63] William James Dally and Brian Patrick Towles. *Principles and Practices of Interconnection Networks*. Morgan Kaufmann Publishers, San Francisco, 2004.

[64] Ilana David, Ran Ginosar, and Michael Yoeli. Self-timed is self-checking. *Journal of Electronic Testing*, 6(2):219–228, 1995.

[65] Mark E. Dean, Ted E. Williams, and David L. Dill. Efficient self-timing with level-encoded 2-phase dual-rail (LEDR). In *Proceedings of the University of California/Santa Cruz Conference on Advanced Research in VLSI*, pages 55–70. MIT Press, April 1991.

[66] Charles Dike and Edward Ted Burton. Miller and noise effects in a synchronizing flip-flop. *IEEE Journal of Solid-State Circuits*, 34(6):849–855, June 1999.

[67] Rostislav (Reuven) Dobkin, Ran Ginosar, and Avinoam Kolodny. QNoC asynchronous router. *Integration, the VLSI Journal*, 42(2):103–115, March 2009.

[68] Rostislav (Reuven) Dobkin, Ran Ginosar, and Christos P. Sotiriou. Data synchronization issues in GALS SoCs. In *Proceedings of the International Symposium on Advanced Research in Asynchronous Circuits and Systems*, pages 170–180. IEEE Computer Society, April 2004.

[69] Rostislav Reuven Dobkin, Yevgeny Perelman, Tuvia Liran, Ran Ginosar, and Avinoam Kolodny. High rate wave-pipelined asynchronous on-chip bit-serial data link. In *Proceedings of the IEEE International Symposium on Asynchronous Circuits and Systems*. IEEE, March 2007.

[70] Hao Dong. Modified berger codes for detection of unidirectional errors. *IEEE Transactions on Computers*, C-33(6):572–575, June 1984.

[71] José Duato, Sudhakar Yalamanchili, and Lionel Ni. *Interconnection Networks: An Engineering Approach*. Morgan Kaufmann Publishers, San Francisco, CA, 2003.

[72] Tudor Dumitraş and Radu Mărculescu. On-chip stochastic communication. In *Proceedings of the Design, Automation & Test in Europe Conference & Exhibition*, pages 10790–10795. IEEE Computer Society, March 2003.

[73] Doug Edwards and Andrew Bardsley. Balsa: An asynchronous hardware synthesis language. *The Computer Journal*, 45(1):12–18, 2002.

[74] Dan Ernst, Nam Sung Kim, Shidhartha Das, Sanjay Pant, Rajeev R. Rao, Toan Pham, Conrad H. Ziesler, David T. Blaauw, Todd M. Austin, Krisztián Flautner, and Trevor N. Mudge. Razor: A low-power pipeline based on circuit-level timing speculation. In *Proceedings of the Annual International Symposium on Microarchitecture*, pages 7–18. IEEE Computer Society, December 2003.

[75] Tomaz Felicijan. *Quality-of-Service (QoS) for Asynchronous On-Chip Networks*. PhD thesis, Department of Computer Science, the Faculty of Science and Engineering, the University of Manchester, 2004. http://apt.cs.manchester.ac.uk/ftp/pub/amulet/theses/TomazPhD.pdf.

[76] Tomaz Felicijan, John Bainbridge, and Steve Furber. An asynchronous low latency arbiter for quality of service (QoS) applications. In *Proceedings of the International Conference on Microelectronics*, pages 123–126. IEEE, December 2003.

[77] Tomaz Felicijan and Steve B. Furber. An asynchronous on-chip network router with quality-of-service (QoS) support. In *Proceedings of the IEEE International SOC Conference*, pages 274–277. IEEE, September 2004.

[78] Chaochao Feng, Zhonghai Lu, Axel Jantsch, Minxuan Zhang, and Zuocheng Xing. Addressing transient and permanent faults in NoC with efficient fault-tolerant deflection router. *IEEE Transactions on Very Large Scale Integration (VLSI) Systems*, 21(6):1053–1066, 2013.

[79] Werner Friesenbichler, Thomas Panhofer, and Martin Delvai. A comprehensive approach for soft error tolerant four state logic. In *Proceedings of the IEEE Symposium on Design and Diagnostics of Electronic Circuits and Systems*, pages 214–217. IEEE Computer Society, April 2009.

[80] Werner Friesenbichler and Andreas Steininger. Soft error tolerant asynchronous circuits based on dual redundant four state logic. In *Proceedings of the Euromicro Conference on Digital System Design, Architectures, Methods and Tools*, pages 100–107. IEEE Computer Society, August 2009.

[81] Steve Furber and John Bainbridge. Future trends in SoC interconnect. In *Proceedings of the International Symposium on System-on-Chip*, pages 183–186. IEEE, November 2005.

[82] Steve Furber and Paul Day. Four-phase micropipeline latch control circuits. *IEEE Transactions on Very Large Scale Integration (VLSI) Systems*, 4(2):247–253, June 1996.

[83] K. T. Gardiner, Alexandre Yakovlev, and Alexandre V. Bystrov. A C-element latch scheme with increased transient fault tolerance for asynchronous circuits. In *Proceedings of the IEEE International On-Line Testing Symposium*, pages 223–230, July 2007.

[84] Gilles Gasiot, Maximilien Glorieux, Sylvain Clerc, Dimitri Soussan, Fady Abouzeid, and Philippe Roche. Experimental soft error rate of several flip-flop designs representative of production chip in 32 nm CMOS technology. *IEEE Transactions on Nuclear Science*, 60(6):4226–4231, December 2013.

[85] Ran Ginosar. Fourteen ways to fool your synchronizer. In *Proceedings of the International Symposium on Asynchronous Circuits and Systems*, pages 89–96. IEEE Computer Society, May 2003.

[86] Ran Ginosar. Metastability and synchronizers: A tutorial. *IEEE Design & Test of Computers*, 28(5):23–35, 2011.

[87] Christopher J. Glass and Lionel M. Ni. The turn model for adaptive routing. *Journal of the ACM*, 41(5):874–902, September 1994.

[88] Stanislavs Golubcovs, Delong Shang, Fei Xia, Andrey Mokhov, and Alex Yakovlev. Modular approach to multi-resource arbiter design. In *Proceedings of the IEEE Symposium on Asynchronous Circuits and Systems*, pages 107–116. IEEE, May 2009.

[89] Stanislavs Golubcovs, Delong Shang, Fei Xia, Andrey Mokhov, and Alex Yakovlev. Multi-resource arbiter decomposition. Technical report, Microelectronic System

Design Group, School of EECE, Newcastle University, February 2009. `http://async.org.uk/tech-reports/ NCL-EECE-MSD-TR-2009-143.pdf`.

[90] Crispín Gómez, María E. Gómez, Pedro López, and José Duato. Exploiting wiring resources on interconnection network: Increasing path diversity. In *Proceedings of the Euromicro Conference on Parallel, Distributed and Network-Based Processing*, pages 20–29. IEEE, February 2008.

[91] María Engracia Gómez, Nils Agne Nordbotten, Jose Flich, Pedro López, Antonio Robles, José Duato, Tor Skeie, and Olav Lysne. A routing methodology for achieving fault tolerance in direct networks. *IEEE Transactions on Computers*, 55(4):400–415, April 2006.

[92] Kees Goossens, John Dielissen, and Andrei Radulescu. Æthereal network on chip: Concepts, architectures, and implementations. *IEEE Design & Test of Computers*, 22(5):414–421, September 2005.

[93] Richard Wesley Hamming. Error detecting and error correcting codes. *Bell System technical journal*, 29(2):147–160, 1950.

[94] Jeremie Hamon and Edith Beigne. Automatic leakage control for wide range performance QDI asynchronous circuits in FD-SOI technology. In *Proceedings of the IEEE International Symposium on Asynchronous Circuits and Systems*, pages 142–149. IEEE, May 2013.

[95] P. Hazucha, T. Karnik, J. Maiz, S. Walstra, B. Bloechel, J. Tschanz, G. Dermer, S. Hareland, P. Armstrong, and S. Borkar. Neutron soft error rate measurements in a 90-nm CMOS process and scaling trends in SRAM from 0.25-μm to 90-nm generation. In *Proceedings of the IEEE International Electron Devices Meeting*, pages 21.5.1–21.5.4. IEEE, December 2003.

[96] Jörg Henkel, Wayne Wolf, and Srimat Chakradhar. On-chip networks: A scalable, communication-centric embedded

system design paradigm. In *Proceedings of the International Conference on VLSI Design*, pages 845–851, 2004.

[97] Jingcao Hu and Radu Mărculescu. DyAD — smart routing for networks-on-chip. In *Proceedings of the Design Automation Conference*, pages 260–263. ACM, June 2004.

[98] Wei Huang, Mircea R. Stan, Kevin Skadron, Karthik Sankaranarayanan, Shougata Ghosh, and Sivakumar Velusamy. Compact thermal modeling for temperature-aware design. In *Proceedings of the Annual Design Automation Conference*, pages 878–883. ACM, 2004.

[99] Henrik Hulgaard, Steven M. Burns, and Gaetano Borriello. Testing asynchronous circuits: A survey. *Integration, the VLSI Journal*, 19(3):111–131, 1995.

[100] Jameel Hussein and Gary Swift. Mitigating single-event upsets, May 2015. http://www.xilinx.com/support/documentation/white_papers/wp395-Mitigating-SEUs.pdf.

[101] P. D. Hyde and G. Russell. A comparative study of the design of synchronous and asynchronous self-checking RISC processors. In *Proceedings of the IEEE International On-Line Testing Symposium*, pages 89–94. IEEE Computer Society, July 2004.

[102] Eishi Ibe, Hitoshi Taniguchi, Yasuo Yahagi, Ken-ichi Shimbo, and Tadanobu Toba. Impact of scaling on neutron-induced soft error in SRAMs from a 250 nm to a 22 nm design rule. *IEEE Transactions on Electron Devices*, 57(7):1527–1538, July 2010.

[103] Masashi Imai and Tomohiro Yoneda. Improving dependability and performance of fully asynchronous on-chip networks. In *Proceedings of the IEEE International Symposium on Asynchronous Circuits and Systems*, pages 65–76. IEEE Computer Society, April 2011.

[104] ITRS. International technology roadmap for semiconductors. Technical report, Semiconductor Industry Association, 2009. http://www.itrs.net/Links/2009ITRS/2009Chapters_2009Tables/2009_Design.pdf.

[105] Wonjin Jang. *Soft-error tolerant quasi delay-insensitive circuits*. PhD thesis, California Institute of Technology, 2008. https://thesis.library.caltech.edu/5260/6/jang-wonjin-2008-thesis.pdf.

[106] Wonjin Jang and Alain J. Martin. SEU-tolerant QDI circuits. In *Proceedings of the International Symposium on Advanced Research in Asynchronous Circuits and Systems*, pages 156–165. IEEE Computer Society, March 2005.

[107] Natlie Enright Jerger and Li-Shiuan Peh. *On-Chip Networks*. Morgan & Claypool Publishers, 2009.

[108] Niraj K. Jha. Separable codes for detecting unidirectional errors. *IEEE Transactions on Computer-Aided Design of Integrated Circuits and Systems*, 8(5):571–574, 1989.

[109] Mark B. Josephs and Jelio T. Yantchev. CMOS design of the tree arbiter element. *IEEE Transactions on Very Large Scale Integration (VLSI) Systems*, 4(4):472–476, December 1996.

[110] Norhuzaimin Julai, Alexandre Yakovlev, and Alexandre V. Bystrov. Error detection and correction of single event upset (SEU) tolerant latch. In *Proceedings of the IEEE International On-Line Testing Symposium*, pages 1–6. IEEE Computer Society, June 2012.

[111] Tanay Karnik, Peter Hazucha, and Jagdish Patel. Characterization of soft errors caused by single event upsets in CMOS processes. *IEEE Transactions on Dependable and Secure Computing*, 1(2):128–143, 2004.

[112] Mark J. Karol, Micheal G. Hluchyj, and Samuel P. Morgan. Input versus output queueing on a space-division packet switch. *IEEE Transactions on Communications*, 35(12):1347–1356, December 1987.

[113] Parviz Kermani and Leonard Kleinrock. Virtual cut-through: A new computer communication switching technique. *Computer Networks*, 3(4):257–286, 1979.

[114] John Kim, William J. Dally, Brain Towles, and Amit K. Gupta. Microarchitecture of a high radix router. In *Proceedings of the International Symposium on Computer Architecture*, pages 420–431, June 2005.

[115] David J. Kinniment. *Synchronization and Arbitration in Digital Systems*. John Wiley & Sons Ltd, December 2007.

[116] J. L. Knighten, N. W. Smith, L. O. Hoeft, and J. T. DiBene II. EMI common-mode current dependence on delay skew imbalance in high speed differential transmission lines operating at 1 gigabit/second data rates. In *Proceedings of the International Symposium on Quality of Electronic Design*, pages 309–314. IEEE Computer Society, March 2000.

[117] Israel Koren and Zahava Koren. Defect tolerance in VLSI circuits: Techniques and yield analysis. *Proceedings of the IEEE*, 86(9):1819–1838, 1998.

[118] Srivathsan Krishnamohan and Nihar R. Mahapatra. A highly-efficient technique for reducing soft errors in static CMOS circuits. In *Proceedings of the IEEE International Conference on Computer Design: VLSI in Computers & Processors*, pages 126–131. IEEE Computer Society, October 2004.

[119] Milos Krstic, Eckhard Grass, Frank K. Gürkaynak, and Pascal Vivet. Globally asynchronous, locally synchronous circuits: Overview and outlook. *IEEE Design & Test of Computers*, 24(5):430–441, September 2007.

[120] Weidong Kuang, Enjun Xiao, Casto Manuel Ibarra, and Peiyi Zhao. Design asynchronous circuits for soft error tolerance. In *Proceedings of the IEEE International Conference on Integrated Circuit Design and Technology*, pages 1–5, May 2007.

[121] Weidong Kuang, Peiyi Zhao, Jiann-Shiun Yuan, and Ronald F. DeMara. Design of asynchronous circuits for high soft error tolerance in deep submicrometer CMOS circuits. *IEEE Transactions on Very Large Scale Integration (VLSI) Systems*, 18(3):410–422, March 2010.

[122] Amit Kumar, Partha Kundu, Arvind Singh, Li-Shiuan Peh, and Niraj Jha. A 4.6Tbits/s 3.6GHz single-cycle NoC router with a novel switch allocator in 65nm CMOS. In *Proceedings of the International Conference on Computer Design*, pages 63–70. IEEE, October 2007.

[123] J. Lach, W. H. Mangione-Smith, and M. Potkonjak. Runtime logic and interconnect fault recovery on diverse FPGA architectures. In *Proceedings of the Military and Aerospace Applications of Programmable Devices and Technologies International Conference*, 1999.

[124] Christopher LaFrieda and Rajit Manohar. Fault detection and isolation techniques for quasi delay-insensitive circuits. In *Proceedings of the International Conference on Dependable Systems and Networks*, pages 41–50. IEEE Computer Society, June 2004.

[125] Reed K. Lawrence and Andrew T. Kelly. Single event effect induced multiple-cell upsets in a commercial 90 nm CMOS digital technology. *IEEE Transactions on Nuclear Science*, 55(6):3367–3374, 2008.

[126] Jakob Lechner, Martin Lampacher, and Thomas Polzer. A robust asynchronous interfacing scheme with four-phase dual-rail coding. In *Proceedings of the International Conference on Application of Concurrency to System Design*, pages 122–131, June 2012.

[127] Jakob Lechner, Andreas Steininger, and Florian Huemer. Methods for analysing and improving the fault resilience of delay-insensitive codes. In *Proceedings of the IEEE International Conference on Computer Design*, pages 519–526. IEEE Computer Society, October 2015.

[128] Jakob Lechner and Varadan Savulimedu Veeravalli. Modular redundancy in a GALS system using asynchronous recovery links. In *Proceedings of the IEEE International Symposium on Asynchronous Circuits and Systems*, pages 23–30. IEEE Computer Society, May 2013.

[129] Soojung Lee. A deadlock detection mechanism for true fully adaptive routing in regular wormhole networks. *Computer Communications*, 30(8):1826–1840, 2007.

[130] Teijo Lehtonen, Pasi Liljeberg, and Juha Plosila. Online reconfigurable self-timed links for fault tolerant NoC. *VLSI Design*, 2007:1–13, 2007.

[131] Teijo Lehtonen, David Wolpert, Pasi Liljeberg, Juha Plosila, and Paul Ampadu. Self-adaptive system for addressing permanent errors in on-chip interconnects. *IEEE Transactions on Very Large Scale Integration (VLSI) Systems*, 18(4):527–540, 2010.

[132] Anthony Leroy, Dragomir Milojevic, Diederik Verkest, Frédéric Robert, and Francky Catthoor. Concepts and implementation of spatial division multiplexing for guaranteed throughput in networks-on-chip. *IEEE Transactions on Computers*, 57(9):1182–1195, September 2008.

[133] Bin Li, Li-Shiuan Peh, and Priyadarsan Patra. Impact of process and temperature variations on network-on-chip design exploration. In *Proceedings of the ACM/IEEE International Symposium on Networks-on-Chip*, pages 117–126, April 2008.

[134] S.-H. Lo, D. A. Buchanan, Y. Taur, and W. Wang. Quantum-mechanical modeling of electron tunneling current from the inversion layer of ultra-thin-oxide nMOSFET's. *IEEE Electron Device Letters*, 18(5):209–211, 1997.

[135] Faiq Khalid Lodhi, Syed Rafay Hasan, Osman Hasan, and Falah Awwad. Low power soft error tolerant macro synchronous micro asynchronous (MSMA) pipeline. In *Proceedings of the IEEE Computer Society Annual Symposium on VLSI*, pages 601–606. IEEE, July 2014.

[136] Kia Seng Low and Alexandre Yakovlev. Token ring arbiters: An exercise in asynchronous logic design with Petri nets. Technical Report 537, Department of Computer Science, University of Newcastle upon Tyne, November 1995. https://eprint.ncl.ac.uk/160499.

[137] Rakan Maddah, Rami G. Melhem, and Sangyeun Cho. RDIS: Tolerating many stuck-at faults in resistive memory. *IEEE Transactions on Computers*, 64(3):847–861, March 2015.

[138] Sohaib Majzoub, Resve Saleh, and Rabab Ward. PVT variation impact on voltage island formation in MPSoC design. In *Proceedings of the International Symposium on Quality of Electronic Design*, pages 814–819. IEEE Computer Society, March 2009.

[139] Alain J. Martin. The design of a self-timed circuit for distributed mutual exclusion. Technical Report CaltechCSTR:1983.5097-tr-83, California Institute of Technology, 1983. http://resolver.caltech.edu/CaltechCSTR:1983.5097-tr-83.

[140] Alain J. Martin. The limitations to delay-insensitivity in asynchronous circuits. In *Proceedings of the MIT Conference on Advanced Research in VLSI*, pages 263–278. MIT Press, 1990.

[141] Alain J. Martin. Synthesis of asynchronous VLSI circuits. Technical Report CaltechCSTR:1991.cs-tr-93-28, California Institute of Technology, 1991. https://resolver.caltech.edu/CaltechCSTR:1991.cs-tr-93-28.

[142] Alain J. Martin and Pieter J. Hazewindus. Testing delay-insensitive circuits. In *Proceedings of the University of California/Santa Cruz conference on Advanced research in VLSI*, pages 118–132. MIT Press, 1991.

[143] Alain J. Martin, Andrew M. Lines, and Uri V. Cummings. Asynchronous circuits with pipelined completion process, December 2002. US Patent 6,502,180.

[144] Juan-Miguel Martinez-Rubio, Pedro López, and José Duato. A cost-effective approach to deadlock handling in wormhole networks. *IEEE Transactions on Parallel and Distributed Systems*, 12(7):716–729, 2001.

[145] Philippe Maurine, Jean-Baptiste Rigaud, Ghislain Bouesse, Gilles Sicard, and Marc Renaudin. Static implementation of QDI asynchronous primitives. In *Proceedings of the International Workshop on Power and Timing Modeling, Optimization and Simulation*, pages 181–191. Springer Berlin Heidelberg, September 2003.

[146] Timothy C. May and Murray H. Woods. A new physical mechanism for soft errors in dynamic memories. In *Proceedings of the Annual Reliability Physics Symposium*, pages 33–40, April 1978.

[147] Timothy C. May and Murray H. Woods. Alpha-particle-induced soft errors in dynamic memories. *IEEE Transactions on Electron Devices*, 26(1):2–9, 1979.

[148] Edward J. McCluskey. Built-in self-test techniques. *IEEE Design & Test of Computers*, 2(2):21–28, April 1985.

[149] Peggy B. McGee, Melinda Y. Agyekum, Moustafa A. Mohamed, and Steven M. Nowick. A level-encoded transition signaling protocol for high-throughput asynchronous global communication. In *Proceedings of the IEEE International Symposium on Asynchronous Circuits and Systems*, pages 116–127. IEEE Computer Society, April 2008.

[150] Joe W. McPherson. Time dependent dielectric breakdown physics — models revisited. *Microelectronics Reliability*, 52(9-10):1753–1760, 2012.

[151] Sarah E. Michalak, Kevin W. Harris, Nicolas W. Hengartner, Bruce E. Takala, and Stephen A. Wender. Predicting the number of fatal soft errors in Los Alamos national laboratory's ASC Q supercomputer. *IEEE Transactions on Device and Materials Reliability*, 5(3):329–335, 2005.

[152] Giovanni De Micheli and Luca Benini. *Networks on Chips: Technology and Tools*. Morgan Kaufmann, 2006.

[153] Ivan Miro-Panades, Fabien Clermidy, Pascal Vivet, and Alain Greiner. Physical implementation of the DSPIN network-on-chip in the FAUST architecture. In *Proceedings of the ACM/IEEE International Symposium on Networks-on-Chip*, pages 139–148. IEEE, April 2008.

[154] Mahim Mishra and Seth Copen Goldstein. Defect tolerance at the end of the roadmap. In *Proceedings of the International Test Conference*, pages 1201–1210. IEEE Computer Society, October 2003.

[155] Kartik Mohanram and Nur A. Touba. Cost-effective approach for reducing soft error failure rate in logic circuits. In *Proceedings of the International Test Conference*, volume 1, pages 893–901, 2003.

[156] Yannick Monnet, Marc Renaudin, and Régis Leveugle. Asynchronous circuits sensitivity to fault injection. In *Proceedings of the IEEE International On-Line Testing Symposium*, pages 121–126. IEEE Computer Society, July 2004.

[157] Yannick Monnet, Marc Renaudin, and Régis Leveugle. Asynchronous circuits transient faults sensitivity evaluation. In *Proceedings of the Design Automation Conference*, pages 863–868. ACM, June 2005.

[158] Yannick Monnet, Marc Renaudin, and Régis Leveugle. Hardening techniques against transient faults for asynchronous circuits. In *Proceedings of the IEEE International On-Line Testing Symposium*, pages 129–134. IEEE Computer Society, July 2005.

[159] Yannick Monnet, Marc Renaudin, and Régis Leveugle. Designing resistant circuits against malicious faults injection using asynchronous logic. *IEEE Transactions on Computers*, 55(9):1104–1115, 2006.

[160] Fernando Moraes, Ney Calazans, Aline Mello, Leandro Möller, and Luciano Ost. HERMES: An infrastructure for low area overhead packet-switching networks on chip. *Integration, the VLSI Journal*, 38(1):69–93, October 2004.

[161] Mahdi Mosaffa, Fataneh Jafari, and Siamak Mohammadi. Designing robust threshold gates against soft errors. *Microelectronics Journal*, 42(11):1276–1289, 2011.

[162] Shubu Mukherjee. *Architecture Design for Soft Errors*. Morgan Kaufmann Publishers, Amsterdam, Boston, 2008.

[163] David E. Muller and W. Scott Bartky. A theory of asynchronous circuits. In *Proceedings of the Annals of Computing Laboratory of Harvard University*, pages 204–243, 1959.

[164] Robert Mullins and Simon Moore. Demystifying data-driven and pausible clocking schemes. In *Proceedings of the IEEE International Symposium on Asynchronous Circuits and Systems*, pages 175–185. IEEE Computer Society, March 2007.

[165] Robert Mullins, Andrew West, and Simon Moore. Low-latency virtual-channel routers for on-chip networks. In *Proceedings of the Annual International Symposium on Computer Architecture*, volume 0, pages 188–197. IEEE Computer Society, 2004.

[166] Robert Mullins, Andrew West, and Simon Moore. The design and implementation of a low-latency on-chip network. In *Proceedings of the Asia and South Pacific Design Automation Conference*, pages 164–169. IEEE, January 2006.

[167] Tadao Murata. Petri nets: Properties, analysis and applications. *Proceedings of the IEEE*, 77(4):541–580, 1989.

[168] Jens Muttersbach, Thomas Villiger, and Wolfgang Fichtner. Practical design of globally-asynchronous locally-synchronous systems. In *Proceedings of the International Symposium on Advanced Research in Asynchronous Circuits and Systems*, pages 52–59. IEEE Computer Society, April 2000.

[169] Javier Navaridas, Mikel Luján, José Miguel-Alonso, Luis A. Plana, and Steve B. Furber. Understanding the interconnection network of SpiNNaker. In *Proceedings of the International Conference on Supercomputing*, pages 286–295. ACM, June 2009.

[170] Ted Nesson and S. Lennart Johnsson. ROMM routing on mesh and torus networks. In *Proceedings of the Annual ACM Symposium on Parallel Algorithms and Architectures*, pages 275–287. ACM Press, 1995.

[171] Chrysostomos A. Nicopoulos, Dongkook Park, Jongman Kim, Narayanan Vijaykrishnan, Mazin S. Yousif, and Chita R. Das. ViChaR: A dynamic virtual channel regulator for network-on-chip routers. In *Proceedings of the Annual IEEE/ACM International Symposium on Microarchitecture*, pages 333–346. IEEE Computer Society, December 2006.

[172] Arthur Nieuwoudt, Jamil Kawa, and Yehia Massoud. Crosstalk-induced delay, noise, and interconnect planarization implications of fill metal in nanoscale process technology. *IEEE Transactions on Very Large Scale Integration (VLSI) Systems*, 18(3):378–391, March 2010.

[173] Jinhyun Noh, Vincent Correas, Soonyoung Lee, Jongsung Jeon, Issam Nofal, Jacques Cerba, Hafnaoui Belhaddad, Dan Alexandrescu, YoungKeun Lee, and Steve Kwon. Study of neutron soft error rate (SER) sensitivity: Investigation of upset mechanisms by comparative simulation of FinFET and planar MOSFET SRAMs. *IEEE Transactions on Nuclear Science*, 62(4):1642–1649, August 2015.

[174] Steven M. Nowick. Design of a low-latency asynchronous adder using speculative completion. *IEE Proceedings — Computers and Digital Techniques*, 143(5):301–307, September 1996.

[175] José L. Núñez-Yáñez, Doug A. Edwards, and Antonio Marcello Coppola. Adaptive routing strategies for fault-tolerant on-chip networks in dynamically reconfigurable systems. *IET Computers & Digital Techniques*, 2(3):184–198, May 2008.

[176] Simon Ogg, Bashir M. Al-Hashimi, and Alexandre Yakovlev. Asynchronous transient resilient links for NoC. In *Proceedings of the International Conference on Hardware/Software Codesign and System Synthesis*, pages 209–214, 2008.

[177] Ümit Y. Ogras, Jingcao Hu, and Radu Marculescu. Key research problems in NoC design: A holistic perspective. In *Proceedings of the IEEE/ACM/IFIP International Conference on Hardware/Software Codesign and System Synthesis*, pages 69–74. ACM, September 2005.

[178] Eiji Oki, Zhigang Jing, Roberto Rojas-Cessa, and H. Jonathan Chao. Concurrent round-robin-based dispatching schemes for Clos-network switches. *IEEE/ACM Transactions on Networking*, 10(6):830–844, December 2002.

[179] Eiji Oki, Nattapong Kitsuwan, and Roberto Rojas-Cessa. Analysis of space-space-space Clos-network packet switch. In *Proceedings of the Internatonal Conference on Computer Communications and Networks*, pages 1–6, August 2009.

[180] J. Olsen, P. E. Becher, P. B. Fynbo, P. Raaby, and J. Schultz. Neutron-induced single event upsets in static RAMS observed a 10 km flight attitude. *IEEE Transactions on Nuclear Science*, 40(2):74–77, 1993.

[181] Carlos Ortega, Jonathan Tse, and Rajit Manohar. Static power reduction techniques for asynchronous circuits. In *Proceedings of the IEEE International Symposium on Asynchronous Circuits and Systems*, pages 52–61. IEEE, May 2010.

[182] Recep O. Ozdag and Peter A. Beerel. High-speed QDI asynchronous pipelines. In *Proceedings of the IEEE International Symposium on Asynchronous Circuits and Systems*, pages 13–22. IEEE Computer Society, April 2002.

[183] Jiwoo Pak, Bei Yu, and David Z. Pan. Electromigration-aware redundant via insertion. In *Proceedings of the Asia and South Pacific Design Automation Conference*, pages 544–549, January 2015.

[184] Thomas Panhofer, Werner Friesenbichler, and Andreas Steininger. Reliability estimation and experimental results of a self-healing asynchronous circuit: A case study. In *Proceedings of the NASA/ESA Conference on Adaptive Hardware and Systems*, pages 91–98. IEEE Computer Society, June 2010.

[185] Giorgos Passas, Manolis Katevenis, and Dionisios N. Pnevmatikatos. A 128 × 128 × 24Gb/s crossbar interconnecting 128 tiles in a single hop and occupying 6% of their area. In *Proceedings of the ACM/IEEE International Symposium on Networks-on-Chip*, pages 87–95. IEEE Computer Society, May 2010.

[186] Suhas S. Patil. Forward acting n x m arbiter. Technical Report 67, Massachusetts Institute of Technology, April 1972. http://csg.csail.mit.edu/CSGArchives/memos/Memo-67.pdf.

[187] Robert Pawlowski, Joseph Crop, Minki Cho, James W. Tschanz, Vivek De, Thomas Fairbanks, Heather Quinn, Shekhar Y. Borkar, and Patrick Yin Chiang. Characterization of radiation-induced SRAM and logic soft errors from 0.33V to 1.0V in 65nm CMOS. In *Proceedings of the IEEE Custom Integrated Circuits Conference*, pages 1–4. IEEE, September 2014.

[188] Li-Shiuan Peh and William J. Dally. A delay model and speculative architecture for pipelined routers. In *Proceedings of the International Symposium on High-Performance Computer Architecture*, pages 255–266. IEEE Computer Society, January 2001.

[189] Song Peng. *Implementing self-healing behavior in Quasi Delay-Insensitive circuits*. PhD thesis, Cornell University, August 2006.

[190] Song Peng and Rajit Manohar. Efficient failure detection in pipelined asynchronous circuits. In *Proceedings of the IEEE International Symposium on Defect and Fault Tolerance in*

VLSI Systems (DFT), pages 484–493. IEEE Computer Society, October 2005.

[191] Song Peng and Rajit Manohar. Self-healing asynchronous arrays. In *Proceedings of the IEEE International Symposium on Asynchronous Circuits and Systems*, pages 34–45, March 2006.

[192] James Lyle Peterson. *Petri Net Theory and the Modeling of Systems*. Prentice Hall, USA, 1981.

[193] Stanislaw J. Piestrak and Takashi Nanya. Towards totally self-checking delay-insensitive systems. In *Proceedings of the International Symposium on Fault-Tolerant Computing*, pages 228–237. IEEE Computer Society, June 1995.

[194] Matthew Pirretti, Greg M. Link, Richard R. Brooks, Narayanan Vijaykrishnan, Mahmut Kandemir, and Mary Jane Irwin. Fault tolerant algorithms for network-on-chip interconnect. In *Proceedings of the IEEE Computer Society Annual Symposium on VLSI*, pages 46–51. IEEE Computer Society, February 2004.

[195] Luis A. Plana, John Bainbridge, Steve Furber, Sean Salisbury, Yebin Shi, and Jian Wu. An on-chip and inter-chip communications network for the SpiNNaker massively-parallel neural net simulator. In *Proceedings of the International Symposium on Networks-on-Chips*, pages 215–216. IEEE Computer Society, April 2008.

[196] Luis A. Plana, David M. Clark, Simon Davidson, Steve B. Furber, Jim D. Garside, Eustace Painkras, Jeffrey Pepper, Steve Temple, and John Bainbridge. SpiNNaker: Design and implementation of a GALS multicore system-on-chip. *ACM Journal on Emerging Technologies in Computing Systems*, 7(4):17:1–17:18, December 2011.

[197] Luis A. Plana, Steve B. Furber, Steve Temple, Mukaram Khan, Yebin Shi, Jian Wu, and Shufan Yang. A GALS infrastructure for a massively parallel multiprocessor. *IEEE Design & Test of Computers*, 24(5):454–463, 2007.

[198] Julian José Hilgemberg Pontes. *Soft Error Mitigation in Asynchronous Networks on Chip*. PhD thesis, Pontifícia Universidade Católica do Rio Grande do Sul, 2012. http://hdl.handle.net/10923/1559.

[199] Julian José Hilgemberg Pontes, Ney Calazans, and Pascal Vivet. Adding temporal redundancy to delay insensitive codes to mitigate single event effects. In *Proceedings of the IEEE International Symposium on Asynchronous Circuits and Systems*, pages 142–149. IEEE Computer Society, May 2012.

[200] Julian José Hilgemberg Pontes, Matheus T. Moreira, Fernando Moraes, and Ney Calazans. Hermes-A — an asynchronous NoC router with distributed routing. In *Proceedings of the International Workshop on Integrated Circuit and System Design: Power and Timing Modeling, Optimization, and Simulation*, pages 150–159. Springer, September 2011.

[201] Martin Radetzki, Chaochao Feng, Xueqian Zhao, and Axel Jantsch. Methods for fault tolerance in Networks-on-Chip. *ACM Computing Surveys*, 46(1):8:1–8:38, July 2013.

[202] David A. Rennels and Hyeongil Kim. Concurrent error detection in self-timed VLSI. In *Proceedings of the International Symposium on Fault-Tolerant Computing*, pages 96–105. IEEE Computer Society, June 1994.

[203] Phillip J. Restle, K. A. Jenkins, A. Deutsch, and P. W. Cook. Measurement and modeling of on-chip transmission line effects in a 400 MHz microprocessor. *IEEE Journal of Solid-State Circuits*, 33(4):662–665, April 1998.

[204] Samuel Rodrigo, Jose Flich, Antoni Roca, Simone Medardoni, Davide Bertozzi, Jesús Camacho Villanueva, Federico Silla, and José Duato. Addressing manufacturing challenges with cost-efficient fault tolerant routing. In *Proceedings of the ACM/IEEE International Symposium on Networks-on-Chip*, pages 25–32. IEEE Computer Society, May 2010.

[205] Roberto Rojas-Cessa and Chuan-Bi Lin. Scalable two-stage Clos-network switch and module-first matching. In *Proceedings of the Workshop on High Performance Switching and Routing*, pages 303–308, June 2006.

[206] Thomas L. Saaty. *Elements of Queueing Theory: With Applications*. McGraw-Hill New York, 1961.

[207] Yoichi Sasaki, Kazuteru Namba, and Hideo Ito. Soft error masking circuit and latch using Schmitt trigger circuit. In *Proceedings of the IEEE International Symposium on Defect and Fault Tolerance in VLSI Systems (DFT)*, pages 327–335. IEEE Computer Society, October 2006.

[208] Steve Scott, Dennis Abts, John Kim, and William J. Dally. The BlackWidow high-radix clos network. In *Proceedings of the International Symposium on Computer Architecture*, pages 16–28. ACM, May 2006.

[209] Norbert Seifert and Nelson Tam. Timing vulnerability factors of sequentials. *IEEE Transactions on Device and Materials Reliability*, 4(3):516–522, September 2004.

[210] Maitham Shams, Jo C. Ebergen, and Mohamed I. Elmasry. A comparison of CMOS implementations of an asynchronous circuits primitive: The C-element. In *Proceedings of the International Symposium on Low Power Electronics and Design*, pages 93–96. IEEE, August 1996.

[211] Delong Shang, Fei Xia, Stanislavs Golubcovs, and Alex Yakovlev. The magic rule of tiles: Virtual delay insensitivity. In *Proceedings of the International Workshop on Power and Timing Modeling, Optimization and Simulation*, pages 286–296. Springer Berlin Heidelberg, 2009.

[212] Abbas Sheibanyrad. *Asynchronous Implementation of a Distributed Network-on-Chip*. PhD thesis, University of Pierre et Marie Curie, 2008.

[213] Abbas Sheibanyrad and Alain Greiner. Two efficient synchronous ⇔ asynchronous converters well-suited for

networks-on-chip in GALS architectures. *Integration, the VLSI Journal*, 41(1):17–26, January 2008.

[214] Abbas Sheibanyrad, Alain Greiner, and Ivan Miro-Panades. Multisynchronous and fully asynchronous NoCs for GALS architectures. *IEEE Design & Test of Computers*, 25(6):572–580, November 2008.

[215] Kenneth L. Shepard and Vinod Narayanan. Noise in deep submicron digital design. In *Proceedings of the IEEE/ACM International Conference on Computer-Aided Design*, pages 524–531. IEEE Computer Society / ACM, November 1996.

[216] Yebin Shi. *Fault-Tolerant Delay-Insensitive Communication*. PhD thesis, University of Manchester, 2010. http://apt.cs.manchester.ac.uk/publications/thesis/YShi10_phd.php.

[217] Yebin Shi, Steve B. Furber, Jim Garside, and Luis A. Plana. Fault tolerant delay insensitive inter-chip communication. In *Proceedings of the IEEE International Symposium on Asynchronous Circuits and Systems*, pages 77–84. IEEE, May 2009.

[218] Keun Sup Shim, Myong Hyon Cho, Michel Kinsy, Tina Wen, Mieszko Lis, G. Edward Suh, and Srinivas Devadas. Static virtual channel allocation in oblivious routing. In *Proceedings of the ACM/IEEE International Symposium on Networks-on-Chip*, pages 38–43. IEEE Computer Society, 2009.

[219] Montek Singh and Steven M. Nowick. MOUSETRAP: Ultra-high-speed transition-signaling asynchronouspipelines. In *Proceedings of the International Conference on Computer Design*, pages 9–17, September 2001.

[220] Montek Singh and Steven M. Nowick. The design of high-performance dynamic asynchronous pipelines: Lookahead style. *IEEE Transactions on Very Large Scale Integration (VLSI) Systems*, 15(11):1256–1269, November 2007.

[221] Charles Slayman. Soft error trends and mitigation techniques in memory devices. In *Proceedings of the Annual Reliability and Maintainability Symposium*, pages 1–5. IEEE, January 2011.

[222] Jared C. Smolens, Brian T. Gold, James C. Hoe, Babak Falsafi, and Ken Mai. Detecting emerging wearout faults. In *Proceedings of the IEEE Workshop on Silicon Errors in Logic — System Effects*, April 2007.

[223] Wei Song. *Spatial Parallelism in the Routers of Asynchronous On-Chip Networks*. PhD thesis, University of Manchester, 2011. https://www.escholar.manchester.ac.uk/uk-ac-man-scw:126142.

[224] Wei Song and Doug Edwards. An asynchronous routing algorithm for Clos networks. In *Proceedings of the International Conference on Application of Concurrency to System Design*, pages 67–76. IEEE Computer Society, June 2010.

[225] Wei Song and Doug Edwards. A low latency wormhole router for asynchronous on-chip networks. In *Proceedings of the Asia South Pacific Design Automation Conference*, pages 437–443. IEEE, January 2010.

[226] Wei Song and Doug Edwards. Asynchronous spatial division multiplexing router. *Microprocessors and Microsystems*, 35(2):85–97, 2011.

[227] Wei Song, Doug Edwards, Jim Garside, and William J. Bainbridge. Area efficient asynchronous SDM routers using 2-stage Clos switches. In *Proceedings of the Design, Automation & Test in Europe Conference & Exhibition*, pages 1495–1500. IEEE, March 2012.

[228] Wei Song, Doug A. Edwards, José Luis Núñez-Yáñez, and Sohini Dasgupta. Adaptive stochastic routing in fault-tolerant on-chip networks. In *Proceedings of the International Symposium on Networks-on-Chips*, pages 32–37. IEEE Computer Society, May 2009.

[229] Daniel J. Sorin. *Fault Tolerant Computer Architecture*. Morgan & Claypool Publishers, January 2009.

[230] Jens Sparsø. Asynchronous design of networks-on-chip. In *Proceedings of the Norchip*. IEEE, November 2007.

[231] Jens Sparsø and Steve Furber. *Principles of Asynchronous Circuit Design — A Systems Perspective*. Kluwer Academic Publishers, Boston, U.S.A, 2001.

[232] Jens Sparsø and Jørgen Staunstrup. Delay-insensitive multiring structures. *Integration, the VLSI Journal*, 15(3):313–340, 1993.

[233] Jayanth Srinivasan, Sarita V. Adve, Pradip Bose, and Jude A. Rivers. The impact of technology scaling on lifetime reliability. In *Proceedings of the International Conference on Dependable Systems and Networks*, pages 177–186. IEEE Computer Society, June 2004.

[234] Mikkel Bystrup Stensgaard and Jens Sparsø. ReNoC: A network-on-chip architecture with reconfigurable topology. In *Proceedings of the ACM/IEEE International Symposium on Networks-on-Chip*, pages 55–64. IEEE, April 2008.

[235] Edward A. Stott, N. Pete Sedcole, and Peter Y. K. Cheung. Fault tolerant methods for reliability in FPGAs. In *Proceedings of the International Conference on Field Programmable Logic and Applications*, pages 415–420. IEEE, September 2008.

[236] Ivan E. Sutherland. Micropipelines. *Communications of the ACM*, 32(6):720–738, 1989.

[237] Ivan E. Sutherland and Scott Fairbanks. GasP: A minimal FIFO control. In *Proceedings of the IEEE International Symposium on Asynchronous Circuits and Systems*, pages 46–53. IEEE Computer Society, March 2001.

[238] A. Taber and E. Normand. Single event upset in avionics. *IEEE Transactions on Nuclear Science*, 40(2):120–126, 1993.

[239] Mehdi Baradaran Tahoori and Subhasish Mitra. Defect and fault tolerance of reconfigurable molecular computing. In *Proceedings of the IEEE Symposium on Field-Programmable Custom Computing Machines*, pages 176–185. IEEE Computer Society, April 2004.

[240] E. Takeda and N. Suzuki. An empirical model for device degradation due to hot-carrier injection. *IEEE Electron Device Letters*, 4(4):111–113, April 1983.

[241] Andrew S. Tanenbaum and David J. Wetherall. *Computer Networks*. Prentice Hall, 5 edition, January 2010.

[242] The Advanced Processor Technologies Research Group, School of Computer Science at the University of Manchester. Spinnaker — a universal spiking neural network architecture. https://apt.cs.manchester.ac.uk/projects/SpiNNaker/.

[243] Yvain Thonnart, Edith Beigné, and Pascal Vivet. Design and implementation of a GALS adapter for ANoC based architectures. In *Proceedings of the IEEE Symposium on Asynchronous Circuits and Systems*, pages 13–22, May 2009.

[244] Yvain Thonnart, Pascal Vivet, and Fabien Clermidy. A fully-asynchronous low-power framework for GALS NoC integration. In *Proceedings of the Design, Automation & Test in Europe Conference & Exhibition*, pages 33–38. IEEE Computer Society, 2010.

[245] Xuan-Tu Tran, Yvain Thonnart, Jean Durupt, Vincent Beroulle, and Chantal Robach. Design-for-test approach of an asynchronous network-on-chip architecture and its associated test pattern generation and application. *IET Computers Digital Techniques*, 3(5):487–500, 2009.

[246] Dean Nguyen Truong, Wayne H. Cheng, Tinoosh Mohsenin, Zhiyi Yu, Anthony T. Jacobson, Gouri Landge, Michael J. Meeuwsen, Christine Watnik, Anh Thien Tran, Zhibin Xiao, Eric W. Work, Jeremy W. Webb, Paul Vincent Mejia, and Bevan M. Baas. A 167-processor computational platform in 65

nm CMOS. *IEEE Journal of Solid-State Circuits*, 44(4):1130–1144, April 2009.

[247] King-Ning Tu. Recent advances on electromigration in very-large-scale-integration of interconnects. *Journal of Applied Physics*, 94(9):5451–5473, 2003.

[248] Leslie G. Valiant and Gordon J. Brebner. Universal schemes for parallel communication. In *Proceedings of the Annual ACM Symposium on Theory of Computing*, pages 263–277. ACM, May 1981.

[249] Sriram R. Vangal, Jason Howard, Gregory Ruhl, Saurabh Dighe, Howard Wilson, James W. Tschanz, David Finan, Arvind P. Singh, Tiju Jacob, Shailendra Jain, Vasantha Erraguntla, Clark Roberts, Yatin Hoskote, Nitin Borkar, and Shekhar Borkar. An 80-tile sub-100-w TeraFLOPS processor in 65-nm CMOS. *IEEE Journal of Solid-State Circuits*, 43(1):29–41, January 2008.

[250] Thomas Verdel and Yiorgos Makris. Duplication-based concurrent error detection in asynchronous circuits: Shortcomings and remedies. In *Proceedings of the IEEE International Symposium on Defect and Fault Tolerance in VLSI Systems*, pages 345–353, November 2002.

[251] Tom Verhoeff. Delay-insensitive codes — an overview. *Distributed Computing*, 3(1):1–8, March 1988.

[252] Daniel Wiklund and Dake Liu. SoCBUS: Switched network on chip for hard real time embedded systems. In *Proceedings of the International Parallel and Distributed Processing Symposium*. IEEE Computer Society, April 2003.

[253] Wayne Wolf, Ahmed Amine Jerraya, and Grant Martin. Multiprocessor system-on-chip (MPSoC) technology. *IEEE Transactions on Computer-Aided Design of Integrated Circuits and Systems*, 27(10):1701–1713, October 2008.

[254] Pascal T. Wolkotte, Gerard J.M. Smit, Gerard K. Rauwerda, and Lodewijk T. Smit. An energy-efficient reconfigurable circuit-switched network-on-chip. In *Proceedings of*

the *IEEE International Parallel and Distributed Processing Symposium*. IEEE, April 2005.

[255] Jian Wu and Steve Furber. A multicast routing scheme for a universal spiking neural network architecture. *The Computer Journal*, 53(3):280–288, 2010.

[256] Jing-ling Yang, Oliver Chiu-sing Choy, Cheong-fat Chan, and Kong-pong Pun. Design for self-checking and self-timed datapath. In *Proceedings of the IEEE VLSI Test Symposium*, pages 417–422. IEEE Computer Society, April 2003.

[257] Jian Yao, Zuochang Ye, Miao Li, Yanfeng Li, R. D. Schrimpf, D. M. Fleetwood, and Yan Wang. Statistical analysis of soft error rate in digital logic design including process variations. *IEEE Transactions on Nuclear Science*, 59(6):2811–2817, December 2012.

[258] Tomohiro Yoneda, Masashi Imai, Naoya Onizawa, Atsushi Matsumoto, and Takahiro Hanyu. Multi-chip NoCs for automotive applications. In *Proceedings of the IEEE Pacific Rim International Symposium on Dependable Computing*, pages 105–110, November 2012.

[259] Qiaoyan Yu. *Transient and permanent error management for Networks-on-Chip*. PhD thesis, University of Rochester, 2011. http://hdl.handle.net/1802/14810.

[260] Qiaoyan Yu and Paul Ampadu. Transient and permanent error co-management method for reliable networks-on-chip. In *Proceedings of the ACM/IEEE International Symposium on Networks-on-Chip*, pages 145–154. IEEE Computer Society, May 2010.

[261] Qiaoyan Yu and Paul Ampadu. Dual-layer adaptive error control for network-on-chip links. *IEEE Transactions on Very Large Scale Integration (VLSI) Systems*, 20(7):1304–1317, 2012.

[262] Kenneth Y. Yun, Peter A. Beerel, and Julio Arceo. High-performance asynchronous pipeline circuits. In *Proceedings of*

the IEEE International Symposium on Asynchronous Circuits and Systems, pages 17–28. IEEE Computer Society, 1996.

[263] Guangda Zhang, Wei Song, Jim D. Garside, Javier Navaridas, and Zhiying Wang. Transient fault tolerant QDI interconnects using redundant check code. In Proceedings of the Euromicro Conference on Digital System Design, pages 3–10, September 2013.

[264] Guangda Zhang, Wei Song, Jim D. Garside, Javier Navaridas, and Zhiying Wang. Protecting QDI interconnects from transient faults using delay-insensitive redundant check codes. Microprocessors and Microsystems, 38(8, Part A):826–842, 2014.

[265] Meilin Zhang, Qiaoyan Yu, and Paul Ampadu. Fine-grained splitting methods to address permanent errors in network-on-chip links. In Proceedings of the IEEE International Symposium on Circuits and Systems, pages 2717–2720, May 2012.

[266] Ying Zhang, Zebo Peng, Jianhui Jiang, Huawei Li, and Masahiro Fujita. Temperature-aware software-based self-testing for delay faults. In Proceedings of the Design, Automation & Test in Europe Conference & Exhibition, pages 423–428, March 2015.

[267] Zhen Zhang, Alain Greiner, and Sami Taktak. A reconfigurable routing algorithm for a fault-tolerant 2D-mesh network-on-chip. In Proceedings of the Design Automation Conference, pages 441–446. ACM, June 2008.